Confr

American Encounters · GLOBAL INTERACTIONS

A series edited by Gilbert M. Joseph and Emily S. Rosenberg
This series aims to stimulate critical perspectives and fresh inter-
pretive frameworks for scholarship on the history of the imposing global presence of the United States. Its primary concerns include the deployment and contestation of power, the construction
and deconstruction of cultural and political borders, the fluid
meanings of intercultural encounters, and the complex interplay
between the global and the local. American Encounters seeks to
strengthen dialogue and collaboration between historians of U.S.
international relations and area studies specialists.

The series encourages scholarship based on multiarchival historical research. At the same time, it supports a recognition of the
representational character of all stories about the past and pro-
motes critical inquiry into issues of subjectivity and narrative. In
the process, American Encounters strives to understand the context in which meanings related to nations, cultures, and political
economy are continually produced, challenged, and reshaped.

MICHEL GOBAT

Confronting the American Dream

NICARAGUA UNDER U.S. IMPERIAL RULE

Duke University Press   Durham and London 2005

© 2005 Duke University Press

All rights reserved

Printed in the United States of America

on acid-free paper ∞

Designed by C. H. Westmoreland

Typeset in Minion by Keystone Typesetting, Inc.

Library of Congress Cataloging-in-

Publication Data appear on the last

printed page of this book.

FOR MY MOTHER AND IN MEMORY OF MY FATHER

Contents

Illustrations

Acknowledgments

IT GIVES ME GREAT PLEASURE to acknowledge the many debts I have incurred in completing this book. I would first like to extend my special thanks to John Coatsworth and Friedrich Katz, my professors at the University of Chicago. I am extremely grateful for the advice, support, and encouragement they have given me every step of the way; their own work has also been a great source of inspiration to me. I am also deeply appreciative for the intellectual and moral support of Jeffrey Gould, Leora Auslander, and Hans Werner Tobler, who guided my first foray into Nicaraguan history.

In Nicaragua, I am profoundly indebted to the staffs of numerous archives and libraries for their unbounded generosity and flexibility, without which I would not have been able to complete this study. I would especially like to thank Alfredo González Vílchez, Ana Rosa Morales, and their colleagues at the Archivo Nacional de Nicaragua; Eliázar Morales Marenco and Juana Blanco Mendoza of the Archivo de la Municipalidad y de la Prefectura de Granada; Margarita Vannini and the staff of the Instituto de Historia de Nicaragua y Centroamérica; Reyna Clark and the staff of the Registro Público de la Propiedad de Granada; and the staff of the Hemeroteca Nacional de Nicaragua, particularly Edmundo Navarro and Cristina Ortega. All allowed me especially broad access to their holdings and provided helpful advice; they were also extremely welcoming to me and supportive of my project. I am also deeply indebted to Silvio Urbina Ruiz and Leopoldo Guevara of the Alcaldía de Granada for allowing me unlimited access to the municipality's historical documents and for backing my work at a key moment in the research. I would also like to express my thanks to Eva Tatiana Torres from the Instituto de Historia de Nicaragua y Centroamérica for providing me with photographs for this book.

I am deeply appreciative of the support and advice I received from many scholars in Nicaragua. I particularly want to thank the following researchers at Managua's Instituto de Historia de Nicaragua y Centroamérica for sharing with me their knowledge of Nicaraguan history and for their intellectual camaraderie: Margarita Vannini, Frances Kinloch Tijerino, Alvaro Argüello Hurtado, and Miguel Angel Herrera Cuarezma. I am especially grateful for Miguel Angel's friendship and hospitality, and for Frances's and Margarita's unwavering support and generosity. Many thanks also go to Germán Romero

Vargas, Jorge Eduardo Arellano, Michelle Dospital, Xiomara Avendaña Rojas, Mercedes Mauleón Isla, Günther Schmigalle, Nelly Miranda, Roberto Cajina, Oscar-René Vargas, Amaru Barahona, and Rafael Casanova Fuertes.

In Granada, I would like to thank the many individuals who welcomed me with such open arms. I cannot express how grateful I am for the hospitality, moral support, and friendship that Dieter Stadler, director of the cultural center Fundación Casa de los Tres Mundos, and his wife, Lydia Quezada, so graciously extended to me. Dieter not only allowed Laura and me to make the Casa our home but has always been there whenever I have needed him. Many special thanks also go to the staff of the Casa de los Tres Mundos, as well as Angel Márquez Leypon, Alvaro Rivas, Fernando López, Mariano Marín, Ana Rosa Morales, Paúl Morales, Bernardo Marenco, and Justin Wolfe for making life in Granada such a wonderful experience. In addition, I am very grateful for the conversations I had with Dela Pérez Estrada viuda de Marín, Graciela Bendaña viuda de Dreyfus, Lola Coronel Urtecho viuda de Chamorro, Jaime Barberena Meza, Francisco Barberena Bendaña, Jimmy Avilés Avilés, Raúl Xavier García, Leopoldo Guevara, the late Gonzalo Meneses Ocón, Luis Mora Castillo, and María Ernestina Chamorro Favilli. I am also greatly indebted to Héctor Mena Guerrero and José Joaquín Quadra Cardenal, both of whom have been so generous with their time and have taught me so much about the history of their city. Special thanks are also owed to Henry Díaz, Julio Díaz, and Verónica Castillo for their outstanding research assistance. My deepest appreciation goes to the late Luciano Cuadra Vega and his wife, Ana Gómez Alfaro, whose friendship and memories made my stay in Granada so special.

In the United States, many colleagues and friends have given me extremely helpful feedback for which I am deeply appreciative. I am forever grateful to Laura Gotkowitz, whose critical comments, challenging questions, and unlimited support have been indispensable to this project. I also benefited greatly from the extensive comments provided by Matilde Zimmerman and the second, anonymous reviewer for Duke University Press. I am especially indebted to Aldo Lauria-Santiago and Richard Warren for their close and critical reading of many chapters, and to Laurie Milner for her editorial advice. For valuable comments and criticism, I would also like to thank Barry Carr, Charles A. Hale, Barbara Weinstein, Nils Jacobsen, José Antonio Cheibub, Michael Schroeder, Jorge Domínguez, Lowell Gudmundson, José Antonio Fernández, Víctor Hugo Acuña, Arturo Taracena Arriola, Iván Molina Jiménez, Völker Wünderich, Julie Charlip, Charles Walker, Aviva Chomsky, Robin Derby, Jeremy Adelman, Jim Giblin, Stephen Vlastos, T. M. Scruggs, and Justin Wolfe. At the University of Iowa, I am very grateful to Colin Gordon and Todd Erickson for producing the maps and to Linda Edge-Dunlap for preparing the photographs. Angela Keysor and Michael Hohenbrink provided much appreciated research assistance. Special thanks go to Laura Moss Gottlieb for preparing the index. I would also like to thank my editor at Duke University Press, Valerie Millholland, for all her help and support, and Mark Mastromarino for his smooth shepherding of the book through the production process.

Funding for this project was generously provided by the following institutions: the MacArthur Foundation (through the University of Chicago's Council on International Peace and Cooperation), the Swiss National Fund for Scientific Research, the Sawyer foundation (through the Harvard University Trade Union Program), the National Endowment for the Humanities, and the University of Iowa (the History Department, Office of the Provost, Office of the VP for Research, International Programs, and the College of Liberal Arts and Sciences).

Finally, I wish to thank my mother, Irmgard Gobat, for all her support and encouragement. My greatest and never-ending thanks go to Laura, my lifelong compañera, for sustaining me with her enthusiasm and love.

Confronting the American Dream

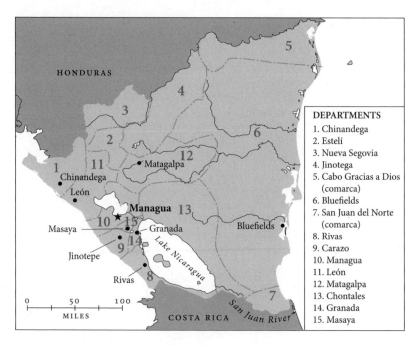

MAP 1 Political map of Nicaragua (1920s)

Introduction

U.S. INTERVENTION HAS MARKED few nations as profoundly as Nicaragua. The most recent incursion was the Reagan administration's undeclared war against the Sandinista Revolution of 1979–90. Yet U.S. efforts to dominate Central America's largest country have a much deeper history, for the United States long believed that its global aspirations depended on controlling Nicaragua's transisthmian passage. As early as 1788 Thomas Jefferson proclaimed his country's interest in using the San Juan River and Lake Nicaragua to build a canal that would link the Atlantic and Pacific oceans.[1] Not until the following century, however, did the United States actually seek to construct such a canal. Although U.S. expeditions accomplished little beyond surveying the projected route, they enjoyed strong local support, since many Nicaraguans valorized the canal as their gateway to the "civilized" world. In June 1902, the United States shocked Nicaraguans when it suddenly decided to build the interoceanic canal in Panama. The abrupt decision did not end U.S. efforts to dominate Nicaragua, however. On the contrary, the United States meddled even more deeply in Nicaraguan affairs, as it sought to prevent other foreign powers from constructing a rival canal. These efforts culminated in the U.S. occupation of 1912–33. In the end, the canal project brought Nicaragua not the expected riches but U.S. intervention. Few better foresaw this tragic outcome than the Nicaraguan journalist who warned his compatriots in 1845, "The waterway across the Isthmus of Nicaragua is the apple in our Eden. It will be our curse."[2]

This book examines the history of U.S. intervention in Nicaragua from the heyday of U.S. Manifest Destiny in the mid-nineteenth century through the U.S. occupation of 1912–33. Covering the two main phases of U.S. expansionism into Latin America, it considers the efforts of diverse U.S. actors to reshape Nicaragua in their own image and according to their own interests. First and foremost, however, it explores how Nicaraguans experienced and confronted U.S. intervention. Time and again, the United States has projected not just its power but its institutions and values—the "American dream"—onto other nations.[3] More often than not, such impositions have triggered fierce nationalist opposition around the world. In Nicaragua, U.S. intervention engendered what may be Latin America's most celebrated anti-U.S. insurgency: the Sandino Rebellion of 1927–33.

While this study examines how Nicaraguans actively resisted U.S. impositions, it also seeks to uncover the deeper, more ambiguous effects of U.S. intervention. Above all, it focuses on two apparent paradoxes that have hitherto escaped scholarly attention: Why did so many Nicaraguans embrace U.S. political, economic, and cultural forms to defend their own nationality against U.S. impositions? And why did the U.S. occupation of 1912–33 push Nicaragua's wealthiest and most Americanized elites to turn against the U.S. ideals of modernity that they had valorized for so long, thus transforming them from leading supporters of U.S. imperial rule into some of its greatest opponents? Both questions challenge us to reassess not only the role of U.S. intervention in Nicaraguan history but the nature and limits of U.S. imperial rule more broadly.

Nicaragua and U.S. Expansionism

The history of U.S. intervention in Nicaragua begins in 1849, when the California gold rush turned the Central American isthmus into a major transit for westbound fortune hunters and a key target for U.S. expansionists. Nowadays, U.S. expansionism under the banner of Manifest Destiny is associated primarily if not exclusively with the conquest of the "American West." Yet the age of Manifest Destiny hardly ended with the United States' annexation of California following its 1846–48 war against Mexico. In fact, this annexation only strengthened North Americans' expansionist impulse. Some sought to spread their country's influence even farther west, as evident in Commodore Matthew Perry's "opening" of Japan in 1853. But many more set their sights southward and viewed Latin America as the new "frontier." These expansionists, the so-called filibusters, invaded Latin American nations without the official backing of the U.S. government. Thousands and thousands of North Americans participated in the private military expeditions. Although some filibusters went as far as Ecuador, most confined themselves to the Caribbean Basin. The only filibuster expedition that achieved lasting control of Latin American territory was the one that ruled Nicaragua between 1855 and 1857.

The Nicaraguan filibusters were led by the era's most notorious apostle of Manifest Destiny: William Walker. After seizing control of Nicaragua in 1855, this former gold rusher strove to "Americanize" the country by replacing the native populace with U.S. colonists and implanting U.S. institutions such as slavery. Extremely popular in the United States, Walker attracted nearly ten thousand North American men and women, making this one of the largest

U.S. exoduses to Latin America ever. For two long years, Walker and his troops waged a brutal war against Nicaraguans and other Central Americans as they tried to create an "American empire" in the region. Despite the racial superiority they believed they embodied, these U.S. expansionists failed miserably and were expelled from Nicaragua in 1857.

The U.S. civil war of 1861–65 curbed the country's expansion into Latin America and across the Pacific Ocean. At the turn of the century, however, the United States once again seized control of major overseas territories. As in the 1850s, this second phase of U.S. expansionism targeted the Caribbean Basin. Except for Puerto Rico, the United States did not formally colonize the region's nations. Instead it turned them into protectorates, allowing them to remain nominally independent while exercising extensive control over their internal and external affairs. A mix of strategic, economic, political, and ideological motives drove the United States to establish its so-called informal empire. Between the 1890s and the early 1930s this renewed expansionism into the Caribbean Basin produced over forty U.S. military interventions.[4] While some were brief, others ushered in lengthy military occupations (see map 2). Of these occupations, none lasted longer than the one suffered by Nicaragua.[5]

The occupation of 1912–33 represented the greatest U.S. effort to turn Nicaragua into "a little United States."[6] Granted, the occupation never engendered a U.S. military government as in Cuba (1898–1902), the Dominican Republic (1916–24), and Haiti (1915–34). Nor did it trigger a massive influx of North American capital. Still, the U.S. occupation profoundly destabilized Nicaragua. Most notably, it produced the protracted guerrilla war waged by Augusto Sandino's peasant-based movement against a combined U.S-Nicaraguan military force. In addition, the occupation led to the disruptive U.S. takeover of Nicaragua's public finances under the aegis of dollar diplomacy. This takeover not only impeded the development of Nicaragua's agroexport economy and fanned political conflicts that culminated in the civil war of 1926–27, it also empowered peasant producers to challenge the economic dominance of large landlords. The occupation further subverted the existing order by facilitating the dramatic spread of U.S. Protestant missionary activities. In seeking to "uplift" the lower classes, U.S. missionaries aggressively promoted Nicaragua's Americanization and undermined the authority of the Catholic Church and its elite allies. Finally, the occupation entailed a fateful democratization campaign that was conducted by the U.S.

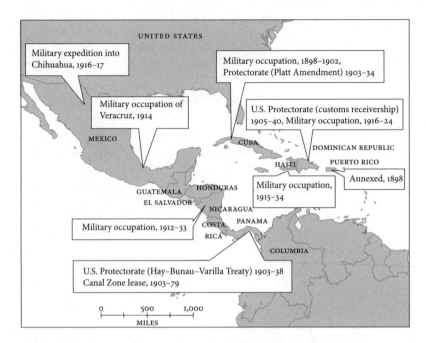

UNITED STATES

Military expedition into
Chihuahua, 1916–17

Military occupation, 1898–1902,
Protectorate (Platt Amendment) 1903–34

Military occupation of
Veracruz, 1914

U.S. Protectorate (customs receivership)
1905–40, Military occupation, 1916–24

MEXICO

CUBA

DOMINICAN REPUBLIC

PUERTO RICO

HAITI

Annexed, 1898

GUATEMALA   HONDURAS
EL SALVADOR
NICARAGUA

Military occupation,
1915–34

Military occupation, 1912–33

COSTA   PANAMA
RICA

COLUMBIA

U.S. Protectorate (Hay–Bunau–Varilla Treaty) 1903–38
Canal Zone lease, 1903–79

0   500   1,000
MILES

MAP 2 Major U.S. interventions in the Caribbean Basin, 1898–1930s

military between 1927 and 1932. While this campaign resulted in some of the fairest elections in Nicaraguan history, it also enabled a U.S.-established military institution—the Guardia Nacional—to become the most powerful political force in the all-important countryside. So deep were the occupation's effects that it helped produce Central America's lengthiest dictatorship, the Somoza dynasty of 1936–79, and its only successful social revolution, the Sandinista Revolution of 1979.

Americanization and Anti-Americanism

Nicaragua's long encounter with U.S. intervention has been generally viewed by both scholars and contemporary observers in dichotomous terms: Nicaraguans either abetted U.S. impositions or bravely rejected them.[7] By the 1850s many Central Americans fretted about how Nicaraguans seemed to be throwing themselves into the arms of U.S. expansionists. Then in the early twentieth century, Nicaragua's wealthiest and most Americanized elite sector—the Conservative oligarchy based in Granada—became so closely associated with the U.S. occupation that its members evolved into some of Central America's most infamous *vendepatrias* ("country sellers"). But of all the possible Nicaraguan culprits, none have been more vilified as agents of U.S. imperialism than the Somoza dictators, who ruled via the most thoroughly U.S.-trained military institution in Latin America: the Guardia Nacional. On the other hand, the list of anti-U.S. heroes is just as long and includes President José Santos Zelaya (1893–1909), whose nationalist policies pushed the United States to engineer one of its first ousters of a foreign government; General Benjamín Zeledón, who died fighting the U.S. invaders of 1912; and of course Augusto Sandino and the latter-day Sandinistas, who gained worldwide support for their revolutionary challenges to U.S. power. These Manichaean images of accommodation and resistance have served as powerful political weapons for Nicaraguans and foreigners alike. Yet they obscure the ambiguities that defined Nicaraguans' encounter with the "northern colossus."

This book seeks to elucidate the deeper, more ambiguous effects of U.S. intervention by examining elite Nicaraguans' embrace of particular U.S. ways, on the one hand, and their anti-Americanism, on the other. It focuses on elites precisely because they were the Nicaraguans whose power and identity were most transformed by U.S. imperial rule. Their response to U.S. influence was also the most ambivalent. In addition, elite formation is a vantage point for exploring why U.S. imperial rule in Nicaragua, unlike elsewhere in the Caribbean Basin, helped "democratize" rural society by weakening landlord hegemony over the peasantry. As we will see, this peculiar impact of U.S. imperial rule was unintended and resulted from the fact that poorer Nicaraguans managed to cope more effectively with U.S. political and economic impositions than was possible for elite Nicaraguans. Indeed, a key goal of this book is to show how Nicaraguans' variegated experiences with U.S. intervention gave rise to different and, at times, competing forms of pro- and anti-Americanism.

After considering how the California gold rush produced the first U.S. intervention in Nicaragua, the book details the ways that the Walker disaster of 1855–57 paradoxically strengthened elite Nicaraguans' infatuation with the U.S. road to modernity. While these elites deemed the United States a grave threat to Nicaraguan sovereignty, they also considered it the most successful model of nation building. Post-Walker elites thus concluded that Nicaraguans could best protect their country against U.S. expansionism by embracing, not rejecting, the liberal ideals of progress embodied in what later became known as the American dream. But elites' "Americanization"—that is, their adoption of U.S. customs and institutions—was not plain mimicry. In general, they looked to the United States more as a paradigm of economic progress and national strength than as a model of political liberty. As a result, they were primarily interested in appropriating the U.S. political, economic, and cultural forms they believed were conducive to capitalist development and state-making. At the same time, elites also believed that the United States could help their country fulfill its own manifest destiny by constructing an interoceanic canal that would transform Nicaragua into the region's most prosperous nation. Americanization was neither a simple U.S. imposition nor an inherent barrier to Nicaraguan independence. Instead it formed the cornerstone of a highly cosmopolitan nationality.

The primary question pursued by the book is an even more paradoxical outcome of U.S. intervention in Nicaragua: Why did the U.S. occupation of 1912–33 lead the country's most Americanized elites—Conservative oligarchs from Granada—to develop an anti-American image of themselves and the nation? This anti-American turn had complex origins, but it issued largely from the efforts of U.S. bankers, marines, and missionaries to spread their own version of the American dream to Nicaragua. In particular, Conservatives' nascent anti-Americanism responded to the 1920s rise of Protestantism, the "modern woman," and other "vices" of modernity emanating from the United States, as well as to the unexpected ways that U.S. efforts to modernize elite economic and political practices weakened the power of large landowners. Conservatives' anti-American turn is key to understanding one of the greatest puzzles of U.S. imperial rule in Nicaragua: why entrenched oligarchs who had long been identified with U.S. ways and interests came to support the anti-U.S. struggle waged by the region's leading revolutionary, General Augusto Sandino. These elite Conservatives not only shared Sandino's opposition to the occupation, they also sought with him, as one oligarch put it, to "expel the contagious American way of life from the popular spirit."[8] Ultimately, Conservatives failed to form a durable political alliance with Sandino largely because their reactionary and elitist brand of anti-Americanism clashed with the guerrillero's utopian vision of a "new Nicaragua" that was not just de-Americanized but classless.

In tracing Nicaraguans' contradictory responses to U.S. imperial rule, this book builds on new trends in the study of Americanization throughout the world. In the past, scholars tended to view the export of the "American way of life" either as a positive means of modernization or as a nefarious tool of U.S. domination.[9] Recent studies, in contrast, have emphasized the ambiguous political meanings of Americanization. For starters, they stress that even within the United States the "American way of life" means many different things. But most of all, they maintain that Americanization abroad results from a complex process of adaptation and negotiation, as non-U.S. societies do not just passively adopt U.S. ways but modify them, and when possible, borrow only those that best fit their needs.[10] For this reason, they also claim that Americanization is hardly a homogenous process but can vary greatly over space and time. Finally, recent research shows that the appropriation of U.S. institutions, practices, and values does not inherently threaten non-U.S. nationalities. On the contrary, this borrowing can strengthen at times national identities, with some subject peoples even turning U.S. ways into a powerful weapon against imperial rule.[11]

While embracing these trends, this book also diverges from much of the recent literature on Americanization in three key ways. First, it shows that Nicaraguans bent on emulating the United States did not simply adapt U.S. consumption and leisure patterns—the typical contemporary definition of Americanization. More important to them was the adoption of the liberal institutions and practices that, in their view, had allowed the United States to become so prosperous and modern.[12] Second, this study emphasizes that Nicaraguans' variegated responses to Americanization reflected not just selective borrowing. Above all, they resulted from Nicaraguans' subjection to diverse modes of U.S. intervention (military, economic, political, and cultural) and from the uneven effects of U.S. intervention on distinct social groups.

Third, and perhaps most important, this book focuses less on Americanization per se than on its tense relationship with anti-Americanism. For many scholars, anti-Americanism reflects nothing more than opposition to U.S. foreign policy and its "way of life."[13] But as the Nicaraguan case underscores, anti-Americanism is not always directed against the United States. At times, it can also be an attack against fellow citizens who have embraced U.S. ways. Not by chance did Sandino justify his anti-Americanization crusade by stating that "imperialism does not grow without a moral base of support within the very populace in which it has its tentacles."[14] Of course Sandino was not alone in making this claim, for Latin American nationalists have frequently criticized the powerful allure of the "American way of life." In 1900 the Uruguayan intellectual José Enrique Rodó famously complained that Latin Americans' "mania for the north" was allowing the United States to "delatinize" the continent and reshape it in its own likeness "without the extortion of conquest."[15] Seven decades later, two supporters of Chile's socialist regime stated in their celebrated book *How to Read Donald Duck* that the main threat to Latin American nationality was not the "American Way of Life" but the "American Dream of Life." In particular, they maintained that "it is the manner in which the U.S. dreams and redeems itself, and then imposes that dream upon others for its own salvation, which poses the danger for the dependent countries. It forces us Latin Americans to see ourselves as they see us."[16]

Not all Nicaraguans who sought to emulate the United States were "accomplices" of U.S. imperialism, however. In fact, some of Nicaragua's most acclaimed nationalists consciously adopted certain U.S. political, economic, and cultural forms in order to defend their country's independence against U.S. expansionism. For example, in 1910, the leading Liberal ideologue Salvador Mendieta publicly exhorted his compatriots to resist the deepening of U.S. imperial rule by embracing ever more strongly the "angloamerican way of being."[17] To Nicaraguan nationalists like Mendieta, valorizing the United States as a model signified anything but a desire to be devoured by the "northern colossus." Their ambivalent view of the United States as both a model and a threat was hardly unique, for numerous nationalist movements throughout Latin America have appropriated U.S. ideologies to challenge U.S. dominance over their countries.[18]

Above all, however, the tension between Americanization and anti-Americanism resulted from Nicaraguans' own contradictory engagements with U.S. intervention and its effects. Such contradictions are especially evident in the competing strategies elite Nicaraguans pursued to counter dollar diplomacy's deleterious impact on their economic fortunes during the 1920s. To cope with their economic anxieties, many upper-class Nicaraguans embraced economic anti-Americanism. Yet in doing so, they also reinforced their identification with U.S. ideals of modernity. Members of the country's most entrenched and Americanized oligarchy, in contrast, responded by developing a new form of cultural anti-Americanism that, ironically, targeted their own wives and daughters who steadfastly clung to the ways of the

Americanized "modern woman"—a figure many Nicaraguans associated with dollar diplomacy. In U.S.-occupied Nicaragua, then, the coexistence of Americanization and anti-Americanism reflected much more than Latin America's alleged "love-hate relationship" with the United States.[19] In reality, it often had less to do with Nicaraguans' ambivalent opinions of the United States than with the internal effects of Americanization and the contrasting ways that Nicaraguans dealt with the realities of U.S. imperial rule.

Imperialism and Its Contradictions

Many U.S. diplomatic historians reject the concept of imperialism as a way of explaining the history of U.S. intervention in Latin America.[20] In their view, U.S. imperialism was a short-lived phenomenon of the 1890s and thus an aberration in the country's history.[21] In contrast, Latin Americanist historians have far fewer qualms about applying the term to describe the continent's relations with the United States. In the case of Nicaragua, I have two principal reasons for using the concept of imperialism.[22] First, I want to stress that the distinct modes of U.S. incursion in Nicaragua were fundamentally related to each other. The book not only shows that U.S. invasions carried out in the 1850s and the early twentieth century were intrinsically connected, it also emphasizes the links between distinct forms of U.S. intervention that Nicaraguans experienced during the same period. Second, I want to highlight that U.S. incursions in Nicaragua occurred in the broader geographical and historical context of U.S. efforts to forge an informal empire in the Caribbean Basin. This emphasis contrasts with many U.S. scholars' denial of their country's imperial aspirations by viewing U.S. interventions as geographically and historically isolated events.[23] As we will see, U.S. intervention in Nicaragua was anything but accidental and anything but un-American.

It is also important, however, to stress the tensions plaguing the imperial project itself. One of the greatest contradictions of U.S. imperial rule lay in its ability to both undermine and strengthen Nicaraguans' nationality by Americanizing them. In key ways, this tension reflects a broader paradox at the heart of U.S. nationalism: as a messianic ideology, it justifies the expansion of U.S. influence in not so much nationalistic as universal and utopian terms.[24] And ever since the era of Manifest Destiny (1830s–50s), the United States has had the power to impose its ways on other nations, particularly in Latin America. As history has shown time and again, such impositions entail tragic consequences—precisely because, as historian Emily Rosenberg notes, U.S. "exporters of the American dream" believe that there can be "no truly enlightened dissent against the ultimate acceptance of American ways."[25] Still, we should not ignore the extraordinary appeal of the "American dream" beyond U.S. borders, particularly its promise of freedom, material abundance, and upward mobility. Indeed, the dream's utopian impulse helps explain why prominent Nicaraguan nationalists could genuinely invoke key U.S. nationalist ideals in their challenge of U.S. impositions.

At the same time, Nicaragua's multifaceted encounters with U.S. imperialism were shaped by differences among the "exporters of the American dream." Between the 1849 gold rush and the 1933 withdrawal of the occupation force, Nicaraguans had to contend with a vast array of U.S. expansionists, from diplomats and marines to missionaries and bankers. Whether young or old, male or female, these North Americans shared a firm belief in Americanization—as a way both to further U.S. influence and to "uplift" Nicaragua. Yet they also had competing aims, preoccupations, and visions. For example, the earliest U.S. expansionists—transient entrepreneurs such as Cornelius Vanderbilt and filibusters like William Walker—wanted to Americanize Nicaragua under the banner of Manifest Destiny. But if Vanderbilt strove to inculcate Nicaraguans with U.S. economic values, Walker waged a "race war" in order to colonize Nicaragua with U.S. settlers. Unfortunately, the elite Nicaraguans who contracted Walker's services wrongly believed that he would pursue the same kind of Americanization project as Vanderbilt. This fatal error would cost them dearly, but it helps explain why they courted the filibuster in the first place.

Complicating matters further, the United States used multiple, inconsistent modes of intervention to dominate Nicaragua. Between 1910 and 1933, for instance, Nicaraguans experienced the following interventions in succession: a U.S.-orchestrated regime change that blocked Nicaragua's incipient democratic opening; a U.S. invasion and subsequent military occupation; the takeover of Nicaraguan public finances by U.S. dollar diplomats; the spread of U.S. missionary activities and culture industries, especially Hollywood; a second full-scale U.S. invasion; the U.S. military's campaign to promote democracy; and a six-year guerrilla war. Not surprisingly, distinct sectors of the Nicaraguan populace responded very differently to these interventions. But even one seemingly cohesive mode of intervention could elicit contradictory responses among the very same group of Nicaraguans. Take again the case of Nicaragua's wealthiest elites—Conservative oligarchs from Granada—and their engagement with dollar diplomacy. While they strongly supported dollar diplomats' controversial political and economic policies, these elites also waged a fierce, albeit much less publicized struggle against dollar diplomats' efforts to Americanize Nicaraguan culture.

In sum, this book compares Nicaraguans' contradictory engagements with forms of U.S. intervention that are often studied separately. Such an approach not only permits a more dynamic analysis but bridges the gap between "culture" and "political economy" marking much of the scholarship on U.S. and European imperialism. Traditionally, the field has been dominated by studies that focused on the structural dimensions of imperial rule, particularly state institutions, economic systems, and class relations. In the last decade or so, the scholarly focus has shifted from the material to the cultural realm.[26] As a result, we now have a more nuanced view of the multiple actors, hierarchies, and processes that shape the imperial encounter. Yet such analytical gains have also come at a cost, for the field's cultural turn has pushed the study of imperialism's political-economic structures to the sidelines. A focus on both "culture" and "political economy" is of course indispensable for studying the complex nature of imperial rule. But as various scholars have stressed, it is not just a question of incorporating the two domains into one analytical framework. We also have to explore their interconnections.[27] Only by considering the cultural dimensions of economic practices and the materiality of cultural practices can we truly understand two puzzling outcomes of U.S. imperialism in Nicaragua: why the entrepreneurial spirit of U.S. gold rushers led Nicaraguans to embrace filibusters like Walker, and why dollar diplomacy pushed Americanized elites to crusade against their country's Americanization.

The Local View

To better trace Nicaraguans' multifaceted encounter with U.S. intervention, this study combines an analysis of Americanization at the national level with a regional focus on the city and the department of Granada. I focus on Granada largely because its Conservative-dominated oligarchy, which had been the country's chief proponent of the U.S. road to modernity, evolved into that path's main opponent. As a result, Granada is an especially good vantage point for exploring Nicaraguans' contradictory and shifting relationship with Americanization and anti-Americanism. This regional focus is also important, as Granadan oligarchs formed the most powerful planter and merchant class in Nicaragua; their encounter with U.S. intervention thus deeply affected the rest of the nation.

Originally, the strength of Granada's elite stemmed from its control of the country's wealthiest and most populous province or "prefecture." For much of the nineteenth century, the prefecture of Granada spanned the future departments of Managua, Carazo, Masaya, Granada, and Chontales (see map 1). While Granadan oligarchs had already established large cattle estates in the plains and hills of Chontales during the colonial era, it was not until the late nineteenth century that they carved out lucrative coffee plantations in the southern uplands of Managua/Carazo and on Granada's extinct volcano (the Mombacho). By the turn of the century, the prefecture system had been abolished and the department of Granada had been dramatically reduced to its current size. In the meantime, however, the wealth of Granadan oligarchs had come to depend increasingly on investments elsewhere in the nation. In addition to acquiring large commercial establishments in other major towns, these oligarchs established sugar estates in the northwestern plains of Chinandega, banana plantations in the tropical lowlands of the Atlantic coast, and coffee estates in the northern mountains of Matagalpa. Politically, Granadan oligarchs also wielded great influence. They not only controlled the Conservative Party, which together with the Liberal Party dominated Nicaraguan political life until the Sandinista Revolution of 1979, but they also ran the Nicaraguan state for most of the period between the 1857 ouster of Walker's regime and the 1933 end of U.S. occupation.

That Granada developed into a bastion of elite power and Americanization had much to do with the city's location. Founded by Spanish conquistadors in 1524, Granada rests on the northwestern shore of Lake Nicaragua, which drains into the Caribbean Sea by way of the San Juan River. Thanks to this waterway, Granada became a major port for Central American trade with the North Atlantic and home to some of the most prosperous merchants and landlords in the isthmus. Granada's close ties with the world economy also made it an unusually cosmopolitan city. The influx of numerous European and U.S. merchants introduced the city's populace to North Atlantic ways and manners. Conversely, international trade enabled many elite Granadans to travel overseas. So even though Granada emerged in the nineteenth century as the seat of Nicaragua's Conservative Party, the city's oligarchs were widely viewed as people unusually open to foreign currents.

This openness contrasted with the great reluctance of Granada's oligarchy to admit outsiders into its ranks. Although it accepted some rich foreigners and Nicaraguan nouveaux riches, since the mid-nineteenth century most of its members have originated from the same families, particularly the Argüellos, Chamorros, Cuadras, Lacayos, Pasos, Urtechos, Vegas, Vivas, and Zavalas. Little wonder that these oligarchs have long been deemed by Nicaraguans to constitute an "aristocracy." Granadan oligarchs tended to intermarry and live near each other, either in the city's center or on its principal commercial street, the Calle Atravesada. The oligarchy's exclusivity was most apparent in the makeup of the city's social club, the institution that mainly determined elite membership and identity. Between the club's founding in 1871 and the 1930s, over three quarters of its members came from "aristocratic" families. As the club's roll further indicates, Granada's oligarchy totaled about two hundred men during the U.S. occupation—or less than 3 percent of the city's adult male population (in 1920 the municipality had about 22,000 inhabitants while the department had 34,000 and the nation 640,000).[28] So controversial was the social exclusivity of Granada's Americanized oligarchy that it became a key target of nationalist campaigns waged by Nicaraguans who did not belong to it.

On the other hand, the department of Granada also serves as an ideal lens to examine how U.S. imperial rule could inadvertently "democratize" rural society, since nowhere else in Nicaragua was land more concentrated than in this elite bastion. Already in the era of Spanish colonialism (1520s–1820), the fertile and well-irrigated plains of Granada were home to large rural properties, particularly cattle, sugar, cacao, and indigo estates. Land in Granada became even more concentrated with the agroexport boom of the late nineteenth-century, as landlords seized large amounts of land previously controlled by small- and medium-scale farmers as well as peasant and Indian communities. Although the boom did not make the majority of rural Granadans landless, it produced a rural society where landlord hegemony was the strongest in all of Nicaragua. During the U.S. occupation of 1912–33, this expansion of elite power came to a sudden halt, for many Granadan estate owners went bankrupt while numerous peasant producers enjoyed renewed prosperity. As the case of Granada illuminates, the occupation's uneven impact on Nicaragua's rural producers was entirely unintended and resulted primarily from the greater ability of small-scale producers to cope with dollar diplomacy's deleterious economic effects.

Finally, a focus on Granada illuminates the nature of the elite divisions that so tragically facilitated U.S. imperial rule. On the basis of limited empirical evidence, scholars have generally assumed that such divisions pitted a Liberal coffee bourgeoisie centered in the northern region of León against a cattle-based Conservative oligarchy based farther south in Granada. In reality, Conservative oligarchs were not only highly diversified economically, but they also spearheaded the development of the country's coffee economy. Moreover, not all Conservative oligarchs were from Granada; many lived in León as well as in other Nicaraguan towns. At the same time, Granada's oligarchy included numerous Liberals who owned large cattle estates but no coffee plantations. As conflicts among wealthy Granadans instead indicate, cultural and ideological differences were far more important in fueling elite disputes than divisions by region, party affiliation, or economic specialization. Especially volatile were the struggles over how to define elite membership and identity. Such struggles were moreover exacerbated by pressures elites faced from below, particularly from peasants and urban artisans. But just as important, elite divisions reflected competing viewpoints that Nicaraguans formed in reaction to a shared experience of U.S. imperial rule.

My point of departure, then, is that the impact of imperialism on subjugated nations can be best understood by analyzing local sources that illuminate the experiences and views of those subjected to imperial rule. While this might sound like an obvious point, many studies of U.S. occupation in Latin America continue to rely disproportionately on U.S. sources and, therefore, to privilege North American viewpoints.[29] Such an imbalance frequently reflects scholars' greater interest in the U.S. experience or strategies of imperial rule. But it also results from the difficulties of locating sources produced by subjects of U.S. imperial rule. In Nicaragua, for instance, much historical documentation has been lost due to warfare and natural disasters, particularly the earthquakes of 1931 and 1972. Moreover, when the U.S. occupiers finally left Nicaragua in 1933, they took with them many Nicaraguan records, including the captured correspondence of Sandino and his followers. As a result, both native and foreign scholars have long assumed that any study of Nicaragua's encounter with U.S. intervention would be based overwhelmingly on U.S. archival materials. Indeed, this book has certainly drawn on the extensive holdings of the U.S. National Archives and other North American depositories.

After the country's last war ended in 1990, it has become increasingly apparent that many more Nicaraguan-based archival sources survived the ravages of the past than is commonly assumed. Little-known Nicaraguan records that have been invaluable to this study include the official and private correspondence of President Adolfo Díaz (1911–16 and 1926–28) held in the National Archive of Nicaragua and the Instituto de Historia de Nicaragua y Centroamérica; local and national newspapers contained in the Hemeroteca Nacional; and the thousands of property titles and mortgage transactions recorded in Granada's property registry. Perhaps the most important re-discovery of Nicaraguan documents pertains to the over sixteen hundred *legajos* (bundles of documents) that form the core of Granada's municipal archive. For decades, these precious sources withered away in a hidden cor-ner of Granada's town hall, crushed in dirty sacks that Nicaraguans use to store basic grains. In 1993, the documents were finally "liberated" and placed in the newly formed municipal archive. While particularly strong for the late nineteenth century, the holdings go from 1856—the year a fire set by Walker's men razed the city—up to the revolutionary triumph of 1979. This archival material is also extraordinarily diverse, for it ranges from court cases and petitions to electoral, tax, and demographic records to political correspon-dence, school reports, and private letters.[30] Thanks to these newly accessible Nicaraguan sources, this study is in a better position to show how the para-doxical outcomes of U.S. imperial rule were shaped by Nicaraguans' own contradictory and multifaceted engagements with distinct modes of U.S. domination.

Organization

Divided into four parts, the book first traces how the projected interoceanic canal tragically entangled Nicaragua's sense of manifest destiny with that of the United States. Chapter 1 explores how, from the very start, U.S. interest in a transisthmian route posed a great risk to Nicaraguan sovereignty. It opens with the 1849 arrival of California-bound gold hunters who introduced Nic-araguans to U.S. ideals of modernity. The chapter's main focus is on "Presi-dent" William Walker (1855–57) and the thousands of U.S. military-colonists whose Americanization efforts devastated Nicaragua. Chapter 2 analyzes how Nicaraguans recuperated from the Walker disaster by coalescing around a cosmopolitan nation-state project. In doing so, elites reembraced U.S. ideals of progress and supported U.S. efforts to build the canal—as long as the United States respected Nicaraguan sovereignty.

Part II explores the illiberal effects of U.S. imperial rule by analyzing how the U.S. intervention of 1910–12 resulted in a failed oligarchic restoration. Chapter 3 considers how the U.S. government helped Conservative oligarchs not only to overthrow the Liberal dictatorship of José Santos Zelaya (1893–1909) but to restore a hierarchical political and social order reminiscent of the pre-Zelaya era. Chapter 4 focuses on the antioligarchic violence and anti-Americanism that marked the U.S. military intervention in the Nicaraguan civil war of 1912.

Part III traces Nicaraguans' confrontations with dollar diplomacy, which defined the U.S. occupation from 1912 to the civil war of 1926–27. Chapter 5 shows how many Nicaraguans, especially those of the Liberal opposition, embraced a new form of economic nationalism directed against dollar diplomacy. In consequence, Nicaragua's most acclaimed nationalists only reinforced their identification with the U.S. ideals of modernity. Chapter 6 explores dollar diplomacy's socioeconomic impact. In particular, it elucidates how dollar diplomats' restrictive fiscal and financial policies inadvertently promoted peasant over estate production and thus helped "democratize" land ownership. Chapter 7 analyzes how dollar diplomacy's "democratizing" impact led elites most closely identified with U.S. imperial rule—the ruling Conservative oligarchs—to forge a new identity constructed against U.S. ideals of modernity. In short, Part III explains why dollar diplomacy's most vociferous opponents fervently clung to the "American dream," while the region's most infamous pro-Americans turned against the dream's modernizing impulse.

Part IV considers how the post-1927 militarization of U.S. imperial rule revolutionized Nicaraguan politics. Chapter 8 examines U.S. efforts to use the military to impose its ideals of democracy in Nicaragua. This democratization campaign not only enabled a U.S.-created military, the Guardia Nacional, to become a major political force, it also led Conservative oligarchs to radicalize their anti-U.S. outlook and embrace quasi-fascist ideals. Chapter 9 explores Nicaraguans' ambivalent attitudes toward the Sandino Rebellion of 1927–33. Above all, it considers how pro-fascist Conservatives (unsuccessfully) sought to forge an alliance with Sandino. This was more than simply an opportunistic act, as Conservative oligarchs identified with Sandino's revolutionary nationalism in key ways. Part IV thus shows how the 1927 shift in U.S. imperial rule pushed Nicaragua's most Americanized elites to reject definitively the liberal values embodied in the "American dream." The book closes with an epilogue that reassesses two key legacies of U.S. imperial rule in Nicaragua: the rise of the Somoza dictatorship (1936–79), and elite support for the Sandinista Revolution (1979–90).

This book seeks to contribute to a better understanding of the effects of U.S. intervention in Nicaragua and in Latin America more broadly. By considering how peasant producers coped with dollar diplomacy better than landlords, it shows that U.S. imperial rule can inadvertently democratize, not just polarize, rural class relations. In addition, the book elucidates how the spread of U.S. missionary activities and culture industries can critically weaken elite authority. On the other hand, it also explains why the United States' efforts to impose its ideals of democracy can facilitate the rise of authoritarian rule. Finally, the book challenges conventional wisdom about the social base of revolutionary nationalism by revealing that the elite sector most supportive of Sandino's struggle against U.S. imperialism was a Conservative, agroexport oligarchy—the very antithesis of the "national bourgeoisie" as commonly defined in Latin America. Since this oligarchy had long been an enthusiastic proponent of the U.S. road to modernity, the Nicaraguan case reveals how the (largely unintended) "democratizing" consequences of U.S. imperial rule can fuel an even more intense rejection of the "American way of life."

PART I · Manifest Destinies, 1849–1910

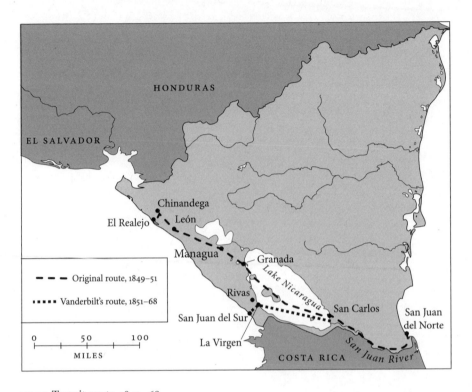

HONDURAS

EL SALVADOR

Chinandega
El Realejo
León
Managua
Granada
Lake Nicaragua
Rivas
San Carlos
San Juan del Sur
San Juan del Norte
La Virgen
San Juan River
COSTA RICA

— — — Original route, 1849–51
▪▪▪▪▪ Vanderbilt's route, 1851–68

0   50   100
MILES

MAP 3 Transit route, 1849–68

1 Americanization through Violence

Nicaragua under Walker

LEADERS OF NICARAGUA'S LIBERAL PARTY enthusiastically greeted William Walker and his band of fifty-seven U.S. mercenaries when they sailed
into the Pacific port of Realejo on 16 June 1855. Months earlier the Liberal
Party had sent emissaries to San Francisco, California, to contract Walker's
services. In exchange for land and money, this well-known soldier of fortune
was to help Liberals overthrow the Conservative government based in Granada. From Realejo, the Liberal delegates accompanied Walker and his men
to Chinandega (see map 3). All along the fifteen-mile dirt road, rural dwellers
came out of their straw-hatched huts to salute the U.S. adventurers; in Chinandega, townspeople enthusiastically greeted them with loud church bells.
From Chinandega, Walker's Nicaraguan hosts took him to nearby León, then
the country's largest city and the seat of the Liberal Party. There the Liberal
chieftain Francisco Castellón cordially received Walker and gave him free
reign to fight the Conservatives in the name of "liberty" and "progress."[1]

The spirited welcome extended to Walker by the local populace stands in
profound contrast to the way latter-day Nicaraguans have remembered his
brief but fateful rule. To them, Walker and his men were nothing but brutal
invaders who tried to enslave their ancestors and destroy their culture.
Walker and his men certainly brought unprecedented violence to Nicaragua
in their efforts to create a new, slaveholding U.S. empire. But these U.S.
expansionists were not invaders: they had been invited by prominent Nicaraguans to their country—not just to wage war but to help "civilize" Nicaragua.[2] In particular, elite Liberals hoped that Walker's men would settle
down as agricultural colonists and help Nicaragua replicate the U.S. path to
political and economic modernity. Nor was Walker's band solely backed by a
handful of misguided Liberal patriarchs, as some scholars would argue.[3]
Poorer Nicaraguans also welcomed the North Americans as "liberators."
Many continued to support Walker even after he became the country's
strongman and attracted up to ten thousand additional (male and female)
U.S. colonists to his cause. In fact, the Nicaraguan masses tended to stay aloof
from the now mythical "National War" that led to the expulsion of Walker
and his U.S. followers in May 1857.

Today, Nicaraguans' warm embrace of Walker in 1855 seems perplexing, for we know the devastation he wrought. But perhaps the greater puzzle is why U.S. expansionism under the banner of Manifest Destiny did not push elite Nicaraguans to join other Central Americans in repudiating U.S. military-colonists like Walker. Central Americans had become especially wary of U.S. expansionism after the United States conquered the northern half of Mexico in the war of 1846–48. Yet this U.S. conquest hardly perturbed elite Nicaraguans, thus leading a Spanish-born diplomat of the era to wonder why Nicaragua could not imagine "that in throwing herself into the arms of American citizens . . . a day would arrive when she would be strangled in those very arms which were so spontaneously open to receive her"?[4] As we will see, the key to this puzzle lies not just in the tragic way Nicaragua's own sense of manifest destiny—the interoceanic canal—became entangled with U.S. expansionism. It also stems from Nicaraguans' expectation that Walker's colonists would embody the same entrepreneurial values as the thousands of California-bound adventurers who had crossed the isthmus since the gold rush began in 1848.

To Nicaraguans' grave misfortune, Walker's military-colonists introduced Nicaraguans to a very different kind of Americanization project than the gold rushers who transited their country. With the transit business, Nicaraguans eagerly adopted a wide array of new U.S. goods and cultural practices as well as U.S. ideals of technological progress and enterprise. In Walker's followers, by contrast, Nicaraguans encountered a highly exclusionary and bellicose strand of U.S. Manifest Destiny that claimed Latin Americans could not be Americanized through the "civilizing" force of U.S. culture and trade but had to be violently subordinated if not physically exterminated. As Walker famously stated in his book *The War in Nicaragua*, "The history of the world presents no such Utopian vision as that of an inferior race yielding meekly and peacefully to the controlling influence of a superior people. Whenever barbarism and civilization . . . meet face to face, the result must be war."[5] But as their enthusiastic reception of Walker's band evinces, many Nicaraguans initially believed in such a "Utopian vision." And it was this faith that Walker and his men would brutally betray.

The Initial Encounter

Ever since the United States started expanding westward in the early nineteenth century, its government and citizens strove to exploit Nicaragua's ideal location for an interoceanic route.[6] But only with the California gold rush of 1848–49 did U.S. entrepreneurs establish a transisthmian route through Nicaragua. Until the U.S. transcontinental railroad was completed in 1869, the Nicaraguan transit and its Panamanian counterpart (established in 1848) were the fastest and most secure pathways between both coasts of the United States. So essential were these transits to the United States that they secured by far the largest foreign investments made by U.S. citizens prior to their country's civil war of 1861–65.[7]

The U.S.-operated transit across Nicaragua followed a route that local residents had been using since well before the Spanish conquest of 1523. Its Atlantic terminus was the sleepy port of San Juan del Norte, where steamers carrying hundreds of gold seekers arrived from New York and New Orleans. There, passengers transferred to smaller dugouts that took them through deep jungle 122 miles up the San Juan River to Lake Nicaragua. After crossing the shark-infested lake to Granada, the travelers rode another 134 miles through the country's most populated areas before boarding San Francisco-bound steamers at the old Pacific port of El Realejo. This 375-mile journey across Nicaragua took about twenty days to complete. In 1851, the travel time dropped dramatically after the U.S. shipping magnate Cornelius Vanderbilt opened a transit route about half as long that required only a twelve-mile land journey between Lake Nicaragua (La Virgen) and the Pacific (San Juan del Sur). Vanderbilt's Accessory Transit Company also made key technological improvements, such as replacing Nicaraguan dugouts with U.S. steamboats and macadamizing dirt paths so that they would no longer become mud trenches whenever it rained. These changes enabled gold-hungry adventurers to cross the isthmus in as little as two days, thus shortening their travel time between New York and San Francisco to about twenty-two days. The Nicaraguan transit route became so popular that, until its closure by warfare in 1856, it carried nearly two thousand travelers a month—a mighty flow for a country of about 250,000 inhabitants.[8]

For better or for worse, the transit business represented the first major U.S. intervention in Nicaragua. Politically, U.S. agents of the Accessory Transit Company alienated native elites by meddling in their country's internal affairs. They even instigated the first major U.S. military action in Nicaragua—the 1854 bombardment of San Juan del Norte—in order to resolve a conflict with local boatmen and authorities. The company also refused to pay the Nicaraguan government the 10 percent royalty on its annual profits stipulated by the original contract. Finally, its agents antagonized native elites by helping rural communities defend their autonomy against the encroaching central state.[9] In particular, they hindered state authorities from pressing peasants into military service; in exchange, the company gained privileged access to much-needed laborers. If elites railed at the company's high-handedness, poorer Nicaraguans living along the transit route often welcomed its intervention.[10]

Even more contradictory was the transit's economic impact. To the dismay of many Nicaraguans, the transit business significantly increased U.S. control over their economy. North Americans not only owned the transit's main means of transport and monopolized the sale of wood needed to fuel the steamboats, they also operated many of the hotels and taverns that catered to the foreign adventurers.[11] In creating this quasi-enclave economy, U.S. entrepreneurs displaced various local businesses, especially boatmen who had long carried most of the country's transisthmian commerce. Yet the transit also brought a whiff of prosperity to Nicaragua. For local laborers, U.S. entrepreneurs offered more secure employment and higher wages. Further, Vanderbilt's modernization of the transport system produced, as a local observer stressed, "a favorable revolution" in the country's commercial sector.[12] Nowhere was this impact more strongly felt than in the rural economy. In addition to facilitating the export of Nicaraguan corn to California, the new transit benefited the many peasants and petty merchants who sold food and liquor to the thousands of gold rushers crossing their country.[13]

This massive flow also produced the first U.S. cultural intervention in Nicaragua. A diverse group, the transients—*californios* in local parlance—introduced a wide variety of U.S. consumption and leisure patterns, including distinct styles of dress and unfamiliar dances.[14] The gold rushers and U.S. transit operators fascinated some Nicaraguans with their entrepreneurial spirit. Native elites, in particular, favorably contrasted the foreigners' "spirit of progress" with the antientrepreneurial attitudes they claimed many of their compatriots had inherited from the Spanish colonizers.[15] No doubt, the closer Nicaraguans lived to the transit route the more they adopted the ways of the transients, a process which native elites often equated with becoming more "civilized." As the prefect of Granada noted in 1850, the "good taste of [the city's] inhabitants, its culture, and civilization [was] being daily enhanced by . . . the influx of foreigners."[16] Yet the Nicaraguans whose lifestyles probably changed the most were the hundreds who worked for the transit company in various capacities, for they had to adapt to a U.S.-based labor regime.[17]

Culturally and otherwise, then, Nicaragua was notably changed by its encounter with the transit company and the *californios*. Yet such changes paled next to the havoc wreaked by William Walker and his band of U.S. expansionists, who advanced, as a U.S. resident in Granada put it, "the grand idea of the Americanization of the entire region of Central America."[18]

Embracing Walker's Filibusters

When Walker's men arrived in Nicaragua, the country was already anything but peaceful. As elsewhere in Latin America, Nicaragua's 1821 independence from Spain had ushered in a long period of upheaval, as competing groups fought to forge a new political community on the ruins of the Spanish colonial state.[19] This conflict certainly had an ideological dimension, for it essentially pitted elite Conservatives, who sought to uphold the colonial order, against elite Liberals, who favored a new order based on liberal principles, such as free trade, the secularization of society, more democratic forms of government, and the privatization of land owned by corporate entities (especially the Catholic Church and indigenous communities).[20] But, as in much of Central America, Nicaraguan Liberals and Conservatives waged war "more for power than principle."[21] And in Nicaragua the battle over the nation-state was especially protracted, as the country possessed two equally powerful regional elites: one based in the Liberal stronghold of León, the other in the Conservative bastion of Granada. If in some parts of Latin America the center had come to control the provinces by the mid-nineteenth century, in Nicaragua the elites of León and Granada—both composed of cattle barons, indigo and cacao planters, and merchants—remained locked in a bloody struggle for power.

Complicating matters, elite conflicts fueled the rise of peasant movements that posed grave challenges to the existing social order. The strength of such movements was especially evident in the rural revolts that rocked Nicaragua in the late 1840s.[22] These revolts sprang largely from popular wrath over efforts of the nascent state to expand its power over the lower classes by imposing new taxes, regulating the commercialization of common goods, increasing demands for labor, and curbing the political autonomy of rural communities. Centered in the Pacific zone, the popular revolts drove Nicaragua's warring elites to join forces for the very first time. Thanks to this unprecedented alliance, elites were able to crush what they deemed "communist" movements.[23] Shortly thereafter, however, elites resumed their internecine war.

It was against this violent backdrop that leaders of the Liberal Party hired Walker and his men to help overthrow the ruling Conservatives. They knew little about Walker other than that he was a political liberal willing to lead U.S. military adventurers against Conservative regimes in Latin America. Their favorable image of Walker, a thirty-one-year-old lawyer-journalist born in Tennessee, stemmed from the well-publicized military expedition he had led in Baja California and Sonora from November 1853 to May 1854. Although unsuccessful, Walker had impressed Nicaraguan Liberals with his ability to wage war against Mexico's Conservative government.[24]

But Nicaragua's hard-pressed Liberals also contracted Walker's services because of their positive experiences with previous U.S. mercenaries.[25] Since the end of the U.S. war against Mexico in 1848, Nicaragua and the rest of the Caribbean Basin had experienced a rise in U.S. military incursions. The participants of such private military adventures came to be known as filibusters, a word derived from the French term for the pirates who had pillaged the Spanish colonies in the Caribbean Basin (*flibustiers*). Like Walker, some filibusters were invited by embattled native elites. Others were outright invaders. None enjoyed the U.S. government's explicit sanction.[26]

Filibusters were agents of U.S. Manifest Destiny, and they saw themselves, to quote Walker, as "the advance guard of American civilization."[27] Still, their personal goals could vary considerably.[28] In the case of Walker's men, some were unemployed veterans of the U.S.-Mexican war enticed by good pay. Others were outlaws on the run who believed that gold-rich Nicaragua was not only a fine refuge but the new "El Dorado." Many more were farmers lured by the promise of land bonanzas. A few others saw their main goal as the evangelization of the "godforsaken" (i.e., Catholic) natives. A significant number joined Walker principally for political reasons. For example, many Southerners went to Nicaragua to defend the institution of slavery in the United States.[29] Others claimed to be political liberals fighting the international battle against the forces of "reaction." This was especially the case of Walker's French and German soldiers, many of whom had emigrated penniless to the United States after participating in the failed European revolutions of 1848.[30] Diverse motivations drove thousands of young men from all parts of the United States to enlist in Walker's filibuster army. Yet no matter how varied a crowd, most apparently supported their leader's main goal: to "Americanize" Nicaragua via the import of U.S. colonists and U.S. institutions.

This goal was partly shared by the Nicaraguan Liberals who hired Walker's filibuster gang and offered each of the mercenaries a farm of 250 acres at the close of the military campaign. Their offer was not simply a ploy to circumvent U.S. laws that prohibited the departure of private military expeditions from U.S. ports but did not restrict U.S. settler-colonists from setting sail for Latin America.[31] Instead, the offer was a genuine attempt to create a U.S. farming colony in Nicaragua's vast stretches of undeveloped land.[32] It thus reflected the ongoing efforts of native elites to replicate the political and economic development of the United States by promoting the massive immigration of U.S. settlers to Nicaragua. Liberals and Conservatives alike considered this matter so important that the contracts their governments signed with Vanderbilt's transit company obliged the latter to establish U.S. agricultural colonies along the transit route.[33]

Nicaraguans' valorization of the U.S. road to modernity impelled their enthusiastic reception of Ephraim George Squier, a U.S. envoy who visited the isthmus in 1849–50 in order to secure the interoceanic canal project for his country. No matter where Squier went, local elites of all political colors received him with open arms and reiterated their belief that the United States was the "most perfect model" for their country.[34] According to Squier, they queried him time and again about ways to promote U.S. immigration. This was even the case of the country's bishop, who apparently told him that all Nicaraguans wanted "an infusion of your people to make this broad land an Eden of beauty, and the garden of the world."[35] Of course, Squier's presentation of Nicaraguan opinions must be taken with caution. In particular, he underestimated the extent to which prominent Conservatives worried about the potential threat the United States posed to their nation's sovereignty. Still, contemporary accounts suggest that Squier was right to stress how many upper-class Nicaraguans eagerly supported the influx of U.S. colonists to their country.[36] Such support was especially striking in its sharp contrast to the anti-U.S. sentiments other Central American elites developed once the United States began its southward expansion in the 1840s.[37] Few elite Nicaraguans shared the opinion of the Honduran president who, following the 1846 U.S. invasion of Mexico, stated the "cause of Mexico is, we may say, our own, and therefore to look upon it with indifference would be a crime meriting opprobrium and execration."[38]

Why, then, did Nicaragua's upper class stand out for its apparent "indifference" toward U.S. expansionism? No doubt, its members hoped that closer ties with the United States would prevent Costa Rica and Great Britain, then the leading power in the Caribbean Basin, from seizing the projected canal route.[39] Elite Nicaraguans had long believed that the canal would make their country, as the era's leading Conservative stated, "the emporium . . . of the entire world."[40] Such lofty dreams, however, became more elusive as the post-1830s expansion in world trade intensified the international scramble for the Nicaraguan canal route. France had joined Great Britain and the United States in seeking to control the Nicaraguan route. In thus clamoring for U.S. immigration, elite Nicaraguans trusted that U.S. colonists would not only restore political order and improve the nation's capacity to defend its sovereignty, but greatly increase the will of the U.S. government to safeguard Nicaragua's gateway to the "civilized" world.[41] On the other hand, elite Nicaraguans also valorized U.S. colonization as a result of their encounter with the U.S. transients whose entrepreneurial spirit they so immensely admired. Indeed, they desired nothing more than to have North American harbingers of progress settle down and help "civilize" what many believed was Central America's most "anarchic" nation.

Many elite Nicaraguans tempered their pro-U.S. views once the transit route boomed after Squier's departure from the isthmus.[42] Most objected to the ways Vanderbilt's transit company intervened in local affairs. In addition, they were disappointed by the U.S. government's failure to oppose British and Costa Rican encroachments on the projected canal route more forcefully. Some also resented U.S. transients' disrespect for their customs and local authorities. Perhaps the greatest scandal these *yanquis* provoked was the riot that broke out in Granada on 21 July 1852 after one transient was jailed for having brawled with another U.S. adventurer.[43]

Still, few elite Nicaraguans ended up forsaking the U.S. ideals of progress embodied by the transients. Even at the height of their conflict with Vanderbilt's transit company, they continued to court U.S. colonists. This was evident when, in 1851, Liberal leaders defied the U.S. government and contracted North American filibusters. In a rejoinder to the U.S. chargé d'affaires in Nicaragua, they stated that these foreign adventurers would "establish liberty and order" as well as help Nicaragua "develop its resources by industry."[44]

Liberals' idealization of the United States as the model of "progress" was shared by their Conservative rivals. After coming to power in 1853, the latter even tried to turn Nicaragua into a U.S. protectorate by claiming they "would make any concessions to [the United States], which were necessary and proper for the purpose."[45] To the U.S. chargé d'affaires, such pleas only reinforced the fear of other Central American governments that "Nicaragua was already . . . passed over into the hands of Americans."[46] Given this backdrop, it should not be surprising that so many elite Nicaraguans viewed Walker's filibusters as their country's "civilizers."[47] Only when it was too late did they realize that the filibusters pursued a very different form of Americanization than the one they had come to embrace.

Walker's Rise to Power

Elite Nicaraguans' admiration for U.S. filibusters was reinforced by the quick victory of Walker's army—the "American Phalanx"—over the Conservative army. Initially, Walker had disappointed Liberal leaders when he landed in June 1855 with only fifty-seven U.S. filibusters rather than the three hundred they had contracted for. He also alienated some by refusing to march immediately toward Granada, seat of the Conservative government. Instead, Walker wanted to first gain control over the San Juan del Sur–La Virgen transit road so that he could more easily replenish his forces with recruits and supplies arriving from the United States.[48] Not until early September did he finally capture the transit road. But then he quickly set his sights on defeating the Conservative forces.

Rather than risk a full-scale battle, Walker staged a surprise attack on the Conservative stronghold of Granada. In perhaps his boldest military move, Walker commandeered one of the transit company's lake steamers docked in La Virgen. By sailing from La Virgen to Granada, Walker's army of about one hundred filibusters and three hundred native volunteers circumvented the superior Conservative forces camped in Rivas and seized their capital without a battle on 13 October 1855 (see map 3). In Granada, the filibusters executed their most prominent prisoner, Foreign Minister Mateo Mayorga; ironically, Mayorga had been one of the country's loudest proponents of U.S. immigration. Walker then threatened to kill many more prisoners unless the remaining Conservative forces surrendered immediately. Fearing for their kin's lives, Conservative generals quickly acceded. In under five months,

Walker had achieved military control over Nicaragua. He then set out to solidify his political power in order to realize his main goal: the creation of an "American empire" in the isthmus.

To Walker's surprise, both prominent Conservatives from Granada and powerful popular caudillos petitioned him to become their country's new president.[49] Yet Walker preferred to rule first through a puppet regime. He pressured the warring Liberal and Conservative elites to form a bipartisan government with the aging Conservative Patricio Rivas of León as its provisional president. Walker nonetheless remained the real power behind the Rivas administration. To control its Nicaraguan members, he forced each minister to have a U.S. filibuster as his deputy. Further, Walker concentrated military power into his filibuster army by disbanding all native forces except for those who had volunteered to fight under his command.

In fortifying his power, Walker was heavily supported by two U.S. entrepreneurs—Cornelius Garrison and Charles Morgan—who had recently seized control of the Accessory Transit Company from Cornelius Vanderbilt. In exchange for his loyalty, Walker secured much-needed funds and arms as well as free shipment of colonists, up to ten thousand of whom (men and women) began to flock to Nicaragua once news of his exploits reached the United States.[50] Thanks to the transit company, Walker's filibuster band swelled to an army of about two thousand soldiers and became perhaps the best-armed force Central America had ever seen.

Ultimately, however, Walker's fortunes hinged on his popularity with the local populace. Indeed, Walker so easily consolidated his political authority only because he was aided by elites throughout the country. Such support was not unlimited; many leading Conservatives fled to the country's interior, where they waged a guerrilla war against the filibusters. Still, many Conservative and Liberal elites welcomed Walker's rise to power and thwarted local efforts to expel the filibusters, as Walker's fiercest detractors grudgingly admitted.[51] Nothing better illuminates the grounds for Walker's elite support than the sermon made by Agustín Vijil shortly after Walker captured Granada.[52] Born in Granada in 1801, Vijil was an influential Catholic priest and one of Nicaragua's first coffee planters. Though an ardent Liberal, he had long been respected by the city's powerful Conservative oligarchs for his intellect and cosmopolitan outlook. His sermon was of further symbolic significance as it was delivered at Granada's most exclusive church, La Merced, in the presence of Walker and his officers. It thus publicized the filibusters' success in gaining the endorsement of some of Nicaragua's most powerful men.

Vijil's sermon illustrates how much Walker benefited from the fascination of Nicaragua's upper classes with U.S. transients and transit entrepreneurs. In justifying his embrace of the filibusters, Vijil reiterated three arguments typically made by proponents of U.S. colonization plans. First, he argued that because Walker hailed from a "civilized" nation he would be able to end the political and social turmoil that had ravaged the country since independence. Second, he maintained that Walker's military-colonists would promote the country's economic development by infusing it with the entrepreneurial spirit allegedly characteristic of North Americans. Third, Vijil stressed how these U.S. colonists would help Nicaragua construct the interoceanic canal. Under Walker, Vijil concluded, Nicaragua would finally become part of the "civilized world." This belief, firmly rooted in the country's first encounter with U.S. Manifest Destiny, largely explains why so many elite Nicaraguans followed Vijil in hailing Walker as their "guardian angel" who would "civilize" their country.

Yet to reshape Nicaragua in his own image, Walker was even more dependent on the backing of nonelite sectors. Not only did his imperial project secretly call for a revolution against the native elite, but, in a country as fraught with political and social conflicts as Nicaragua, popular movements exerted much power. And for a while Walker enjoyed great popular support. Even his main Nicaraguan foe admitted that, at least until early 1856, "the public mind was still in favor of Walker."[53] Such support manifested itself in popular songs that glorified Walker. For example, when he traveled from his capital of Granada to León in June 1856, local musicians greeted him by chanting, in Spanish, the following ode:

O Patriots, sing
A thousand happy hymns
To the redeemer
Of our freedom.

The world amazed
Shall obey and respect
The intrepid son
Of the great Washington.

And Free Nicaragua
Shall forever proclaim,
Hail the conquering Walker!
Hail our Liberator![54]

No doubt, Walker gained much support from León's predominantly Liberal populace simply for having conquered its longtime nemesis: the Granada-based Conservatives. But Walker's victory was also celebrated by popular sectors well beyond León's orbit.

Rural communities reached out to Walker in the hope that the filibuster would reverse efforts of past regimes to expand the power of the central state at their expense. As evident in the 1840s uprisings, these communities especially resented state authorities' efforts to curtail communal control over labor and the commercialization of lucrative products such as tobacco and *aguardiente* (a liquor brewed from sugarcane). They thus welcomed Walker's abolition of forced military conscription. In addition to saving them from military service, this decree reinforced the autonomy of their communities, especially over labor.

Walker's apparent willingness to consider popular demands also helped him gain the trust of rural powerbrokers. Leaders of indigenous communities trekked from near and far to enlist Walker's aid in their struggle for political, economic, and cultural autonomy. One case involved the indigenous community of Masatepe, then an important producer of tobacco and aguardiente. In petitioning Walker for help, the community's leaders sought to recuperate some of the economic power they had lost to "the Tyrant," their name for the encroaching central state. They also believed that Walker and his filibusters would be much more sensitive to their demands than the mestizo authorities who, in their words, showed nothing but "contempt" for their "caste."[55] In gaining the support of indigenous authorities, Walker clearly benefited from their strained relations with both the central state and neighboring mestizo communities.

Local priests were another set of authorities that to the chagrin of the nationalist opposition helped strengthen the filibusters' hold over the local populace. No doubt, numerous priests supported Walker, as they were Liberals who had been persecuted by the previous Conservative regime.[56] But in all likelihood many more backed Walker because they shared Vijil's enthusiasm for U.S. colonization projects. Thanks to these priests, Walker successfully countered the efforts of his enemies to use the fear of Protestantism as a way of mobilizing popular opposition to his regime. In fact, so close were Walker's relations with native priests that some anticlerical filibusters broke with him.[57]

Yet Walker's main native allies turned out to be the leaders of popular movements that had long battled local elites and the expanding central state. Coming from all over the country's Pacific zone, such popular caudillos included Mariano Méndez of León, Máximo Espinoza of Rivas, Francisco Bravo of Masaya, and Ubaldo Herrera of Granada.[58] But the most powerful was León's José María Valle, commonly known as El Chelón, who had helped lead the popular uprisings that rocked Nicaragua in the late 1840s.

Among the very first Nicaraguans to fight for Walker, Valle facilitated the filibusters' rise to power. Walker's dependence on Valle was even recognized by the U.S. public, as evident in the celebration of him in the 1856 Broadway hit *Nicaragua, or, Gen. Walker's Victories.*[59] Despite its racist bent, the musical correctly suggests that Walker was able to achieve his main military victories only with Valle's help. However, it fails to tell its U.S. audience that this one-legged Nicaraguan caudillo was also key to Walker's political fortunes. When Walker appointed Valle governor of Segovia—a vast, mountainous department bordering Honduras where many of Walker's elite opponents had sought refuge—the choice of territory was surely not random. Walker doubtlessly hoped that his principal native ally would allow him to gain control over a cattle- and mineral-rich region where peasant and indigenous communities were particularly powerful. For a while, Valle more than satisfied Walker's hopes.

Valle left no known record explaining his support for Walker other than his statement that the filibuster was fighting for the same "sacred" cause as he was, that is, for "true democracy."[60] We do know, however, that Valle was also an enthusiastic advocate for the projected interoceanic canal. In an 1845 speech to his troops, for instance, he claimed that the construction of the canal would turn Nicaragua into a "grand emporium."[61] Undoubtedly, Valle believed that Walker would help realize the canal project. In addition, he might have emulated other popular caudillos in idealizing the United States as a political and economic model.[62]

The reasons that motivated Valle to support Walker seem similar to those given by Vijil and other elite Nicaraguans. Yet if elites like Vijil firmly believed that Walker would defend the existing social order, Valle surely hoped for the exact opposite. How could he not? Not only had he long waged an antielite struggle but, as Walker's closest native ally, Valle probably knew about the filibuster's secret desire to destroy the native elite.

Walker's Revolution from Above

Walker waited until he had usurped the presidency in July 1856 to launch his attack against native elites. In his own mind, Walker's efforts to reshape Nicaragua constituted a full-fledged revolution. Indeed, he believed that a key difference between North Americans and Latin Americans was that the latter were "less fit for the real work of revolution than the robust children of the North."[63] Yet however loudly Walker proclaimed himself a revolutionary, elite Nicaraguans came to view him as a reactionary.

To them, no act better symbolized Walker's regressive bent than his promotion of slavery. Due to Walker, Nicaragua has the infamy of being the only country in Spanish America that legally reinstituted African slavery after it had already been abolished.[64] Walker maintained that this colonial institution would solve Nicaragua's perennial labor shortage and thus promote its capitalist development. He also believed that slavery would help "separate the races and destroy the half-castes who cause the disorder, which has prevailed in the country since the independence."[65] Walker justified his efforts to exterminate the "amalgamated race" that dominated Nicaragua by drawing deeply on Manifest Destiny, an ideology that most North Americans then associated with progress, not regression.[66] But in Nicaragua, Walker's racial views only reinforced his reactionary image as they echoed the age-old arguments Spanish colonizers had made to defend their caste system.

Walker's ideal vision of the nation-state also elicited contradictory reactions. Once his filibuster army became large enough, Walker hoped to rule as the supreme patriarch of a militarized, aristocratic state that was to be independent of the United States.[67] In exchange for their fealty, his U.S. followers would reign as paternalist plantation owners over indentured Indians and imported African slaves. For Walker, the formation of such a military aristocracy was a progressive enterprise. But for upper-class Nicaraguans, it mirrored the patriarchal nation-state conservative elites had sought to build around the extended hacienda family of colonial origin.[68] Of course, there was one key difference: In Walker's Americanized Nicaragua there was no place for native elites. Walker never realized his ideal state. He even failed to implement his most infamous decree, the establishment of a slave regime. Yet this did not prevent Walker and his men from unleashing a violent attack against the Nicaraguan elite.

Time and again, the filibusters justified their antielite attack as a struggle for the "regeneration" of Nicaragua. In the United States, "regeneration" was a powerful frontier myth that had shaped the country's expansion from the very start. As the historian Richard Slotkin has argued, it represented the redemption of the "American spirit" as something to be achieved by wars of racial extermination.[69] Following this logic, Walker and many of his men believed that regeneration entailed the violent displacement of Nicaraguan "mongrels" by Anglo-Saxon Americans. Yet some of Walker's men understood regeneration to mean instead the uplifting of Nicaraguans by North Americans.[70] To them, the people—not the land—should be regenerated.[71] They advocated the implementation of progressive, liberal principles then in vogue in the United States. Indeed, Walker's revolution occurred against the backdrop of a highly intensive and broadly encompassing reform movement that engulfed much of the United States. This fervor for radical social and political change was shared by some of Walker's men, particularly supporters of the "Young America" movement and veterans of the 1848 European revolutions. But filibusters who favored uplifting Nicaragua also believed that the local populace had long suffered from the "misrule" perpetrated by, as Walker put it, a "degraded aristocracy."[72] Thus no matter how differently Walker's men understood their mission of regeneration, they all clamored for a revolutionary assault against the Nicaraguan elite.

The filibusters unleashed their revolution on two fronts. On the one hand, they attacked the political basis of elite power by trying to monopolize the reins of government. Ironically, such efforts entailed the democratization of the country's electoral system. In the past, elite-controlled electoral colleges had selected the country's president, congressional deputies, and senators. Walker, by contrast, decreed that elections be decided by direct popular vote. He also dispensed with the property and income requirements that had previously excluded the overwhelming majority of Nicaraguans from the electoral process. According to the filibusters' bilingual newspaper *El Nicaragüense*, Walker extended the franchise to "every male inhabitant of eighteen years, against whom there is no criminal prosecuting, and who is not charged with being a dissolute and vicious man."[73]

Of course, Walker's new system was highly flawed, as evidenced by the massive electoral fraud that allowed him to capture the presidency in July 1856. Still, it represented a revolutionary challenge to the old political order. Above all, Walker's election ensured that for the first time since independence native elites no longer represented the nation-state. This election also set an important precedent as it was the first in Central America to be based on the principle of direct popular vote.[74] In doing so, it shifted control of national elections from the elite-dominated electoral college to communal authorities. Walker's electoral reforms thus gave popular sectors new institutional means to undermine elite rule. They enabled rural communities to strengthen their political autonomy, and empowered popular caudillos to determine the course of national politics. Perhaps fear of such a power shift, and not Walker's usurpation of the presidency alone, explains why his supporters among the Nicaraguan elite were so troubled by his insistence on holding direct elections.[75]

Even more dramatic was the filibusters' assault on the economic power of the native elite. As Walker was well aware, power in Nicaragua resided heavily in the ownership of landed estates. Consequently, he and his men believed that the most effective way to destroy the native elite was by confiscating its rural properties. This confiscation campaign began immediately after Walker usurped the presidency in July 1856. Walker's main goal was to redistribute the seized estates to his filibusters and the thousands of U.S. colonists flocking to Nicaragua. He also sought to sell some to prominent U.S. investors in order to raise much-needed funds. In both cases, the confiscation campaign represented the main means through which Walker sought to create his "American empire."[76]

The campaign proved a quick success due to the capacity of the Nicaraguan popular caudillos who directed many of the seizures.[77] Within two months, Walker's regime had expropriated over a hundred landed estates belonging to at least eighty elite families.[78] Most expropriated estates consisted of cacao plantations that dotted the southern region of Granada/Rivas and large cattle ranches centered in the great plains and hills of Chontales. This was hardly a coincidence. These cacao and cattle estates were among the most valuable in all of Nicaragua, and were often owned by Walker's main enemies, Conservative oligarchs from Granada. Still, pro-Walker elites also came to fear the confiscation campaign.[79] For some time, they had supported the distribution of land to filibusters as a way of "civilizing" Nicaragua. But they expected that these North Americans would colonize the country's large tracts of uncultivated land. Never did they imagine that the filibusters would instead want to seize their own estates and thus destroy them.

Once Walker's elite supporters recognized the revolutionary thrust of his Americanization project, most united with their erstwhile enemies to expel the filibusters. This unification was sealed by the Liberal-Conservative pact of 12 September 1856. Deposed president Rivas and his coterie justified their turnabout as a necessary response to the filibusters' sudden attempt to destroy the existing order. They not only rejected Walker's usurpation of the presidency but also denounced his electoral reforms and confiscation campaign. In addition, they claimed that Walker intended to "extinguish" the country's religion.[80] To be sure, in the United States Walker was widely celebrated as a Protestant hero waging a just war against Catholicism.[81] But in Nicaragua he made every effort to cultivate good relations with the Catholic clergy. The claim that Walker was out to destroy the Catholic Church thus seems baseless. Yet, as Walker himself acknowledged, it represented a shrewd ploy of elite Nicaraguans to tap the powerful force of popular Catholicism and use it to rally the masses against the predominantly Protestant filibusters.[82]

In closing their ranks against Walker, Nicaragua's upper classes responded very similarly to the way they had reacted to the revolutionary crisis that had engulfed the country in the late 1840s. However, there were two key differences. First, elites felt much more threatened by Walker's revolution from above than by the popular rebellions of the previous decade. While this greater threat did not make the pact of 1856 easier to forge, it ensured that over the long run elite unity would be far firmer. Second, the filibusters' threat to elite authority was so wide-reaching that it enabled Nicaragua's anti-Walker opposition to form a military alliance with other Central American rulers. This joining of forces was an extraordinary step for a region where elite rivalries had destroyed the Central American Federation of 1824–39. In the tumultuous decade of the 1840s alone, Nicaraguan elites had tried four different times to reestablish some form of Central American unity.[83] Yet such efforts bore fruit only after Walker and his filibuster army appeared on the scene.

The "National" War

Like their Nicaraguan counterparts, Central American elites feared Walker's attempt to revolutionize the region's political and social structures. Costa

Rica's president Juan Mora thus stated that in fighting for Walker's ouster he mainly sought to extinguish "this revolutionary spirit that has been the greatest of our enemies."[84] In their public proclamations, however, Mora and other Central American leaders followed the lead of their Nicaraguan allies, highlighting the filibusters' "godlessness" and their efforts to enslave the native populace—surely because they believed these were the issues most likely to inspire popular support.[85]

The Central American governments began their so-called National War against the filibuster regime immediately following Walker's "victory" in the presidential elections of June 1856.[86] While Costa Rican forces had already fought the filibusters in April, only after Walker usurped the presidency did the other Central American nations join the struggle. In mid-July, a force of over one thousand Guatemalan, Salvadoran, and Honduran troops invaded northwestern Nicaragua and quickly dislodged the filibusters from the region around León. This offensive greatly circumscribed the geographic scope of Walker's revolution and spurred his Nicaraguan enemies to intensify their guerrilla war in the north-central departments of Matagalpa and Chontales. After a series of setbacks, the Allied forces, now totaling about eighteen hundred men, captured the important towns of Managua and Masaya in early October. At about the same time, Costa Rica's army began advancing from the south. Unable to recapture Masaya, Walker withdrew his army of about fifteen hundred filibusters from his capital of Granada to Rivas so that he could better defend the transit road. However important Granada was to Walker's political fortunes, he could not afford to lose his lifeline to U.S. recruits and supplies.

Walker left Granada ordering his men to burn the city down. Still furious over the desertion by his former elite allies, Walker believed there was no better way to punish them than by destroying the city that best symbolized elite power.[87] The fire lasted for about ten days and razed one of the continent's oldest cities. Walker's intoxicated men looted and raped as they torched house after house, working from the suburbs toward the city's center.[88] When allied forces finally captured the smoldering city little was left intact except for a sign reading "Here was Granada." Walker's men made sure to leave it behind.

The loss of Granada was a great blow to the filibusters. Yet Walker still believed that his army would prevail over the Allied forces. Walker's optimism stemmed largely from his racist belief that Anglo-Saxons were inherently superior to Central Americans. It also reflected the dispirited state of his enemies. Not only had the Allies suffered much higher casualties from combat and cholera alike, their leaders also began to quarrel bitterly over military strategy, political control, and personal prestige. More important to Walker was the Allies' apparent inability to enlist the Nicaraguan masses in their struggle. Until the end, Walker maintained that "the people adhered to the Americans [while] the *calzados*, those wearing shoes, deserted to the enemies."[89] Indeed, the filibusters continued to be supported by Valle and other influential caudillos. As Walker later admitted, these popular leaders "aided to keep the people . . . from joining in the crusade the Allies preached against the 'filibusters.' "[90]

Yet Walker's popular support eroded as the National War progressed. According to filibuster accounts, the Nicaraguan masses were not necessarily upset over Walker's usurping the presidency, his Protestant faith, or even his proslavery stance—issues that Central American elites emphasized in trying to drum up popular support.[91] What the Nicaraguans truly dreaded, the filibusters claimed, were the unprecedented violence and the cholera epidemic brought on by the outsiders waging the National War. We also know that many urban dwellers were greatly troubled by the antivagrancy and labor-contract decrees Walker passed in September 1856 so that his regime could more easily coerce poor Nicaraguans to work on the confiscated plantations. The rural masses, in turn, resented the filibusters for raiding their farms for food and livestock once the war intensified.[92]

These resentments, however, did not induce Nicaraguans to join the Allies en masse. True, members of indigenous communities from Matagalpa and the island of Ometepe (in Lake Nicaragua) played a key role in the guerrilla war waged by Walker's elite enemies.[93] Still, Nicaraguans made up only about an eighth of the Allied forces, even though the National War was waged exclusively on their territory. So if an astounding 3.5 percent of Costa Rica's population went to war, only about half a percent of all Nicaraguans participated in what they would later celebrate as their nation's foundational event.[94] Whatever their motives may have been, Nicaraguans' aloofness from the war did not hinder Walker, for his filibuster army was not dependent on native troops.

Walker's days were nonetheless numbered. Ironically, the deathblow was delivered by the United States in the person of Cornelius Vanderbilt. Vanderbilt intervened in the National War to spite Walker's most important U.S.

business allies: Charles Morgan and Cornelius Garrison. Both had infuriated the "Commodore" after usurping his lucrative Accessory Transit Company in 1853. And once Walker began to defend the interests of Morgan and Garrison, he too became an enemy of the second richest man in the United States.[95] At first, Vanderbilt simply exhorted the U.S. government to prevent Morgan and Garrison from forwarding recruits and arms to Walker. His hopes were not misplaced as the administration of President Franklin Pierce had initially opposed Walker's filibustering expedition. But the administration ultimately bowed to public pressure and allowed U.S. adventurers to sail to Nicaragua on ships operated by Morgan and Garrison. As a result, Vanderbilt took matters into his own hands and began to provide the Allies with much-needed funds and arms. Then, in January 1857, his agents helped Costa Rican troops capture strategic forts along the San Juan River and confiscate all the transit steamers. Thanks to Vanderbilt, the Allies controlled the transit route from the Atlantic coast to Lake Nicaragua. By early April, they had also seized its western portion, depriving Walker of his last supply line and escape route.

The loss of the transit sealed the fate of the filibusters besieged in Rivas. With desertion and cholera rapidly depleting his starving ranks, Walker surrendered on 1 May 1857. To the dismay of its Nicaraguan members, the Allied leadership allowed Walker and his men to escape unharmed and sail for the United States under the protection of the U.S. Navy. Thus ended Nicaragua's first dramatic encounter with U.S. imperialism.

Conclusion

Walker returned to the United States a popular hero. He continued to be obsessed with Nicaragua and its potential to become the world's commercial center. Thrice he led filibuster expeditions to resurrect his regime. The last occurred in 1860, when Walker sought to enter Nicaragua via the Honduran coast. Caught by the British navy, he was handed over to Honduran authorities, who promptly executed him. By then, Walker's star in the United States had dimmed; the nation was now far more concerned with self-preservation than expansion. Significantly for Latin America, the U.S. Civil War of 1861–65 put an end to filibusterism.

Although Walker's rule lasted only two years, the violent impulse of U.S. filibusterism has remained etched in Nicaraguans' consciousness to the present day. This is not surprising, for Walker and his men left behind a trail of plundered farms, destroyed cities, and thousands of dead. Such bitter memories were refreshed by future U.S. interventions. Yet Nicaraguans would repress a key aspect of their fatal encounter with Manifest Destiny: They forgot that their forefathers initially embraced the filibusters as a result of an infatuation with the U.S. ideals and practices that were introduced by the gold rushers. Perhaps because the betrayal of Walker was so great, it buried elite Nicaraguans' memories of their own complicity in the filibuster's rise to power. Indeed, the Walker fiasco only strengthened the will of elite Nicaraguans to replicate the U.S. road to modernity as a means to strengthen their own nationality and state institutions.

2 Americanization from Within

Forging a Cosmopolitan Nationality

ALTHOUGH WALKER'S RULE BROUGHT great destruction to Nicaragua, its end ushered in a long period of political stability. The foundations of this new order were laid in the final moments of the National War. Profoundly shocked by Walker's revolution from above, elite Nicaraguans made every effort to settle the protracted battle over the nation-state. For the first time, Liberals and Conservatives jointly ratified a new constitution in 1858 and agreed to share power more generally. Thanks to this elite convergence, an unprecedented number of presidents—six Conservatives—succeeded each other in an orderly fashion. This lengthy phase of Conservative rule ended in 1893, when dissident Conservatives helped the Liberal José Santos Zelaya establish an autocratic regime that lasted until 1909. Despite its distinct style of governance, Zelaya's Liberal dictatorship represented more a continuation than a break with the previous Conservative governments. Not only did both regimes enjoy much bipartisan support, they pursued the same cosmopolitan nation-state project that linked the nation's interest and identity with the country most likely to build the canal: the United States.

Post-Walker elites' embrace of a cosmopolitan nation-state project might seem paradoxical, for cosmopolitanism is often viewed as the antithesis of nationalism.[1] But in Latin America, it has long served as a crucial means to strengthen the nation-state.[2] Nicaragua's most famous cosmopolite, the poet Rubén Darío (1867–1916), articulated this melding of ideas when he proclaimed that Latin Americans could forge "a national spirit" only if they were "nationalistic inward and cosmopolitan outward."[3] Darío was not the first Latin American to advocate a cosmopolitan nationality. Cosmopolitan nation-state projects had existed since the continent became independent in the 1820s. But such projects were not implemented until the consolidation of the liberal nation-state in the second half of the nineteenth century. Above all, Latin American cosmopolitanism invoked a greater insertion of the nation into the world economy, largely via the export of agrarian and mineral products. It also entailed the nation's opening to foreign immigrants, principally Europeans and North Americans. As a result, it often implied the desire to whiten the nation. Finally, cosmopolitanism called for the citizenry to embrace the ideas and ways that marked North Atlantic models of "prog-ress." Most Latin American ruling elites did not simply imitate these models but molded them to their countries' peculiarities.[4]

Indeed, what made Nicaraguan cosmopolitanism distinct was the very factor that most attracted international interest to the country: the canal. And since the canal was so entangled with the interests of the United States, Nicaraguan cosmopolitanism deviated from the general Latin American path in a key way: rather than promoting the Europeanization of life as it did in most other Latin American nations, it strengthened Nicaraguans' embrace of the "American way of life."

Reembracing Americanization

At first, however, the Walker fiasco fanned anti-U.S. sentiments in Nicaragua. The rise of anti-Americanism manifested itself in the proliferation of anti-filibuster tales and songs, some of which survived well into the twentieth century. The most enduring song to emerge in the wake of the Walker fiasco was "Mama Ramona," which told of a woman who ran a boarding house in Masaya. Drawing on the ancient trope of the female traitor, the song de-nounced the immorality of Walker's enterprise and valorized Nicaragua's nationalist struggle. The trauma Walker inflicted on Nicaraguans' psyche can also be seen in the rise of new popular sayings that evoked the filibusters' infamous deeds. One proverb that Nicaraguans still use when discussing a misfortune is "Nada eso es, para lo que pasó en Granada" [That's nothing compared to what happened in Granada], which refers to Walker's infamous burning of the city.

Yet ample evidence suggests that the anti-Americanism engendered by the Walker episode was weaker than scholars have generally assumed.[5] In fact, following Walker's expulsion, government officials privately fretted about the populace's will to resist future filibuster invasions.[6] A U.S. diplomat similarly noted in 1858 that "among the subordinate population, who do all the labor, and bear all the burdens of the State, there is a strong undercurrent in favor of 'Walker,' which is the name in which they embody the idea of American domination." But he also added that the poor "would gladly embrace any change to relieve them from their present masters, and the abominable sys-tem of military recruiting and forced contributions to which they are subjected."[7] As during the National War, many of the rural poor appeared bent more on defending communal autonomy than on either embracing or rejecting "American domination."

By contrast, Walker's main victims—native elites—more clearly shed their former enthusiasm for U.S. colonization. Various political leaders labored to block U.S. migration to their country; some even sought to expel U.S. residents. The rise of elite anti-Americanism was also noticeable in the government's refusal to reopen the transisthmic transit. As a prominent Conservative oligarch stressed, ruling elites feared that the transit would "infallibly result in the sweeping of their country by hordes of filibusters."[8] Such fears also drove the Nicaraguan government to ask for French and British help against future U.S. invasions. Although this call went unheeded, it highlighted to U.S. officials that the Walker imbroglio had pushed Central America's hitherto most pro-U.S. elite to develop a strong "hatred of our race."[9]

Some elite Nicaraguans even developed a new, anti-U.S. national identity based on the amorphous concept of a "raza latina." In 1858 a U.S. envoy claimed that elites' anti-Americanism derived from their desire to preserve "the dominion and ascendancy of what they are pleased to call the 'razalatina' or latin race."[10] In constructing this "latin race," against the "rapacious, evergrasping irreligious barbarians of the North," Nicaraguans appropriated the emerging French discourse of Latinity.[11] Used by the French to expand their influence over the continent, this discourse celebrated the common culture allegedly shared by speakers of the Latin-based languages of Spanish, Portuguese, and French.[12] Throughout Latin America, elites leery of U.S. expansionism appreciated Latinity, as they believed the example of France challenged U.S. notions that Catholic nations could not be as developed as Protestant ones.[13]

In the end, however, an anti-U.S. nationality failed to grow in post-Walker Nicaragua, as many elites reembraced U.S. ideals of progress.[14] This reembrace reflected elites' enduring faith in the entrepreneurial spirit of North Americans. But above all it resulted from their belief that the main way they could defend Nicaraguan nationality was by emulating the U.S. paradigm for state-making. In rebuilding post-Walker Nicaragua, elites desperately sought to create a strong nation-state capable of fending off future filibuster invasions. And to them, the United States continued to be their best and only model. The drafters of the 1858 constitution were thus guided by the example of the U.S. Constitution, particularly in their efforts to strengthen the executive branch.[15] In addition to selectively adopting U.S. political forms, Nicaragua's ruling elites wanted the masses to assimilate what the leading Liberal Gregorio Juárez called the U.S. "national spirit." For Juárez, this spirit consisted principally of "the liberality with which [the United States] offers citizenship to all the inhabitants of the world."[16] In a similar vein, the Conservative editors of the government newspaper claimed in 1858 that Nicaraguans needed to embrace the U.S. way of life in order to survive: "Nicaragua needs . . . its sons to change their character, customs, and lifestyle: they need to undergo, in a word, a complete metamorphosis."[17]

That Nicaragua's ruling elites would exhort the citizenry to adopt the institutions and lifestyle of the nation that most threatened their independence might seem odd. But it is also striking that this belief was widely shared by elite Nicaraguans no matter their political affiliation. Consider, for example, the case of Mexico, the Latin American country most damaged by U.S. expansionism in the age of Manifest Destiny. Mexico's devastating defeat in the 1846–48 war with the United States polarized elite attitudes toward the United States and sharpened their ideological divisions.[18] In Nicaragua, by contrast, U.S. expansionism pushed native elites to settle their longstanding conflicts as they converged around a cosmopolitan nationalist project based on the U.S. experience. No doubt, this difference reflects the greater role elite divisions played in facilitating U.S. intervention in Nicaragua. But perhaps more important still, elite Nicaraguans differed from their Mexican counterparts in believing that their country's manifest destiny—the canal—was tied with that of the United States.

For only a fleeting moment, then, did the Walker disaster push Nicaraguans to equate antifilibusterism with anti-Americanism. This equation did not greatly trouble those Nicaraguan leaders who most strongly believed in the U.S. model of development. For example, Gregorio Juárez, who served as foreign minister in the first post-Walker government, acknowledged in 1858 that "the Nicaraguan people has collapsed the filibuster with the North American, and has been so zealous of its own independence that it mistrusts the government of that nation." But he added that this "deplorable situation, while seemingly alarming, lacks importance if we consider it in light of the philosophy and policies of both countries."[19] Juárez proved right; anti-Americanism did not flourish in post-Walker Nicaragua.

Forging a Cosmopolitan Nation-State

After a brief turn inward, ruling elites spent the rest of the century forging a cosmopolitan nation-state. Time and again, they proclaimed that the country's cosmopolitan future hinged on the realization of the canal project.[20] Such statements echoed the views of pre-Walker rulers like José Laureano Pineda (1851–53), who declared that the canal would transform Nicaragua into a "cosmopolitan nation" by making it the world's greatest emporium and a center of foreign immigration.[21] But post-Walker governments undertook much greater efforts than their predecessors to disseminate their canal-based nationalist imagery in order to gain the necessary local and foreign support.

At home, ruling elites propagated their cosmopolitan project largely via the country's expanding educational system and newspaper industries. Some papers, like the *Canal de Nicaragua*, were founded to promote the country's canal and immigration projects. Two other important venues were townhall-like meetings where local citizens would debate the canal issue; and public celebrations of canal resolutions, treaties, or visiting survey expeditions.[22] How the government's canal-based nationalist project was received by the local populace remains an open question. No doubt, many Nicaraguans believed that the canal would never be built. Others feared that it would only attract a second Walker to their country. But local accounts suggest that the canal project excited broad sectors of the urban populace.[23]

Nicaragua's rulers also strove to spread their cosmopolitan project abroad. In doing so, they greatly benefited from the late-nineteenth-century expansion of world's fairs. Centered in North Atlantic metropolises, these fairs embodied cosmopolitan nationalism, as they celebrated the civilizing mission of free trade as well as nationalist aspirations.[24] For the Nicaraguan state, world's fairs were an ideal forum to publicize its canal-centered image of a cosmopolitan nation. Not coincidentally, the Nicaraguan exhibit at the era's greatest fair—the Paris Universal Exposition of 1889—was dominated by an enormous relief of the projected canal.[25] It was the only Latin American exhibit that did not project a national imagery based on its current exports or cultural past. For example, the showcase of Bolivia's pavilion was a tunnel of silver, highlighting the country's leading export product and the economic basis of the Sucre-based ruling elite. Argentina, a rising exporter of beef, presented a cattle-based image of itself. Mexico featured an Aztec palace and Ecuador an Inca temple of the sun.[26] Few of these national images resembled the realities they purported to represent, yet none centered on such a hopeful projection as Nicaragua's.

To Nicaragua's ruling elites, their nationalist project was more than a hope, for they firmly believed that the United States would soon build the canal. Their faith in the United States was not misplaced. True, the completion of the U.S. transcontinental railroad in 1869 eliminated the need for a U.S. passenger transit through Central America. But influential U.S. investors and their government remained impassioned about constructing a transisthmic canal, with most favoring the Nicaraguan over the Panamanian route. At first, U.S. backers of the Nicaraguan canal simply stressed its economic benefits for the United States.[27] Many maintained that the canal would transport freight between the U.S. coasts much cheaper than the transcontinental railroad. Others went further, arguing that the Nicaraguan canal would allow U.S. manufacturers along the Atlantic seaboard to wrest control of the booming Asian trade from their European rivals who, they claimed, had greatly benefited from the 1869 opening of the Suez Canal. From the late 1880s onward, proponents of the Nicaraguan canal increasingly stressed its military importance, claiming that such a waterway was indispensable for transforming the United States into a world power. Among the most vocal of such canal promoters was Alfred Thayer Mahan, then one of the world's leading naval strategists and publicists.[28]

A mix of economic and strategic concerns thus fueled U.S. efforts to build the Nicaraguan canal. While the U.S. Congress established canal commissions to secure the necessary political and financial support, the White House periodically sent surveying expeditions to Nicaragua (see figure 1). These efforts in turn sparked the founding of private U.S. canal syndicates. In the end, all such enterprises failed, with many running out of funds. This fate befell the Maritime Canal Company, the only syndicate to undertake actual work on the Nicaraguan canal. Like most plans of the era, the company's projected waterway followed Vanderbilt's transit route. After construction began at the canal's Atlantic terminus in 1889, costs quickly ran high. In addition to employing two thousand well-paid laborers, the company needed to import food and expensive machinery such as dredges. Unable to attract additional capital, the company discontinued work after a financial crisis shook the United States in 1893; shortly thereafter it went bankrupt.[29] Paradoxically, such collapses only solidified Nicaragua's canal dreams as they pushed the U.S. government to more vigorously seek the canal's completion.

1. Nicaraguan workers on U.S. canal survey expedition, 1884.
Courtesy of U.S. National Archives.

The vicissitudes of the canal project compelled Nicaragua's rulers to walk across a diplomatic tightrope. While striving to maintain U.S. enthusiasm for their canal project, they sought to block efforts of the U.S. government to gain exclusive ownership of the canal zone. And until 1901, they were largely successful, as the United States was repeatedly forced to sign canal treaties that safeguarded Nicaragua's territorial integrity.[30] Nicaragua clearly bene-fited from the post–Civil War rise of antiexpansionist sentiments within the U.S. Congress, which shaped U.S. canal policy during the late nineteenth century.[31] Nicaraguan officials also exploited U.S.-European competition over the canal to wrest important concessions from the United States.[32] But their ability to withstand U.S. pressure primarily resulted from the strong state Nicaraguans had built on the ruins of Walker's failed empire.

Putting an end to "anarchy" had always been key to elites' cosmopolitan project. After the Walker disaster, it became the sine qua non for their very survival. And since elites believed that their own internal conflicts had facili-tated Walker's rise to power, they became obsessed with unity.[33] As a first step, Conservative and Liberal leaders agreed to share power by forming a bipartisan government that included members of the country's two principal regional elites: those of León and Granada. Tainted by having invited Walker to Nicaragua, Liberals ceded the presidency to the Conservatives. In exchange, Conservative presidents persistently nominated Liberals to key government ministries. Also, if most presidents came from the Conservative-dominated region of Granada-Rivas, leaders of Congress tended to emanate from the Liberal stronghold of León. Finally, Liberals were allowed to exert great influence over municipal politics, even in Conservative bastions like Granada. Exemplary of post-Walker elites' desire to create a more cohesive ruling class was their decision to move the capital to Managua. Located halfway between León and Granada, this town was one of Nicaragua's first centers of coffee production. Bustling Managua was more than a regional compromise. It embodied the new, cosmopolitan nation-state the country's ruling elites sought to forge.

Even if the Walker episode discredited the Liberal Party, liberal ideals guided the construction of the post-Walker state.[34] Politically, Nicaragua's rulers built an administrative infrastructure that greatly strengthened the autonomy and power of the central state. They created notable state institutions such as public schools, land registries, local militias, a national military, agricultural judgeships, rural police forces, regional financial administrative offices, a bureau of demographic and agricultural statistics, prisons, and a ministry of development. Economically, government officials pursued liberal policies to stimulate agroexports. They tried to liberalize land and capital markets, and they used state resources to improve the country's communication and transport systems.[35]

Finally, post-Walker elites went to great lengths to impose a culture of modernity on the local populace. Their goal was both to forge a stronger "national spirit" and to turn poorer Nicaraguans into more productive and cosmopolitan citizens. To do so, they promoted the secularization of society via public schools, liberal laws, civic rituals, and state regulation of social norms.[36] Emulating the United States, they also fostered the rise of an independent press and the creation of civic associations such as scientific and literary societies, social clubs, and agricultural organizations[37]—institutions that, in practice, remained closed to nonelite sectors. But above all it was through public schools that governing elites sought to inculcate, as the minister of education put it in 1883, "the habits . . . that produce a civilized and socially acceptable person."[38]

Far from stymieing the rise of a liberal, cosmopolitan state, then, the Walker episode accelerated this process.[39] True, Conservatives benefited politically from Liberals' fatal alliance with Walker. Yet liberalism—in this case, the valorization of free trade, immigration, secularization, land privatization, and anticorporatism—became the dominant ideology of the post-Walker elite. And it was the Granada-based Conservatives who were mainly responsible for implementing the liberal reforms that fostered the rise of a dynamic export economy, a centralized state apparatus, and a more secular society.[40] So strongly did Conservatives embrace the liberal banner of "progress" that a prominent ideologue from the Liberal Party quipped they were "more red" than Karl Marx himself.[41] Even the grand patriarch of Conservatives, Pedro Joaquín Chamorro Alfaro, embraced liberalism. In fact, under his presidency (1875–79), the Nicaraguan state carried out the most extensive liberal reforms and infrastructure improvements of the post-Walker era. An ardent nationalist who fiercely opposed Walker from the very start, Chamorro followed most of his fellow elites in viewing the world's premier liberal nation—the United States—as his "model Republic."[42] This valorization might strike some as a mere gesture of cultural mimicry. But for Chamorro, the need to emulate the United States was a key lesson he had carried away from his country's traumatic encounter with Walker. As the case of Chamorro exemplifies, Conservative oligarchs who had led the Nicaraguan struggle against Walker came to believe that the only way to protect their country against future U.S. expansionists was by replicating the U.S. road to modernity.

Due to the post-Walker elite convergence, Nicaragua developed into arguably the most stable country in Central America. From Walker's fall to 1900, Nicaragua experienced the fewest violent transfers in presidential power (one) and the most orderly presidential transitions via elections (six). Still, the efforts of Nicaraguan elites to forge a cosmopolitan nation-state did not go unchallenged. On the contrary, in 1881 these reforms provoked the largest uprising on the isthmus in the late nineteenth century. This rebellion also reveals how cosmopolitanized Nicaragua had become.

Challenging Cosmopolitanization

The uprising that stunned Nicaragua in 1881 consisted of two separate insurrections: the rural rebellion of several thousand Matagalpan Indians, and the riots that convulsed the country's urban centers. If the Matagalpan insurgents were largely Indian men, the urban protestors were a mixed group that included Indians and non-Indians (*ladinos*), rich and poor, men and women. Although hardly the first violent upheavals of the post-Walker era, they were the largest and most powerful. The uprisings reflected popular opposition not so much to the spread of commercial agriculture (as often claimed) but, rather, to the expanding state and the country's cosmopolitanization.[43]

Matagalpa's massive revolt was sparked by government efforts to force local Indians to build roads and telegraphs for little to no wages, yet the insurgents were fueled by deeper grievances.[44] Like rural people elsewhere in Nicaragua, Matagalpan Indians were troubled by state authorities' gnawing at their community's economic and political autonomy. It was thus to the thundering cries of "Death to the Government" that over one thousand Indians rose up on 30 March 1881. The rebels also targeted elite efforts to cosmopolitanize the nation, defending what their leaders called an "Indian Nation."[45] However amorphous this indigenous nationalism might have been, it challenged the elite, cosmopolitanist imagining of the nation as void of Indians. By fighting for an "Indian Nation," the insurgents sought to invert the racial order underpinning the nationalist project of cosmopolitan elites, who tended to equate Indianness with "barbarism" and "backwardness." Still, indigenous nationalism did not present the main threat to cosmopolitanism, partly because more Nicaraguans had come to share elites' anti-Indian vision of the nation-state.[46]

The greater danger lay in the religious thrust of the Matagalpan Indian rebellion. According to indigenous prisoners, the rebels launched their second attack, in August 1881, in the name of Catholicism.[47] In particular, they protested the government's recent expulsion of the Jesuit order, whose members had (wrongly) been accused of instigating the March uprising. Yet the rebels' defense of religion went beyond simple loyalty to their Jesuit allies. They more generally resisted the efforts of cosmopolitan elites to secularize schools, festivals, and other aspects of local society and culture. Above all, Matagalpan Indians fought to preserve control over religious institutions and practices that regulated economic and political relations within their community. Little wonder that Matagalpa's 1881 rebels launched their first attack during Holy Week.[48]

Concern for the nation's Catholic identity also drove many non-Indians to participate in the demonstrations that shook urban Nicaragua in mid-1881.[49] Unlike the Matagalpa rebellion, these protests involved not just the poor but also dissident elites, the *iglesieros*. Consisting largely of wealthy Conservative merchants and estate owners, iglesieros spearheaded the 1881 riots that paralyzed the country's largest city, León. Their main goal was to close the Instituto de Occidente, a state-funded male primary and secondary school that had been established in March 1881 by the city's wealthiest families. From the start, iglesieros waged a vitriolic campaign against the school's European professors, whom they denounced as Freemasons bent on destroying Nicaragua's Catholic identity. When the expulsion of the Jesuits triggered a mass uprising in May, León's iglesieros sought to harness the force of popular Catholicism to its crusade against the Institute. Like the Matagalpan insurgents, the urban rebels carried out their attacks while shouting anticosmopolitan slogans such as "Death to the Masons!" and "Long live religion!" Despite rallying much popular support, they were defeated by government troops; the same fate befell the Matagalpan rebels.

Iglesieros' participation in the urban revolts of 1881 reveals that not all elites supported the country's cosmopolitanization.[50] Initially, iglesieros opposed official efforts to "cosmopolitanize" key laws such as the freedom of worship.[51] Post-Walker governments sought these legal changes in order to facilitate the assimilation of foreign immigrants. To help "make the immigrant a citizen," they argued, would only strengthen Nicaraguan nationality. Iglesieros, by contrast, charged that such laws threatened the country's national identity, for they would not only undermine Catholicism, the nation's spiritual core, but transform Nicaraguans into "cosmopolitan subjects" void of any nationality.[52] In doing so, iglesieros criticized the governing elites for what the former saw as thoughtless and dangerous "imitation" of foreign trends.[53]

Long peaceful, iglesieros' anticosmopolitan crusade took a violent turn once the struggle over the country's national identity shifted into the realm of education. Whether they advocated a cosmopolitan or a Catholic Nicaragua, elites agreed that schools represented the main means to impose a national project on society. After public education expanded in the late 1870s, cosmopolitan and anticosmopolitan elites struggled fiercely for control of schools. Exacerbating these tensions was the emergence of state schools, which competed with religious ones established by Jesuits and other Catholic missionaries who arrived in the 1870s. As the clash over education more generally suggests, Nicaragua's cosmopolitanizing state collided with a reinvigorated Catholic Church and with the popular religiosity that fueled the growth of lay

Catholic organizations such as the Apostolado de la Oración and the Hijas de María.[54] This collision between cosmopolitanism and Catholic revival occurred at many different levels, including struggles between religious and secular women's organizations for control of public welfare.[55] But nowhere was it more deeply felt than in the 1881 uprisings.

These revolts pitted not so much antimodern against modern forces as competing nationalist projects against each other. However much leaders of both camps cast their conflict as one between the forces of modernity and tradition, the iglesieros were just about as modern as cosmopolitan elites.[56] Not only did the iglesieros aggressively use modern means, particularly the media, to wage their anticosmopolitan crusade, they also upheld liberal-democratic and republican values that were then hallmarks of modernity.[57] Similarly, popular insurgents of 1881 did not reject modernity outright. For governing elites who believed that the telegraph represented the "triumph of civilization," nothing better highlighted the rebels' antimodern thrust than the destruction of telegraph posts by Matagalpan Indians.[58] Actually, the indigenous rebels attacked the telegraph not for fear of things modern but to defend their communal autonomy against an encroaching state. Moreover, many Nicaraguan Indians apparently accepted reigning notions of modernity such as liberal property and political rights.[59] Fighting for a Nicaragua that was at once Catholic and modern, the 1881 insurgents rejected governing elites' belief that "there can never be a marriage between Mr Modern Progress and Mrs Catholic Religion."[60]

Yet the swift defeat of the 1881 rebels also shows how entrenched the cosmopolitan nation-state had become since the Walker fiasco. Never before did cosmopolitan elites have a stronger state apparatus at their disposal. More important, elites had become more united in supporting their country's cosmopolitanization. The only elites manifestly opposed to cosmopolitanism were the iglesieros. Yet this minority faction of the Conservative Party never succeeded in wrestling control of the state from liberal Conservatives and their Liberal allies. By 1881, governing elites had so thoroughly embraced cosmopolitanism that the textbook most widely used in Nicaraguan public schools was the *Libro de lectura* authored by the Argentine statesman Domingo Sarmiento, arguably Latin America's most prominent proponent of a cosmopolitan nationality.[61]

Cosmopolitan elites' nation-state project also seems to have enjoyed greater popular support than commonly believed. While contemporary accounts stress that the majority of the Nicaraguan populace opposed the expulsion of the Jesuits and the secularization of the public sphere more generally, recent studies show that urban and rural dwellers had increasingly come to accept the liberal state as a legitimate authority.[62] And popular support for liberal ideals key to the cosmopolitan project grew as more peasants benefited from the post-1870s expansion in export agriculture.

The Agroexport Boom

Nicaragua's ruling elites had long deemed trade with North Atlantic nations as essential to their efforts to make the country more cosmopolitan. But not until the post-Walker state was consolidated could they exploit the industrialized world's booming demand for cash crops such as coffee. Nicaraguan governments followed the general Latin American path by providing extensive subsidies to export producers, modernizing the transportation and communication systems, and enacting wide-reaching liberal reforms that produced an institutional environment more conducive to export production. Taking advantage of an accommodating state, easier access to foreign capital, and new market opportunities, Nicaraguan landlords as well as numerous small-scale farmers created what became Central America's second fastest growing export economy.[63] And as we will see in the next section, the profits generated by the post-1870s export boom enabled elite Nicaraguans to increase their consumption of U.S. goods and their identification with U.S. leisure practices.

Nicaragua's agroexport economy stood out not just for its dynamism but also for its diverse base. As in much of Central America, the boom was fueled by coffee exports. In the 1870s and 1880s, most new coffee fields were established in the southwestern uplands that stretched from Managua to Carazo and Granada.[64] In the following decade, coffee cultivation also expanded into the north-central region of Matagalpa. By the 1900s, Nicaragua had two major coffee zones that generated about half of the country's export revenues. Still, other cash crops continued to dominate the country's rural landscape. Some were new export products like bananas, which were cultivated on the Atlantic coast. Yet many other products, such as sugar, cacao, corn, and cattle, were of older origin and largely served the Central American market. Nicaragua's so-called coffee revolution was thus driven not only by coffee but by a wide range of cash crops.

2. Elite residence in Granada. *Courtesy of U.S. National Archives.*

The spectacular growth of commercial agriculture also enabled cities to undergo a stunning facelift. This change was especially noticeable in Granada, home to the country's wealthiest agroexport producers. For a long time, the city had been unable to recover from the massive destruction suffered during the National War. Time and again, foreign travelers sadly noted how few of Granada's churches, homes, and government buildings had risen from their ashes. As a British visitor stated in 1866: "In the city itself there is nothing further to describe; it is but a heap of ruins. . . . Granada is a dream of desolation—a nightmare—a horror unspeakable."[65] Funds from the post-1870s export boom allowed Granadans to go on an unprecedented building spree that sought to resurrect old Granada by remaining faithful to its pre-Walker layout. Yet the rich also gave the city a modern look by constructing two-story homes, churches, and public buildings in the neoclassical and eclectic styles then in vogue among cosmopolitan elites throughout Latin America (see figure 2).[66] In addition, municipal officials and local elites imported U.S. materials to establish one of Central America's most modern lighting, water, communication and streetcar systems. Finally, by founding a new indoor market, large stores, a theater, and a central park, Granadans reconstituted the city's center as a site of not only public affairs but consumption and leisure. By the 1890s Granada had regained its former bustle and developed, in the eyes of many Nicaraguans, into a center of modernity.

The agroexport boom did not benefit all Nicaraguans. But nor did it thoroughly impoverish and proletarianize the rural masses, as is often claimed.[67] Rather, it created a more stratified peasantry, with kinship and patronage key to peasants' changing fortunes. Above all, the expansion of commercial agriculture accelerated the disintegration of communal properties, leading many peasants to lose their traditional access to land. While some of the dispossessed migrated to towns to join the swelling ranks of urban poor, most survived by working under cruel conditions on commercial farms with many, particularly women and children, becoming debt peons.[68] Still, a surprisingly large number of peasants took advantage of the export boom, the availability of capital, and the privatization of communal land to expand their holdings or establish new ones, including coffee farms.[69] Much of this expansion occurred at the expense of fellow peasants.

Differences in entrepreneurial spirit surely help explain the boom's unequal impact on Nicaragua's rural populace. But the peasants best positioned to exploit the boom were often those with privileged access to state resources. Especially advantageous were connections with rural municipal councilors, who often belonged to powerful clan-based patronage networks.[70] These councilors not only controlled the sale and rental of common lands but also regulated access to rights of way and water. Moreover, they nominated local judges and police authorities, who were key actors in disputes over material resources. Not by chance were municipal councilors and their cliques among the rural folk who most benefited from the post-1870s boom in commercial agriculture.

The conflict-ridden rise of such a prosperous peasant strata was not limited to frontier regions. It also occurred in places like Granada, where land concentration and landlord hegemony was great. In fact, even after the hacienda expansion peaked in the 1900s, much of Granada's rural landscape was dotted with nonelite landholdings—albeit now in the form of small and medium-sized private farms, not communal properties.[71] Consider, for example, the dramatic changes in land tenure experienced by the rural dwellers of Diriomo, an old Indian village of about four thousand inhabitants that lay at the foot of Granada's Mombacho volcano. Prior to the agroexport boom, Diriomo's land was mainly held communally and used to cultivate basic grains. By the 1900s, the common lands had been privatized.[72] Moreover, the village lost nearly all of its most precious territory on the Mombacho to landlords and merchants from the neighboring towns of Granada and Nandaime, who established large coffee plantations on the volcano's fertile slopes. Not surprisingly, many who came to toil on the Mombacho during the coffee harvest were from Diriomo.[73] Still, in 1900 very few (less than 5%) of Diriomo's inhabitants were landless. Instead, most villagers (nearly 80%) owned small plots ranging from five to fifteen manzanas (seven to twenty-five acres), while a strong minority (about 20%) were middling producers, with some even owning coffee farms on the Mombacho.[74]

Nicaraguan elites were also unevenly affected by the post-1870s growth of export agriculture. Many landlords crumbled under the economic pressures generated by the boom and, in the process, lost much of their land. As with peasants, landlords who most benefited from the boom stood out for their privileged access to political power. The link between political power and economic success was especially noticeable in the 1880s scramble to secure profitable coffee estates on Granada's Mombacho volcano. Initially, the main losers were peasants from Diriomo and the neighboring village of Diriá, but once rich townsfolk from Granada and Nandaime had taken the villagers' newly staked lands, conflicts among these local elites quickly intensified.[75] The winners of this battle for what became known locally as "the bourgeois mountain" were Conservative oligarchs from Granada who had close links to large-scale moneylenders and their highly diversified investment portfolios. But perhaps more important still, they tended to belong to the region's most powerful patron-client networks, led by families such as the Chamorros, the Cuadras, and the Lacayos.

Contrary to conventional wisdom, then, the agroexport boom did not engender a new Liberal coffee bourgeoisie based in Managua and León, displacing a traditional, cattle-based Conservative oligarchy centered in Granada. In reality, it produced an agroexport elite that included Liberals and Conservatives from all of the nation's leading regions. Further, its members were diversified economically, with the allegedly backward Conservatives of Granada pioneering the takeoff of the country's dynamic coffee, sugar, and banana industries. Granada's Conservative oligarchs underscored their entrepreneurialism by establishing in 1890 what would long remain Central America's largest and technologically most advanced agroindustrial enterprise: the San Antonio sugar mill in the northwestern department of Chinandega (see figure 3). With political influence key to economic success, tradi-

3. San Antonio sugar mill (located in the department of Chinandega), 1910.
Courtesy of Instituto de Historia de Nicaragua y de Centroamérica.

tional oligarchs who controlled rural politics dominated the ranks of the agroexport elite. Foreigners certainly came to own many large coffee estates, especially in frontier regions like Matagalpa. But in the country's most commercialized regions, entrenched oligarchs continued to hold sway. Still, scholars are right to stress that the agroexport boom produced a new bourgeoisie. This bourgeoisie, however, was new not so much in its social origins as in its embrace of the U.S.-influenced "bourgeois spirit."

The Rise of a "Bourgeois Spirit"

As elsewhere in Latin America, the enormous wealth generated by the agroexport boom enabled elite Nicaraguans to afford new forms of leisure and consumption widely identified with bourgeois behavior and taste.[76] Export earnings further provided elites with a wider range of educational and professional opportunities that infused them with new ideals and expectations. At the same time, the export boom facilitated the diffusion of new lifestyles by fueling the expansion of the print media. The boom's modernizing impact on transport and communication systems also helped to break down barriers that had impeded elites from developing extraregional patterns of social interaction. Just as important, improved maritime transportation increased Nicaraguans' access to North Atlantic cultures. In more ways than one, the export boom pushed elites to dissociate themselves from the rustic traditions of the patriarchal family and instead embrace a new, cosmopolitan identity that came to be known as the "bourgeois spirit."[77]

As contemporary accounts stress, Nicaragua's "bourgeois spirit" stood out for its celebration of "modern" manly and feminine values emanating from the United States and Europe.[78] Many of these ideals were introduced by foreign teachers who arrived in the 1880s. For example, Nicaraguans often associated bourgeois notions of manliness with the Masonic ideals and practices disseminated by Europeans who taught at the country's most exclusive boys' schools, including León's Instituto de Occidente.[79] With regard to femininity, the bourgeois spirit was closely identified with the ideals of domesticity spread by U.S. teachers at Granada's Colegio de Señoritas (Young Ladies College), the nation's leading boarding school for young elite women (see figures 4 and 5). With good cause a prominent chronicler claimed that the new "bourgeoisie" differed from the old "oligarchy" not in social origins but in the "modern" ideologies it acquired at foreign-run schools.[80]

In the end, however, Nicaragua's bourgeois spirit hinged on two older ideals that elites had long valorized but could not truly attain until the agroexport boom set in. First and foremost, the bourgeois spirit celebrated entrepreneurialism. And if the bulletin of the Nicaraguan government is to be believed, this manly virtue remained elusive to native elites at least until 1881, when the bulletin complained about "the lack of initiative and entrepreneurial spirit on the part of our capitalists."[81] Yet such complaints quickly turned into praise after elites helped to establish one of the region's most dynamic agroexport economies. Nothing better validated elites' newly found confidence than the numerous medals Nicaraguan coffee producers won internationally, from the Paris Universal Exposition of 1889 onward. Since most prizes went to Granada's Conservative oligarchs—architects of Nicaragua's export boom—they also became the most visible native exponents of entrepreneurialism and the bourgeois spirit more generally.[82] As a leading intellectual of the era put it, "the so-called oligarchy of Granada is, in essence, nothing else but a bourgeoisie."[83]

The second longstanding bourgeois ideal that the export boom enabled

4. U.S. teachers at Granada's Young Ladies College, 1884.
Courtesy of U.S. National Archives.

5. Students of Young Ladies College, 1884.
Courtesy of U.S. National Archives.

6. Interior of elite household in Granada, 1884.
Courtesy of U.S. National Archives.

elites to realize was consuming imported goods. Nicaraguans had long valorized foreign wares as a sign of modernity. But not until the post-1870s surge
in their export earnings could elites afford luxury imports such as French
fashion, English hats, Austrian rocking chairs, German toiletries, Italian oil,
and U.S. wheat flour (to make white bread).[84] This internationalization of
native consumption patterns was especially evident at upper-class weddings,
traditionally the chief family ritual and thus a formative site for elite self-
representation. According to a contemporary, at elite weddings in turn-of-
the-century Granada "all the bride's trousseau and jewels, as well as the
china-, glass-, and silverware . . . were imported from Paris."[85] Whether at
weddings or elsewhere, the consumption of European and U.S. products
marked bourgeois identity. Yet this did not mean that elite Nicaraguans
wanted to be European or North American. On the contrary, the wealthy
avidly consumed imported wares to assert a cosmopolitan Nicaraguan nationality (see figure 6).[86]

For the local populace, the bourgeois spirit was perhaps most noticeable in elites' embrace of more commercialized leisure pursuits, many of which were imported from abroad. Thanks to the boom in export earnings, Nicaragua's urban centers witnessed the rapid spread of new public places of entertainment, such as theaters, social clubs, sporting arenas, restaurants, and billiard halls.[87] Their primary consumers were the wealthy, but the less affluent participated in these new forms of recreation as well. For example, in 1896 a U.S. traveler noted how Granada's theatergoers came from all walks of life, though he also stressed their spatial segregation, with "the dark-haired, bright-eyed ladies [seated] in the many boxes, the substantial-looking gentlemen in the orchestra chairs, and the Indians grouped at the rear."[88] As this account underscores, the theater and other similar forms of public entertainment—however segregated their audience—provided a new space for different classes to socialize among themselves in proximity to each other. In addition, they diminished the centrality to elite social life of traditional family gatherings. As a result, public institutions increasingly replaced domestic ones in defining elite membership and identity—a shift scholars deem key to bourgeois class formation.[89]

Few institutions shaped the meaning of Nicaragua's bourgeois spirit more than the male social clubs that emerged during the export boom. The first was founded in 1871 by elite Granadans inspired by similar institutions they had encountered in their U.S. and European travels.[90] From Granada, social clubs spread to all other major urban areas in western Nicaragua. Most clubs developed close ties, thus ensuring that bourgeois beliefs and practices were diffused nationally. Underscoring their bourgeois character, the clubs were much more of a public institution than the traditional family salons (*tertulias*) they sought to replace. For example, club members met not in a private home but in the clubhouse, which was generally located in the city's center and consisted of a grand, two-story building with a lavish interior. In addition, the clubs' rituals, ceremonies, sports activities, and cultural events allowed their members to forge a common bourgeois identity based on modern notions of manliness. These clubs also had formal constitutions, making them more accountable to the public. Thanks to regulated entry requirements, kinship ties and social origins did not guarantee club membership. Economic success and political influence were equally important.

Social clubs were therefore deemed more inclusive than family salons, as evidenced by a contemporary chronicler's contrast of the "aristocratic salon" with the "popular club of the bourgeoisie."[91] Of course the clubs were anything but "popular." They excluded women and entailed high membership fees, and so remained bastions of men born to privilege. For example, forty years after the founding of the Club de Granada, only 20 percent of its members were nouveau riche, while the rest were of elite origin.[92] Even if this notion of openness was more imagined than real, it was nonetheless a myth essential to the bourgeois image elites sought to construct of themselves.

In developing this image, elites benefited from their growing ability to travel overseas. True, the expansion in foreign trade and investment promoted the influx of North Americans and Europeans, who introduced Nicaraguans to new customs and commodities that became part of their bourgeois lifestyle. Yet the more important agents of cultural change were the many Nicaraguans who traveled abroad, particularly to the United States. If Nicaraguans initially went north mostly for pleasure or business, over time more went for schooling. This travel bug affected men and women; men generally pursued a college or university education, while women tended to study at private high schools. Not surprisingly, these young and highly impressionable students were the most zealous importers of new beliefs and practices emanating from the North Atlantic nations. And because most studied in U.S. schools (located mainly in Washington, DC, Philadelphia, and New York) at a time when such schools fervently sought to assimilate the growing immigrant population, these students helped ensure that turn-of-the-century Nicaragua would be more Americanized than Europeanized.[93]

Nothing better illustrates the Americanizing impact of U.S.-educated students than their success in making a U.S. sport—baseball—into Nicaragua's national pastime. Baseball first arrived in Nicaragua in 1888 when a U.S.-German merchant introduced it, together with cricket, to the residents of Bluefields on the Atlantic coast.[94] Since the links between the country's two coasts were still tenuous, baseball was not played in western Nicaragua until 1891, when the game was brought back by native elites who had studied in the United States.[95] Thanks to these youthful returnees, baseball quickly became the principal sport of male elites. In the 1900s, U.S.-educated elites spread the sport to urban artisans and later to the rural populace. As early as the 1920s, arguably, baseball had replaced cockfighting as the national pastime. Baseball's rise was anything but inevitable, for it had to compete with European team sports such as cricket, rugby, and especially soccer, which eventually became the national game in the rest of Central America. The U.S. occupation of 1912–33 contributed to baseball's nationalization by providing Nicaraguans with a key means to express their nationalist sentiments. Still, baseball had captured the imagination of urban Nicaraguans well before the arrival of U.S. troops. By the early 1910s, Granada boasted ten baseball teams but only one soccer club.

Baseball's rise exemplifies the key role U.S. customs played in elite efforts to make themselves and their nation more cosmopolitan. Nicaraguans studying in the United States could have embraced other sports, such as football, the most popular college game in the United States at the time. Why they adopted baseball remains unclear. Perhaps Nicaraguan students found it easier to learn or just more fun than football. But it is also possible that they embraced baseball precisely because it was the North American national pastime and thus the U.S. leisure pursuit that best served as a paradigm of progress.[96] As evinced in newspaper articles and congressional debates, elites firmly believed they could use the U.S. national pastime to further their efforts to create a cosmopolitan Nicaragua.[97] In particular, they argued that baseball promoted modern, "civilized" notions of manliness that challenged older, "barbaric" manly values symbolized by cockfighting. In their view, the U.S. team sport inculcated bourgeois virtues such as self-control, physical vigor, orderly competition, work ethic, and cooperation; the blood sport, by contrast, perpetuated the violent, corrupt, irrational, and socially unruly attributes of a "backward" manhood rooted in Spanish colonialism. In practice, these distinctions were hardly clear-cut, especially since baseball games spurred riots where the blood spilled was not animal but human. Yet such violence did not deter the rich from linking baseball with gentlemanly behavior.

Elites were so invested in baseball's virtuous image precisely because they saw the sport as a path to cosmopolitan nationality.[98] Tellingly, the attractive uniforms of numerous clubs were adorned with the names of foreign places like Japón, Boer, Yorktown, Alemania, Chile, New York, and Buffalo. Of course, baseball did not smoothly produce a modern sense of nationality. In fact, it often intensified traditional local allegiances, to the point that fans of a defeated home team would attack the victorious out-of-towners. Still, it was this quest for a cosmopolitan nationality—and social control—that motivated elites to transmit their passion for the "American game" to the rest of society.[99]

Nicaragua's Americanization from within only deepened as expanding export earnings enabled elite families to send child after child to U.S. schools.

One family that epitomizes this process is the Urtechos from Granada. The first to go to the United States, in 1871, was twenty-one-year-old Juan Ignacio Urtecho Cabistán, who went to study at Jefferson Medical College in Phila-delphia. As with many U.S.-educated Granadans of the era, Urtecho be-longed to a family that had been victimized by Walker's antielite revolution. This experience, however, failed to quench his thirst for U.S. culture. On the contrary, Urtecho enthusiastically embraced local customs during his three-year stay in Philadelphia. After returning in 1873, he shared his admiration for the "American way of life" with his large family and fellow Granadans. As his grandson José Coronel Urtecho recalled, Juan Ignacio viewed "the United States as a moral and material world that was much superior to anything else from the past, the apex of progress . . . where mankind, helped by science, would never repeat the fatal errors that had been committed in Europe."[100] Thanks to his thriving coffee plantation, Juan Ignacio Urtecho was able to send four of his five daughters (he had no sons) and two nephews to study in the United States. They, too, eventually returned to Granada and shared their U.S. experiences with those who stayed at home. One nephew who had studied engineering at the University of Pennsylvania wrote newspaper arti-cles that lauded the "American way of life."[101] Reinforcing the family's link with U.S. lifestyle, three of Urtecho's daughters married U.S.-educated Nic-araguans, while other close relatives, such as the three baseball-playing Arellano brothers, also studied in the United States. When the next genera-tion emerged around 1900, most members of the Urtecho household were able to speak English.[102]

    U.S. cultural practices were certainly embraced by elite families throughout Nicaragua. Yet those of Granada, which had the wealthiest upper class, were probably the most Americanized of all. As José Coronel Urtecho stressed, nearly all of his peers in turn-of-the-century Granada were "linked one way or the other with the United States."[103] In addition, foreign travelers noted that many elite Granadans spoke English very well. One even claimed that English was "almost as common at a fashionable dance in Granada as in Washington."[104] Yet Granadans also cultivated U.S. consumption and leisure patterns. The U.S.-educated and baseball-playing "Sugar King" Adolfo Be-nard Vivas could thus boast that his city was much more "americanized" than its chief rival, León.[105] This was likely true. But elites in León had also come to embrace U.S. customs. In 1908, for example, the city's most famous son, Rubén Darío, noted with much surprise how strongly local elites had come to embrace "foreign ways" since his last visit fifteen years before. To him, nothing highlighted their transformation better than the sight of U.S.-educated señoritas flaunting their "North Americanized manners" in the streets of León.[106]

Darío had a right to express surprise at this transformation of elite culture. The Americanization of elite households contradicted the Europeanization trend of fin de siècle elites in most other parts of Latin America. Indeed, many elite Nicaraguans themselves followed their Latin American counterparts in deeming European consumer tastes superior to those of the United States.[107] They also enjoyed greater local contact with Europeans, for the latter's colony was at least four times as large as the North American one. Finally, Nicaraguan exporters were oriented more toward European than U.S. markets—an orientation that some scholars assume should have led to a predominantly Europeanized outlook among native elites.[108]

Nevertheless, elite Nicaraguans wound up becoming more Americanized than Europeanized for three key reasons. First, the greater propensity of Nicaraguans to study in the United States than in Europe ensured that U.S. ways, particularly U.S. leisure pursuits, had a greater impact on elite lifestyle. Second, elites' allure for things American deepened as, from the late 1890s onward, more imported goods came from the United States than anywhere else. Third, and perhaps most important, was the very factor that had led their forefathers to embrace the U.S. road to modernity in the first place: no matter how much they preferred European tastes, Juan Ignacio Urtecho and his peers continued to idealize the United States as their principal political and economic model. In consequence, U.S. practices and values remained elites' main means to a cosmopolitan nationality.

Of course, elites' faith in the U.S. model also hinged on the widespread assumption that the United States would construct the canal through their country. Yet just when the United States was on the verge of realizing Nicaragua's manifest destiny, it abruptly decided to build the canal in Panama instead. The northern colossus shattered more than Nicaraguan dreams of prosperity; it jeopardized elites' cosmopolitan nation-state project.

Shattered Dreams

The fate of the Nicaraguan canal was sealed in June 1902 when the U.S. Congress voted for the Panama route. This decision represented an astounding reversal, since Nicaragua had long been the preferred site for the United States. As late as February 1902, the influential U.S. admiral Alfred Thayer Mahan maintained that as "regards the canal I have always been a Nicaragua man. . . . It has been the American idea all along."[109] So greatly did U.S. opinion support the Nicaraguan canal that it came to be identified in many North American minds with, as one U.S. analyst put it in 1896, "the manifest economic destiny of their country."[110] Such support only deepened after the U.S. conquest of Pacific and Caribbean territories in the 1898 war against Spain. Mirroring public opinion, turn-of-the century U.S. newspapers tended to report much more favorably on the Nicaraguan route than on the competing route in Panama.[111] In addition, Congress had repeatedly endorsed the Nicaragua option, most recently in January 1902 when the House voted 308 to 2 in its favor. Even Teddy Roosevelt firmly believed, on entering the White House in September 1901, that the canal would be built in Nicaragua.[112] Yet shortly thereafter, Roosevelt and Congress opted for Panama. Any remaining Nicaraguan hopes that the United States would reverse its decision disappeared once construction on the Panama canal began in 1904.

If Nicaragua had long been identified as "the American route," why did the United States ultimately decide against it? For scholars of Nicaraguan history, the surprising decision resulted from U.S. exasperation with the stubborn efforts of President José Santos Zelaya (1893–1909) to defend Nicaragua's sovereignty over the canal.[113] By the end of his lengthy regime, Zelaya had certainly become the principal nemesis of the United States in Latin America. But his nationalism had not always been directed against the northern colossus. In fact, Zelaya (1853–1916) had been born into a rich family that had initially supported William Walker's regime.[114] And until the United States opted for the Panama canal route, Zelaya had arguably been the most pro-U.S. president in Nicaraguan history.

Although educated in France, Zelaya followed most elite Nicaraguans in valorizing the United States as the model of economic and political development. It was no coincidence that Zelaya proclaimed his regime's most important reform project—the liberal constitution of 1893—on U.S. Independence Day.[115] He also made sure that government newspapers published articles lauding the United States as the ideal of modernity.[116] But Zelaya's pro-U.S. stance was most evident in the unparalleled efforts his regime undertook to have the United States build the Nicaraguan canal. These efforts culminated in Zelaya's willingness to sign, in May 1902, a U.S.-proposed treaty that would have given the United States not only perpetual ownership of the Nicaraguan canal but exclusive police authority over the six-mile-wide canal zone and the right to station troops.[117] No other president had gone this far in abdicating Nicaraguan sovereignty over the canal. Little wonder that, until 1902, the United States had nothing but praise for Zelaya.[118]

Rather than Zelaya's alleged intransigence, two key developments in the United States explain its decision to build the canal in Panama. The first was the aggressive effort of the so-called Panama lobby to sway the U.S. Congress, which had hitherto consistently supported the Nicaraguan route.[119] The lobby's most notorious action was distributing a recently issued Nicaraguan postage stamp that showed an erupting volcano (the Momotombo near León) to all U.S. Senators three days before their June 1902 vote. The lobbyists sought to exploit the volcano scare that engulfed the United States after a 14 May eruption had killed thirty thousand people on the Caribbean island of Martinique. Since Panama had no volcanoes, they hoped the stamp would raise enough fears about Nicaragua's seismic instability to tilt the vote in their favor. The second factor explaining the Congress's action was new scientific research countering longstanding assumptions that Nicaragua was the technically superior route.[120] Panama was found to offer advantages such as better natural harbors, a shorter canal transit, a lower summit evaluation, fewer locks and curvatures, the existence of a completed railroad, and a partial excavation—all of which would make the Panama canal cheaper to construct.

The U.S. decision in favor of Panama devastated elite Nicaraguans, whose cosmopolitanism so greatly depended on the canal's construction. And with the loss of the canal as a unifying project, elite conflicts became more volatile. As elsewhere in Latin America, elite cleavages in Nicaragua had grown as export-led growth and cyclical economic crises heightened existing social tensions. In addition, elite discontent with Zelaya intensified as his regime became more corrupt and authoritarian. Yet until 1902 these conflicts remained easily mediated, largely because elites knew that their country's greater political stability was a key reason why U.S. policymakers favored the Nicaraguan canal route over Panama's.[121] Their canal hopes shattered, disgruntled elites no longer showed such restraint and enlisted other disaffected social groups, especially urban artisans and peasants, in their political battles. At the same time, elites became more susceptible to the divisive effects of meddling foreign business groups and states. No force played a greater role in destabilizing Nicaragua than the U.S. government, which actively encouraged dissident elites and neighboring states to overthrow Zelaya.[122]

Once again, the U.S. turn against Zelaya had little to do with his alleged anti-Americanism. On the contrary, no matter how stung by the U.S. decision for the Panama route, Zelaya persisted in his belief that the emulation of U.S. ways represented a key means to strengthen Nicaraguan nationality. Not only did his regime keep sending elite youths to the United States for schooling, it also opened up densely populated western Nicaragua to some of the most fervent exporters of U.S. culture: Protestant missionaries.[123] In addition, Zelaya steadfastly promoted the spread of U.S. economic practices to Nicaragua by continuing to grant U.S. entrepreneurs monopolist control over key sectors of the local economy such as logging, mining, communications, electricity, and the banana trade. In fact, Zelaya's 1909 downfall was precipitated largely by the local populace's revulsion against the special concessions his regime awarded to large U.S. companies notorious for their exploitative practices.[124]

U.S.-Nicaraguan government relations soured after 1902 precisely because the canal dreams of both countries began to collide. Zelaya defied the United States by seeking to have its main international rivals build an alternative canal through Nicaragua. After unsuccessfully courting Great Britain and France, Zelaya turned to Germany and Japan, both of which expressed strong interest in his canal plans.[125] In addition, Zelaya's efforts to develop Nicaragua's economy via large European loans contradicted the 1904 Roosevelt Corollary to the Monroe Doctrine, which called for U.S. financial predominance over the Caribbean Basin. Finally, Zelaya's diplomatic and military campaign to unite Central America under his leadership directly clashed with the hegemonic ambitions of the United States. In all three instances, Zelaya attacked more than just the strategic and economic interests of the United States. His nationalist policies posed an unprecedented challenge to what U.S. officials claimed was their country's manifest destiny: the transformation of the Caribbean into an "American lake." This is why the United States turned against an ally it had trusted and supported for so long.

U.S. efforts to overthrow Zelaya culminated in the 1909 revolution instigated by General Juan José Estrada, the Liberal governor of Nicaragua's Atlantic coast. Initially, Estrada's uprising hardly threatened the Zelaya regime. But just as government troops were about to crush Estrada's forces, they executed two U.S. citizens caught fighting for the rebels. This execution was the pretext the U.S. government had been waiting for to openly support the anti-Zelaya revolt. On 1 December 1909, U.S. Secretary of State Philander Knox sent a letter to the Nicaraguan embassy in Washington notifying it that diplomatic relations were severed.

Published widely in U.S. and Nicaraguan newspapers, the so-called Knox Note denounced Zelaya's regime as a "blot upon the history of Nicaragua" and called for its overthrow.[126] Knox's bellicose letter appears to have been the most hostile ever sent by the U.S. government to a Latin American country.[127] One U.S. newspaper compared it to "a Western sheriff's proclamation against some outlaw."[128] This was an apt comparison, for Knox drew on the 1904 Roosevelt Corollary's assertion that the United States had the duty to intervene as an "international police power" in Latin American nations allegedly plagued by "chronic wrongdoing."

To back up his fighting words, Knox dispatched a naval force with one thousand marines to Nicaraguan waters. The next day, Zelaya undertook the one measure he hoped would stop the looming U.S. invasion: he went into exile after handing the presidency to José Madriz, a longstanding Liberal critic of his regime. So overwhelming was Madriz's support among Nicaraguans that the revolutionary movement quickly disintegrated. Yet when government troops encircled the few remaining rebels in Bluefields on the Atlantic coast, U.S. warships suddenly intervened on the latter's behalf. Shortly thereafter Madriz's government collapsed and Nicaraguans became subjected to U.S. imperial rule for the first time since the Walker episode of the 1850s.

Conclusion

The U.S. intervention of 1910 marked the first of many regime changes the United States would orchestrate in twentieth-century Latin America. Had the United States not intervened against Madriz, Nicaragua would probably have regained much of the political stability it had enjoyed since Walker. Even the fiercest opponents of the Zelaya dictatorship acknowledged that Madriz's short-lived regime drew support from all sectors of Nicaraguan society.[129] U.S. policymakers, however, insisted that Madriz and all other leading Liberals were dangerous "Zelayistas" bent on undermining U.S. hegemony over the region. To the world, the U.S. government claimed that it was restoring "order" to strategically important Nicaragua. But as a German diplomat correctly noted, it was the United States that had "welcomed disorder" in what had long been Central America's most stable country.[130]

The U.S. intervention of 1910 crippled the cosmopolitan nation-state project that Nicaraguan elites had so doggedly pursued since their disastrous encounter with Walker. For fin de siècle Latin America, there was nothing unusual about this Nicaraguan quest to construct a strong, cosmopolitan nation by emulating North Atlantic institutions and ways. In 1907, a German diplomat reported from Mexico, "The cosmopolitans [Mexico's ruling *científico* elite], . . . paradoxical as this may sound, see precisely in economic dependency the guarantee of political independence, insofar as they assume that the large European interests that have investments here constitute a counterweight to American annexationist appetites and that they will pave the way for the complete internationalization and neutralization of Mexico."[131] Like the Científicos, elites of post-Walker Nicaragua embraced cosmopolitanism in order to defend their country's sovereignty against U.S. expansionism. But unlike their counterparts in Mexico and much of Latin America, elite Nicaraguans believed that the main means to a cosmopolitan nationality was not Europeanization but Americanization. And few better embodied this faith in the nationalist impulse of Americanization from within than President Zelaya. The United States severely tested elites' trust in Americanization, first when it opted for the Panama canal route and then when it used gunboat diplomacy to turn Nicaragua into a U.S. protectorate.

PART II · Restoration, 1910–1912

3 Challenging Imperial Exclusions

Nicaragua under the Dawson Pact

THE VICTORY OF THE U.S.-SUPPORTED REBELS in August 1910 threw Nicaragua into disarray. With U.S. warships lurking on the Atlantic coast, Nicaraguans anxiously wondered how the "northern colossus" would shape their immediate future. Many feared the United States would destroy Nicaraguan nationality by turning their country into a U.S. colony. Others believed that the United States would instead strengthen their nationality by extending to them its ideals of "progress" and "liberty."[1] In the end, the United States neither colonized Nicaragua nor spread its liberal model of development. Rather, the United States turned Nicaragua into its protectorate by means of an illiberal political intervention—the so-called Dawson Pact.

This pact was forged in October 1910 between the U.S. special envoy Thomas Dawson and the leaders of the new U.S.-backed regime: the Liberal president Juan José Estrada, the Conservative vice president Adolfo Díaz, and the Conservative generals Luis Mena and Emiliano Chamorro.[2] Like many U.S. officials of the era, Dawson believed that Nicaraguans lacked the financial responsibility and political maturity necessary to run a stable, pro-U.S. government. His pact thus called for U.S. officials to take over the management of Nicaraguan state finances—a plan patterned after the financial protectorate Dawson had imposed on the Dominican Republic in 1904. But it would take a full-scale U.S. military invasion—that of 1912—before the United States could truly turn Nicaragua into a financial protectorate.

Instead, the beginnings of U.S. imperial rule in Nicaragua were mostly marked by the Dawson Pact's second goal: to create an exclusionary political order that served U.S. strategic interests. Above all, the pact concentrated power in the hands of its four Nicaraguan signers and their U.S. patrons. And, since Dawson deemed elections "at present impracticable and dangerous to peace," he ordered their suspension for at least two years.[3] At the same time, the pact enabled Conservative oligarchs to seek the "restoration" of a hierarchical order they claimed was reminiscent of the Conservative-dominated ancien régime of 1857–93.[4] In reality, the 1910 restoration shared little with its alleged predecessor. Post-Walker elites had established a political order designed to stop, not further, U.S. expansionism. Moreover, their order stood out for its spirit of inclusion. The U.S.-engineered restoration, in contrast, explicitly promoted the politics of exclusion.

This regressive impulse of U.S. imperial rule shocked those Nicaraguans who had long associated the United States with the promise of progress and liberty. But the U.S. intervention in Nicaragua also contrasted with the reformist impetus of most U.S. occupations of the era. Whether in the Caribbean or the Philippines, post-1898 U.S. interventions generally strove to "uplift" local societies by modernizing the economy and the state along liberal lines. At times, they also sought to promote their vision of democracy. Ultimately, such interventions rarely produced more "progress" and "liberty."[5] Yet in Nicaragua, the United States did not even try to implement its "liberal-developmental" project.[6] This certainly reflected low U.S. interest in Nicaragua's economy. But it also responded to the recent decline in the U.S. public's support for costly interventions abroad. As a result, the U.S. government sought to control Nicaragua by the least costly means possible, via the imposition of an exclusionary order.[7]

Designed to produce stability, the U.S. intervention instead polarized Nicaraguan society to the breaking point. In particular, the United States gravely underestimated the populace's ability to resist imperial and oligarchic impositions. Dawson and other U.S. policymakers viewed Nicaragua's political conflicts as personal power struggles waged between seemingly omnipotent caudillos. Yet, the country's political culture was much more complex, for the power of caudillos rested on an intricate web of distinct elite allegiances, as well as complex alliances with rural communities and urban artisan organizations. In addition, Nicaraguans had just freed themselves from a lengthy and corrupt dictatorship. When Dawson arrived in Nicaragua, he encountered a country gripped by an unprecedented level of political debate and social mobilization. By overlooking such intricacies, U.S. officials were ill prepared when conflicts within the ruling Conservative oligarchy opened space for a myriad of groups, including women, urban artisans, and indigenous communities, to advance their struggles for greater political and social rights. Three principal conflicts divided elite Conservatives: the debate over the "religious question," the controversy over the U.S.-Nicaraguan loan treaty, and the clash over elite status triggered by the reopening of Conservative-dominated social clubs. All three conflicts were exacerbated and peculiarly shaped by popular challenges to the exclusive political order embodied in the Dawson Pact. It was against this volatile backdrop that in mid-1912 a drought-induced food shortage pushed the country to the brink of what the U.S. government most feared: a social revolution.

The Religious Debate:
Divided Elites, Unruly Women, and Rebellious Artisans

From the start, U.S. efforts to promote an exclusionary order were undermined by ideological debates waged within Nicaraguan civil society. After seventeen years of dictatorship, many Nicaraguans refused to remain silent. Whether through newspapers, handbills, or street demonstrations, men and women of all social classes participated in the struggle to reshape state and society. Although these popular protests antagonized the ruling Conservatives, the latter were unable to curb what they deemed were acts of "exaggerated liberty."[8]

Initially, no debate more divided Nicaragua's burgeoning civil society than the conflict over the "religious question." The debate broke out in January 1911, when a Constituent Assembly sought to reform the Constitution of 1905. Discord erupted after Conservative deputies headed by General Emiliano Chamorro (1871–1966) introduced a motion to declare Catholicism the state religion. Opposing the motion were the so-called Progressive Conservatives, led by Chamorro's chief rival, General Luis Mena (1865–1928).[9] Since Chamorro's adherents dominated the Assembly, the religious article was incorporated into the new constitution of April 1911. But clerical sectors could not savor their victory for long. In December 1911 a new, pro-Mena Assembly nullified the religious article.

The debate over the religious question was fueled by the power struggle among the signers of the Dawson Pact. But it also revealed the extent to which the ruling Conservatives had become ideologically divided over key issues, especially the compatibility of Catholic and liberal tenets. This schism ultimately reflected, as the official bulletin of the National Assembly stressed, Conservatives' competing visions of how to "reorganize" state and society after the fall of Zelaya.[10] The debate's intensity is rather striking since most elite Conservatives had tended to favor a liberal, cosmopolitan nationality over a Catholic one. Yet in the final years of the Zelaya dictatorship, an antiliberal, proclerical ideology emerged that gradually undermined the

ideological unity of elite Nicaraguans. So even if many Conservatives maintained a highly liberal outlook, some had recently embraced, as a Liberal
ideologue noted, a "reactionary tendency that . . . Conservatism never had
before."[11] This "reactionary tendency" represented a new antiliberal current
that had begun to make important inroads in Latin America at the turn of the
century.[12] In particular, it was heavily influenced by Catholic social thought
expressed in the 1891 papal encyclical *Rerum novarum*, which attacked the
excesses of liberal capitalism and called for social reform.

As their speeches in the Assembly evince, proclerical Conservatives worried about how liberalism was undermining the Catholic fabric of Nicaraguan society.[13] They complained that Zelaya's liberal policies had opened the
country to foreign Protestant missionaries. But they were even more troubled
by the anticlerical sentiments prevailing among elite youth. According to a
prominent Conservative, "liberal theory" so dominated the minds of "young
Conservatives" that even they deemed "liberal ideas a sign of intelligence
and Catholic thought a sign of backwardness."[14] To thus curb elite anti-
Catholicism, proclerical forces sought to transfer the reins of the country's
education from secular forces to the Catholic clergy.

The proclerical view that liberalism promoted Catholicism's decay was
rejected by Conservative deputies opposed to the proposed religious article.
In speech after speech made to the Assembly, they insisted that Catholicism
was thriving and that its advance could only be upheld if the Church remained separate from the state.[15] True, many Progressive Conservatives
agreed with their proclerical adversaries that Nicaragua had decayed morally during the previous Liberal regime. Yet they claimed that this had resulted not from the proliferation of liberal ideas but from Zelaya's corrupt
rule. Upholding their faith in a cosmopolitan nationality, these Progressives
staunchly criticized proclerical forces for seeking to dismantle secular education and, more generally, for blocking the country's economic and political
modernization.

Typical of this period, the religious debate was exacerbated by pressures
that feuding congressional factions faced from their own social base. As one
leading Conservative confessed, his mitigation efforts failed because extra-
parliamentary forces had pressured proclerical deputies to adopt a more
intransigent position.[16] Some of the most vocal proclerical zealots were elite
women. Not only did they submit countless petitions demanding the ratifica-

tion of the religious article, these prominent women also took their cause to the streets of the capital by leading popular demonstrations.[17] And for the first time, women participated in a congressional debate. From the galleries of the all-male Assembly, they heckled deputies who spoke against the proposed religious article. Unnerved, some anticlerical deputies tried to force the women out of the chamber.[18]

While women left no written records explaining their crusade for a Catholic nationality, male journalists said a great deal about female proclerical actions. But whether pro- or anticlerical, they all made the simple point that women were inherently more religious than men. What they overlooked was the possibility that women's strident proclerical stance might have had a political logic, as the proposed religious article would have likely enhanced women's role. In particular, the religious article sought to strengthen the very institutions—Catholic schools and charities—that historically had provided wealthy women with an effective tool to challenge their marginalization from the male-dominated public sphere.[19] In addition, the public status of upper-class women had increased during the Zelaya dictatorship, as many participated in antigovernment activities; this was especially true of women whose husbands had been driven into exile. The political influence gained by elite women threatened to evaporate with the return of their spouses following the U.S.-orchestrated regime change. A leading Conservative deputy admitted that his congressional faction strove to banish women from "political society" and relegate them to "the sacred temple of the home."[20] Such threats were consistent with the exclusionary politics characteristic of the Dawson Pact. By thus fighting for the proposed religious article, women also challenged their threatened exclusion from the public sphere.

If elite women represented the shock troops of proclerical forces, their anticlerical counterparts were urban artisans. Much of the latter's opposition to the proposed religious article was ideological, as artisans believed that secular education was fundamental to the construction of citizenship.[21] But even more so than proclerical women, artisans' participation in the debate over the religious question was fueled by political concerns. They feared that proclerical Conservatives were using the cloak of religion to curb the power of artisan organizations. While artisans had long been an important factor in municipal elections, their political clout increased toward the end of the Zelaya regime when they spearheaded the urban opposition to the dictatorship.[22] Moreover, artisans had just begun to establish their own voluntary organizations, such as the Clubes Sociales de Artesanos. Traditionally, artisans had tended to meet at places where all social strata intermingled, like canteens, billiard halls, and cockpits. In the 1900s, however, organizations emerged that represented a public space specifically reserved for male artisans. In addition to political objectives, these new artisan societies served a broader cultural purpose: to forge among the heterogeneous artisan population a more common identity as *artesanos* or *obreros*.[23]

With the U.S. intervention of 1910, nascent artisan organizations suddenly faced increased competition from urban associations promoted by Catholic orders and proclerical Conservatives interested in broadening their popular support. In Granada, for instance, newly founded Conservative/Catholic groups included the Club Conservador de Artesanos (Conservative Club of Artisans), the Sociedad para los intereses Católicos (Society for Catholic Interests), and the Casa de Obreros (Workers' House). Conservative elites and priests often presided over the inauguration of these organizations; at times, they even directed them. As the competition thus grew, artisans increasingly feared that proclerical Conservatives were bent on curtailing the political and cultural autonomy they had recently gained.[24] Largely because of this fear, Liberal artisans from Managua, led by President Estrada—a carpenter by trade—attempted to expel the Conservatives from the government shortly after the Constituent Assembly ratified the religious article on 4 April 1911.[25] The coup failed miserably. Not only did U.S. diplomats force Estrada into exile, they secured the rise of Adolfo Díaz (1877–1964) to the presidency. The Conservative takeover of the government was now complete.

Though unsuccessful, Estrada's coup suggests that U.S. officials underestimated the power of nonelite sectors. In particular, they failed to realize that the artisans who promoted Estrada's failed coup resented the attempt by Conservative oligarchs to curtail their newly gained political influence. And it was this resentment that led artisans nearly to trigger what the U.S. government desperately sought to avoid: a costly armed intervention in Nicaragua. Such an invasion was not far off, however. Civil war broke out in July 1912, and U.S. troops intervened on behalf of the beleaguered Díaz government. This war was largely rooted in the dramatic turnabout in another major controversy generated by the Dawson Pact: the nationalist campaign against the U.S.-Nicaraguan loan treaty of June 1911, which called for the U.S. takeover of Nicaragua's public finances.

Reimagining the Nation:
The Campaign against the U.S.-Nicaraguan Loan Treaty

Like the struggle over the religious article, the campaign against the loan treaty displayed civil society's powerful confrontation with the U.S.-backed restoration of the oligarchy. Yet there was a crucial difference. If the religious debate centered on conflicts over society's organization, the loan controversy highlighted competing definitions of the nation. In particular, the treaty's opponents challenged the dominant elite vision of a cosmopolitan national-ity, advocating instead a more inward-looking and inclusionary national project that celebrated the country's various nonwhite ethnicities. Initially, the nationalist campaign was spearheaded by Liberal artisans, who organized boisterous street demonstrations. Over time, however, it came under control of elite Conservatives led by General Mena. Thanks to this campaign, Mena evolved into a powerful icon of anti-U.S nationalism.

Although many Nicaraguans opposed a U.S. takeover of their country's financial system, U.S. officials remained confident that the all-important loan treaty was not doomed. Their confidence was based on two important as-sumptions. First, they believed that power in Nicaragua rested in the hands of the signers of the Dawson Pact. So even though much of civil society rejected the loan treaty, U.S. diplomats felt that the opposition could be ignored as long as the treaty was supported by the pact's signers. Second, they assumed that the pact's signers staunchly supported the controversial loan treaty sim-ply because elite Conservatives were, as Dawson put it, "universally pro-American."

Assumptions about Conservatives' unequivocal "pro-American" stance were further reinforced when the Constituent Assembly ratified the Knox-Castrillo loan treaty on 6 June 1911. Based on the Dawson Pact, the treaty provided that Nicaragua would receive a loan of fifteen million U.S. dollars from U.S. bankers to place its finances "upon a sound and stable basis."[26] To guarantee this loan, Nicaragua was to cede to U.S. officials control of the custom's collectorship—the state's most lucrative source of income—and the Banco Nacional de Nicaragua (National Bank of Nicaragua). After the U.S. Senate rejected the Knox-Castrillo treaty, the U.S. government arranged for the Wall Street banks Brown Brothers and J. and W. Seligman to grant Nicaragua a short-term loan of one and a half million dollars in exchange for the same guarantees provided by the Knox-Castrillo treaty. And since this amount proved insufficient, both U.S. banks gave the Nicaraguan government a second loan of $725,000 in March 1912. In return, they received from the Nicaraguan government 51 percent of the stocks belonging to the National Railway, which also owned the country's steamers and wharves.[27] To the great surprise of U.S. diplomats and bankers, Nicaragua's Constituent Assembly refused to ratify the second loan convention when it first came up for vote on 14 March 1912. The Assembly reversed its decision five days later. Still, the convention's initial rejection revealed that even the ruling Conservatives increasingly opposed U.S. efforts to impose a financial protectorate on Nicaragua.

The rise of such nationalist views overshadowed the visit U.S. Secretary of State Philander Knox paid to Nicaragua on 5 and 6 March 1912. U.S. diplomats were not surprised that Knox was greeted by violent anti-U.S. street demonstrations led by Liberal artisans.[28] But they were taken aback when the president of the Assembly, the U.S.-educated Conservative Ignacio Suárez, officially welcomed Knox with a speech highly critical of the U.S. intervention. The high point came when Suárez told Knox, "It cannot be denied . . . that your visit . . . has awakened fears and misgivings in timid minds, who see in it a peril to our autonomy."[29] Like most Conservative deputies, Suárez had supported the Knox-Castrillo treaty. But by early 1912, he had evolved into a vocal critic of the U.S. project in Nicaragua. Suárez's evolution was by no means unusual, for it symbolized the growing strength of anti-U.S. sentiment among the ruling Conservatives.

How are we to explain the evolution of prominent Conservatives from pro-U.S. stalwarts to opponents of the U.S. intervention? For most U.S. officials, this evolution was simply a Machiavellian scheme designed to promote the presidential ambitions of General Luis Mena (see figure 7). As late as September 1911, the U.S. chargé d'affaires still considered Minister of War Mena "the staunchest friend and supporter of the entire American program."[30] But relations between U.S. officials and the Conservative general soured when the Constituent Assembly in October 1911 elected Mena as the country's next president for the term beginning in 1913. This election outraged U.S. officials, for it was undertaken without prior U.S. approval.[31] Undoubtedly, U.S. diplomats were right to insist that Mena was using the popular opposition to the loan treaty to propel his own political ambitions. But they never truly considered the possibility that Mena and his Conservative supporters opposed the treaty for patriotic reasons as well.

7. General Luis Mena,
1911. *Courtesy of
Instituto de Historia
de Nicaragua y de
Centroamérica.*

Indeed, Mena and other "pro-American" Conservatives had long been secretly opposed to the surrender of Nicaragua's financial autonomy. This was even the case of David Arellano (1872–1928), widely known as the "premier Yanquista" of Nicaragua. A prominent Conservative lawyer, merchant, moneylender, and cattle baron from Granada, Arellano had lived eight years in the United States and studied at Fordham College in New York City. After returning home, Arellano became famous for avidly promoting U.S. cultural practices such as baseball. Like his uncle Juan Ignacio Urtecho (the U.S.-educated doctor discussed in chapter 2), Arellano firmly believed that Nicaraguans needed to adopt the political and economic institutions and practices that had allowed the United States to become the "most powerful nation on earth."[32] Still, Arellano shared Mena's nationalist misgivings about U.S. efforts to turn Nicaragua into a financial protectorate. That Arellano's efforts to Americanize Nicaragua did not preclude him from defending Nicaraguan nationality is illustrated in a confidential letter he wrote after the signing of the Dawson Pact. Arellano begins the letter by acknowledging that "no one is a more fervent supporter of American influence in Nicaragua than I am."[33] But then he insists that Nicaragua should not "suffer unnecessary damage to its national dignity." Singling out the proposed loan treaty, Arellano complains that "everybody knows that without control of public finances any form of rule is ridiculous in America" and concludes: "It would be better to surrender our weapons than the customs and control of national revenues." Because such nationalist views were initially made in private, Conservatives' opposition to the U.S. intervention remained hidden from U.S. officials.

But as U.S. opposition to General Mena's presidential ambitions increased, pro-Mena Conservatives felt freer to denounce the "American program" openly. Such attacks only enhanced Mena's nationalist credentials. Nothing boosted his popular appeal more than the report in the Conservative daily *El Periódico* that "the General" would be willing to risk a war with the United States in order to defend Nicaraguan sovereignty. Accordingly, Mena insisted that he would not let the United States intimidate him with a Knox-like note as Zelaya had. Instead, if "the Yankees want to intervene . . . they will have to land troops and fight it out with us."[34] In reality, these fighting words had been made not by Mena but by a close political ally, the Conservative Granadan oligarch Manuel Zavala Chamorro. Nevertheless, many Nicaraguans believed that these had been Mena's own words—a belief that found its way even into Costa Rican newspapers.[35]

While evolving into a nationalist hero, Mena made sure never to state explicitly his opposition to the U.S. intervention. In countless interviews, he was pressed by the so-called nationalist press for an anti-U.S. statement. But the minister of war never did them the favor, as evident in an interview he gave to the Liberal paper *Diario Moderno*. When asked about the Dawson Pact, Mena smiled and answered, "The pacts? . . . Well there they are. I seldom go out into the street and thus don't know what people think of them." Despite his purported ignorance, the article claimed, "Mena does not believe in the Dawson pacts."[36] This habit of putting anti-U.S. words in the general's mouth was not unusual. It represented a skillful ploy used by the nationalist press to construct Mena as a champion of anti-U.S. sentiment.

Politically, Mena's silence helped him keep the door open to both the U.S. government and the nationalist forces opposed to the U.S. intervention. But it also permitted him to court the political support of many Conservative artisans who maintained a contradictory stance toward the U.S. intervention. On the one hand, Conservative artisans joined their Liberal counterparts in criticizing the U.S.-backed regime for pursuing an overly liberal trade policy with the United States.[37] In particular, they argued that U.S. manufactured imports like shoes threatened to destroy Nicaragua's artisan industry. But unlike their Liberal counterparts, Conservative artisans supported the loan convention, largely because it called for a monetary reform.

Ironically, these artisans defended the loan convention with the same kind of prolabor arguments made by U.S. officials defending the proposed monetary reform.[38] In an open letter to the Constituent Assembly, Conservative artisans stated that this reform would effectively curtail the exploitation of the "working class" by the "privileged, rich minority" composed of coffee exporters, miners, and large-scale merchants.[39] They maintained that under the existing monetary system, this "rich minority" reaped enormous profits by selling its products in stable foreign currencies such as the U.S. (gold) dollar, while paying salaries in the rapidly depreciating Nicaraguan (silver-based) currency. Indeed, between 1900 and 1912 the value of the Nicaraguan peso had depreciated from forty-eight to six U.S. cents, due largely to the government's excessive printing of paper money.[40] In the eyes of Conservative artisans, the new currency (the gold córdoba) would do away with this inequity and thus increase the purchasing power of the Nicaraguan working class.

Coincidentally or not, artisans' language of class struggle echoed the anticapitalist discourse of proclerical Conservatives, most of whom supported the loan convention. For this reason, Conservative artisans were often denounced by the Liberal press as lackeys of the *vendepatria* (sellout) elites in power. But as Mena was well aware, Conservative artisan organizations formed an autonomous group that had recently shown its ability to mobilize urban masses and wage bitter labor strikes.[41] And because the general wanted to secure their political support, he could not antagonize them by publicizing his opposition to the proposed loan convention. Hence his silence.

If Mena's silence was an effective political ploy on his part, it also allowed his figure to become an open field on which the nationalist press could promulgate an anticosmopolitan and mixed-race nationality. Whether Liberal or Conservative, such newspapers emphasized the cultural differences separating Mena from his rivals within the ruling Conservative elite.[42] On the one hand, they sought to portray this forty-seven-year-old Conservative general as a "son of the people" who embodied the Nicaragua of the "inditos, zambos, mulatos, or mestizos."[43] This contrasted their image of Mena's Conservative rivals, who were depicted as un-Nicaraguan, U.S.-educated, "Spanish" (i.e., white) aristocrats who stood out for their "cosmopolitan" ways and "mania to Americanize us." In making this contrast, the nationalist press often highlighted Mena's links to his birthplace, Nandaime, a provincial town where mulatto and mestizo identities had traditionally been differentiated from the "Spanishness" of the regional elite seated in adjacent Granada. In fact, *Mena* was a common surname among Nandaimes who descended from black Jamaican slaves.[44]

On the other hand, nationalist papers also stressed Mena's class attributes. Though of "humble" origins, the general had succeeded in climbing the social ladder through his honorable and hard work as a pioneering banana planter in the jungles of the Atlantic region. His Conservative rivals, by contrast, were painted as lazy, champagne-drinking parasites who had enriched themselves by looting the national treasury. Along similar lines, the pro-Mena press contrasted the military prowess this physically imposing general had demonstrated in the 1894 conquest of the Mosquito Reserve—a British protectorate on the Atlantic coast—and the 1909–10 civil war with the cowardly and effeminate traits of elite Conservatives who defended the loan conventions with U.S. banks. A typical characterization was that by Rubén Darío, a bitter opponent of the Dawson Pact, who idealized Mena as a "rustic and awesome general . . . a man of the machete and of popular values."[45]

In promoting Mena's public persona, the nationalist press conveniently ignored that he possessed many of the negative traits it foisted on elite Conservatives supportive of the loan convention. They never mentioned that Mena accumulated much of his wealth between 1910 and 1912, when he enjoyed privileged access to state funds as the country's powerful minister of war.[46] Further, few Nicaraguans knew that this alleged economic nationalist owned stocks in the U.S.-controlled La Luz and Los Angeles Mining Company.[47] This gold-mining enterprise was a favorite target of Nicaraguan nationalists because it was closely associated with the two principal exponents of the U.S. intervention: Secretary of State Knox, the former lawyer of the company's primary owners (the Fletcher family from Pittsburgh), and President Adolfo Díaz, the company's longtime bookkeeper.

Mena was also more closely associated with Granada's "aristocratic" elite than the nationalist press let on. Mena, whose father owned a medium-sized cattle ranch and was a former mayor of Nandaime, shared a long history with the Chamorro family, which had helped him establish a banana plantation on the Atlantic coast in the 1880s. In addition, Mena married into one of Granada's oldest elite families, the Montiel, who descended from an eighteenth-century Spanish governor of Costa Rica. Still, Mena's kinship, business, and political ties with Granada's "aristocrats" did not preclude him from remaining an outcast in the latter's eyes. As their private correspondence reveals, Granadan oligarchs like the Chamorros labeled Mena a "negro" or "semisavage Indian" who was unfit to belong to their "civilized" circle.[48]

Mena's inability to be fully accepted by Granada's oligarchy enabled anti-U.S. forces to map an alternative national project on the general's body. Above all, Mena came to incarnate a Nicaragua that valorized popular culture and the country's diverse non-Spanish ethnicities. It was a much more inclusive national project than the dominant elite vision of a cosmopolitan Nicaragua. To a certain extent, this project resembled the nationalist discourse of *mestizaje* that was then emerging in Nicaragua, which valorized the racially mixed "mestizo" as the embodiment of the nation.[49] But there were at least three important differences that separated the Menista vision from that of a "Nicaragua mestiza." First, while the Menista national project openly celebrated Nicaragua's ethnic diversity, contemporary Nicaraguan proponents of mestizaje sought to suppress such differences in the name of cultural homogeneity. Second, if this form of mestizaje emerged largely in opposition to indigenous identity, the Menista national project was constructed against the "cosmopolitanism" and "whiteness" of the country's wealthiest elites. Third, Menista nationalist discourse had a much stronger anti-U.S. thrust—at least until a more revolutionary variant of mestizaje emerged during the Sandino Rebellion of 1927–33 (see chapter 9).

In promulgating their alternative nationality, the Menistas were playing with fire. In particular, they led Nicaraguans to believe that nationalists under Mena's leadership would actively resist a U.S. military invasion. Their belligerent discourse thus raised the stakes in the silent war between Mena and U.S. officials. Equally dangerous was their attempt to distinguish themselves socially and culturally from their "vendepatria" opponents, as it helped prepare the ground for the antielite terror perpetrated during the 1912 civil war (see chapter 4). But what made this nationalist discourse most explosive was its intertwinement with the conflict that broke out when social clubs—the institution that principally defined elite status—reopened their doors in early 1912. Centered in competing definitions of elite identity, this conflict unexpectedly radicalized civil resistance to the U.S.-sponsored oligarchic restoration.

"Aristocrats" versus "Bourgeois": The Conflict over Elite Status

The reopening of elite social clubs occurred against a hostile political backdrop. Yet the social context was perhaps even more volatile, for the U.S. intervention of 1910 came at a time when the rapid growth of Nicaragua's agroexport economy was heightening social tensions. In addition to transforming relations among social groups, the boom promoted their internal differentiation and thus complicated the reproduction of existing social identities. As for elites, the closing of social clubs during the final years of the Zelaya dictatorship momentarily masked the extent to which a common elite identity had been unmade. But when these clubs reopened in early 1912, struggles over elite identity resurfaced ever more forcefully, further inflaming an already charged atmosphere. Although these struggles failed to impress U.S. officials in Nicaragua, they helped induce the nightmarish scenario of "anarchy" that would impel the United States to invade Nicaragua later that year.

At first, elites expected that the reopening of their beloved social clubs would help unify their fractured class. Even Granada's polemical nationalist daily *El Periódico* hoped that this reopening would promote "conciliation."[50] Such hopes were hardly misplaced, for in the past social clubs had helped unify elites. Not only had they provided a neutral ground where elites could socialize without having to resolve their political and ideological differences, they had also helped them forge a common "bourgeois" identity. To elites' chagrin, the clubs' reopening had the opposite impact, as they quickly developed into arenas of conflict.

Reflecting the deep divisions plaguing the ruling Conservatives, much of this controversy was centered in their bastion of Granada. As elsewhere, the city's upper classes initially desired that their club would once again represent the epitome of "culture."[51] Yet shortly after its reinauguration in March 1912, a fierce conflict broke out when four prominent Conservatives from old elite families—Joaquín Gómez Rouhaud, Gustavo A. Argüello, Salvador Jiménez, and Manuel Zavala Chamorro—were not elected to the club's board of directors, allegedly because they were political supporters of General Mena.[52] Similar conflicts rocked reopened clubs elsewhere in Nicaragua.

The greatest storm, however, arose when the reopened clubs failed to admit individuals considered parvenus, in the process triggering a fierce debate over the criteria of club membership. As evident in letters and articles published in local newspapers, club members bitterly disagreed over what role factors such as wealth, profession, kinship ties, and racial and social origins should play in the admission of new members. The volatility of such struggles over elite identity was especially apparent in a highly publicized case that embroiled the Club de Granada in April 1912 and involved José de la Rosa Sandino, a pro-Mena Conservative from Nandaime (no relation to the future guerrilla leader Augusto Sandino). For his supporters, Sandino's failure to be admitted to the Club de Granada exemplified how social and racial prejudice prevented many parvenus from being accepted as equals by the local "aristocracy."

In many ways, Sandino's climb up the social ladder paralleled the path taken by his political patron Luis Mena.[53] Born in 1875, Sandino was raised in the milieu of Nandaime's medium-sized cattle ranches. During his youth, he labored as a foreman on large cattle haciendas owned by prominent Granadan oligarchs. Thanks to the support of one such landlord (Ernesto Selva), Sandino struck it rich in the agroexport sector; however, he made his fortune in coffee, not bananas. Like Mena, Sandino accumulated enough wealth and status to marry into one of the oldest elite families of Granada, the Argüellos. Benefiting from his wife's wealth and business connections, Sandino further expanded his economic interests. By 1912, this parvenu had established himself as an important entrepreneur in the city of Granada and the coffee-growing district of Carazo. But probably even more satisfying to Sandino was his success in becoming a leading cattle rancher in his native region of Nandaime. After Sandino had established himself economically, he began to expand his political influence. Like many other Conservatives, he benefited from the U.S.-induced regime change of August 1910, first serving as mayor of Granada and then as the *jefe político* (governor) of the department of Granada. In June 1911, Sandino reached the pinnacle of his political power, becoming the country's minister of finance.

In April 1912, Sandino took the most important step toward legitimizing his hard-won elite status by applying to the Club de Granada. Club members so bitterly opposed the parvenu's application that he withdrew his bid before it came up for a vote. No doubt, many club members rejected Sandino to spite his patron General Mena. But the uproar Sandino's bid caused among elite Granadans suggests that his exclusion was not based solely on political differences. Why had the club just accepted other outspoken pro-Mena Conservatives? As Managua's leading Liberal daily, *Diario Moderno*, argued, Sandino's rejection reflected the club's policy of social and racial discrimination toward social climbers: "The club members don't forgive him for having ousted Manuel Lacayo from the ministry [of finance], the man whose haciendas Sandino had once managed, and they reproach him for his humble origin and his Nandaime roots. They adamantly refuse to admit that he is white, for they consistently call him the black [*negro*] Nandaime, an upstart [*advenedizo*], etc."[54]

Diario Moderno saw Sandino's rejection from the Club de Granada as a product of three distinct yet interrelated forms of exclusion. First, the term *negro* underscored that Sandino remained in the eyes of elite Granadans a racialized other. Second, his racial status was reinforced by his connection with Nandaime. As the line "A mi me dicen negro porque de Nandaime soy" (They call me black because I am from Nandaime) in a popular song indicates, Granadans tended to differentiate themselves from Nandaimes by representing the latter as "negros"[55]—a legacy of the colonial era, when African slaves were sent to Nandaime to toil on haciendas owned by Granadan landlords. Third, much of the controversy over Sandino's exclusion from the Club de Granada centered on whether this "upstart" had acquired his wealth through "honorable" or "illicit" means. Sandino's supporters maintained that he had struck it rich thanks to his entrepreneurial spirit. Sandino's opponents in Granada, by contrast, deemed him a moral outcast who had enriched himself by stealing from the national treasury. Some went so far as to paint on the city's walls that Sandino was both a "thief" and a "leper."[56]

The exclusion of parvenus like Sandino from elite social clubs generated a debate in local newspapers that quickly transcended the personal level and seemed to pit a modernizing "bourgeoisie" against an "aristocracy" steeped in colonial attitudes. A key protagonist was the pro-Mena Conservative daily *El Periódico* of Granada, which championed the "bourgeois" cause. Although run by members of the city's traditional elite families, the paper supported the admission of parvenus like Sandino to the social club. In doing so, it tended to stress the entrepreneurial character of "self-made" men. More frequently, *El Periódico* contrasted the inclusionary beliefs of this nascent "bourgeoisie" with the "exclusionary" social and political practices of the colonial-like "aristocracy" whose power, it claimed, was based on social and racial origin rather than on individual merit.

Highlighting these distinct elite outlooks, *El Periódico* published testi-monies by elites who had distanced themselves from their "aristocratic" origins in order to embrace a "bourgeois" identity. For example, "Bourgeois Chatter" ("Cháchara burguesa") tells how a member of Granada's "nobility of lineage" rejected the feudal-like cultural values of his own class and instead embraced a bourgeois work ethic acquired during a sojourn in England.[57] In a similar vein, a renegade, pro-Mena Conservative "aristocrat" describes his revulsion at the "exclusivist" cultural practices that prevent social climbers from ever being accepted by the "nobles." As one of these "nobles"—his uncle—succinctly put it: "A Brahmin is always a noble . . . just like a plebeian can never stop being a pariah." In addition, his testimony recounts how "nobles" have scorned him and like-minded "sans-culottes" for having re-nounced their "aristocratic" origins and embraced the "vulgarity" of popular culture. However, the main goal of this elite testimony is to situate competing elite cultural practices in their broader political context. Not coincidentally, it ends with the narrator's uncle stating: "After the triumph of the [1910] Revo-lution I took the path of honesty, while you took the opposite one, following that demagogue Luis Mena. Despite having degenerated yourself, you still have much honor: I congratulate you, but don't forget that History is full of restorations."[58]

Like *El Periódico*, other nationalist papers sought to challenge the U.S.-sponsored oligarchic restoration by whipping up class-based resentments against elite Conservatives who supported the U.S. intervention.[59] Time and again, they framed the political divisions plaguing the ruling Conservatives in class-based terms: While Mena's elite supporters embodied the socially inclusive bourgeoisie, anti-Mena Conservatives belonged to an "aristocracy of blood" that sought to preserve its power and status by caste-based princi-ples of social exclusion.

In practice, however, the "bourgeois" elites championed by the nationalist press were not as inclusive as they claimed to be. Like the much-despised "aristocrats," they sought to exclude individuals of nonelite origin from the social club. Their exclusionary practices became apparent in yet another incident that rocked Granada's social club in April 1912: its refusal to admit the young artisan Santiago Arauz. A jeweler, Arauz was surely not an average artisan. In addition to owning his own workshop, he was one of the few master artisans of Granada who advertised his business in newspapers that circulated in Managua. Like other wealthy Granadan artisans, Arauz also owned some rural property. Still, his most important capital was not economic but social: he was engaged to the daughter of Alberto Chamorro, a leading coffee planter and a member of the country's most powerful clan.[60] Despite the backing of the Chamorros and other "aristocratic" families such as the Cuadras, the Pasos, and the Lacayos, Arauz's application to the Club de Granada was rejected.

The club's rebuff of Arauz was quickly exploited by "aristocrats," who charged that the "bourgeois" nouveaux riches were the ones guilty of practicing social "exclusivism." For example, the principal paper of Granada's "aristocracy of blood," *El Diario Nicaragüense*, claimed that the club's "bourgeois" members rejected Arauz because he was an artisan and thus did not possess sufficient wealth.[61] But money, the paper's editors argued, should not be the main criteria for club membership. More important were "complete honesty, good manners, and correct values"—moral qualities that Arauz abundantly possessed. Such arguments were echoed in letters various "aristocrats" wrote to *El Diario Nicaragüense*. They could explain Arauz's rejection only in terms of class: he was a simple "artisan," a "humble son of the people" who did not possess the necessary economic capital to satisfy the parvenu members of Granada's social club. To them, the Arauz incident more generally highlighted how parvenu elites differed from traditional elites by defining social status in terms of "money" rather than "morality."[62]

Inverting the logic of the pro-Mena nationalist press, one letter writer even attacked the parvenus for being a "nobility" themselves. "But what nobility, Holy God!," he exclaimed, "It is a nobility of mulatos, mestizos, and quadroons [*cuarterones*]." He claimed further that, unlike the "aristocracy of blood," this new, racially impure "nobility" was neither "illustrious" nor "generous"; nor was it "a social class distinct from the common townsfolk." Instead, their claim to "nobility" was solely based on "his majesty the money."[63] In general, "aristocrats" claimed that this new "nobility" was born of the "corrupt" dealings that allegedly flourished during the Zelaya dictatorship. Or as the leading Conservative politician Carlos Cuadra Pasos would remark in less passionate terms, the Zelaya era produced the displacement of a "Creole [white] patriarchy of colonial origin" by a "bourgeoisie of new rich."[64]

But how many "new rich" actually belonged to elite social clubs? The controversy over their entrance policies suggests that the clubs were evenly divided between old elites of the "aristocracy of blood" and parvenus who comprised the "nobility of mulatos, mestizos, and quadroons." In reality, the "aristocrats" outnumbered the parvenus by far; this disparity reflected traditional oligarchs' continued domination in the ranks of Nicaragua's agroexport elite. In Granada, for example, nearly three quarters of the sixty-eight men who reopened the club in March 1912 belonged to families that had achieved elite status prior to 1890, that is, before Nicaragua's agroexport boom began to produce nouveaux riches like José de la Rosa Sandino.[65] In contrast, only a fifth of the club's members fit the profile of a parvenu; and of these, a bit more than half were foreigners, while very few were of rural upbringing or identified themselves as master artisans. The club's rejection of Sandino and Arauz was thus no exception but the rule, as the former typified the parvenu of rural/provincial origin and the latter the master artisan. Had they been united, traditional elites should have been easily able to dictate the club's entrance policy. Yet after decades of extraordinary unity, these elites had become highly divided.

It was hardly a coincidence that such cultural divisions centered on social climbers' efforts to be admitted into the principal institution that defined elite status. Social identity, as Pierre Bourdieu has argued, "lies in difference, and difference is asserted against what is closest, against that which represents the greatest threat."[66] In Granada, many Conservative elites viewed Conservative "upstarts" like Sandino as most proximate and therefore the most threatening. Not only were these parvenus politically and economically linked to Granada's Conservative "aristocracy," they were at times tied to them through kinship. Given this social proximity, Granada's Conservative "aristocrats" asserted their difference from Conservative parvenus more easily through cultural markers such as race and family background than through political or socioeconomic distinctions. No wonder the controversial entrance policies of the newly opened social clubs engendered such a fierce debate.

This controversy was primarily fanned by pro-Mena papers, which used the language of class struggle to attack the "aristocracy of blood." In the process, they antagonized prominent pro-Mena Conservative nationalists, pushing more and more of them to join the anti-Mena forces. Not surprisingly, many of these deserters belonged to "aristocratic" families. One such "turncoat" was David Arellano, Nicaragua's "premier Yanquista," who had so bitterly opposed the projected U.S. takeover of Nicaraguan finances. Another was Fernando Guzmán Bermúdez, whose grandfather (Fernando Guzmán

Solórzano) had been president of Nicaragua between 1867 and 1871 and who as jefe político of Granada was an important ally of General Mena. Typically, Guzmán stated that he could no longer tolerate the campaign of "hate" that pro-Mena nationalists were waging against "honorable families" such as the Chamorros and Cuadras.[67] But no matter how much this campaign troubled Guzmán and his "aristocratic" friends, they surely never foresaw that it would help pave the way for the extraordinary violence perpetrated by the "nobility of mulattoes, mestizos, and quadroons" against men and women of the "aristocracy of blood" during the civil war that broke out in late July 1912.

On the Brink of Revolution:
Hunger and the Spread of Social Violence

By early July, Nicaragua's political crisis had sunk to the point that commentators from across the political spectrum feared the country was on the brink of a social revolution. Such fears certainly responded to the escalating war of words among elite Conservatives. But the increasingly revolutionary ambiance was further fueled by popular outrage over the food shortages that engulfed Nicaragua in the spring of 1912. From the end of March onward, the urban and rural poor began to go hungry. And since the rich were less affected by skyrocketing prices, the food shortage only fanned antielite sentiments. Throughout western Nicaragua, it triggered social violence. Above all, however, the food shortage radicalized popular opposition to the U.S. intervention, for many Nicaraguans blamed the Díaz government and its U.S. sponsors for their plight.

The crisis sprang from the drought of March–July 1912, which severely reduced the output of basic food crops. As the food shortage spread, many families from rural areas in central and northern Nicaragua sought refuge in urban areas, thus worsening the already precarious situation in cities like Managua, León, and Granada. The situation further deteriorated when, at the end of the coffee harvest, thousands of laid-off seasonal laborers migrated to the cities in search of food.[68] With demand rapidly rising, the price of basic grains shot up in urban areas, and soon only the wealthiest could afford these staples. To relieve the growing food shortage, municipal authorities attempted to import corn and wheat.[69] As the drought affected most of Central America, such imports had to come from distant markets like California. To finance these unexpected imports, numerous congressional deputies tried to pass a law authorizing the Díaz government to seek a domestic loan. National authorities, however, balked at the import of basic grains, arguing that such a measure not only violated prevailing customs law but would promote speculation.[70] The U.S. official in charge of Nicaragua's custom duties also opposed these imports on grounds that they would increase the nation's public debt.[71]

The government's seemingly fatalistic view coupled with the intransigence of the U.S. customs collector galvanized antielite and anti-U.S. sentiment throughout Nicaragua. A leading Conservative from Matagalpa reported that many of the region's poor believed they were on the brink of starvation simply because "the Conservatives sold the country and the gringos don't care if the people of Nicaragua die of hunger."[72] The government's inability to curb the spreading food shortage was exploited by the opposition press, which framed the crisis in terms of class warfare, pitting an uncaring and decadent governing elite against the starving "proletariat."[73] At first, government forces simply complained that their rivals were tactless to manipulate the spreading food shortage for political purposes. But popular pressure in the form of street demonstrations soon grew to such an extent that in early July 1912 the government relented and allowed municipal authorities to import basic grains.

Rather than solving the crisis, the grain imports deepened popular opposition to the U.S.-backed regime. True, the arrival of these imports provoked much jubilation. In Managua, for example, a huge crowd accompanied by a marching band greeted the first train transporting fifteen hundred bags of corn and one thousand bags of beans. Yet the populace's initial euphoria quickly turned to anger as the imported grain became the object of price speculation.[74] The principal culprits were foreign coffee traders, who, thanks to their international connections, received the grain imports first. It was from these foreigners that desperate municipal authorities bought the over-priced grains that they subsequently distributed to the populace through a network of local merchants.

Not all municipal authorities resisted the temptation to exploit the populace's hunger. In Granada, for example, Mayor Leopoldo Lacayo and other young "aristocrats" were accused of reaping profits of over ten thousand U.S. dollars by selling corn at a price one third higher than that charged by authorities in Managua.[75] Such price speculation enraged popular organizations with which Lacayo and his cronies were politically allied. Responding to pressure from Granada's Club Conservador de Artesanos, Lacayo's political patron, General Emiliano Chamorro, forced the municipality to lower the price of corn.[76] Adding to the populace's plight, the distribution of imported grains was further hampered by regional rivalries, as authorities from different municipalities vied with each other for scarce foods. Distribution difficulties coupled with rampant acts of speculation militated against efforts by local and national authorities to defuse social tensions caused by the food shortage.

Progovernment newspapers sought to convince a hostile public that the growing hunger crisis did not result from the government's indifference to the plight of Nicaragua's "needy class." Instead, they tried to make a case for the deeper structural roots of the crisis. In general, they argued that the booming agroexport economy was sapping capital, labor, and land traditionally allocated to the production of basic grains.[77] More specifically, Granada's El Diario Nicaragüense claimed that the current grain shortage was rooted in the lengthy Zelaya dictatorship, when "in order to fill our chests with coffee, sugar, and dairy products, we neglected to grow cereals, which form the base of our nourishment."[78] The paper found small producers most guilty of having forsaken the production of grains to plant more lucrative cash crops. For a government desperate for popular support, such criticism was hardly opportune, but it accurately reflected the crucial role small producers played in driving the country's post-1870s agroexport boom.

Although public attention centered on the hunger crisis, the drought of 1912 also intensified pressure on scarce water resources, thus exacerbating social tensions in the countryside. In regions of recent hacienda expansion, the drought pushed peasants to use violence to reclaim access to better-irrigated fields. Such was the case of Masaya's indigenous community, which sought to recover over twenty-five thousand acres of fertile land in the plains of Tisma.[79] Since this land was adjacent to Lake Nicaragua, Lake Managua, the Tipitapa River, and Tisma Lagoon, it was exceptionally well irrigated and suited to grain production. Masaya's indigenous community had lost its access to these lands during the late nineteenth century, when the agroexport boom led elites from the city of Granada to establish large cattle haciendas in Tisma. To make matters worse, Granadan cattle barons not only fenced their properties with barbed wire but drilled new wells that drained vast tracts of traditionally well-irrigated lands.[80] With the 1910 regime change, Masaya's indigenous community sought to recover its land by appealing to the new

Conservative authorities, to no avail. Then, at the height of the dry season of 1912, over one hundred armed Indians from Masaya violently occupied their former lands in Tisma, singling out haciendas belonging to Liberal cattle barons from Granada.[81]

It is possible that Masaya's Indian community had been mobilized by certain cattle barons to attack the estates of other landlords with whom they disputed property boundaries.[82] But the timing of the attack suggests that the violent turn in the Tisma land conflict was also driven by Indians' thirst for better irrigated land at a moment of crisis. Indeed, similar acts of violence occurred in other parts of rural Granada, where the 1912 drought sharpened conflicts over water use.[83] Peasants who waged such conflicts often believed that natural water resources were a public good, and that landlords had no right to fence them.

Finally, the drought-induced rise in rural violence apparently led more and more peasants to steal food and rustle cattle from neighboring haciendas. In the rich cattle regions of Boaco and Chontales, peasants reportedly snuck out at night in small bands to steal "animals, corn, cheese, and other goods of lesser importance."[84] Such thefts occurred even in areas where elite control over the rural populace was exceptionally strong, as in the Granada district El Sitio, where the powerful Chamorro family owned large haciendas. Although the inhabitants of El Sitio were some of the Chamorros' most dependent political clients, they too suffered from the inability of their patrons to resolve the growing shortage of food.[85]

The sudden upsurge in rural violence revealed how elite control over the rural populace was rapidly eroding. Although hardly mentioned in urban-based newspapers, this erosion of elite power clearly troubled rural political brokers like Matagalpa's Bartolomé Martínez, then the main ally of General Emiliano Chamorro in northern Nicaragua. Already in April 1912 this large-scale coffee grower and future president (1923–24) had forewarned Chamorro that "the masses driven by hunger could revolt at any moment." As the crisis sharpened over the next month, Martínez's fears worsened. By the end of May, he was convinced that the escalating conflicts between Matagalpan coffee barons and peasants or Indians over natural resources threatened to turn antielite sentiment into a violent uprising.[86]

A general sense of eroding elite authority overtook urban centers as well.[87] Most noticeably, starving plebeians took to the streets to protest local authorities' failure to solve the food shortages. In addition, rent disputes proliferated as urban dwellers—the overwhelming majority of whom were renters—found it harder to pay, surely because an increasing portion of family earnings went to soaring food costs.[88] Antielite sentiments were further fanned by the inability of local, elite-owned water companies to resolve the water shortage. As the lack of water paralyzed construction and other artisanal activities, it also contributed to rising urban unemployment. But plebeians were not the only ones to feel the country's deepening crisis: the soaring urban crime rates led local elites, particularly wealthy women, increasingly to fear for their safety. As Managua's *Diario de Nicaragua* stressed in its 31 May issue, "banditry has begun to spread due to hunger, and women are the victims." Given that the poor could hardly afford the price of food, this Liberal paper feared "the wretched populace" would "struggle with the dagger, with force, with whatever is in its reach to obtain a piece of bread and thus calm the cries of its empty stomach."

As social violence spread, more and more newspapers dreaded that the country was sliding into a bloody abyss. Under the banner "On the Verge of Anarchy," *Diario de Nicaragua* warned its readers on 28 June 1912 that the country was experiencing a "social breakdown." On 12 July, Managua's leading Liberal daily *Diario Moderno* went a step further, exclaiming that Nicaragua was on the brink of a "social revolution." The paper emphatically warned that this "is the worst of all revolutions [for it represents] the war to death of the destitute, the humble, of those who are hungry and thirsty . . . against the rich, the haughty, the powerful . . . whose heads will be cut off by the pike of the helpless who will refuse to pardon any 'señor.'" Not even a month later, these words would prove prophetic, particularly in the elite bastion of Granada.

Conclusion

The increasingly revolutionary situation in early-twentieth-century Nicaragua was in itself not unusual. Throughout Latin America, decades of profound economic change and oligarchic rule had heightened social and political tensions to the breaking point. Numerous regimes sought to defuse the mounting crisis by accommodating the varied demands of excluded groups, particularly the middle classes. Those that refused to open up the political system risked violent upheaval, as was the case with the Porfirio Díaz dictatorship in Mexico (1876–1911). Under President Madriz, who succeeded

Zelaya, Nicaragua first embarked on a democratizing path. Yet its political opening was cut short by the U.S. intervention of 1910. The nation that saw itself as the world's premier promoter of liberal democracy instead imposed an antiliberal, exclusionary political order on Nicaragua. Of course there is nothing inevitable about revolutions. But if any U.S. intervention has made revolution inevitable, as historian Walter LaFeber suggests, the Dawson Pact of 1910 came very close to doing so.[89]

The polarized political culture that emerged under the shadow of the Dawson Pact met six preconditions often deemed necessary for revolutionary upheaval.[90] First, this U.S.-imposed arrangement so greatly deepened divisions within the ruling elite that its members were willing to take up arms against each other. These divisions, in turn, weakened the government's capacity to rule. But they also helped politicize nonelite sectors, who intensified their struggle for greater political rights and better access to economic resources such as fertile land. Further, the U.S.-ordered proscription of Liberals and postponement of popular elections ensured that many Nicaraguans viewed the U.S.-backed regime as illegitimate. By enabling General Mena's evolution into a nationalist hero, the Dawson Pact moreover provided Nicaraguans with a clear and popular alternative to the U.S.-backed regime. Finally, the inability of U.S. officials and national authorities to curb the spread of hunger and social violence ensured that a wide range of social groups—not just the poor—suffered from worsening social and economic conditions, and thus became potential supporters of revolutionary change.

With good reason, then, local observers feared that the political crisis engendered by the Dawson Pact had deteriorated into an impending social revolution, a "war to death" against the "señores." Given these fears, ruling elites were probably not surprised that the civil war that broke out in late July 1912 was marked by a high degree of antielite violence. But they never imagined that its principal instigators would come from within their own ranks.

4 Bourgeois Revolution Denied

U.S. Military Intervention in the Civil War of 1912

THE BRIEF BUT BRUTAL CIVIL WAR of 1912 was a watershed for Nicaragua. Above all it triggered the country's first full-scale U.S. invasion since the Walker fiasco of the mid-1850s. Occurring when the anti-U.S. rebels were on the verge of victory, the 1912 invasion ushered in a U.S. occupation that lasted for just over twenty years—the lengthiest occupation in Latin America. For many latter-day Nicaraguan nationalist leaders, this U.S. intervention represents one of the most tragic events in their country's history. With Tomás Borge—the powerful interior minister of the Sandinista Revolution (1979–90)—they lament that the 1912 invasion "frustrated . . . a bourgeois democratic revolution, which never again raised its head."[1] Indeed, the leaders of the 1912 rebellion not only cast their struggle as a "revolution" waged by a modernizing "bourgeoisie" against a backward "aristocracy," they also claimed to be fighting for a more democratic order and greater national autonomy.

But what did this "bourgeois revolution" actually stand for? Nowadays, most Nicaraguans associate the 1912 war exclusively with General Benjamín Zeledón's famous last stand against the U.S. invaders. Most of the rank-and-file revolutionaries shared Zeledón's nationalist views and were willing to fight until the bitter end. But in the case of the revolutionary leadership, Zeledón's martyrdom was the exception, for all other leaders chose to surrender rather than defend Nicaragua's sovereignty. As promised, however, the rebel leaders did attack the U.S.-sponsored oligarchic restoration of 1910. In the name of liberty and equality, the revolutionaries persecuted progovernment elites. And for most contemporaries, it was this violence, not the struggle against U.S. imperial rule, that primarily defined the "revolution" of 1912.

Not coincidentally, the antielite violence occurred mostly in Granada, where both insurgent forces and the ruling Conservative oligarchs were based. For two full months, rebels tortured and publicly humiliated prominent Granadan men and women. Most surprising are the identities of those chiefly responsible for this violence: pro-Mena parvenu "bourgeois" who belonged to the same Conservative Party as their victims. Of course, we should not fully disregard the victims' claims about the "savage" and thus irrational nature of the 1912 violence. Still, the violence clearly represented a revolutionary attack on the hierarchical social order. Rebel leaders tapped into widespread resentment against the ruling, pro-U.S. "aristocrats" in order to incite, as one contemporary noted, "the downtrodden to rise up against those at the top."[2] But once these leaders lost control over the violence, they believed that they had no other choice than to embrace the U.S. invaders as their protectors. Or as an antirevolutionary "aristocrat" put it, when "the specter of anarchy commenced to raise its horrible face . . . the same chiefs who had risen in arms against the legitimate Government, frightened at their own words, sought the protection of the American marines, and delivered to them the government of [their strongholds]."[3] This "deliverance," and the violence that caused it, were perhaps the most poignant legacies of Nicaragua's frustrated "bourgeois revolution."

For Liberty, Equality, and Autonomy: Revolutionary Nationalists on the Attack

The 1912 civil war erupted when General Luis Mena rebelled against the Conservative government of Adolfo Díaz on 29 July. The revolt occurred only hours after Mena had been forced to resign as minister of war, ostensibly because he had sought to overthrow the Díaz government.[4] Thanks to the mediation of U.S. Minister to Nicaragua George Weitzel, Mena was spared arrest after promising to refrain from any violent actions against the Díaz government. Yet Mena refused to give up that easily. Shortly after nightfall, the deposed minister of war fled with about six hundred loyal troops to Masaya, a Liberal stronghold fifteen miles south of Managua. Simultaneously, Conservative forces led by Mena's son captured control of Granada.

Once in Masaya, Luis Mena established a powerful military and political alliance composed of Conservatives and Liberals. In letters to leading Liberals, Mena stressed the nationalist and bipartisan nature of his cause.[5] Mena's pleas met with resounding success as he quickly amassed over three thousand men to form the so-called Allied Army (Ejército Aliado). By most accounts, the bulk of Mena's army consisted of artisans, small-scale farmers, and students.[6] To ensure bipartisanship, Mena shared command with the Liberal general Benjamín Zeledón. He also declared that the force's insignia would consist of both red and green bands, the traditional colors of the Liberal and Conservative parties.[7] In numbers, the Allied Army rivaled the government troops centered in Managua. But in terms of firepower, the rebels possessed a clear advantage, as Mena had previously transferred the bulk of the Nicaraguan army's arsenal to the Granada fortress commanded by his son. Further, Mena had the political momentum on his side. Prominent Conservatives and Liberals flocked from all corners of the country to join him. In Masaya, Mena reconstituted a National Assembly that included most of the prewar congressional deputies, an act that the rebels believed greatly legitimized their cause.[8]

Masaya's revolutionary assembly wasted little time in challenging the core of the U.S. imperial project. First, it replaced the staunchly pro-U.S. president Díaz with his second alternate Marcos Mairena, a pro-Mena Conservative.[9] The assembly then reignited the democratization process by calling for free elections in which all Liberals could participate.[10] Finally, the assembly sought to recuperate Nicaragua's sovereignty by renationalizing the country's railroad and steamships, which had been acquired by U.S. bankers with the second loan convention of June 1912. This renationalization act was more than an empty declaration, as the rebels had already seized six of the company's eleven locomotives and its two steamers. Of great military value, the railroads facilitated the movement of troops and arms, while the steamers enabled the rebels to control the country's strategic waterways. Yet the steamers and, in particular, the railroad were also key symbols of national sovereignty. The reestablishment of Nicaraguan control over the railroad was frequently mentioned by revolutionary leaders in their efforts to win public support.[11]

The socially diverse insurgents bonded equally, if not more, in their struggle against the 1910 oligarchic restoration. From the start, rebel leaders sought to harness class resentment against the ruling "aristocrats" to their nationalist project. For example, their first communiqué denounced "Wall Street bankers" and the "handful of Nicaraguan oligarchs" for perpetrating the "misery of the middle and lower classes."[12] In addition, these leaders wove into their nationalist rhetoric a liberal discourse of rights. General Zeledón, for example, tried to fire up his troops by echoing popular demands for a more democratic order: "Citizens, we will win back our rights: Equality before the law will shine on all of us, whether rich or poor. . . . Without liberty there is no life; without equality there is no light; without national autonomy chaos reigns. . . . No more intervention in our internal affairs. . . . We want to have true welfare for all the downtrodden [and] . . . the anonymous whom the oligarchy disparagingly calls 'cannon fodder.'"[13]

So greatly did this rhetoric appeal to the local populace that many foreign observers were certain the rebels would swiftly defeat the U.S.-backed Díaz government.[14] Indeed, in the week following Mena's flight to Masaya, rebel forces quickly gained command over southwestern Nicaragua. In addition, they captured the strategic railway that ran from the Pacific port of Corinto to Granada and strengthened their control over the country's most important waterways.

Prodded by the U.S. minister to Nicaragua, President Díaz sought to stave off defeat by officially requesting a U.S. military invasion on 3 August.[15] The following day, a small force of one hundred U.S. troops arrived in Managua from the Pacific port of Corinto, where a U.S. gunboat had recently anchored. But differences between U.S. military and civilian authorities in Washington delayed a full-scale U.S. military intervention until the end of August.

In the meantime, the insurgents disregarded U.S. warnings and continued their advance. On 11 August they launched their long-awaited assault on the capital. Over the next four days, the revolutionaries lay siege to Managua, combining massive bombardments with infantry charges. During this battle, more than a thousand Nicaraguans were killed, their corpses strewn across the fields.[16] To their own surprise, revolutionary forces failed to capture the capital. Yet this setback did not slow the rebels' advance. Moving north, they gained control of León after a revolutionary uprising ended in the massacre of over five hundred government soldiers (see figure 8). The insurgents then captured Chinandega and made important inroads in the north-central department of the Segovias.[17] By late August, much of Nicaragua was in rebel hands, with government control reduced to Managua and Corinto.

Revolutionary Violence as a "Social War"

Once in control of their territory, local revolutionaries quickly established what some contemporaries called a "reign of terror." The most brutal acts of revolutionary violence occurred during the war's initial phase, when insurgents assaulted progovernment elites and looted their properties. The violence escalated once again with the landing of the U.S. invasion force in early September. In this second wave, rebels also targeted foreign residents, particularly U.S. citizens. The last outburst of violence occurred at the war's end when the revolutionary rank-and-file vented their anger against their leaders'

8. Anti-U.S. revolutionaries marching in León, 1912. *Courtesy of Instituto de Historia de Nicaragua y de Centroamérica.*

peaceful surrender to the U.S. invaders. The strongest outbreak of antielite violence since the Walker revolution of 1856, the 1912 terror was deemed by its main victims a "social or communist war."[18]

Nowhere was the "social war" more fiercely waged than in Granada, which was not only the bastion of the ruling Conservative oligarchs but home to the principal revolutionary leaders. Contemporary accounts tended to blame Granada's violence on outsiders such as "peons," "Indians," or Liberals from León.[19] In reality, its chief perpetrators were Granadan Conservatives.[20]

To the outside world, renegade Conservative oligarchs represented the public face of Granada's revolutionary movement. With few exceptions, these scions of old elite families belonged to the Conservative Party's pro-Mena, "progressive" faction that had opposed the religious article and the U.S.-Nicaraguan loan treaty.[21] Many had held important political positions and possessed great social status; all were members of Granada's exclusive social club. In general, these oligarchic insurgents identified with the "new" bour-geoisie that allegedly opposed the old-line "aristocracy of blood." But as we have seen, such a contrast was anything but clear-cut. Moreover, many revo-lutionary oligarchs were closely linked with antirevolutionary "aristocrats," either via kinship, membership in Granada's social club, or as simple neigh-bors.[22] Yet political and ideological divisions within Granada's Conservative oligarchy had become deep enough that a sizeable minority embraced the call for an antioligarchic revolution.

Despite the prominence of dissident oligarchs, Granada's revolutionary movement was mainly led by upwardly mobile Conservatives of nonelite origin.[23] One leading revolutionary parvenu was José de la Rosa Sandino, whose recent exclusion from Granada's social club had been such a cause célèbre. Much of the power wielded by Granada's revolutionary parvenus rested on their complete control over local rebel troops. In fact, not one oligarch was represented in Granada's revolutionary military leadership. This absence contrasted with the plethora of Granadan oligarchs in the military leadership of the government troops besieged in Managua. The two main military leaders of Granada's rebel army—General Luis Mena and the thirty-five-year-old Alberto Osorno—embody the two types of parvenus who di-rected Granada's revolution. If Mena typified the revolutionary parvenu who emerged from the social milieu of owners of medium-sized cattle ranches in rural Granada, the merchant/farmer Osorno represented the upwardly mobile urbanite who owned agricultural enterprises.

Whether of urban or rural origins, Granada's revolutionary parvenus shrewdly used local patron-client networks to mobilize over five hundred rebel troops.[24] Their mobilization efforts were undoubtedly aided by the recent upsurge in antigovernment and anti-U.S. sentiment. But Granada's revolutionary leaders also benefited from the material and symbolic author-ity they exerted over the rural populace. Many revolutionary parvenus rented unused land to local peasants, often in exchange for labor, and extended them small loans. Politically, they tended to dominate important loci of power such as the municipal governments and local political clubs.[25] These leaders also had great status in their rural communities, as evidenced by their presiding over a local cofradía (a lay religious brotherhood that honors a specific saint). For example, the principal officer (mayordomo) of Malaca-toya's Nuestra Señora de los Desamparados cofradía was the forty-two-year-old Nazario Chavarría, owner of a large cattle ranch in Malacatoya and a high-ranking officer in Granada's revolutionary forces.[26] As mayordomo, Chavarría sponsored the patron-saint festival of Malacatoya held annually on 26 and 27 April, an event that surely enhanced his authority among the local populace.

Granada's urban revolutionary leaders, in turn, benefited from their close links to the politically influential artisans. This was particularly true for two chief perpetrators of Granada's revolutionary violence: Alberto Osorno, who presided over the city's leading mutualist organization, the Sociedad de Obreros y Socorros Mutuos; and the forty-eight-year-old Liberal merchant Valeriano Torres, who led the artisan-dominated paramilitary group Cuadro Rojo (Red Cadre) during the 1912 war.

In certain cases, Granada's revolutionary parvenus derived much political and economic capital from their kinship ties to old elite families. These links tended to be forged less by those who hailed from the frontier-like region of Malacatoya or the city of Granada than those who lived in Nandaime—a region where medium cattle ranchers had historically been key clients of Granada's most powerful patronage networks. Still, as evident in the experiences of Luis Mena and José de la Rosa Sandino, such ties did not ensure that parvenus would be fully accepted as equals by members of Granada's "aristocracy." Instead they often remained racialized others. This racially based social exclusion was especially apparent in the reluctance of Granada's social club to accept parvenus. If all of Granada's revolutionary oligarchs were club members, only one of their parvenu comrades (the thirty-eight-year-old cattle baron Hildebrando Rocha) belonged to this exclusive circle.

It was against representatives of this racist, hierarchical social order that Granada's parvenu revolutionaries unleashed their "social war."[27] Not content to loot their opponents' stores and haciendas, the revolutionaries imprisoned and tortured many progovernment Conservative oligarchs in their main fortress, the San Francisco Church located in the city's center. Most of the evidence about this torture comes from prisoners' testimonies and thus needs to be treated with caution.[28] Yet even some of the revolutionaries' firmest supporters acknowledged that such violent acts had been committed by Granada's revolutionaries. For example, the pro-Mena *La Información* of Costa Rica reported after the war's end that the much-celebrated rebels of Granada had tortured their opponents with "a savagery befitting the Middle Ages."[29]

For the most part, this "savage" violence consisted of incarceration under hideous conditions. The revolutionaries bound their male and female victims, locked them together in a dark and filthy cell, and forced them to sleep on the ground, which was covered with horse manure. Numerous prisoners fell gravely ill as their captors deprived them of water and food for days. Occasionally, the revolutionaries shoved the heads of prominent political prisoners into extremely filthy toilets and held them there for five minutes before allowing them to eat their food. It is likely that women suffered more than men, especially since numerous women were reportedly raped. Although such acts of violence did not result in any known deaths, let alone executions, they were among the worst ever suffered by members of Nicaragua's wealthiest regional elite.

What most traumatized the elite victims of Granada's revolutionary violence was the way they were publicly humiliated. Indeed, one testimony suggests that attacking the victims' honor was the principal purpose of Granada's "social war."[30] This observation is corroborated by many elite victims who later testified that they had been constantly insulted by lower-class revolutionaries.[31] Equally scandalous, the revolutionaries often paraded their elite victims on horseback facing backward through the streets of Granada before locking them up.[32] The greatest public humiliation occurred when the revolutionaries stripped prominent prisoners and forced them to walk naked through the streets of Granada. One such victim was the wealthy landlord Martín Benard Vivas. A highly influential Conservative politician, the forty-two-year-old Benard was the co-owner of the country's largest sugar mill (the Ingenio San Antonio) and a driving force behind the reopening of Granada's social club, which his father had helped found in 1871. Like many other members of Granada's "aristocracy of blood," Benard was arrested by the 1912 revolutionaries and taken to a nearby police station. There, as his friend Salvador Chamorro later testified, the revolutionaries "stripped him, outraged him in a horrible manner [and] menaced him with being shot."[33] After blindfolding Benard, they had him walk naked to their main prison, the San Francisco Church.

Benard's humiliating march underscores that the 1912 revolutionaries staged some of their violent acts as public spectacles. In doing so, they dramatized the breakdown of the authority wielded by the country's most prominent elites. As historian Dorinda Outram has argued, the physical body has often served "as an image of the order of state and society: the bearing, features and physical dignity . . . of rulers and great men has traditionally been the means . . . by which power is wielded and authority imposed."[34] Since the body is such an important resource of power, contemporaries surely read Granada's spectacle of violence as an attack on the hierarchical social order incarnated by its main victims.

Another manifestation of the terror's political nature was the revolutionaries' physical abuse of elite women. Not only did they mistreat prominent female prisoners, they also assaulted elite women in their private homes and at the country's most exclusive boarding school for girls.[35] To escape persecution, many wives and daughters of local "aristocrats" went into hiding. Some risked their lives by passing from house to house across slippery rooftops. A few found refuge in their country homes close by, only to be victimized yet again by marauding revolutionary bands. As elite women later testified, what they most feared was the loss of their "honor" to the "perverse" revolutionaries.[36] Since the authority of elite men hinged on their capacity to protect the honor of their women, the sexualized nature of Granada's violence was integral to the "social war" the rebels waged against the "aristocracy of blood."[37]

Granada's revolutionary violence suddenly expanded with the landing of the U.S. invading force in early September. In particular, the invasion triggered a rise in attacks on a new group of victims: foreign merchants. And unlike the violence perpetrated against Granada's "aristocrats," the revolutionaries chiefly implicated in terrorizing foreign merchants were not parvenu elites but poorer urban artisans.[38] At first, popular revolutionaries simply looted the properties of U.S. merchants and hurled at them insults such as "Yankee pigs." But very quickly they also began to ransack stores owned by European merchants. Rebels even vandalized the homes of Granada's foreign residents who had displayed their native flags in an effort to secure immunity from the terror. For example, the Italian merchant Antonio Cassinelli stated that on 11 September a rebel squad broke into his house and "proceeded to commit violently all kinds of abuses." The rebels robbed him and nearly killed his wife. Two days after Cassinelli complained to Granada's revolutionary leadership about this "barbarous act," mounted guards returned to his house at midnight, cut down the Italian flag, and fired their rifles at the house.[39]

Rebel attacks against foreign merchants reflected popular anger at a group widely suspected of hoarding and overpricing food. This anger existed on the eve of the war's outbreak, when much of the country suffered from a food shortage. The hunger crisis worsened during the 1912 war as Granada's insurgents plundered stores and market stalls to stock up on food. Meat also became scarce, since the revolutionaries seized much cattle from adjacent haciendas. Marauding revolutionaries robbed farmers so frequently that the latter no longer dared to bring their produce to the city's market. As the food crisis deepened, popular anger at foreign merchants increased, especially at those who, to quote a British merchant, "didn't miss a chance of supplying hungry people with food but for cash only."[40]

The violence perpetrated against foreign merchants also suggests that parvenu elites were beginning to lose control over Granada's revolutionary violence. This shift is underscored by the testimony of the prominent "aristocrat" Salvador Chamorro (father of General Emiliano Chamorro), who claimed that local artisans had taken control over Granada's "reign of terror" toward the war's end.[41] In particular, he singled out four artisans as its chief perpetrators: the carpenters José María Pérez and Manuel Balmaceda, and the barbers Francisco Marenco and Francisco Obando, who also was the president of the artisan-dominated dance club El Eden. No doubt, Granada's artisan revolutionaries carried out numerous violent acts against the will of their leaders. Given their close relations with European merchants, neither the oligarchic nor the parvenu factions of Granada's revolutionary leadership would have supported the antiforeign violence perpetrated by their artisan followers. Similarly, it is hard to believe that Granada's revolutionary leaders condoned the pillaging of stores, landed estates, and homes owned by prorevolutionary oligarchs.[42] Such acts included the infamous 23 September incident in which artisan-led bands terrorized the city's main elite neighborhood in charivari-like manner.[43] The growing inability of Granada's revolutionary leaders to protect their own friends largely explains why they surrendered the city to the U.S. invaders without a fight.

When U.S. troops first entered Granada on 24 September, their commander, Major Smedley Butler, observed how feelings between pro- and antirevolutionaries were "so bitter as to be scarcely understood by civilised people." Given the extent of the revolutionary terror, Butler feared "the certainty of reprisals of a possibly barbarous nature."[44] Although Granada's popular sectors had clearly suffered from the revolutionary violence, those who had the greatest reason to be "bitter" were men and women of the city's entrenched oligarchy.

How are we to explain this violence that so greatly traumatized the country's most powerful elite sector? Revolutionary leaders certainly used it to extort money from the country's richest families. Time and again, they justified this practice as a means to recuperate state resources the Díaz government had distributed to compensate its elite backers for losses allegedly suffered during the Zelaya dictatorship. When the immense payments (the largest totaled three hundred thousand U.S. dollars) were leaked to the press in early 1912, they outraged the Nicaraguan public. Tapping into this widespread discontent, revolutionary leaders promised to recover the "illegitimate" payments. Apparently, this promise greatly helped the revolutionaries mobilize popular support for their cause.[45]

But the 1912 violence also had broader political aims. Indeed, political violence is often wielded in the idiom of a society's distinctive history.[46] Since Granada had recently experienced profound structural changes engendered by the agroexport boom, was it a coincidence that some of the violence, such as floggings, stocks, or dehumanizing prison conditions, resembled forms of punishment prevailing on many of the region's landed estates?[47] And why were some young male prisoners, likely of elite origin, assigned to "forced labor" as if they were hacienda peons? Granada's antielite violence could be seen as an attempt by the revolutionary rank and file to invert the "culture of violence" prevailing in rural Granada.[48]

Whatever its structural roots, the antielite violence of 1912 was further conditioned by recent political developments. Above all, it represented a revolutionary attack by parvenu elites against the U.S.-engineered oligarchic restoration of 1910. This restoration had triggered a war of words among local elites that provided the idiom in which the intraelite violence of 1912 was perpetrated. To a lesser extent, the 1912 violence also sprang from the prewar struggles of nonelite sectors against the illiberal effects of the 1910 oligarchic restoration. For example, revolutionary artisans' attack on elite women could be seen in the context of the bitter fight the two groups had waged over the religious article. As we saw in chapter 3, many artisans feared that proclerical forces—who enjoyed strong support from elite women—were using this controversial article to circumscribe the political influence they had recently attained. Finally, the 1912 violence revealed the strength of nationalist sentiments among the more popular elements of the local revolutionary forces. Such sentiments increased dramatically after the U.S. invasion force landed in early September. But as the next section shows, the invasion alone did not intensify the revolutionary violence. Popular revolutionaries expanded the scope of their reign of terror only after their leaders failed to confront the "Yankee" invaders.

Between Accommodation and Resistance:
Encountering the U.S. Invaders

To the revolutionaries' initial relief, the full-scale U.S. military intervention in the 1912 civil war developed more slowly than anticipated due to conflicts among U.S. policymakers. From the start, State Department officials advocated a more aggressive stance than their military colleagues. In part, they feared that the revolutionaries were receiving support from Germany, which they perceived as the greatest threat to U.S. hegemony in the Caribbean.[49] But, more important, the State Department fretted that the triumph of Nicaragua's revolutionary movement would encourage other Caribbean Basin nations also to resist U.S. efforts to turn the Caribbean into an "American lake."[50] War Department officials, by contrast, claimed that the Nicaraguan revolution did not sufficiently threaten U.S. security interests to merit a larger armed intervention. In their view, the State Department was calling for an invasion simply to defend U.S. business interests in Nicaragua.[51] This view was widely shared by U.S. officers who, as one historian has noted, deeply resented that their "high codes of honor [were] being prostituted for commercial ends."[52]

Despite the U.S. military's grave reservations, President Howard Taft eventually authorized a full-scale invasion of Nicaragua. Between 28 August and 4 September, twenty-three hundred marines and sailors, led by Admiral William Southerland, landed in Corinto. It was the largest U.S. military detachment yet to set foot in Central America. The invaders' stated objectives were "to observe strict neutrality between the government and revolutionary forces, to permit no fighting in the vicinity of the railroad, [and] to permit no bombardment of unfortified towns or any act contrary to civilized warfare."[53] In reality, this invading force was anything but a neutral player, for its main goal was to suppress the revolution against the U.S.-engineered oligarchic restoration.

After U.S. invasion plans became a reality, Nicaragua's revolutionary leaders were confronted with the dilemma of whether to risk an outright war with the very nation they still idealized as their political and economic model. The first real test came on 25 August, when the northern revolutionary leadership based in León sought to capture the port of Corinto, the presumed launching pad for the impending U.S. invasion.[54] The rebels could have easily captured the port from the twenty U.S. sailors stationed there. Yet they adhered to the U.S. demand that no Nicaraguan armed force enter Corinto. This decision foreshadowed the policy of appeasement that most revolutionary leaders would embrace in confronting the U.S. invaders. But if the U.S. invasion led revolutionary leaders to mollify their anti-U.S. rhetoric, it had the opposite effect on many of their popular followers.

From the invasion's start the revolutionary leadership struggled hard to control the anti-U.S. sentiments it had previously fanned. Such was the case when popular revolutionaries ambushed fifty U.S. sailors in León on 21 August, the day President Taft ordered the invasion. Led by Commander Warren Terhune, this U.S. force had been stationed in Managua since the outbreak of the civil war. Once the invasion order was issued, Terhune and his men left Managua by rail to secure the beachhead at Corinto for the invading force. Since his troops needed to pass through León, Terhune asked for a safe-conduct from local revolutionary leaders, a request that was readily granted. But as Terhune's men entered León, they were attacked by hundreds of revolutionaries, including women armed with machetes.[55] The assailants tore off the U.S. flag adorning the locomotive, that icon of Nicaraguan nationhood. Completely outmatched, Terhune's men abandoned the train and sought refuge in the arms of León's revolutionary leaders. In private, these leaders warned Terhune that they would be unable to "restrain the mob from attacking" his men if they were to continue to Corinto.[56] Heeding their warnings, Terhune's fear-stricken force decided to leave the train in León and commenced the fifty-five-mile trek back to Managua in pouring rain.

Publicly, León's revolutionary leaders gladly took responsibility for Terhune's humiliating retreat. To foreign journalists, the leadership stated that it would never "permit American troops to travel by rail, especially not with the flags of that nation on Nicaraguan locomotives and wagons."[57] In reality, León's leaders had been willing to allow Terhune and his men to go to Corinto in a train bearing the U.S. flag. Rather, it was the revolution's popular supporters who had cowed Terhune's force into submission. Even before the arrival of the massive U.S. invasion force, the accommodating position embraced by many revolutionary leaders had begun to clash with the more aggressive stance of their popular supporters.

The landing of the U.S. invasion force only deepened the rift between the northern revolutionary leaders and their rank and file. Once again, tensions arose when U.S. troops sought to pass through the revolutionary stronghold of León. This time it was Admiral Southerland who requested a safe-conduct for his force. He further demanded that the northern revolutionaries relinquish control over the Corinto-León-Managua railroad to the U.S. invaders. This demand posed a grave military and political threat to the revolutionaries. In addition to using the railroad to transport arms and troops, the revolutionaries' seizure of the railroad symbolized their attempt to recuperate Nicaragua's nationhood from the much-vilified U.S. bankers. Not surprisingly, then, northern revolutionary leaders rejected Southerland's demands. They let Southerland know that, while they still revered the United States as their model nation ("escuela práctica"), they would never accept it as their colonizer.[58] Yet the next day the northern revolutionary leadership suddenly acceded to all of Southerland's demands. This abrupt reversal can certainly be explained, as one participant suggested, by the leaders' realization that any armed resistance to the "mightiest" invading force Nicaragua had ever witnessed was utterly futile.[59]

But the leadership's quick surrender to Southerland's demands was also driven by its fear over the growing radicalization of its rank and file. Not coincidentally, the leadership's change of heart occurred immediately after popular revolutionaries attacked a train carrying members of a Central American peace mission.[60] Since León's revolutionary leaders closely identified with the mission's political position, the attack served as warning to local revolutionary leaders not to negotiate with the U.S. invaders but rather to engage them in battle.[61] Frightened by the waning of their control, León's revolutionary leadership caved in to Southerland's demands moments after the attack on the peace mission.

At first, revolutionary leaders seemed to benefit from their accommodating stance as Southerland pursued a policy of "strict neutrality" that enabled the rebels to consolidate their power. The admiral's policy infuriated the State Department, which was clamoring for a speedy end to a rebellion it had just labeled as "the most inexcusable in the annals of Central America."[62] To its dismay, Southerland undertook peace negotiations with the northern revolutionary leaders, most of whom were willing to lay down their arms provided they would have a say in the future government.[63] In addition, the admiral rebuffed U.S. Minister Weitzel by refusing to capture the southern revolutionary leaders Luis Mena and Benjamín Zeledón. He also antagonized U.S. diplomats by prohibiting the forces of the Díaz government from using the railroad.

Southerland's policy of "strict neutrality" so exasperated President Díaz that on 23 September he threatened to resign. In a letter to a U.S. bank official, Díaz complained that the U.S. invasion force had "done much to assist rebel cause and nothing to help [his] Government."[64] Díaz's protest was justified for, even after the landing of Southerland's troops, the revolutionaries had been able to expand their control in northern Nicaragua while maintaining their ground in the south.[65]

But only a day after President Díaz threatened to resign, the supreme commander of the Allied Army, General Luis Mena, unexpectedly surrendered to 350 U.S. marines led by Major Butler. This U.S. force had left Managua on 15 September in order to seize control of the Managua-Granada portion of the railway. Despite being bedridden with rheumatism, Mena was still the effective head of the powerful revolutionary army at the time of his surrender. In Granada, he possessed a well-armed and motivated fighting force of at least five hundred men. Moreover, three days after Butler's troops had set up camp on the outskirts of Granada, Mena's troops were reinforced by about five hundred revolutionaries from León. Well in range of Butler's force, these reinforcements entered the city with much fanfare and to shouts of "Death to the Americans!"[66] As Mena later admitted, most of the revolutionary forces in Granada "wished to continue fighting even though they had to fight against marines as well."[67] But Mena proved to be less enthusiastic and, on 24 September, he accepted Butler's demand for unconditional surrender. Two days later, Mena was placed on a U.S. ship bound for Panama, having been forced to promise never to return to Nicaragua.[68]

In part, Mena's surprising surrender came on the heels of Southerland's abrupt turn against the southern revolutionary leadership. Initially, the admiral wanted Butler's force to simply gain control of the Managua-Masaya-Granada railway. But once in Granada, Butler was ordered to obtain Mena's surrender. For various U.S. scholars, the hardening of Southerland's position toward Mena represented a belated victory of the State Department's uncompromising policy.[69] In reality, this shift was of Southerland's own doing and resulted from the unexpected resistance he faced from pro-Mena revolutionaries in Masaya.

The crisis originated on 17 September, when a group of rebels blocked Butler's train as it reached the town of Masaya. Unable to negotiate with the revolutionaries, Butler's men were left stranded. To break the impasse, Southerland traveled to Masaya in the belief that his presence would quickly resolve the problem. The situation facing Southerland resembled the crisis he

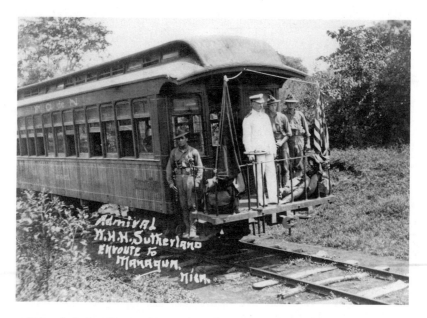

9. U.S. Admiral William Southerland en route to Managua, 1912.
Courtesy of Instituto de Historia de Nicaragua y de Centroamérica.

had mastered in León. But to the admiral's consternation, Masaya's revolutionary delegation, led by Mena's representative, Federico Lacayo, refused to succumb. For local observers, Lacayo's intransigence was not surprising, as this Conservative oligarch had stood out for his opposition to U.S. imperial aspirations.[70] According to a U.S. observer, Southerland resented Lacayo's "affront to the United States," and later vilified him and his superior, General Mena, as "land pirates." Unable to move Lacayo, the admiral returned to Managua (see figure 9), but not without warning him that Butler's train "was going through if armed force had to be employed."[71] Two days later, the revolutionaries apparently gave in and allowed Butler's train to advance to Granada. But just as it passed the Masaya station, a group of revolutionaries fired on the train, wounding four of Butler's men. Once notified of this attack, an enraged Southerland immediately abandoned his "neutrality" and ordered Butler to seek Mena's defeat. Never did the admiral expect that Mena would surrender without a fight.

From Mena's own perspective, the only alternative to surrender was a certain death. Impeded by illness, Mena was convinced that he and his men in Granada stood alone in their struggle against the U.S. invaders. He came to this conclusion after his most important ally, General Zeledón, allowed Butler's troops to pass through Masaya.[72] Actually, Zeledón had tried to set up a trap that would have allowed his troops and Mena's men to jointly attack Butler's force. But Mena never learned about Zeledón's secret plan as government forces intercepted the latter's message to him.[73] In addition, Mena probably did not know the true size of Butler's force. Due to the general's illness, civilian leaders from Granada's revolutionary movement conducted the negotiations with the U.S. attackers encamped on the edge of the city. Since Butler was concerned about the numerical inferiority of his forces, he made elaborate preparations that led Mena's civilian delegates to believe that he had thousands of men under his command.[74] With no escape route at his disposal, Mena was well aware that if he did not surrender, he would have to risk a military confrontation with Butler's force. One can only wonder to what extent Mena's inflated sense of Butler's military strength dissuaded him from taking such a risk.

At the same time, Mena's surrender responded to the recent radicalization of the antielite violence perpetrated by Granada's popular revolutionaries. As we have seen, the city's revolutionary leadership began to lose control over the violence following the U.S. invasion of early September. In particular, artisan-led bands defied their leaders by terrorizing foreign merchants. Then, with the advance of Butler's force, they began to target revolutionary oligarchs and their family members. Not surprisingly, the violence's radicalization greatly troubled Granada's revolutionary leaders, especially those who hailed from the city's Conservative oligarchy. Although these oligarchs wielded little influence over Granada's rebel forces, they dominated the delegation that met with Butler. Given how much revolutionary oligarchs must have wanted to end Granada's deepening "reign of terror," they likely seized the opportunity presented by Butler's arrival to secure the unconditional surrender of their own military forces. It was for this reason that a well-informed foreign correspondent in Nicaragua claimed Mena's capitulation was the work of "prestigious Conservatives."[75]

However rational his motivations, Mena's surrender stunned his soldiers. The U.S. officer who conducted Mena into exile observed that "rebels throughout the route from Granada to Corinto did not seem to believe that he had surrendered."[76] Mena's submission also startled his comrade-in-arms Zeledón. Just a day earlier, this Liberal general had written a letter expressing little doubt that Mena would wage war against the U.S. invaders.[77] Indeed, Mena's surrender contradicted his well-publicized vow, "I will not be like Zelaya; the Americans will not chase me away with a simple note." So shocking was the surrender of Nicaragua's leading anti-imperialist that it engendered the popular saying "Esta!, dijo Mena," which refers to a boastful person who breaks his or her promise. The persistence of this saying up to the present suggests how profoundly Mena's failure to attack the U.S. invaders disillusioned Nicaraguans.

Mena's capitulation had a lasting impact on popular memory because it contrasted so sharply with the fate of his ally Benjamín Zeledón, who died in the only full-scale battle that the 1912 revolutionaries waged against the U.S. invaders. Nowadays, Mena and Zeledón are depicted as polar opposites, with the former representing cowardice and the latter heroic martyrdom.[78] In fact, these comrades-in-arms were quite similar. Like Mena, the thirty-three-year-old Zeledón was of nonelite origin (his father was a carpenter) and a former minister of war who hailed from a provincial town (Estelí).[79] In addition, he shared Mena's anticlerical, liberal views and his valorization of the United States as a political and economic model.[80] Finally, Zeledón had also been able to marry into a rich elite family; his father-in-law, the prominent Conservative Jerónimo Ramírez, was a wealthy coffee planter from Carazo. Still, the co-commanders of the Allied Army represented two distinct kinds of parvenu elites who led Nicaragua's revolutionary movement. Unlike Mena, Zeledón did not strike it rich in the agroexport sector; a trained lawyer, he instead made his mark by climbing the ladder of the ever-expanding state bureaucracy. If Mena thus embodied the entrepreneurial bourgeois, Zeledón epitomized the professional one.

With the surrender of Mena's troops in Granada, Zeledón and his men became the primary target of the U.S. invading force. Not only did the U.S. military seek to punish Zeledón for the attack on Butler's train, but Masaya was the only part of the country's railway not under U.S. control. Within a week, one thousand U.S. troops and four thousand soldiers of the Díaz government managed to encircle Zeledón and the eight hundred men under his command. Believing that Zeledón would follow Mena's example and "crawl down," the U.S. field commander Colonel Joseph Pendleton gave the rebel chief twenty-four hours to submit his unconditional surrender.[81] Although their water, food, and arms supplies were running precariously low, Zeledón and his outnumbered men refused to budge. In rejecting Pendleton's ultimatum, Zeledón reiterated the nationalist arguments previously put forth by Luis Mena and León's revolutionary leaders. And like them, he invoked the United States' self-defined mission to spread the ideals of liberty.[82] Only Zeledón, however, fulfilled his promise to defend Nicaragua's sovereignty "until the last cartridge."[83]

Zeledón's posthumous nationalist fame had much to do with the nature of his death. The same day that Pendleton gave his ultimatum, Zeledón was visited by his father-in-law, Jerónimo Ramírez. The meeting had been arranged by President Díaz, who desperately wanted to avert the first full-fledged battle between Nicaraguan and U.S. troops since the National War against Walker. When Ramírez pleaded with Zeledón not to leave him a widowed daughter and four fatherless grandchildren, the latter retorted: "If my children will suffer from poverty, they should suffer it from this moment onward; but I shall not bequeath to them comfort with cowardice."[84] While aware of the hopeless situation, Zeledón reiterated his willingness to die in defense of Nicaragua's "dignity and sovereignty."[85] No doubt, Zeledón was still traumatized by Mena's surrender. Yet he also resented the appeasing stance of the northern revolutionary leadership. By dying on the battlefield, Zeledón apparently hoped to restore Nicaraguans' faith in the struggle for national autonomy—a faith he believed had been betrayed by the failure of nationalist leaders to stand up to the "Yankee" invaders. As eyewitness accounts stress, Zeledón's sacrificial defiance made a strong impact on his own men, and through them on popular memory.[86]

The battle of Masaya was a quick victory for the U.S. troops and their Nicaraguan allies. While most of the revolutionaries were killed or captured, a small force led by General Zeledón managed to escape. Their flight ended when the group was ambushed by Government troops ten miles south of Masaya. The Díaz government claimed that Zeledón had been mortally wounded. But U.S. accounts state that he was "put to death" by his captors.[87] Government soldiers paraded Zeledón's corpse through the adjacent hamlets before burying him in Catarina, a village about two miles south of Masaya. According to popular memory, this macabre parade was to warn the local populace against joining future antigovernment rebellions.[88] To some, however, it instilled the contrary sentiment. Among the witnesses was the seventeen-year-old Augusto Sandino, who lived near Catarina. Fifteen years later, as he led a guerrilla struggle against U.S. troops, Sandino recalled that this parade was the event that awakened his national consciousness; in waging war against the U.S.

occupiers, Sandino said, he was carrying the stone Zeledón had initially lifted in order to "bring the light of freedom to our peoples."[89]

After its victory over Zeledón's army, the U.S. military marched north to confront the remaining revolutionary forces centered in the towns of León and Chinandega. Even before the battle of Masaya, northern revolutionary leaders had begun secretly to negotiate with U.S. officers the surrender of their forces.[90] Mena's capitulation certainly pushed them to enter these negotiations. But as in Granada, northern revolutionary leaders were also driven by fear of their more radical followers. Not only did the leaders' policy of appeasement clash with the willingness of popular revolutionaries to attack the U.S. invaders, they and their kin had also become targets of the antielite violence perpetrated by popular revolutionaries. On the eve of the battle of Masaya, a Swedish resident thus reported that León's revolutionary leaders had become "powerless to avoid bloodshed and destruction" committed by their popular supporters and were now "afraid for their lives themselves."[91] The next day popular revolutionaries defied their leadership when they attacked a small group of U.S. marines stationed at Chichigalpa, an important sugar-growing town near Chinandega. To the cries of "Death to the Americans!," the revolutionaries wounded five marines, but not without losing thirteen of their own. While U.S. sources claim the revolutionaries died during the skirmish, local memory maintains that they were executed by U.S. marines on the steps of the local church well after the battle ended.[92]

Perturbed by the Chichigalpa incident, U.S. officers abandoned their mediation efforts and went on the offensive. In justifying this change, the region's U.S. commanding officer admitted that the logic of the U.S. attacks on León and Chinandega was "not apparent from a military point of view." Nevertheless, he stressed that these actions were necessary "on the account of the condition of anarchy which exists . . . because the rebel leaders with whom [he] had been negotiating were losing control of their own men."[93]

The rapid disintegration of elite authority complicated U.S. efforts to capture the northern revolutionary strongholds. On 5 October, the day after their victory at Masaya, five hundred U.S. troops joined their 750 comrades already encamped on the outskirts of León. To ensure a safe surrender, local revolutionary leaders accompanied the U.S. forces when they entered the city the next day.[94] Their presence did not dissuade a group of about two hundred popular revolutionaries from shooting at the U.S. intruders and killing three of them. A similar hail of bullets met U.S. troops at Chinandega, even though revolutionary leaders there too had shown "a strong desire to assist" the U.S. takeover.[95]

As the prominent revolutionary oligarch Leonardo Argüello later acknowledged, the Leonese assault on U.S. forces reflected popular wrath against the leadership's decision to surrender peacefully.[96] Once news spread that U.S. forces were to enter the city unhindered, outraged citizens gathered outside Argüello's house, intending to shoot him and other leading revolutionary oligarchs gathered there. Making matters worse, rumors suddenly circulated that the revolutionary leadership had been bribed into surrendering the city. This explosive charge brought popular wrath against León's revolutionary leaders to the boiling point. But popular revolutionaries could not prevent U.S. forces from capturing León and Chinandega. Within a week, all remaining revolutionary pockets had fallen and an uneasy peace had returned to Nicaragua.

With their victory secured, U.S. troops briefly waged a political campaign to conquer the hearts and minds of the local populace. Astutely recognizing the prevalence of strong anti-U.S. sentiments, Admiral Southerland sent mounted U.S. expeditions throughout Nicaragua to "disabuse . . . the minds of the inhabitants of their previously formed erroneous ideas of Americans."[97] Such efforts came to an end in mid-November 1912, when the United States withdrew its occupation force from Nicaragua.

Southerland's diplomatic campaign clearly had too little time to succeed. But it was also undermined by the public ceremonies and banquets ruling Conservative oligarchs staged to honor the victorious U.S. invaders. These events conspicuously celebrated Nicaragua's subjugation to the United States.[98] Moreover, they clashed with the prevailing food shortage that still plagued most of the population. Popular disdain for the celebrations was captured by a poet in Zeledón's ranks, who wrote: "Ladino [white] mercenaries fill their stomachs / In the banquets given to the despised bourgeoisie / While misery advances without making noise."[99] As these verses highlight, the war ended with a "bourgeoisie" greatly delegitimized.

Conclusion

Although relatively brief, the 1912 civil war was exceptionally violent. Confined to the country's most populated zones in the Pacific region, the war claimed between two thousand and five thousand lives.[100] It also caused widespread destruction to cities and landed estates. The material and human losses Nicaragua suffered in 1912 were the worst since the National War against Walker, and they were not surpassed until the Sandinista insurrection of 1978–79. Moreover, ruling elites were subjected to perhaps the most traumatic forms of public humiliation and violence in the country's modern history, visited on them, most shockingly, by tormentors with whom they shared long-standing political and, in some cases, kinship ties. To come to terms with this trauma, elite victims first sought to represent the violence's chief perpetrators as "barbaric" outsiders, whether in terms of race, class, or region. Over time, they simply silenced their traumatic past by refusing to narrate it to their descendents.[101] As a result, this "social or communist war" has now been effectively erased from elite memory and Nicaraguan historiography.[102]

This erasure notwithstanding, the revolutionary violence of 1912 had grave political consequences for Nicaragua. It critically weakened the authority of local elites by pushing them to embrace the highly unpopular U.S. invasion. As in 1855, a specific elite sector requested the U.S. military intervention of 1912. While mid-nineteenth-century elites ultimately united to defeat Walker's filibuster army, most of the 1912 revolutionary leaders surrendered to the U.S. invaders without firing a shot. This they did against the explicit will of their rank and file. To a certain extent, they made this choice believing that an attack on U.S. forces was futile. But perhaps more important, they surrendered out of fear of their own social base.

If the sole revolutionary leaders to resist the U.S. invaders were those encamped in Masaya, this can largely be explained by the fact that these leaders did not fear their base. While revolutionary leaders in Granada and León were homegrown, those in Masaya were outsiders who had arrived there only after the war's outbreak. And since social relations in the elite bastions of Granada and León were more polarized than in Masaya, the former experienced greater antielite violence than the latter. Revolutionary leaders in Granada and León thus had more reason than their comrades in Masaya to fear the growing radicalization of popular revolutionaries in their strongholds. Once the violence veered out of their control, they turned to the U.S. invaders for protection. This choice allowed them to survive the war intact, but it came at a price: the erosion of their political and moral influence over their fellow citizens.

By contrast, the 1912 war greatly enhanced U.S. power in Nicaragua. It demonstrated that U.S. invasion threats were anything but empty. Underscoring how deeply the invasion had affected the popular psyche, Nicaraguan mothers long invoked the U.S. capture of Luis Mena to frighten their children, warning them, "Hush! Major Butler will get you."[103] The United States also benefited from the invasion's thorough delegitimation of the leaders of Nicaragua's anti-U.S. nationalist movement. As the persistent resonance of the phrase "Esta!, dijo Mena" suggests, popular memory of the 1912 war was principally shaped by the failure of General Mena, then Nicaragua's most revered nationalist leader, to back up his belligerent anti-U.S. words with action. The surrender of Mena was so significant precisely because his example, not Zeledón's martyrdom, was the path followed by most revolutionary leaders of 1912. With Nicaragua's nationalist movement in shambles, conditions in postwar Nicaragua seemed propitious for the United States to implement a relatively new form of imperial domination: dollar diplomacy.

PART III · Dollar Diplomacy, 1912–1927

5 Economic Nationalism

Resisting Wall Street's "Feudal" Regime

AFTER ITS 1912 INVASION, the United States pursued a unique strategy for securing its domination over Nicaragua. Unlike in the territories it seized in 1898—Cuba, Puerto Rico, and the Philippines—and the countries it invaded in 1915 (Haiti) and 1916 (the Dominican Republic), the United States did not establish a military government in Nicaragua. Instead, it withdrew the bulk of its invasion force, leaving behind only one hundred men to guard the U.S. legation in Managua. Eschewing traditional military means, the United States essentially ruled Nicaragua through a handful of U.S. bank representatives, who managed the country's public finances. In justifying this new form of imperial rule, President Taft claimed that his country was seeking to spread its power by "substituting dollars for bullets."[1] And until the Great Depression of 1929, Taft's so-called dollar diplomacy drove U.S. policy toward much of Latin America, especially the Caribbean Basin and the Andes.[2]

In most countries, dollar diplomacy entailed U.S. supervision of state finances in exchange for an unprecedented influx of U.S. loans. Nicaragua, however, suffered the former without benefiting from the latter. In fact, it received less U.S. investment than nearly any other nation in Latin America during the Wall Street–fueled loan frenzy of the 1920s, the infamous "dance of the millions." As its architects readily acknowledged, dollar diplomacy's main goal in Nicaragua was not economic but strategic: to prevent rival powers from exploiting the country's allegedly "chronic" instability to build an alternate interoceanic canal.[3] After the 1912 war between pro- and anti-Mena Conservatives, U.S. officials could no longer blame Nicaragua's political "troubles" on the Liberal supporters of the Zelaya regime. But rather than acknowledging the war's revolutionary thrust, U.S. policymakers viewed it as a simple fight between corrupt, unproductive elites for control of the national treasury. As a result, they came to believe that Nicaragua's political conflicts resulted primarily from elites' politicization of public finances. To solve this "problem," U.S. policymakers forced the Nicaraguan state to hand over its revenues and expenditures to Wall Street bankers who, in turn, were obliged to pursue a restrictive fiscal policy. Pressured by its own government, Wall Street excluded Nicaragua from its "dance of the millions"—a rare case of dollar diplomacy where dollars helped diplomacy much more than the other way around.[4]

But dollar diplomacy in Nicaragua was not just a low-cost weapon of U.S. domination. It also represented a novel diplomacy of modernization rooted in the Progressive reform movement that then held sway in the United States.[5] True, U.S. officials had previously taken over government finances in Puerto Rico, the Philippines, and the Dominican Republic. Yet the Nicaraguan protectorate was the first based on a loan contract with private U.S. bankers, not a diplomatic treaty with the U.S. government. It thus initiated the brand of dollar diplomacy in which "the hitherto 'public' extension of U.S. imperial control shifted into the 'private' sphere."[6] Moreover, if in most parts of Latin America dollar diplomacy's modernizing impulse lay in the export of U.S. corporate values like consumerism, a more institutional vision of modernity defined its application to Nicaragua.[7] In particular, dollar diplomacy rested on Wall Street's control of Nicaragua's national bank, its customs receivership, and the mixed commission that regulated state expenditures. Via these institutions, U.S. officials hoped to ensure Nicaragua's stability by inculcating native elites with the technocratic, apolitical ideals that marked the U.S. ideology of Progressivism. For its architects and enforcers, dollar diplomacy was a universal project that could be seamlessly applied anywhere. In practice, however, it not only promoted a U.S. vision of "progress" but was a means to imperial control and thus inherently disruptive.

Dollar diplomacy's perils were readily apparent to prominent Nicaraguans who had supported the U.S. invasion of 1912 but pleaded with Washington not to turn their country into a full-fledged U.S. financial protectorate.[8] Well aware of how nationalist opposition to the U.S.-Nicaraguan loan treaty had precipitated the 1912 war, they argued that any attempt to complete Wall Street's takeover of Nicaragua's public finances would only provoke another violent anti-U.S. uprising. Such warnings were dismissed by President Taft and his chief advisors. In fact, the 1912 war only strengthened their resolve to impose dollar diplomacy's modernizing project on Nicaragua. Moreover, they hoped to use Nicaragua as a showcase to promote this new form of U.S. domination in other Caribbean Basin nations. In the end, the Nicaraguan warnings proved prophetic. While dollar diplomacy restored a remarkable degree of fiscal solvency to Nicaragua, it failed to produce the political stability U.S. officials so greatly desired. Its tumultuous reign ended in 1927 with yet another U.S. invasion of Nicaragua.

In Nicaragua, dollar diplomacy ensured that economic nationalism became the binding ideology for local resistance to U.S. imperial rule. Above all,

Nicaraguan nationalists came to vilify this much-vaunted diplomacy of modernization as the main obstacle to their country's economic development. Politically, Nicaraguan denunciations of dollar diplomacy's nefarious economic impact shaped the struggles that culminated in the 1927 U.S. invasion. But it also left a deep cultural imprint, as exemplified by the era's most important novels. As we will see, these novels attacked dollar diplomacy for driving Nicaraguan agroexport producers to ruin, with many of them losing their precious enterprises to the dominant villains of their time: the Wall Street banks that controlled Nicaragua's public finances. Even worse, the banks were charged with letting the foreclosed estates waste away. Like the authors of these novels, many Nicaraguans came to identify "Wall Street" with a backward, "feudal" economic regime. In doing so, they turned dollar diplomacy's discourse of "primitivism" on its head. If dollar diplomats, and the U.S. media more generally, represented U.S. protectorates like Nicaragua as "backward" and "primitive," Nicaraguans used the very same representations to castigate Wall Street for blocking their country's economic development.[9]

Nicaraguans' vilification of Wall Street contrasts sharply with most Latin American elites' embrace of it as a symbol of modernity.[10] Latin American elites' enthusiasm for Wall Street sprang mainly from the 1920s' "dance of the millions." And since many used this financial bonanza to modernize their economic enterprises, they often associated Wall Street with modernity. In some instances, however, Wall Street came to be denounced as a monstrous modernity that endangered local culture and society; this was particularly the case in Caribbean nations where U.S.-owned sugar companies reigned supreme.[11] Nicaragua, by contrast, did not experience an expansion of U.S. direct or indirect investment. Moreover, it was arguably the only Latin American nation where dollar diplomacy led to a reduction, not growth, of public improvement projects. It makes sense, then, that Nicaraguans associated Wall Street with an antimodern impulse. This peculiar economic anti-Americanism profoundly marked Nicaragua's nationalist campaign against dollar diplomacy.

Modernization via the Mixed Commission

Nowadays, dollar diplomacy's rule in Nicaragua is mostly associated with Wall Street's control of the national bank, the railway, and the customs receivership. Yet it was through the mixed commission that dollar diplomats primarily sought to modernize Nicaragua's political and economic culture.[12] Although its name varied over time—Mixed Claims Commission (1911–15), Public Credit Commission (1917–18), and High Commission (1919–44)—the panel always consisted of two U.S. bank representatives and a single Nicaraguan. Initially, much of its work centered on lowering the claims that natives and foreigners had made against the Nicaraguan government for material losses suffered during the Zelaya dictatorship, the civil war of 1909–10, and the 1912 revolution. Heavily burdening the Nicaraguan state, these claims represented about 40 percent of the country's public debt in 1913. By reducing this debt, the commission hoped to ensure Nicaragua's political stability.

Its more fundamental goal was to depoliticize Nicaragua's public finances. The commission sought to redefine the relationship between the state and economic activity by insulating the national treasury from politics. Time and again, its U.S. members sought to impress on native elites that state institutions should serve not the vested interests of those in power but the universal interests of civil society. Accordingly, Nicaragua's "troubles" were thought to derive principally from the country's politicized and thus inefficient economic organization in which policies, laws, and institutions were "mere tools" in the hands of a small ruling elite. For example, Arthur Thompson of the first mixed commission claimed in an article titled "Renovating Nicaragua" that in Nicaragua the "original idea of a government of laws has become distorted into a government of persons."[13] Such an interventionist and arbitrary institutional environment, Thompson argued, blocked Nicaragua's political and economic development. To him, then, teaching Nicaraguans how to run an impartial and effective institution was the main way the commission could "renovate" Nicaragua.

Yet the commission's depoliticizing mission was compromised from the start, as U.S. officials allowed the Nicaraguan government to influence its work significantly. Not only did the Nicaraguan president nominate the commission's native member and one of its U.S. representatives, all claims were also subjected to prior screening by local authorities with clear political interests. Little wonder that the commission operated both partially and politically. Nowhere did the mixed commission better reveal its partisan character than in its rulings on the 1912 claims. While the commission rejected all those submitted by anyone who had suffered damages at the hands of government or U.S. troops, it willingly approved damages caused by the

1912 insurgents to the property of government supporters.[14] When the commission disposed the last claims in late 1914, few were surprised that its rulings had primarily favored elite supporters of the Díaz regime: Although governing elites had submitted less than 10 percent of the total 7,911 claims filed, they received about 55 percent (one million U.S. dollars) of the total amount approved; another 27 percent went to 66 U.S. plaintiffs.[15]

Oppositional elites thus had good reason to denounce the mixed commission's political bias.[16] Their frustration with the commission's rulings is exemplified by the case of José León Román y Reyes, a prominent Liberal from the department of Carazo. Román submitted a claim demanding compensation for losses resulting from the 1912 civil war. Like many other prorevolutionary elites, Román had been victimized by popular revolutionaries who had looted his commercial establishment, raided his cattle and coffee haciendas, and robbed him of about US$8,700. Román's claim was one of the few lodged by a 1912 rebel that was not rejected outright by the mixed commission. Still the commission recognized only 3 percent of the total US$830,000 he demanded. In an angry letter to ex-president Adolfo Díaz, Román contrasted his case with those of ruling Conservatives. Although the basis of their claims had been the same as his, the mixed commission recognized about 80 percent of their original amount. "Isn't it true don Adolfo," Román wrote, "that there is no reason to believe in the impartiality of the commission's judges?"[17]

Surprisingly, the commission's rulings also engendered conflicts among Conservatives who had opposed the 1912 revolution. Consider the case of Felipe Bartolomé Ibarra, an ardent supporter of General Emiliano Chamorro and owner of a large soap factory in Managua.[18] In submitting his claim for five thousand U.S. dollars, this forty-eighty-year-old Conservative sought reimbursement for the "unjust taxes" he had been forced to pay in 1911 for the import of raw materials. After a two-year wait, Ibarra was shocked to learn that the commission had rejected his claim. Like those he opposed in the 1912 revolution, Ibarra believed his claim had been declined for political reasons. In particular, he argued that he was being punished for not supporting the Conservative faction led by Carlos Cuadra Pasos, the Nicaraguan representative on the mixed commission. Ibarra's was hardly an isolated case, as other antirevolutionary Conservatives also believed their claims had been rejected solely due to intraparty intrigue.[19]

In time, the mixed commission even antagonized the successful claimants since the approved claims could not immediately be paid. A public uproar ensued and, as its U.S. members stated, the commission's offices were swamped by daily visits from "ragged men and women, many crippled and blind . . . who pathetically beg for the payment of their small claim."[20] The commission used its limited funds to reimburse awards that did not exceed one hundred U.S. dollars—a move designed to shore up the battered legitimacy of both the commission and the Conservative government.[21] It thus cancelled 4,618 claims with a total value of US$157,700.

The more substantial claims began to be paid only after the U.S. Senate ratified the Bryan-Chamorro treaty in July 1916. Through this treaty, the U.S. government gave Nicaragua three million U.S. dollars in exchange for the exclusive rights to build a canal and a Pacific naval base on its territory. Since the U.S. Senate determined that the treaty's funds would be used to cancel Nicaragua's debt to U.S. bankers, only US$335,000 was allocated to the mixed commission. This amount enabled the cancellation of a third of the outstanding claims; the rest had to be paid in custom bonds. To the anger of their holders, these bonds quickly depreciated to about a fourth of their original value. Nearly two thirds of them remained to be liquidated a decade later.[22]

The commission's inability to cancel all claims unnerved the ruling Conservatives, who had placed high hopes in the "canal money." Their expectations grew dramatically as the economic crisis caused by the outbreak of World War I deepened. Before the war, elites had depended on Europe as a market for their products and a source of credit. After the war shut down this all-important market, elites hoped for a massive influx of U.S. capital to offset their credit crunch. Although Nicaragua was dollar diplomacy's showcase, such hopes never materialized. Of the fifteen million U.S. dollars promised by the 1911 loan treaty, Nicaragua received just a bit over two million. Further fueling elite bitterness, the Nicaraguan government was forced to pay exorbitant salaries to the commission's members and other dollar diplomats. And when Nicaragua finally received the "canal money," only about 10 percent went to cover the outstanding claims.[23] As predicted by its U.S. members, the commission's failure to fully reimburse the largest claimants greatly weakened governing elites' belief in the efficacy of dollar diplomacy.[24]

Nicaraguans' faith in the commission's competence sank even further as it became clear that this highly touted institution could not depoliticize access to precious state resources. Even U.S. officials acknowledged that ruling Conservatives used the mixed commission to promote their own interests. Such opinions were forcefully voiced on the eve of the 1916 presidential elections, when the U.S. embassy opposed the candidacy of Carlos Cuadra Pasos (1879–1964), a member of the Nicaraguan family most identified with dollar diplomacy. Between 1911 and 1915, Cuadra had been the Nicaraguan representative on the mixed commission, while his older brothers Eulogio and Pedro Rafael were, respectively, minister of finance and Nicaragua's financial agent in Washington. Since many Nicaraguans resented the brothers' control of the institutional apparatus established by dollar diplomacy, the U.S. embassy feared that Cuadra's election would trigger an anti-U.S. revolution.[25] After the arrival of U.S. battleships, Carlos Cuadra gave in to U.S. pressure and conceded the presidency to his chief rival, General Emiliano Chamorro. To the chagrin of U.S. officials, Chamorro's presidency (1917–20) and that of his uncle Diego Manuel Chamorro (1921–23) only reinforced Nicaraguans' belief that the U.S.-controlled mixed commission served primarily as an instrument of enrichment for those in power.

The principal source of this controversial enrichment—funds provided by the 1916 canal treaty—cemented Conservatives' infamy as "vendepatrias" (sellouts). If Conservatives hoped the treaty would help them realize Nicaragua's manifest destiny, their political opponents claimed the opposite: that it served to prevent the canal's construction by rival foreign powers. Making matters worse, President Díaz supported Secretary of State Bryan's proposal to incorporate into the treaty a provision identical to what the Platt Amendment established for Cuba: Bryan-Chamorro would have given the U.S. government the right to intervene militarily in Nicaragua whenever it wished. Although nullified by the U.S. Senate, the provision greatly discredited the ruling Conservatives.[26] Finally, Conservatives reinforced their antipatriotic image by accepting the Financial Plan of 1917. While this U.S.-imposed plan enabled Nicaragua to receive the canal funds, it also allowed the much-vilified dollar diplomats to increase their control over the Nicaraguan state.[27]

Liberals shrewdly exploited the controversy over the mixed commission to paint the ruling Conservatives as unabashed "vendepatrias" and cast themselves as the true defenders of Nicaraguan sovereignty. While Liberals waged their nationalist campaign largely in print, they also staged highly publicized attacks against dollar diplomats and their local "cronies." For example, Liberals from León generated a scandal when they assaulted the U.S. customs collector, who was attending a party at the local elite social club.[28] Liberals also gained much publicity for their nationalist cause by mocking dollar diplomats and their native allies at Masaya's popular *toro-venado* carnival.[29] As in the 1912 war, however, the nationalist stance of leading Liberals was shifting and often mere posturing. On the eve of the 1916 elections, the leader of the most nationalist wing of the Liberal party, Julián Irías, held secret negotiations with U.S. officials. Desperate for the presidency, Irías promised to accept the proposed canal treaty even if it contained the infamous Platt Amendment provision.[30] Irías made his promise to no avail, as U.S. officials barred the Liberal party from the elections—a proscription that did not end until martial law, in effect since 1913, was lifted in 1924.

The apparent chasm between Conservative "vendepatrias" and Liberal nationalists was hardly so clear. Yet this was not the public perception in Nicaragua or elsewhere in Latin America. In fact, the 1916 canal treaty so thoroughly stigmatized elite Conservatives that when Emiliano Chamorro's grandnephew Pedro Joaquín Chamorro Cardenal (1924–78) traveled to revolutionary Cuba in 1959, Ernesto "Che" Guevara greeted him coldly with the words, "Pedro Joaquín Chamorro, as in the Chamorro-Bryant [*sic*] Treaty?"[31] In Nicaragua, however, Conservatives' "vendepatria" reputation sprang not so much from the treaty per se as from the mixed commission's partisan disbursement of its funds. To many Nicaraguans, this disbursement underscored the fact that dollar diplomacy was neither an effective nor an apolitical diplomacy of modernization.[32]

Confronting Wall Street's Antimodern Impact

Nicaraguans' negative views of dollar diplomacy were critically reshaped by the world depression of 1920–21. To overcome this crisis, most Latin American governments undertook public improvements to promote the agroexport economy. These efforts included the modernization of the transport system, the creation of new state-controlled credit institutions catering to agroexporters, and the establishment of state-owned mercantile institutions. This heightened state activism was largely financed by the post-1921 boom in U.S. loans to Latin America.[33] Nicaragua, however, failed to benefit from this capital inflow, as U.S. bankers refused to extend large loans. Moreover, dollar diplomats ideologically opposed Nicaraguan efforts to enhance the state's economic role. As a result, Nicaragua failed to develop the kind of state interventions implanted elsewhere in Latin America. If "Wall Street" succeeded in restoring fiscal stability to Nicaragua, it came at the cost of being newly vilified as a promoter of economic backwardness.

The rise of anti–Wall Street sentiments is reflected in the 1923 economic survey commissioned by President Bartolomé Martínez (1923–24).[34] The survey asked prominent Nicaraguans from all political, regional, and economic sectors to identify the causes of the country's "distressing economic problem." Of forty-two responses published in newspapers, thirty-seven blamed dollar diplomacy. Many pointed out that dollar diplomats had promoted a highly politicized and thus inefficient administration of public finances or, as one complained, "too much politics and too little administering."[35] They also criticized dollar diplomats for blocking important public investment projects, as well as for their racist views.

Most, however, reserved their harshest criticism for Wall Street's control of Nicaragua's main financial institution: the Banco Nacional de Nicaragua. Above all, they lashed out at the bank's extreme reluctance to provide credit to agroexporters. Indeed, the 1920–21 depression had led the bank to reduce its output of loans drastically.[36] Although international markets recuperated shortly thereafter, the bank continued its restrictive lending practices. Moreover, its Wall Street owners prevented Nicaragua from participating in the post-1921 financial bonanza that swept much of Latin America. To most respondents, then, Wall Street was the main force blocking Nicaragua's development. Or, as one put it, dollar diplomacy was nothing but "a source of misery for Nicaraguans [and] an insurmountable wall for any honorable effort to promote the nation's progress."[37] More than anything, the 1923 survey underscores how dollar diplomacy generated much elite anxiety at a time when many Latin American upper classes were enjoying renewed prosperity. This discrepancy only reinforced Wall Street's peculiarly antimodern image in Nicaragua.

Nowhere did Nicaraguans more vividly depict Wall Street's antimodernism than in literature. The most acclaimed of such novels was Hernán Robleto's *Los estrangulados*.[38] Linked via kinship to parvenu elites, Robleto (1892–1969) was a prominent Liberal journalist who had fought with General Zeledón in the 1912 revolution. Set in the 1920s, *Los estrangulados* [The Strangled Ones] traces how "Wall Street" drove the twenty-four-year-old Gabriel Aguilar to bankruptcy. Like the author's family, Aguilar owns a large coffee plantation in the Sierra of Managua. In charting Aguilar's economic downturn, the novel denounces the U.S.-owned Banco Nacional for forcing the country's most entrepreneurial producers to turn to "antiquated methods of exchange or barter: cacao beans, corn, and other grains for salt, butter, and basic medicine."[39] But the novel also vividly illustrates that Wall Street's stranglehold over Aguilar and his like is not limited to financial matters, as the Banco Nacional monopolizes the coffee trade through its subsidiary, the Compañía Mercantil de Ultramar (Overseas Mercantile Corporation); owns the country's sole railroad; and controls the all-important customhouses. Working in unison, Wall Street's chosen instruments are depicted as forming a diabolical machine bent on paralyzing Nicaragua's coffee economy. So great is Wall Street's regressive impact that local producers are forced to turn to premodern forms of credit and transportation. If Wall Street thus fueled the engines of "progress" in most Latin American countries during the 1920s, *Los estrangulados* stresses that in Nicaragua it forced the economic vanguard to turn to "antiquated" business methods.

Yet Robleto's *Los estrangulados* is more than just an attack against Wall Street. It chronicles how Wall Street nefariously undermines the virility of Nicaraguan agroexporters. For this purpose, *Los estrangulados* begins by presenting the successful, modernizing coffee hacendado Gabriel Aguilar as the paradigm of (elite) manliness. It goes to great length to describe not only Aguilar's mental and business capacities but the physical prowess of this man "formed by fieldwork, strong, a bundle of muscles and nerves."[40] The tragedy that then unfolds centers on Aguilar's heroic yet futile efforts to maintain his economic independence, the basis of modern manhood. His economic problems begin with the sudden fall in international coffee prices—surely a reference to the depression of 1920–21. This unexpected drop prevents Aguilar, who never before faced financial problems, from repaying the loan he had recently received from the Banco Nacional at extremely onerous conditions. For Aguilar, there is no doubt that "Wall Street" orchestrated the devastating decline in coffee prices. And however much he tries to find a way out of the quagmire, Wall Street throws one obstacle after another in his way. In the end, Aguilar succumbs to Wall Street's "diabolical machine" and joins the long line of prominent Nicaraguans whose coffee fincas had been swallowed up by the "Ultra-tomb," that is, the Compañía Mercantil de Ultramar. As the narrator emphasizes, "the most characteristic trait of [Nicaragua's] current men is that they have been unable to defend themselves or defend a legacy of dignity."[41]

Many prominent Nicaraguans shared the view that dollar diplomacy had triggered a crisis of elite masculinity. A leading Liberal politician denounced the Banco Nacional and the Compañía Mercantil de Ultramar as "octopuses that have impoverished and dishonored many of our capitalists."[42] And one of Nicaragua's most famous Liberal ideologues, Salvador Mendieta, claimed that dollar diplomats were "emasculating" (*desvirilizando*) his countrymen.[43] So acute was this concern that "Crisis of Men" was the title a Granadan newspaper chose for an article that denounced dollar diplomats for having ruined many agroexport producers.[44] The 1920s campaign against dollar diplomacy was thus not just about recovering Nicaragua's sovereignty. It sought to rescue elite entrepreneurs and the economy from Wall Street's "diabolical machine."

The first "shot" fired in the anti–Wall Street crusade was President Martínez's commissioning of the 1923 economic survey. The survey asked elites not just to identify the causes of the country's economic crisis but to propose solutions. Most responded by clamoring for the immediate nationalization of the Banco Nacional. This urgent call, as Martínez's chief advisor later admitted, was what the government had secretly hoped for in launching the survey.[45] And in less than a year, the Nicaraguan state recovered full ownership of its bank. Although bitterly opposed by dollar diplomats in Nicaragua, the bank nationalization enjoyed the tacit support of the State Department.[46]

Martínez's successful nationalization campaign represented an important if contradictory watershed in Nicaragua's encounter with U.S. imperial rule. Above all, it fostered a degree of elite unity not seen since the fall of Zelaya. From the start, the Liberal opposition supported Martínez's quest to Nicaraguanize the Banco Nacional. Liberals then accepted Martínez's invitation to forge a nationalist coalition with the Conservative faction opposed to dollar diplomacy. Together, these former foes from the 1912 civil war triumphed in the 1924 elections over the *genuino* Conservative ticket headed by former president Emiliano Chamorro. Once in power, the bipartisan coalition worked hard to complete Martínez's program of liberating Nicaragua from Wall Street's "yoke."[47] As evident in its bipartisan makeup and nationalist agenda, the 1924 coalition seemed to have resurrected the 1912 revolutionary movement headed by Martínez's former adversary, General Mena. But unlike its 1912 counterpart, the 1924 coalition enjoyed the support of the U.S. government.

Officials of the U.S. government undoubtedly would have blocked the coalition's 1924 victory had the nationalist discourse of Liberals not shifted dramatically. While in the 1910s Liberals directed their nationalist ire principally against the U.S. government, after the 1920–21 depression Wall Street became their chief target. Once again, Liberals were not opposed to the U.S. road to modernity. On the contrary, they fought for its realization in Nicaragua. As the prominent Liberal and future president (1929–32) José María Moncada publicly stated, if "Greece received [civilization] from Egypt [and] Italy was aided by the progress of Greece, . . . for us this civilization will come from the United States."[48] Liberals like Moncada thus stressed that their opposition to Wall Street should not be confused with a rejection of U.S. values and institutions.[49] They once again warmed to the United States after Washington sought to phase out its financial protectorate over Nicaragua in 1923.[50] Since this effort was openly opposed by U.S. bankers and dollar diplomats, Liberals hoped that their anti–Wall Street sentiments would resonate with the U.S. government, which until recently had branded them Central America's worst "troublemakers."[51]

Perhaps because of this emerging common ground, Liberal leaders believed they could publicly seek the support of the U.S. State Department without being denounced by their popular followers as "vendepatrias." Some even pleaded for a U.S. military intervention to break the Conservatives' stranglehold on the state apparatus.[52] Such public calls for a U.S. intervention differed sharply from the extreme secrecy with which the Liberal leader Julián Irías courted U.S. support during the 1916 elections. But if Liberals' shifting nationalist discourse coincided with the deepening cleavage between the U.S. government and Wall Street's Nicaragua project, it also paralleled elite Conservatives' growing anger at the control "Wall Street vampires" exercised over the government's finances.[53] In more ways than one, anti–Wall Street sentiments brought together longstanding adversaries.

At the same time, however, the nationalist campaign against dollar diplomacy deepened chasms within the Conservative elite itself. Initially, Conservatives were split by their competing programs for national development. Supporters of the bank nationalization favored strengthening state control of the economy.[54] Although they called their campaign "the economic liberation of Nicaragua," these Conservatives hardly advocated an anticapitalist or autarkic path to development. In fact, they fought for something Wall Street had failed to promote: foreign investment. In practice, then, the economic nationalism of pro-Martínez Conservatives was quite moderate. But so ardently did they attack Wall Street and defend their statist views that dollar diplomats branded them rabid anti-U.S. "Bolsheviks."[55]

Conversely, Conservatives opposed to the bank nationalization upheld an antistatist model of development. This vision was promoted most forcefully by Granada's *El Diario Nicaragüense*, then the country's leading Conservative newspaper.[56] Like dollar diplomats, it claimed that the proposed bank nationalization would only politicize producers' access to credit. Moreover, it argued that the bank's high purchase cost would drain the financial resources of the Nicaraguan state. Although critical of dollar diplomats' restrictive fiscal and financial policies, *El Diario Nicaragüense* did not advocate stronger government regulation of the economy but the opposite. Only a deregulated economy, it argued, could provide Nicaraguan producers with much-needed access to foreign capital.

At first sight, the intra-Conservative controversy over dollar diplomacy's economic regime mattered little. Not only did economic nationalists easily win the struggle over the bank nationalization, but most elite Conservatives blamed Nicaragua's economic woes on dollar diplomacy and supported export-led growth driven by foreign investments. Still, the controversy had lasting significance as it led the country's most entrepreneurial elites (Conservative oligarchs from Granada) to be recast by Liberal nationalists as the embodiment of economic backwardness. This recasting eventually became central to powerful strands of Nicaraguan nationalism.

Economic Vanguard as the Embodiment of Backwardness

During the 1924 electoral campaign pro-Martínez sectors began to represent the intra-Conservative conflict as a more fundamental clash between "modern" and "backward" elites. In particular, they equated their rivals' opposition to greater state intervention with Wall Street's alleged antimodernism. Whether in newspapers or on the campaign trail, pro-Martínez Conservatives and their Liberal allies repeatedly contrasted their nationalist, "modernizing" economic program with the "feudal," pro–Wall Street agenda pursued by Emiliano Chamorro, presidential candidate of the *genuino* Conservatives. And since most leading *genuinos* hailed from Granada, the city's Conservative oligarchy came to be more generally associated with Wall Street's antimodern impulse. It was thus during the 1924 campaign that Granada's Calle Atravesada, home to the city's richest residents, became widely known as the

"Wall Street" of Nicaragua.[57] And if Granada's oligarchy had previously been denounced for its colonial social practices, it now was identified with backward economic practices as well—even though it continued to be the country's economic vanguard.

One of the earliest and most influential efforts to misrepresent Conservative oligarchs as antientrepreneurial was *Historia de Diriamba* (1920), by the prominent Liberal ideologue and lawyer Juan Manuel Mendoza. This controversial book explores the transformation of Mendoza's hometown Diriamba (located in the department of Carazo) from a sleepy cattle town into a dynamic center of coffee production. In doing so, it depicts Conservatives as feudal-like, ladino (here "white") oligarchs who, weighted down by ignorance and fear, are incapable of guiding Nicaragua into modernity. For Mendoza, Conservatives' backwardness is most noticeable in their ownership of large and under-utilized cattle haciendas. In fact, such "feudal" ranching practices reflected a capitalist logic attuned to existing market and credit conditions.[58] Further distorting historical reality, Mendoza states that Nicaragua's coffee revolution had been driven not by Conservative oligarchs but by Liberal parvenus of humble social origins. To him, only these "new" men possessed the entrepreneurial spirit to propel Nicaragua out of colonial backwardness. Like other nationalist ideologues, Mendoza maintains that parvenus' entrepreneurialism sprang partly from their mestizo origin.[59] But he also stresses how they honed it through practice. Whereas feudal oligarchs had accumulated capital by exploiting the ignorant Indian, the "new" men extolled the physical rigors of work. Moreover, the latter enhanced their entrepreneurial spirit by participating in games of chance that tested their ability to take risks. If "backward" oligarchs undertook such risks in cockfights, the modernizing entrepreneurs tested themselves in the most capitalist pastime: the stock exchange. Finally, Mendoza contrasts the ability of these "new" men to make productive use of capital with the disposition of Conservative oligarchs to squander it on a conspicuous lifestyle. Mendoza's rereading of Nicaraguan history can come to only one conclusion: that dollar diplomacy was stymieing Nicaragua's development by favoring an antientrepreneurial (Conservative) "vendepatria" oligarchy over a modern (Liberal) national bourgeoisie.

Given their modernizing bent and economic prowess, why were Granada's Conservative oligarchs so successfully recast as "backward" economic actors? No doubt, Conservatives themselves reinforced an antimodern image with the moralizing crusade they had recently launched against the "modern woman" (see chapter 7). But it could not be denied either that many of them suffered well-publicized bankruptcies just when nationalists intensified their anti–Wall Street campaign. As these cases affected Nicaraguans who seemingly benefited the most from dollar diplomacy, they lent further credence to nationalists' charges that their elite rivals lacked the entrepreneurial spirit characteristic of "modern" economic actors. Perhaps the most prominent of such bankruptcies was that of the large-scale coffee producer Pedro Rafael Cuadra Pasos, who had long served as Nicaragua's financial agent in Washington and was thus closely identified with dollar diplomacy's regime. Cuadra Pasos's economic decline was not an isolated case, as many coffee barons of all political colors joined him in bankruptcy court (see chapter 6). But if elite nationalists blamed their misfortunes on "Wall Street," they represented their rivals' economic downturn as indicative of an antimodern spirit.

What most enabled nationalists to successfully recast elite identities was the open support dollar diplomats lent to the Conservative campaign against the projected bank nationalization. Like their Conservative allies, dollar diplomats were ideologically opposed to statist economic policies. Moreover, they feared that a Nicaraguan takeover would imperil the country's fiscal and financial stability—the core of their self-proclaimed modernizing mission in Nicaragua.[60] The main beneficiary of dollar diplomats' support was Emiliano Chamorro (see figure 10). Ironically, Chamorro endorsed the bank's nationalization in principle; in fact, his government of 1917–20 had taken the first steps to renationalize both the bank and the railroad. As later acknowledged by its chief architect (Toribio Tijerino), Martínez's project of "economic liberation" was the logical culmination of the nationalist policies initiated by Chamorro, his former political patron and business partner.[61] For political reasons, however, Chamorro sought to delay Martínez's nationalization scheme until after the presidential elections of October 1924. In particular, he feared that if the bank were to fall under Martínez's control its financial resources would be used to promote the candidacy of Carlos Solórzano, Chamorro's chief rival in the 1924 presidential elections.[62] After losing the elections, Chamorro supported dollar diplomats in their struggle to block the new government from replacing the bank's U.S. directors with native officials. This struggle abruptly ended in October 1925, when Chamorro overthrew Solórzano's bipartisan coalition.

Many Nicaraguans (incorrectly) believed that U.S. bankers and dollar dip-

10. President Emiliano
Chamorro, ca. 1926.
In Denny, *Dollars for
Bullets*.

lomats had masterminded Chamorro's coup as a last-ditch attempt to prevent the bank's "de-Americanization."[63] Chamorro's government of 1925–26
lent credence to such views by allowing U.S. bankers to reconsolidate their
control over the Banco Nacional's management. In addition, Chamorro
sought to resell the bank to Wall Street firms in order to raise funds for his
financially strapped government. But he also hoped that his overtures to the
U.S. bankers would entice the U.S. government to recognize his regime.
These hopes proved futile, as the U.S. government clung to the Central
American treaty of 1923, which called for the nonrecognition of unconstitutional governments.[64] Chamorro's inability to sway the U.S. government only
deepened his regime's dependence on U.S. bankers and dollar diplomats. Not

surprisingly, this dependence reinforced the image of pro-Chamorro Conservatives as "accomplices" of Wall Street.

Internationally, nothing more enhanced Conservatives' pro–Wall Street infamy than the civil war that broke out in May 1926 and culminated in a U.S. invasion. Encouraged by the U.S. government's opposition to Chamorro's illegitimate regime, supporters of the deposed bipartisan coalition launched their revolt by taking over towns on the Atlantic coast. From the start, the insurgents stressed that they were fighting to free Nicaragua from "an onerous and irresponsible banker rule."[65] Not coincidentally, they began their revolt by attacking local symbols of Wall Street such as the Atlantic branch of the Banco Nacional and U.S.-manned customhouses. These attacks led U.S. bankers and dollar diplomats to fear for the safety of the bank's branches in western Nicaragua. With Chamorro's support, they pressed the U.S. government to recognize the bank as a U.S. entity.[66] Based on their 1912 experience, the U.S. bankers hoped that such recognition would provoke a full-scale U.S. military intervention to defend U.S. properties. The U.S. government, however, failed to grant Wall Street's request, for Washington was desperate to end dollar diplomacy's reign in Nicaragua. Refusing to yield, Chamorro intensified his efforts to sell the Banco Nacional to U.S. investors, while the bank's U.S. manager allowed his regime to appropriate its funds improperly.

In the end, Wall Street bankers and dollar diplomats could not save their Nicaraguan ally. On 11 November, Chamorro yielded to State Department pressure and handed power to former president Adolfo Díaz. Much to the dismay of U.S. officials, this regime change failed to slow the insurgents' advance. On the contrary, it impelled the rebels to attack government forces in western Nicaragua (see figure 11). To prevent a rebel victory, President Calvin Coolidge ordered in late December a full-scale U.S. military invasion of Nicaragua. This intervention generated worldwide outrage and sealed the "vendepatria" notoriety of Conservative oligarchs.[67]

Embracing Intervention

International censure of the U.S. invasion reflected the recent rise of anti-imperialist movements in Europe and the Americas that bitterly opposed dollar diplomacy in Latin America.[68] Much of the initial outcry focused on the pro–Wall Street rhetoric President Coolidge used to justify the deployment of about three thousand U.S. troops to Nicaragua. Made on 10 January

11. Female combatants in the civil war of 1926–27.
Courtesy of U.S. National Archives.

1927, Coolidge's speech shocked even State Department officials, who cringed at his claim that the Nicaraguan insurgents "seriously" threatened U.S. economic interests.[69] As they correctly pointed out, Coolidge grossly exaggerated U.S. investment in Nicaragua, then among the lowest in Latin America. Moreover, although he denied that "big banking interests" were dictating U.S. policy toward Nicaragua, the tone of his message pointed otherwise.

Unlike the president, the State Department defended the invasion not in economic but strategic terms. Officially, it claimed that the intervention would foil the efforts of Mexico's revolutionary regime to set up "Bolshevist control in Nicaragua and thus drive a wedge between the United States and the Panama Canal."[70] Privately, however, State Department officials hoped the invasion would restore the international "prestige" the United States had lost because of its inability to control its protectorate.[71] In the end, Coolidge's speech made the greater impact on public opinion. Anti-imperialists could therefore represent the invading force as a "collecting agency" for Wall Street, when the intervention actually accelerated the end of dollar diplomacy in Nicaragua.[72]

Unbeknownst to its foreign critics, the U.S. invasion was tacitly supported by the rebel leaders. They did not reject outright President Díaz's request for a hundred-year U.S. military and financial protectorate over Nicaragua. True, rebel leaders fiercely opposed Díaz's attempt to strengthen U.S. bankers' control over local finances. Yet many openly endorsed the military aspects of Díaz's proposed protectorate, particularly the imposition of a U.S. military governor.[73] The revolutionaries' willingness to accept a U.S. military protectorate but not a financial one perplexed high-ranking U.S. officials not fully aware of local circumstances. This was true of Henry Stimson, whom President Coolidge had sent to Nicaragua to mediate a peaceful end to the civil war. As Taft's secretary of war, Stimson had unsuccessfully opposed State Department demands for a full-scale U.S. intervention in the Nicaraguan civil war of 1912. Based on this experience and the worldwide outcry against the 1927 invasion, Stimson was fully prepared to meet anti-U.S. revolutionary leaders when he arrived in Nicaragua on 17 April. To his surprise, most were not only "friendly" to the United States but "earnestly seeking our intervention."[74]

On 12 May 1927, Stimson got all revolutionary chieftains—except General Augusto Sandino—to sign a peace treaty with the ruling Conservatives. Under the Tipitapa Agreement, the insurgents agreed to demobilize in exchange for the guarantee that U.S. troops would supervise forthcoming municipal and national elections. Stimson's success certainly resulted from his threat to unleash the hitherto "neutral" U.S. troops against the advancing rebel forces. But if the unwillingness of insurgent generals to risk such a battle paralleled the submissiveness of the 1912 revolutionary leadership, the underlying motives differed sharply. In 1912, most revolutionary leaders failed to act on their bellicose anti-U.S. discourse for fear of losing even more control over their radical popular followers. The passivity of their 1927 counterparts, by contrast, concurred with rather than contradicted their nationalist ideology.

Despite its anti–Wall Street tone, Nicaragua's revolutionary nationalism of the 1920s no longer denounced U.S. government interference in local affairs. In part, this was because the State Department supported, if only tacitly, the economic nationalism that united the insurgent leadership. Many U.S. policymakers thus agreed with ex-secretary of the Navy Josephus Daniels that, in Nicaragua, "dollar diplomacy is the lion in the path of friendly relations."[75] On the other hand, Nicaragua's rebel leaders knew that the Coolidge administration would not accept the military defeat of the Díaz regime. In consequence, they believed that their claims to state power would only materialize if U.S. troops were to supervise truly competitive elections;[76] this view dovetailed with Washington's new emphasis on promoting democracy in Nicaragua (see chapter 8).

Compared to their 1912 counterparts, then, rebel leaders of 1927 were less inclined to view the U.S. intervention as a hostile invasion. Few better embodied this shift than Enoc Aguado, a Liberal lawyer from León and the country's future vice president (1929–32). In early 1912, twenty-two-year-old Aguado gained much fame with a law thesis that lambasted U.S. "expansionism."[77] When a civil war broke out later that year, Aguado quickly emerged as a vocal anti-U.S. leader of León's revolutionary movement. Like other Liberals, Aguado eventually modified his anti-U.S. views, especially after the U.S. government dropped its political proscription of the Liberal Party. Thanks to this shift in U.S. policy, Aguado and other Liberals were elected to the Nicaraguan Congress in 1924. When another civil war broke out in 1926, Aguado once again became a rebel leader. Only this time, the former anti-U.S. agitator supported the U.S. invasion. His claim that the invasion was both "inevitable" and "desirable" neatly sums up the passive yet approving stance the rebel leadership took toward the U.S. intervention of 1927.[78]

Curiously, Aguado and other insurgent leaders did not incur much popular wrath for their open embrace of the 1927 invasion. If the 1912 revolutionary leaders fearfully acknowledged to U.S. officers that their followers were bent on engaging U.S. troops in battle, none of their 1927 counterparts voiced such fears. Underscoring this popular apathy, the U.S. invasion triggered no significant protest among the urban populace. The only documented anti-U.S. protest occurred on 16 May, when a large crowd in León jeered an honor guard of U.S. sailors drawn up to salute two recently fallen U.S. Marines. A well-informed U.S. journalist noted that in 1927 "few people in Nicaragua were really interested in throwing the Americans out of the country, even though they might not love them."[79]

Nicaraguans' ambivalent response to the 1927 invaders was certainly a legacy of the 1912 invasion. For example, the persistence of the motherly warning "Hush! Major Butler will get you" suggests that the memory of the 1912 invaders continued to inspire fear. Moreover, as evinced by the saying "Esta!, dijo Mena," popular sectors undoubtedly remembered how the 1912 revolutionary leaders had betrayed their followers' trust by failing to back up their bellicose, anti-U.S. discourse. Still, mistrust and fear alone do not explain why so many Nicaraguans seemed unwilling to confront the 1927 invaders. We must also consider the fact that they did not become radicalized by the war itself. In 1912, popular participation in the revolutionary "reign of terror" proved to be a formative, radicalizing experience for many. In 1927, few Nicaraguans shared this experience, as all the revolutionary strongholds were on the sparsely populated Atlantic coast.

The failure of the 1927 rebels to inspire large-scale urban uprisings also suggests that preexisting popular enthusiasm for revolutionary upheaval was weaker in 1926–27 than in 1912. If the Nicaraguan press of 1912 echoed widespread elite fears about an impending social revolution, such fears were absent in newspapers on the eve of the 1926–27 civil war. Not surprisingly, then, rebel leaders espoused a much more radical political discourse in 1912 than in 1926–27. While the 1912 leaders promised greater political rights and social justice for the "downtrodden," those of 1926–27 repeatedly stressed the conservative, not revolutionary, nature of their cause. The civilian leader of the 1926–27 insurgents, the Liberal Juan Bautista Sacasa, forcefully contested claims that his movement was seeking "to subvert social order in Nicaragua."[80] If revolutionary leaders were branded by the embattled Conservative government as bloodthirsty "Bolsheviks," they represented themselves as anything but social revolutionaries.

Why, then, did popular sectors pose a lesser revolutionary threat in 1926–27 than in 1912? No doubt this change responded to the recent populist turn in elite politics. Unlike the 1912 war, that of 1926–27 did not come on the heels of a lengthy, personalistic dictatorship marked by a concerted elite attack on the political autonomy of the rural populace. Instead, it unfolded against the backdrop of intense intraelite competition for popular electoral support. Despite the U.S.-dictated proscription of Liberals, post-1912 elections were much more competitive than generally assumed. Not only did Liberals actively participate in municipal elections, Conservatives also competed against each other at all electoral levels in order to secure control of the state apparatus. Elite factions generally sought votes by promising to enact populist economic and social policies. With their control of the state, ruling Conservatives were best positioned to put such promises into practice. And as historian Jeffrey Gould showed, the post-1912 Conservative regimes indeed enacted land and labor reforms that improved the well-being of many rural communities.[81] Such elite populism undoubtedly mitigated the social conflicts that had helped produce the revolutionary violence of 1912.

Economic Nationalism's Limited Appeal

Perhaps most important, popular sectors were little moved by the economic nationalist sentiments that gripped the rebel leaders of 1926–27. In part, this was because of dollar diplomacy's unintended "democratizing" impact on rural society. As we saw in chapter 3, the protorevolutionary fervor of 1912 emerged largely in response to the polarized economic growth that mainly had benefited agroexport elites. In the 1920s, the general socioeconomic context differed sharply, for U.S. bankers' stranglehold on Nicaragua's financial system weakened the economic power of local elites, particularly large agroexport producers. Nonelite agricultural producers, by contrast, suffered far less; in fact, many benefited from this new financial environment to expand their landholdings (see chapter 6). If the 1912 crisis highlighted popular discontent with an elite-led economic offensive, the 1926–27 war revealed instead elite resentment at dollar diplomacy's control of Nicaragua's public finances.

The economic nationalist policy most likely to electrify popular sectors was the nationalization of the Nicaraguan railroad. Already during the 1912 war the revolutionary rank and file had stood out for its zeal in seeking to recover Nicaraguan sovereignty over the railroad. In the following decade, urban popular sectors staged demonstrations against the railroad's U.S. management. Popular wrath targeted management's efforts to expel women and children who sold fruit and beverages from local train stations. At times, such agitation triggered urban riots, as happened in Masaya in 1919 and 1922.[82] Yet it is unclear how greatly these struggles deepened anti–Wall Street sentiment in the popular consciousness. Tellingly, the future guerrilla leader Augusto Sandino never referred to Masayans' confrontations with the railroad in his writings, although he lived in an adjacent village and was an astute chronicler of local struggles against U.S. imperialism.[83]

Anti–Wall Street sentiment even failed to stir the few popular sectors directly affected by the U.S. economic presence in Nicaragua. These sectors consisted primarily of the approximately eleven thousand workers—about 6 percent of the country's labor force—employed by U.S. mining, banana, and logging companies centered in eastern Nicaragua.[84] True, discontented enclave workers were among the first to join Sandino's anti-U.S. guerrilla force in 1927. Yet they were motivated not so much by anti-U.S. sentiment as by the political violence perpetrated by local power holders.[85] Besides, the economic anti-Americanism of the 1926–27 revolutionary elites targeted Wall Street's stranglehold on local finances, not U.S. companies active in Nicaragua. As such, it differed sharply from that of contemporary Latin American nationalists who viewed U.S.-dominated economic enclaves as a far greater threat to national sovereignty than Wall Street bankers.[86] Moreover, if labor actions against U.S. enterprises fueled popular anti-Americanism throughout Latin America, in Nicaragua such enterprises enjoyed an unusual degree of labor peace during the 1920s; the few conflicts that did erupt centered on Spanish-speaking workers' opposition to the recruitment of black laborers from the West Indies.[87] By most scholarly accounts, enclave workers and the surrounding populace generally accepted the U.S. corporations that arrived during the heyday of dollar diplomacy. Not coincidentally, it was in the 1920s that Miskitu Indians—the Atlantic coast's main ethnic group—began to use the term *pawanka* (development) to describe admiringly the values and goods spread by U.S. companies.[88]

In all likelihood, urban artisans were the nonelite group most receptive to the anti–Wall Street agenda of the 1926–27 insurgent leadership. Even so, their support was not univocal. To be sure, artisans criticized Wall Street's control of the customs collectorship.[89] In particular, they resented dollar diplomats for refusing to raise import tariffs on foreign goods that competed with their own products, such as shoes and textile products. Their complaints were legitimate, as dollar diplomacy coincided with a rise in U.S. imports that competed with artisanal products.[90] Still, artisans' economic nationalism did not simply mirror that espoused by the 1926–27 rebel leadership. In fact, many artisans supported dollar diplomats' refusal to devalue the local currency, which was a key demand of elite economic nationalists. As elsewhere in Latin America, artisans (rightfully) feared that such a devaluation would dramatically lower the wages and purchasing power of the "laboring classes."[91] These class-based differences over a key economic issue mitigated popular support for the anti–Wall Street campaign waged by the revolutionary leaders of 1926–27.

Conclusion

As in 1912, the U.S. invasion of 1927 prevented the victory of insurgent forces. But if the first military intervention consolidated dollar diplomacy's rule over Nicaragua, the second signaled its demise. To its architects, dollar diplomacy was to have secured political stability by modernizing the seemingly "backward" economic culture of native elites. Instead, dollar diplomacy produced a political culture where U.S.-controlled institutions—the mixed commission, the national bank, and the customs receivership—became the focal point of controversy. Dollar diplomacy thus provoked economic anti-Americanism in a country historically marked by the weak presence of U.S. corporations.

But if such nationalist sentiments facilitated the convergence of previously antagonistic elites, it hardly moved the masses. Like the 1912 revolution, then, the 1926–27 war failed to enhance the popular legitimacy of native elites most identified with the defense of Nicaraguan sovereignty. And it was against this backdrop that both the Sandino-led peasant revolutionaries and self-proclaimed elite reactionaries would develop their respective nationalist projects during the U.S. military occupation of 1927–33. Seemingly antipodal, both explicitly challenged the premise of modernity underlying the U.S. imperial project. This challenge, as chapter 9 explicates, posed a greater threat to U.S. hegemony than the economic nationalism promoted by the rebel leaders of 1926–27. Indeed, however critical of dollar diplomats, elite economic nationalists ultimately shared their adulation of the ideals underpinning the U.S. road to modernity.

Nowhere was this adulation more apparent than in the attempt by elite Liberals to identify themselves as "modern" and vilify their elite opponents as "backward." Clearly, this form of differentiation had already characterized the discourse of the 1912 revolutionaries. But dollar diplomacy added a stronger economic twist to such elite self-representations. If the term "backward" was used initially to attack Conservative oligarchs' exclusionary social practices, by the 1920s it primarily referred to their economic practices, which allegedly revealed them to be in league with Wall Street and, together with the U.S. bankers, blocking Nicaragua's development. In reality, Conservative oligarchs were anything but economically backward. After spearheading the most important period of economic modernization in Nicaraguan history, they continued to maintain their position as the country's economic vanguard under dollar diplomacy. Finally, if the financial environment created by dollar diplomats did drive many Conservative oligarchs into bankruptcy, this fate also befell their nationalist rivals. Given these material realities, the distinction between economically "backward" "vendepatrias" and "modern" nationalist elites was a discursive construction.

Elite nationalists constructed this distinction largely in response to dollar diplomacy's debilitating impact on their economic power. In particular, the Banco Nacional's foreclosure of many coffee plantations generated much anxiety among local elites—anxieties that were often represented as a crisis of masculinity. Elites' angst sharpened during the 1920s as their economic misfortunes starkly contrasted with the other Central American elites' rapid expansion of their economic power. But perhaps even more threatening, peasant producers also succeeded in expanding their economic influence during the 1920s. As such, they exhibited an entrepreneurial spirit many elite producers idealized yet failed to realize. To thus assuage its increasing anxiety, Nicaragua's elite, and its nationalist sector in particular, sought to reinforce its self-identification with "modern" economic values. At the same time, its members blamed their economic downturn on the "feudal" economic policies implemented by dollar diplomats and their Conservative allies. In consequence, the crisis of (elite) masculinity under dollar diplomacy powerfully reinforced the distinction between "modern" and "backward" elites by recasting it in economic terms. This recasting of elite divisions had a lasting impact on Nicaraguan nationalism. But if such divisions were more imagined than real, elite anxieties, as the next chapter will show, did accurately reflect dollar diplomacy's deleterious impact on their material fortunes.

6 Anxious Landlords, Resilient Peasants
Dollar Diplomacy's Socioeconomic Impact

DURING THE HEYDAY OF DOLLAR DIPLOMACY, Nicaragua and the rest of Central America experienced fundamental socioeconomic changes. Hit hard by the disruption of trade and capital flows in World War I, Central America's export sector recuperated quickly and boomed in the postwar decade. Briefly interrupted by the depression of 1920–21, the boom allowed agroexport producers to consolidate their dominance over the region's economy. While it strengthened the power of U.S. banana and logging corporations active on the Caribbean coast, elsewhere in Central America the boom triggered a broad offensive of local coffee elites against peasant producers.[1] This did not occur in the coffee-growing areas of western Nicaragua, where most of the country's population resided. On the contrary, countless Nicaraguan landlords were driven to financial ruin during the boom. At the same time, many nonelite producers expanded their farms. If the 1920s export boom produced an unprecedented concentration of wealth and power in much of Central America, in western Nicaragua the boom instead weakened elite control over the rural economy.

As we have just seen, Nicaragua's otherwise fractious elites showed remarkable unity in blaming dollar diplomacy for their economic predicament. According to them, dollar diplomacy blocked not only the growth of Nicaragua's economy but also its modernization. Yet historical records reveal a far more contradictory and unexpected outcome. On the one hand, they confirm that dollar diplomats' restrictive fiscal and financial policies hindered the modernization of Nicaragua's economy, particularly of its all-important coffee industry. But they also indicate that dollar diplomacy did not block the growth of its agroexport economy. More important still, the data reveal a previously unrecognized dynamism within the "traditional" agricultural sector, which produced basic foodstuffs and was dominated by nonelite producers. If elite Nicaraguans thus had good reason to blame dollar diplomacy for their misfortunes, they were wrong to represent their own economic anxieties as a crisis that plagued the nation as a whole. No matter how many insecure landlords littered Nicaragua's landscape in the 1920s, many more peasant producers enjoyed renewed prosperity.

The boom's uneven impact on Nicaragua's rural producers challenges widespread views that U.S. intervention in agrarian societies inherently widens the gap between the rich and the poor.[2] These views stem largely from the process of land concentration that occurred in U.S.-occupied countries like Cuba and the Dominican Republic, as well as in economic enclaves that U.S. companies created elsewhere in Latin America.[3] In addition, the dollar diplomacy–induced "dance of the millions" enabled many Latin American landlords to increase their power at the expense of the peasantry during the 1920s.[4] Why, then, did Nicaragua's encounter with dollar diplomacy instead entail the "democratization" of rural property relations? Although some dollar diplomats espoused egalitarian ideals, this surprising effect of imperial rule was unintended. Above all, it resulted from the greater resilience small- and medium-scale farmers showed in coping with the peculiar form of dollar diplomacy that allowed Nicaragua's rural economy to grow without making it much more modern.

Growth without Development

In the two decades prior to dollar diplomacy's advent, Nicaragua had the second fastest growing export economy in Central America (see Table 1). After 1912 it became the region's least dynamic export economy—a ranking that did not improve until the end of the U.S. occupation in 1933. Nicaragua's post-1912 fall down the economic ladder surely reinforced elites' view that dollar diplomacy was thwarting the growth of their country's export economy. In reality, however, this economy expanded under dollar diplomats' watch. Even though Nicaragua's export economy of 1912–33 fell behind its Central American counterparts, it still managed to grow twice as fast as it did during the "golden" age of Zelaya's Liberal dictatorship (1893–1909).

Elite criticism notwithstanding, the country's most "modern" rural industries helped fuel the post-1912 expansion of Nicaragua's export economy. Coffee accounted for nearly half of the export revenues generated in the 1910s and 1920s. And contrary to conventional wisdom, the coffee industry was far more productive under dollar diplomacy than in its best years under the Zelaya regime, that is, from 1905 to 1909.[5] In fact, between 1910 and 1930 Nicaraguan coffee growers were, together with their Salvadoran counterparts, the most dynamic in Central America (see Table 2). Coffee growers in the southern uplands of Managua/Carazo/Granada increased production mostly by adding trees to existing coffee farms, while those in the north-

TABLE 1. Central America: Annual average rates of growth of total exports at constant 1980 prices (%), 1890–1940

	Nicaragua	Costa Rica	Guatemala	Honduras	El Salvador
1890–1912	1.0	-0.8	-0.2	-1.6	1.3
1912–32	2.5	3.5	5.4	11.0	2.6
1932–40	5.6	-5.8	-0.3	-7.6	3.8

NOTE: Panama is not included, as most Central Americans during the period of the table did not consider it a Central American nation.

SOURCES: Bulmer-Thomas, *Economic History*, 65; *Statesman Yearbook*, 1912–1920; Mitchell, *International Historical Statistics*, 425–30; Schoonover and Schoonover, "Statistics," 116–17; Young, *Central American Currency*; Bulmer-Thomas, *Political Economy*, 326–27. For price conversion, Mitchell, *International Historical Statistics*, 690–92.

central highlands of Matagalpa did so by expanding the acreage of coffee. Nicaragua's next leading exports were bananas, gold, and timber, all of which were produced chiefly in eastern Nicaragua by U.S. companies. As elsewhere in the Caribbean Basin, these U.S.-controlled enclave economies grew significantly after the end of World War I. Sugar was the final export crop that Nicaraguans associated with modernity. Unlike the other "modern" sectors, Nicaragua's sugar industry became export-oriented only after the onset of dollar diplomacy's reign. But once it did, sugar production soared to unprecedented levels. Under dollar diplomacy, then, Nicaragua's export economy continued to be the most diversified in all of Central America.

Yet the most peculiar aspect of Nicaragua's economic growth under dollar diplomacy was the exceptional strength of its traditional agricultural sector. Typically for Central America, this sector was dominated by the production of cattle and basic grains, especially corn. So strong were Nicaragua's cattle and cereal economies that even during the 1920s export boom they produced nearly three times as much revenue as the country's coffee, banana, and sugar industries taken together. In fact, when measured by output per capita, Nicaragua's traditional agricultural sector was likely Central America's most productive industry of the 1920s.[6] The strength of Nicaragua's traditional agriculture was certainly rooted in its domination of crop acreage. In 1925, for instance, corn was grown on about two thirds of the total farmland, while coffee occupied only about an eighth.[7] But Nicaragua's cereal and cattle

TABLE 2. Central America: Volume (lbs.) index of coffee export production, 1905–34 (1905–9 = 100)

	Nicaragua	Costa Rica	Guatemala	El Salvador
1905–9	100	100	100	100
1910–14	108	100	96	108
1915–19	123	95	105	125
1920–24	136	107	115	145
1925–29	156	126	123	159
1930–34	151	159	119	188

NOTE: Honduras is not included, as it did not become a major coffee exporter until the 1950s.
SOURCE: Williams, *States and Social Evolution*, 265–73.

industries were also highly dynamic. This was particularly evident during the 1920s agroexport boom, when Nicaragua was the only Central American country whose traditional agricultural sector grew sufficiently fast (about 5 percent per year) to ensure that food imports and prices of locally produced foodstuffs did not have to be increased.[8]

The dynamism of Nicaragua's cereal and cattle industries was hardly noticed by foreign journalists and diplomats, as few chose to venture into the countryside. Those who did, however, could not help but marvel at the productivity of the country's traditional agricultural sectors. For example, many U.S. troops who came to be stationed in rural Nicaragua after the 1926–27 civil war (see chapter 8) commented on the relative prosperity of the country's cereal farmers and cattle ranchers. Not surprisingly, the most glowing reports came from the northwestern lowlands of Chinandega/León—the country's granary—and the central plains of Chontales, which produced the most cattle in Nicaragua. Yet U.S. troops also wrote about flourishing cereal producers and cattle ranchers in remote areas such as the northern frontier region of the Segovias where, as a U.S. Marine reported, "one sees nothing but fields of corn and rice besides many cattle."[9]

Ironically, the main factor spurring the 1920s growth of Nicaragua's inward-oriented cereal and cattle industries lay outside of the country. Above all, Nicaraguan farmers and ranchers profited from the inability of their Central American counterparts to adequately supply local demand for basic foodstuffs.[10] This inability stemmed from two economic processes that affected Nicaragua the least during the 1920s. First, elites and the state reallocated crucial resources—more labor and capital than land itself—from the cereal and cattle economies to the expanding coffee and banana industries. Second, the era's boom in large-scale public works further drained the region's labor resources away from the traditional agricultural sectors and heightened rural migration to urban centers. Unable to meet the needs of a growing, more urbanized population, Nicaragua's neighbors were forced to import many provisions from abroad. While most food imports came from the United States, many were of Nicaraguan origin. In particular, Central American nations came to depend on Nicaraguan corn and cattle.[11]

Nicaragua's ranchers and cereal producers relied so heavily on the export market that theirs was the only traditional agricultural sector in Central America that contracted during the Great Depression.[12] Nicaraguan food exporters primarily suffered from the declining purchasing power of neighboring agroexport producers. Yet they were also victimized by the protective tariffs Central American governments imposed on Nicaraguan foodstuffs after the 1929 stock market crash. Numerous U.S. officers observed how the sudden downturn in international market conditions hurt small- and medium-scale producers throughout Nicaragua. In 1930, a U.S. Army captain reported from Chontales that "money is very scarce and the owners of the ranches are land poor. They raise about 40,000 head of cattle annually, but there is no market. Formerly the cattle were driven to Costa Rica for market but now there is no market there."[13]

But if Nicaragua's diverse, rural-based economy expanded steadily until the crash, this growth hardly produced greater development. In fact, Nicaragua was the only Central American nation that failed to modernize its agricultural economy significantly during the postwar agroexport boom. In the 1920s, Nicaraguans imported by far the smallest quantity of modern agricultural implements, be they plows, mills, fertilizers, windmills, tractors, or coffee-processing machines. As a result, Nicaragua regressed to perhaps the lowest level of agricultural mechanization in the isthmus.[14] Even in the country's wealthiest agricultural region—Granada—nearly all of the plowing continued to be done by oxen and wooden plows.[15]

Elite Nicaraguans believed that the underdeveloped nature of their country's economy was most noticeable in the coffee industry, their paradigm of modernity. This belief was further echoed by contemporary surveys, which showed that the technology of Nicaragua's coffee industry lagged far behind that of Guatemala, El Salvador, and Costa Rica.[16] In these surveys, foreign experts mainly criticized Nicaraguans' backward techniques of harvesting and pruning coffee trees, as well as their general failure to use chemical fertilizers. They also noted that even Nicaragua's largest-scale coffee processors tended to use much more primitive machinery than that employed elsewhere in the isthmus. Although this technological lag did not block the growth of Nicaragua's coffee exports, it led Nicaraguans to produce the lowest-quality coffee in Central America and thus the one that fetched the lowest price on international markets. Nothing more reminded elite Nicaraguans of their country's economic backwardness than its inability to produce a coffee bean as lucrative as that of its neighbors.[17]

What most stymied Nicaragua's economic development was its failure to modernize the public infrastructure.[18] In particular, the country's transportation system became the least developed in the region under dollar diplomacy. If between 1910 and 1930 the length of open railway expanded in Guatemala, El Salvador, and Honduras by 43, 89, and 845 percent, respectively, in Nicaragua it increased only by 2 percent. Even Costa Rica, which in 1910 had the region's most developed railroad network, experienced more railroad expansion (7 percent).[19] Although supported by national governments, the expansion of Central America's all-important railroads was mostly financed by U.S. companies like the United Fruit Company. To the chagrin of native elites, dollar diplomats discouraged such U.S. investments in Nicaragua. Even more irritating, they blocked the Nicaraguan government from using its resources to construct long-awaited railroad projects such as the Pacific-Atlantic connection and the extension to the coffee-growing zone of Matagalpa. As a result, Nicaragua remained the only Central American nation whose railroad lines did not connect all of its most important coffee zones with the coastal ports.

Some privately financed roads were built in Nicaragua under dollar diplomacy. But since elites lacked the funds to maintain them, most quickly deteriorated and became mud banks during the rainy season. Nicaragua's road network remained so underdeveloped that even as late as 1934 the U.S. minister to Nicaragua noted how "roads outside of Managua [were] almost impassable by automobile."[20] If trucks and trains assumed an ever greater role

12. Rural transport conditions, ca. 1927. *Courtesy of U.S. National Archives.*

elsewhere in Central America during the 1920s, traditional means of transportation—pack mules, oxcarts, and boats—remained the fastest way of hauling goods in much of Nicaragua (see figure 12).

Nicaragua's grave lag in development mainly resulted from the peculiar brand of dollar diplomacy that the U.S. government imposed on its protectorate. In the name of fiscal stability, dollar diplomats not only blocked Nicaragua's participation in the "dance of the millions" that funded the postwar modernization of so many Latin American economies, they also prevented the Nicaraguan state from using its own resources to develop the economy. So hell-bent were dollar diplomats on slashing public debt that Nicaragua's government expenditures dropped far behind the rest of Central America in the 1920s.[21] Moreover, nowhere did a smaller portion of the state budget flow into public investment programs than in Nicaragua. If most Central American states spent between 10 to 20 percent of their annual budgets on public works during the 1920s, dollar diplomats ensured that in Nicaragua this figure hovered at a mere 5 percent.[22] Dismissing public improvement projects as wasteful works of prestige and political patronage, U.S. officials allocated much of Nicaragua's state budget to finance the reduction of public debt. By massively restricting state expenditures, dollar diplomats succeeded in cutting Nicaragua's external public debt by half—a drop that sharply contrasted with the massive increase in the external debt of other U.S. protectorates and Central American countries.[23] By the late 1920s, dollar diplomats succeeded in their mission to restore stability to Nicaragua's public finances. Yet this success came at a great cost, for dollar diplomats' restrictive fiscal policies delayed the much-needed modernization of Nicaragua's public infrastructure.

Dollar diplomacy's constraint on public investment also had wide-reaching social consequences. In particular, dollar diplomats' refusal to modernize Nicaragua's transport system prevented local landlords from expanding their economic power as forcefully as their Central American counterparts. Poor roads, for example, greatly hampered elite efforts to recruit laborers, especially at harvest time. In addition, higher transportation costs both weakened Nicaragua's competitiveness on the international coffee market and diminished the profit margins of its coffee exporters. Above all, Nicaragua's primitive road network undermined elite power by militating against the centralization of the coffee-processing industry. As elsewhere in Central America, many of Nicaragua's coffee barons sought to enhance their profits by processing the coffee of small- and medium-scale growers. Yet the radius serviced by processing plants depended on local transport conditions because the harvested berries had to be brought to the mill as quickly as possible to prevent spoilage. Thanks to the 1920s improvement of internal transport facilities, large coffee processors throughout Central America massively expanded their clientele. Moreover, this improvement promoted monopsonist market conditions that drastically weakened the bargaining position of nonelite growers.[24] In Nicaragua, by contrast, poor roads perpetuated the decentralized state of the processing industry, thus enabling small- and medium-scale coffee growers to play off elite processors against each other more easily than elsewhere in the region. Unexpectedly, then, dollar diplomats' restrictive fiscal policies helped nonelite coffee growers better defend their economic independence at a time when their Central American counterparts were being squeezed by coffee barons.

But Nicaragua's underdeveloped transport system hardly inhibited nonelite producers from exporting cattle and corn to other Central American countries. Of course, many farmers complained about having to haul their produce on poor roads. Still, small- and medium-scale ranchers who drove their cattle to Costa Rica and Honduras were adequately served by traditional land routes and waterways. Ranchers from cattle-rich Chontales made good use of Lake Nicaragua and the *camino real*, a north-south cart road built in the colonial era that linked the lake's western shore with the rest of Central America. In addition, nonelite cereal producers from the Pacific zone benefited greatly from the Corinto-Granada railroad in exporting their goods to lucrative market centers elsewhere in the isthmus. One such railroad user was the future anti-U.S. guerrilla leader Augusto Sandino, who in his youth was a merchant of corn and beans.[25]

Nicaraguan food exports gained an unexpected boost in the 1920s, when neighboring countries massively improved their road and railway networks. While these improvements aimed to lower transportation costs for coffee exports to Europe and the United States, they also facilitated the import of Nicaraguan foodstuffs. The dollar diplomacy–induced modernization of other Central American transport systems thus inadvertently helped Nicaragua's nonelite cereal and cattle exporters enjoy renewed prosperity when similar producers elsewhere in the isthmus were largely on the economic defensive.

Promoting Peasant over Estate Production

Yet dollar diplomacy mainly weakened the economic power of Nicaraguan landlords in the realm of private, not public finances. Elite producers denounced dollar diplomacy most loudly for "strangling" their access to capital. They particularly criticized the restrictive lending policies of the country's leading financial institution: the U.S.-controlled Banco Nacional. These policies, elites alleged, prevented Nicaraguan farmers from modernizing their methods of production and drove countless "virtuous" landlords to ruin.[26] Such criticisms were certainly justified, as dollar diplomacy ensured that Nicaragua had the most restrictive financial environment in Central America. Yet because this credit crunch unexpectedly "democratized" access to local credit markets, dollar diplomacy ended up better meeting the capital needs of peasant producers than those of landlords.

That Nicaraguan landlords suffered the worst lending conditions in the isthmus during the booming 1920s is beyond question. If coffee elites elsewhere in Central America deemed annual interest rates of 10 to 12 percent as outrageously high, those rates were favorably regarded by their Nicaraguan counterparts.[27] Similarly, the total value of bank loans provided to Nicaraguans was much smaller than that granted to other Central Americans. In

1925 Nicaragua received, per capita, barely two U.S. dollars in bank loans, while Salvadorans and Guatemalans obtained an amount three times as large.[28] And as Central American banks then catered principally to large-scale coffee producers, even more damaging to Nicaragua's coffee elite was the fact that bank loans made up at most 25 percent of the country's coffee export revenues; in Guatemala and El Salvador that percentage was more than twice as high.

Dollar diplomats' restrictive lending policies hurt Nicaraguan landlords so much precisely because their economic fortunes hinged on having regular access to large amounts of credit. True, capital concerns affected all sorts of commercial farmers, and the Banco Nacional was not their sole source of credit. Many small-scale producers borrowed money from private lenders for various reasons—whether to survive bad harvests, acquire more land, plant new cash crops, hire workers, buy tools, or finance nonagricultural activities. Still, landlords frequently required loans of the magnitude that only the Banco Nacional could grant. Furthermore, they were extremely vulnerable to a credit crunch, mostly because they needed large sums to pay their workers. Small- and medium-scale producers, by contrast, more easily survived such crunches, as they and their kin did most of the farming.

This key difference in capital needs was especially pronounced in the coffee sector. Obviously, coffee was a lucrative crop. In the mid-1920s, for instance, the price of a pound of export coffee was about seven times higher than that for exported corn.[29] But coffee was also extremely labor intensive, requiring about three times the labor per acre needed for corn.[30] Typically, coffee growers weeded their groves and pruned coffee trees two to three times a year.[31] They also had to maintain irrigation ditches, control pests, and care for young coffee trees in the nursery and under shade trees (usually plantains). Yet the greatest amount of labor went into the coffee harvest. Ideally, pickers would go over the trees multiple times, as coffee berries on one tree do not ripen at the same time. Once collected, the berries were then hauled to a nearby processing plant. Finally, the harvest waste had to be buried. Thanks to family labor, small-scale coffee growers carried out all of these tasks with little outside help. The opposite was true for large-scale growers. While coffee barons of Matagalpa continued to depend heavily on tenants (*colonos*), sharecroppers, and forced laborers, those in the southern uplands had come to rely primarily on wage workers.[32] The wealthiest planters employed up to one thousand pickers. But the average coffee baron hired around 150 men, women, and children during the picking season and about 40 male workers for the rest of the year. Coffee planters paid their workers low wages; in the mid-1920s wages for coffee pickers ranged between twenty-five and fifty cents per day.[33] But because elite planters produced well over one hundred thousand pounds of coffee, they required annual cash advances of at least six thousand U.S. dollars just to cover labor costs.[34] And since many processed and shipped their coffee to the Pacific port of Corinto, where the best price was fetched, their credit needs increased by at least another two thousand dollars. These were enormous capital needs for a country that had an estimated annual per capita income of about forty dollars.[35]

With credit so vital to elite producers, why were U.S. officials of Nicaragua's Banco Nacional unusually stingy about funneling it? No doubt, their restrictive lending policies sprung from the bank's shortage of capital. In the mid-1920s, the bank's total capital (three hundred thousand U.S. dollars) was five to twenty times smaller than that held by the largest banks in the other Central American countries.[36] This capital gap had been much smaller during the 1910s but widened in the 1920s because dollar diplomats prevented Nicaragua from participating in the "dance of the millions." Moreover, dollar diplomats steadfastly rejected Nicaraguan demands to raise the capital of the Banco Nacional, as such an increase would have contradicted the U.S. goal of reducing Nicaragua's public debt. And since dollar diplomats expressed little confidence in native banking habits, the Banco Nacional further tightened its credit policies by keeping an unusually high percentage (50–150 percent) of cash reserves against private deposits. The bank's U.S. managers also privileged mortgages on coffee plantations to counter what they believed was Nicaraguans' "penchant" to seek overly large loans.[37] In doing so, they increased the financial risks of the few coffee barons who actually received a loan, since the latter could no longer mortgage their less valuable urban dwellings and cattle estates.

Yet as much as the Banco Nacional was criticized for its capital constraint, dollar diplomacy did not cause local credit markets to collapse. On the contrary, these markets grew significantly under dollar diplomats' watch. Consider, for example, how the mortgage market in Nicaragua's wealthiest department—Granada—expanded from 1910 to 1925, that is, from the eve of dollar diplomacy's rule to its apex. Between these years, the total value of mortgages (adjusted for inflation) grew by 58 percent (135 percent in current dollars), while the number of loans granted increased by 236 percent.[38] U.S.

banking officials could hardly take credit for this rapid growth, since the Banco Nacional provided less than 9 percent of the total value of mortgage loans made in 1925. Instead, the expansion of Granada's credit market was driven by private moneylenders. While a few lenders represented foreign merchant houses specializing in the coffee trade, the overwhelming majority came from the city of Granada. And perhaps more than anywhere in Nicaragua, Granada's private lenders tended to be rich. Large merchants, wealthy professionals (doctors and lawyers), and elite women each accounted for about 30 percent of all the mortgage loans made in 1925.

Unfortunately for landlords, Granada's creditors were unable to grant loans as large as those of foreign-controlled merchant houses and the Banco Nacional. But luckily for countless small- and medium-scale farmers as well as artisans and petty merchants, Granada's private lenders accepted mortgages on all kinds of property. They even granted credit to the smallest-scale cereal producers like Ramona Escorcia, whom the neighboring landlord Guillermo Argüello Vargas lent twenty-four U.S. dollars in exchange for a mortgage on her cornfield of not even one manzana.[39] The case of Escorcia also illustrates that private lenders did not shy away from providing credit to women. In fact, women received about 40 percent of all the mortgage loans made in Granada in both 1910 and 1925. As elsewhere in Nicaragua, Granada's private lenders provided credit to the plethora of economic actors snubbed by the Banco Nacional.

In consequence, Nicaragua's small- and medium-scale farmers enjoyed ever greater access to capital at a time when many of their Central American counterparts suffered a severe credit crunch.[40] This was even the case in Granada, which then had the highest degree of land concentration in Nicaragua and where the power of smallholders was hence the weakest. For example, between 1910 and 1925 the rural population's share of all mortgage loans made in Granada more than tripled, from 5 to 17 percent (see Table 3). And since nearly all of Granada's rural borrowers were nonelite producers, it is not surprising that they increased their share particularly within the smallest loan bracket (US$0–100). Further reflecting the greater availability of credit to peasant producers, small borrowers mortgaged rural properties with much greater frequency in 1925 (40 percent) than in 1910 (19 percent). At first glance, it seems that medium-scale farmers failed to benefit from the post-1910 expansion in Granada's credit market, as between 1910 and 1925 the percentage of medium-sized mortgages (US$101–500) on rural proper-

TABLE 3. Granada's mortgage market by loan size: 1910 and 1925 (in current US$)

Loan size	$0–100		$101–500		$501–1,000		$1,000+		Total/ Cumulative ·Average or %	
	1910	1925	1910	1925	1910	1925	1910	1925	1910	1925
Number of loans	42	58	17	105	1	24	15	65	75	252
Value in $1,000	1.9	4.7	4.0	33.4	0.8	19.4	96.3	184.3	103.0	241.8
Average value ($)	45	81	235	318	800	810	6,419	2,835	1,373	959
Average monthly interest rate (%)	2.1	2.0	1.6	1.5	2.0	1.3	1.1	1.2	1.8	1.5
Mortgages on rural properties within loan bracket (%)	19	40	50	19	0	17	53	49	32	31
Debtors from rural Granada within loan bracket (%)	5	41	6	14	0	8	7	5	5	17

NOTE: Based on all mortgage transactions made in 1910 and 1925 that are recorded in Granada's property registry.
SOURCE: RPPG, *Libros de propiedades*, vols. 1–61; RPPG, *Libro de diario*, vol. 19.

ties sank from 50 percent to 19 percent. In reality, however, the majority of medium-sized mortgages on urban properties made in 1925 were used to finance rural enterprises. Perhaps the most significant development in Granada's credit market was the declining ratio of the largest mortgages ($1000+) to medium-sized ones ($101–500); between 1910 and 1925 the ratio fell from 24:1 to 6:1. With credit so important to commercial farming, this decline suggests just how significantly elite control over agricultural production weakened under dollar diplomacy.

Why, then, did credit allocation apparently become more "democratic" in Nicaragua than elsewhere in the isthmus?[41] While dollar diplomats actively curtailed elite access to bank loans, they were never committed to providing credit to nonelite producers. Instead, the democratization of local credit markets resulted largely from a major shift in elite lending patterns. As the case of Granada suggests, local elites were more willing to invest in small-scale agricultural enterprises in 1925 than in 1910. This willingness reflected elites' grave concern with the financial environment emerging under dollar diplomacy. On the one hand, the tight credit policies of the Banco Nacional made it very difficult for large-scale producers to finance their capital-intensive enterprises. At the same time, the bank aggressively foreclosed large estates. As a result, elite lenders increasingly feared that insolvent landlords would drag them to financial ruin. In fact, this fate befell various elite families; in Granada, the most prominent casualty was the Cardenal family.[42] With more and more landlords unable to repay their debts, prudent lenders increasingly opted to invest in a more secure venture: lending smaller amounts of money at higher interest rates to nonelite producers.

Few better exemplified this shift in elite lending patterns than the lawyer Juan Francisco Lugo, Granada's undisputed "king" of moneylenders during the 1920s. Born in 1875, Lugo belonged to an oligarchic family that derived its wealth from cattle ranching, coffee production, and urban commerce. Like other elite lenders, Lugo had long provided large loans to local landlords. But by 1925 he had so greatly diversified his clientele that twenty-eight of the thirty-four mortgage loans he made that year went to individuals who borrowed five hundred dollars or less.[43] About half of these small- and medium-sized loans financed urban entrepreneurs, particularly petty merchants and artisans. The other half went to small- and medium-scale farmers who produced coffee, cereal, and/or livestock in rural Granada. Two of these farmers eventually lost their properties to Lugo after defaulting on their loans, but they were the exception.

Indeed, the case of Granada suggests that many Nicaraguan farmers were able to pay back their debts during the 1920s agroexport boom. In 1925, for instance, close to 90 percent of the total loans made on Granada's mortgage market were repaid. More important still, defaulted properties were not tilted lopsidedly toward nonelite sectors but evenly distributed throughout all credit brackets. This equal distribution is surprising given the onerous credit conditions suffered by small debtors, who were required to repay loans not only within a shorter time but at a higher interest rate.[44] Moreover, when a small farm was acquired due to insolvency, moneylenders tended to resell them very quickly to small-scale producers—at times even to the original owner. Consider the case of Pedro Sabonó, a cereal producer from rural Granada who owned a farm of nine manzanas (about fifteen acres) in Nandaime, an area dominated by large sugar and cattle estates. In 1925 a local court ordered Sabonó to sell his farm to an elite lender from the city of

Granada in order to pay off a debt of US$120. Within a year, Sabonó had already recovered this plot.[45] Sabonó's ability to maintain ownership of his farm, exorbitant monthly interest rates of 2 percent notwithstanding, more generally points to a peculiar trend noticeable in property sales made in Granada during the 1920s agroexport boom. If Central American elites expanded their landholdings primarily at the cost of indebted nonelite producers, Granada's landlords acquired foreclosed farms mostly from within their own ranks.

Nicaragua's distinct form of hacienda expansion forcefully underscores the peculiar evolution of its credit markets under dollar diplomacy. Although dollar diplomats' restrictive lending policy did not weaken such markets, the persistence of high interest rates indicates that it prevented them from growing as strongly as other Central American capital markets. On the other hand, elites' shifting lending patterns suggest that dollar diplomacy engendered a financial environment more conducive to peasant than to estate production. And nothing better underscored the greater efficiency of small-scale producers than their ability to repay loans at the same rate as landlords even though they had to pay interest rates that were nearly twice as high. Thanks to these resilient smallholders, Nicaragua's rural class structures became less polarized under dollar diplomacy.

"Democratizing" Rural Class Structures

An ideal place to trace dollar diplomacy's peculiar "democratizing" impact is rural Granada, as land was more concentrated and landlord hegemony greater in this elite bastion than anywhere else in Nicaragua.[46] When a U.S. traveler passed through Granada in the early 1920s and told local elites how he had been struck by "the number of peasant proprietors" in Costa Rica, a younger Granadan oligarch fittingly responded: "That's just like Leon [sic]. You see some dirty fellow over there and he has his little patch of land. It's very different over here. Everything's in fine big estates."[47]

At the same time, Granada is a vantage point to explore how dollar diplomacy affected rural areas with distinct socioeconomic structures. As map 4 indicates, rural Granada consisted of five subregions with varied cultivation and land-tenure patterns. Farthest north lay the cattle zone of Malacatoya, a plain bound by the Malacatoya River and Tisma Lagoon. While Malacatoya had many large cattle estates, it was still a frontier-like area dotted with small

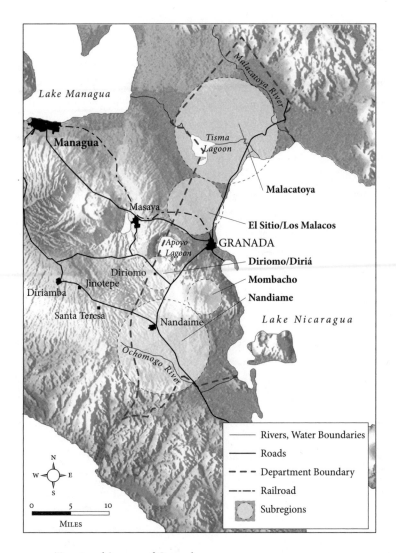

MAP 4 Topographic map of Granada

and medium-sized cattle ranches as well as some corn and rice farms. From Tisma to the city of Granada stretched El Sitio/Los Malacos, whose fertile farmlands were of volcanic origin. This subregion was home to estates of colonial origin that specialized in sugar, cereal, and livestock production, but it also had a smattering of small farms that cultivated corn. The third subregion consisted of the Mombacho volcano—the "bourgeois mountain"— where coffee plantations reigned supreme. By contrast, small and medium-sized farms dominated the hills and narrow valleys surrounding the colonial Indian villages of Diriomo and Diriá. While some of these farms grew coffee, they mostly produced basic grains. Farthest south lay the well-irrigated plains of Nandaime, where sugar, cacao, and cattle estates existed alongside smaller cattle and cereal farms. These five subregions ensured that Granada had the most polarized class relations in rural Nicaragua by the advent of dollar diplomacy. Yet each subregion had developed its distinct social structure, with landlord hegemony strongest in the Mombacho and weakest in Malacatoya.

Dollar diplomacy's impact on class relations in rural Granada is best measured by exploring how it affected land tenure in the region. Not only did contemporaries view land ownership as the ultimate sign of power, officials also collected more complete and reliable data on land than for other class indicators, such as the amount of labor used by agricultural producers, their taxable wealth, or the mean production of their farms. Our two main sources are the annual hacienda surveys that, for tax purposes, recorded farms whose goods were sold in the city;[48] and Granada's property registry, which listed most commercial farms in the department.[49] Both sources tended to record the farm's size, its location, and the type of crop it cultivated. This information is critical if we use land to differentiate the class position of agricultural producers, for one manzana (1.7 acres) of a lucrative cash crop, such as coffee, generates far more income than a manzana of a basic foodstuff like corn. To facilitate comparative analysis, I have followed the lead of other Central Americanists and divided Granada's agricultural producers into three classes: medium-scale producers cultivated fifty to five hundred manzanas in basic grains; fifteen to sixty-five in coffee; fifty to two hundred in sugar; or two hundred to one thousand in livestock.[50] Small-scale producers grew less than the amount corresponding to medium-scale ones, and large-scale producers more.

Large-Scale Producers How then did dollar diplomacy help "democratize" the social structures of rural Granada? First and foremost, it weakened the region's landed elite by producing significant turnover in its membership. Contrary to conventional wisdom, such changes occurred largely at the cost of the ruling Conservatives, the elite faction that not only dominated Granada's landed elite but benefited the most politically from the U.S. occupation. Granted, some Conservative landlords expanded their economic power or regained lands that they had lost during the Liberal era of Zelaya. Yet many more faced serious economic difficulties and were forced to sell their coveted estates.

Dollar diplomacy's detrimental impact on Granada's landed elite is neatly reflected in the changing composition of its most important sector: the exclusive club of individuals owning large coffee plantations on the Mombacho volcano. Of the fourteen largest Mombacho planters recorded in the national coffee survey of 1909, more than half lost their estates under dollar diplomacy.[51] Except for one, all were close to the ruling Conservatives.[52] Also, all thirteen people who entered the ranks of Granada's coffee elite during dollar diplomacy's lengthy reign were Conservatives; only seven of them maintained more than an ephemeral foothold in this elite.[53]

Underscoring this instability, the few Mombacho planters who expanded their coffee farms under dollar diplomacy generally did so at the cost of other coffee barons, not peasant producers. Between 1912 and 1933, Granada's ten largest coffee plantations changed ownership a total of twenty-four times, with nearly all changes due to acute financial difficulties faced by the seller. Most ownership changes did not occur after the Great Crash of 1929, as traditionally stressed by Central American agrarian historians. Instead, they happened during the agroexport boom of the 1920s. For example, the ten largest coffee plantations in Granada experienced nine ownership changes between 1904 and 1911 and another nine during the following eight years. From 1920 to 1927, this figure climbed to eleven, only to sink to five for the subsequent eight years. The case of Granada thus suggests that the 1920s boom produced much instability in the ranks of Nicaragua's coffee elite—an impact that contrasted with the boom's tendency everywhere else in the isthmus to help consolidate coffee elites.

The boom's destabilizing effect on Nicaragua's coffee elites reveals the contradictions of coffee production, an extremely profitable but risky business. While coffee planters then averaged profit margins of about 35 percent, they also had to deal with international coffee prices that fluctuated widely.[54] For example, between 1917 and 1918 the (f.o.b. Corinto) price for one hundred pounds of Nicaraguan coffee fell from $10.60 to $8.80; it then soared to $20.40 in 1920, only to plunge the following year to $8.10.[55] In addition, coffee growers' high profit margins contrasted sharply with the extreme difficulties they faced in obtaining the necessary capital to cover their high production costs. As we saw above, their credit squeeze stemmed largely from dollar diplomacy's restrictive lending policies. But such capital constraints worsened significantly with the world depression of 1920–21.

While this economic crisis hurt large coffee growers throughout Central America, those in Nicaragua were particularly battered. This was partly because the poorer quality of Nicaraguan coffee ensured that its international price would sink the furthest. In addition, Nicaragua's underdeveloped processing industry prevented its coffee barons from following the example of their Costa Rican and Salvadoran counterparts, who passed their losses on to small-scale producers whose coffee they processed.[56] And because Nicaraguan coffee barons primarily used wage labor, which necessitated a large and continuous cash flow, they also lacked the financial cushion that service tenancy and forced labor provided for many coffee planters elsewhere in the region, particularly Guatemala.[57] But perhaps most important, government-affiliated banks throughout Central America responded to the 1920–21 crisis by providing embattled coffee elites with generous financial support. In Nicaragua, the U.S.-controlled Banco Nacional instead cut back sharply on its loans to coffee producers and became even more aggressive in taking over foreclosed properties.

Dollar diplomats even refused to help their main native allies, Conservative landlords, from going bankrupt. The most prominent of such bankruptcies befell Pedro Rafael Cuadra Pasos, a Granadan who had helped implement dollar diplomats' controversial policies between 1913 and 1916 while serving as Nicaragua's financial agent in Washington. On leaving the government, the fifty-six-year-old oligarch bought three coffee estates on the Mombacho.[58] To finance this purchase, Cuadra sold his and his wife's share of an immense cacao plantation that belonged to her family, the Chamorros.[59] In addition, he might have used the large sum that he had recently received from the Mixed Commission.[60] To operate his new estates, Cuadra borrowed nearly thirty thousand U.S. dollars per year, mostly from fellow Granadan oligarchs and foreign coffee traders.[61] All appeared to be going well until coffee prices plummeted in 1920. Although they rebounded the next year, coffee prices did not surpass their 1920 level until 1925. Because of this price drop, Cuadra struggled to meet his debt payments and production costs. He even had trouble repaying local merchants for luxury goods purchased by his wife.[62] Finally, in 1924 a judge forced Cuadra to sell his coffee estates to impatient creditors.[63] According to the Conservative senator Carlos Cuadra Pasos, politics had driven his brother Pedro Rafael over the edge. In particular, Carlos accused his rivals in the Conservative Party of forcing the Banco Nacional to reject Pedro Rafael's request for emergency loans.[64] This is certainly possible. But since coffee barons of all political colors landed in bankruptcy court, it is more likely that dollar diplomats snubbed Cuadra because they deemed him too great a financial risk.

That coffee planters like Cuadra Pasos fell victim less to political intrigue than to a credit crunch and risky investments becomes clearer when we consider dollar diplomacy's distinct impact on Granada's cattle elite. As in the coffee sector, most Granadan landlords who were forced to sell their sprawling cattle ranches belonged to the city's Conservative oligarchy. But even if some famous cattle estates disintegrated, the composition of Granada's cattle elite remained more stable under dollar diplomacy than that of its coffee elite. This stability seems especially surprising since cattle barons received very little financial support from the Banco Nacional. In Granada, for example, owners of cattle estates obtained only 5 percent of the loans that the bank granted between 1912 and 1932, while those mortgaging a coffee farm received 82 percent of such loans.

Still, cattle barons dealt more easily with dollar diplomacy's adverse financial environment since cattle ranching, though about six times less lucrative than coffee production, was far less risky.[65] In general, cattle ranchers were less susceptible to crises in foreign markets, as local demand for meat and dairy products was much stronger than for coffee.[66] More important still, cattle barons were less affected by the scarcity of credit since their production costs were far lower than those facing coffee planters. Not only did cattle barons need fewer workers, they also paid them lower wages, for they frequently employed sharecroppers and tenants whom they granted parcels of land in exchange for their labor.[67] Little wonder that fewer cattle barons faced economic ruin than large coffee planters under dollar diplomacy. Underscoring this difference, twenty coffee plantations in Granada were foreclosed or threatened with foreclosure between 1912 and 1927, while only six cattle estates suffered such a fate, even though the region had at least three times more cattle than coffee estates.

Dollar diplomacy nonetheless engendered much anxiety among Granada's cattle barons. This was largely because more and more cattle barons were losing significant portions of their ranches to nonelite ranchers. An unusually perceptive U.S. consul noted in 1925 that "some of the large [cattle] holdings have diminished, but there has been an increase of breeding among the small farmers."[68] This observation dovetails with the shift in land tenure patterns that occurred in Granada's cattle sector during the 1920s. Typically, the few cattle barons who expanded their estates did so at the cost of fellow landlords. The most successful buyer of indebted cattle estates was Adolfo Benard Vivas, who amassed about four thousand manzanas of prime pasture in Nandaime, much of it from the Cuadra family. While Benard used most of this land for cattle ranching, he set apart about one thousand manzanas to establish what quickly became the region's premier sugar plantation: the Ingenio Amalia. Yet Granada's "Sugar King" was the exception to the rule, as much, if not most, of the pasture land sold in Granada in the 1920s was acquired by nonelite producers.

Small- and Medium-Scale Producers As elsewhere in Nicaragua, Granada's peasantry had become more socially differentiated with the post-1870s growth in export agriculture. By the advent of dollar diplomacy, a vibrant middling sector had emerged that was more active in cattle ranching and cereal production than in the coffee and sugar industries. Compared to the rest of Nicaragua, an unusually high number of the region's medium-scale producers resided in urban areas, especially in the town of Nandaime and the city of Granada, where many doubled as either artisans or shopkeepers. Small-scale producers, by contrast, lived mostly on the land—either in the rural hamlets of Malacatoya, El Sitio/Los Malacos, and Nandaime, or in the villages of Diriomo and Diriá (see map 4). While small-scale producers from El Sitio/Los Malacos cultivated mostly corn and beans, those from Malacatoya were primarily dedicated to small-time cattle ranching, including the production of milk and cheese. Those of Diriomo and Diriá generally possessed small plots covered with fruit, vegetables, sugar cane, and, at times, coffee trees and tobacco plants. But above all they produced rice, corn, and beans. Finally, small-scale producers from Nandaime tended to live from both cereal production and cattle ranching; like their counterparts in Mala-catoya, they often sold their dairy products to medium- and large-scale producers who marketed them in the city of Granada. As these activities underscore, the peasantry in Nicaragua's most commercialized region had hardly become a landless rural proletariat. Still, many Granadan peasants were forced to wage a defensive struggle against the post-1870s expansion of elite landholdings. Under dollar diplomacy, this expansion came to a surprising halt.

The sudden termination of elite encroachment on peasant lands was especially noticeable in Granada's coffee sector. True, numerous peasants sold plots appropriate for coffee cultivation, particularly during the 1920s export boom. Yet much of this land was bought by fellow peasants. In 1925, the boom's apex, small- and medium-scale farmers sold thirty-eight properties in the broader Mombacho/Diriomo/Diriá area, where land suited for coffee cultivation was concentrated.[69] Thirty-three of these went to individuals from rural communities and only five to Granadan landlords. Most important, nonelite buyers succeeded in acquiring all those with coffee trees, thus enabling some small- and medium-scale producers to expand their coffee fincas. Even when nonelite coffee growers had their farms foreclosed, they frequently mobilized family resources to recover their lost land.

Consider the typical case of the Pavón family from Diriomo. In 1924, this family had been forced by the local judge to auction its mid-sized coffee finca in order to cancel outstanding debts owed by the family's recently deceased patriarch, Simón Pavón. The property was acquired for forty dollars by Eufracio Flores, another medium-scale farmer from Diriomo. After re-measuring the finca, Flores realized that it totaled 33 manzanas and not 18.5 manzanas as he and the Pavón family had originally assumed. Taking advantage of this error, Flores sought to resell the finca. He most likely first approached the neighboring coffee baron Sebastián Uriza, a prominent Conservative oligarch who would briefly be Nicaragua's president in 1926. Like other landlords, Uriza was then in dire financial straits and little disposed to expand his property. Unable to find a buyer, Flores divided the finca into various plots, averaging about three manzanas, and in the following years sold most of them to the Pavón family for a total of US$420. While Flores made a profit of nearly 1,000 percent from this sale, the Pavóns were able to recover about 85 percent of their former finca.[70] In contrast to the Pavóns, not a single Granadan landlord recovered a foreclosed coffee estate in the 1910s and 1920s.

This startling difference suggests just how much better equipped family-based growers were than wage-dependent planters in coping with the capital constraint that marked dollar diplomacy's rule in Nicaragua.

That dollar diplomacy inadvertently favored nonelite producers is also noticeable in the purchase by many medium-scale ranchers of lands freed by the breakup of large cattle estates in Granada. A paradigmatic case was the fragmentation of the Nandaime cattle hacienda La Camarona, which measured about three thousand manzanas. The process began in 1924 when large debts drove the family of the recently deceased Conservative oligarch Pablo Guadamuz to sell various hacienda tracts to medium-scale ranchers from the vicinity.[71] Much of this land was bought by the Lara family from Santa Teresa, a town in the department of Carazo located about ten miles northwest of Nandaime (see map 4). The last tract of La Camarona was sold in 1931 after Carlos Alberto Guadamuz—then considered by U.S. officials a wealthy and prominent politician[72]—defaulted on a loan; once again, the buyer came from the Lara family. As the contrasting fortunes of the Guadamuz and Lara families highlight, dollar diplomacy created an environment that enabled numerous medium-scale ranchers to strengthen their economic position at the cost of landlords.

Nothing better underscores the strength of nonelite producers than their acquisition of most farms sold in Granada during the 1920s agroexport boom. Typically, these land sales occurred in the subregions where land pressure was more limited. In 1925, for example, ninety-four registered rural properties changed hands in the department of Granada. Of all these sales, 6 percent occurred in the Mombacho, 46 percent in Diriomo/Diriá, 17 percent in Nandaime, 15 percent in Malacatoya, and 8 percent in El Sitio/Los Malacos.[73] Small- and medium-scale producers failed to get a single finca in the Mombacho and bought only about a third of those put on sale in Nandaime. By contrast, they fared much better in areas where landlord hegemony was weaker, as they bought 62 percent of the farms sold in El Sitio/Los Malacos, 79 percent of those offered in Dirioma/Diriá, and more than 90 percent in Malacatoya. If small- and medium-scale producers bought, overall, fewer properties from large producers than vice versa (5 and 10 farms respectively), they nonetheless acquired over twice as much land from large producers (at least 650 manzanas) than the latter did from them (320 manzanas).

This extraordinary activity attests to the dynamism of Nicaraguan peasant producers in a period when many of their Central American counterparts were on the defensive.[74] Of course, their dynamism had its limits. The relative decline of elite power did not reach the point where Nicaraguan peasants could purchase profitable lands en masse from impoverished landlords. As evident in the coffee fields of the Mombacho, the most valuable farmland remained concentrated in elite hands. But since many of its members went bankrupt, this elite consisted of anything but confident men.

Conclusion

In 1933, when dollar diplomacy was on the wane in Nicaragua, Granada's *El Correo* published a leading article titled "Crisis of Men."[75] This Conservative daily sought to settle accounts with the much despised dollar diplomats. Echoing longstanding elite lamentations, it claimed that dollar diplomats' restrictive fiscal and financial policies had thrown agricultural producers into a profound crisis. At first glance, this elite discourse seems puzzling since Nicaragua's rural-based economy enjoyed spectacular growth rates during the 1920s export boom. In certain ways *El Correo* was right, as Nicaragua's "crisis of men" had a real, material foundation, but the perception was only correct if we consider it a crisis of *elite* men. As chapter 7 will show, this crisis reflected male anxieties about the recent rise of the "modern woman." But above all, the crisis resulted from dollar diplomacy's "democratizing" impact on Nicaragua's rural class structures.

For leading dollar diplomats, there was nothing surprising about the fact that Nicaragua's nonelite farmers fared better than their elite counterparts under dollar diplomacy. For example, W. W. Cumberland claimed in his influential economic survey of 1927 that in "the long run a system of small landholdings yields far better economic as well as political and social results than do large plantations."[76] While Cumberland's views were rooted in an ideological bias for the Jeffersonian society of yeoman farmers, they accurately reflected the contrasting economic fortunes peasant and elite producers were experiencing during his stay in Nicaragua. Yet it would be wrong to suggest, as Cumberland did, that this difference was rooted simply in the inherently greater resilience of small farming.

Instead, Nicaragua's peasant producers benefited from three particularly deleterious, but unintended, effects dollar diplomacy had on elite power. First, by exacerbating intraelite conflicts, dollar diplomacy increased the political leverage of nonelite sectors. As a result, peasants were able to extract from the Conservative governments of the 1910s and 1920s not only favorable economic policies but also laws that enabled them to resist elite appropriation of their land and labor more easily. Second, dollar diplomats created a financial environment that unexpectedly better served the interests of peasant producers than those of the elite. In particular, the restrictive lending practices of the U.S.-controlled Banco Nacional militated against capital-intensive enterprises. Small- and medium-scale producers, by contrast, coped much better with this capital constraint as they generally used family rather than wage labor. And if they did have credit needs, these were modest enough to be satisfied by local moneylenders. Third, market conditions of the 1920s enabled many nonelite farmers to export grain and livestock to the rest of the isthmus. The Central American demand for Nicaraguan foodstuffs resulted largely from the radically different nature of dollar diplomacy in these countries. If dollar diplomacy brought Nicaragua nothing but U.S. financial supervision, in the rest of the isthmus it entailed primarily the massive influx of U.S. portfolio investment—an influx that significantly weakened the region's domestic-use agriculture, the traditional domain of peasant producers. As the next chapter will show, dollar diplomacy's "democratizing" socioeconomic impact so greatly unnerved Nicaraguan landlords that it helped trigger the anti-American turn of the country's most pro-U.S. elites.

7 Cultural Anti-Americanism

The Caballeros Católicos' Crusade against U.S.
Missionaries, the "Modern Woman," and the
"Bourgeois Spirit"

IN 1931, THE YOUNG BUT INFLUENTIAL Granadan oligarch José Coronel Urtecho published the manifesto "Against the Bourgeois Spirit" in the country's leading Conservative newspaper, *El Diario Nicaragüense*.[1] Coronel Urtecho called on Nicaraguans to defend their nationality by waging "war" against the native "bourgeoisie" and its modernizing "spirit." These forces had facilitated the U.S. occupation and thus brought unprecedented ruin to their country, he charged. Many Nicaraguans took this oligarchic scion at his word and viewed the influential treatise as the mark of a new, elite outlook constructed against U.S. ideals of modernity. No doubt, Coronel Urtecho's staunch opposition to liberal democracy was a relatively recent phenomenon (see chapter 8). But there was nothing new about his attack against the Americanized, cosmopolitan spirit then prevailing among the rich, nor about his identification of the nation's traditions with premodern, patriarchal values rooted in the Spanish colonial order. More than the mark of new trends, Coronel Urtecho's 1931 manifesto celebrated and called public attention to a cultural anti-Americanism that some of the country's most prominent men, the Caballeros Católicos (Catholic Knights), had been developing since the end of World War I.

Nicaragua's antibourgeois spirit mirrored the reactionary nationalism espoused by upper classes throughout Latin America during the Roaring Twenties. Staunchly Catholic, Latin America's antimodern elites stood out for their moralizing crusade against the "modern woman" and other "vices" of modernity allegedly emanating from the United States. For most scholars, the rise of antimodernism in postwar Latin America stemmed largely from upper-class anxieties over the rapid socioeconomic and political change the continent was then experiencing.[2] Urbanization, economic modernization, spreading consumerism, popular mobilization, and expansion of the state are some of the forces most often mentioned. Elite attacks on modern lifestyles also proliferated as a result of the postwar revolution in communications. With the expansion of the film, record, magazine, and radio industries,

Latin Americans suddenly enjoyed more extensive and speedier exposure to the newest foreign trends in music, dance, fashion, and so on. It was largely against this postwar spread of "modern conditions" that conservative elites throughout Latin America constructed a new, more agrarian-based and inward-looking image of the nation.

If Nicaragua's antibourgeois spirit matched cultural trends elsewhere in Latin America, there was also something unique about it. Nicaragua's anti-modern elites did not have a long history of attacking U.S. ideals of modernity. In fact, the Nicaraguans who spearheaded the antibourgeois spirit were Conservative oligarchs from Granada—the country's wealthiest and most Americanized elites, whose forefathers had stood out for their cosmopolitan, modernizing views. Conservatives' surprising embrace of cultural anti-Americanism was complexly rooted. It certainly had much to do with the postwar spread of new U.S. cultural goods and practices. But it also reflected their anxieties over the dramatic rise of U.S.-based Protestant missions. Above all, Conservatives' anti-American turn responded to the "crisis of men" brought about by dollar diplomacy's peculiar attack on the authority of Nicaragua's most powerful elite sector.

From Liberal Conservatives to Caballeros Católicos

The antibourgeois spirit that flourished in Nicaragua during the 1920s did not appear out of thin air. Nor was it a simple throwback to the anticosmo-politanism valorized by late-nineteenth-century *iglesieros*. Instead, it represented a new antiliberal ideology developed by a small but influential group of Conservative oligarchs at the turn of the century. Not only did they attack liberal principles such as the separation of church and state, these oligarchs also voiced anticapitalist and social reformist sentiments. In doing so, they were heavily influenced by Catholic social thought expressed in the 1891 papal encyclical *Rerum novarum*. This antiliberal tendency was strengthened by the U.S. interventions of 1910 and 1912.

Still, elite Conservatives of the early 1910s had yet to fully embrace the antibourgeois spirit that would pervade the 1920s. For example, their attacks on the social consequences of economic liberalism were relatively timid. And the effects of liberalism's cultural project of modernity hardly troubled them. Proclerical Conservatives of the early 1910s thus talked little about the need for a thoroughgoing moral regeneration of society. Nor did they advocate an inward-looking agrarian nationalism that exalted the patriarchal, rural idyll of the colonial past. On the contrary, as the heated debates over the controversial U.S.-Nicaraguan loan treaties of 1911 and 1912 illustrate, proclerical Conservatives explicitly defended the longstanding nationalist ideal of a cosmopolitan Nicaragua.

Attacks on elite power eventually eroded many Conservatives' faith that a cosmopolitan nation could be crafted. The first blow came with the disastrous civil war of 1912, which sealed Nicaragua's status as a U.S. protectorate. And if this did not suffice, the First World War weakened its coffee industry— then considered the chief engine of the country's march to progress. The postwar economic recovery of Nicaragua did not end the cultural malaise plaguing the Conservative elite. In fact, the opposite occurred. As elsewhere in Latin America, elite anxieties were partly exacerbated by the recent rise of organized labor. Many Conservatives also feared that the postwar expansion in the missionary activities of U.S. Protestants gravely endangered their country's national identity. In addition, they were greatly troubled by the "immoral" cultural practices (elite) women began to adopt after the war's end. But perhaps most important, the postwar growth in elite anxieties was a response to the unexpected ways that dollar diplomacy weakened elite's economic power. As more and more landlords were driven to financial ruin, elite ideals of a cosmopolitan nation seemed less tenable. Confronting this crisis, many elite Nicaraguans reinforced their self-identification with things modern. A smaller but powerful group of elite Conservatives led by Granada's Caballeros Católicos reacted differently by embracing antimodern ideals ever more forcefully.

Granada's Conservative oligarchs established the all-male Liga de Caballeros Católicos in January 1918.[3] The timing was hardly a coincidence. The Liga's founding occurred just as the country's economic crisis hit its nadir and U.S. Baptists began to expand their missionary activities in Nicaragua. In addition, this elite association emerged at a time of heightened labor mobilization that led to the founding of Nicaragua's first socialist party (the Partido Obrero) and national labor federation (the Federación Obrera Nicaragüense). At about the same time, Nicaraguan women also established the country's first feminist organization and women's magazine. These moves only heightened the anxieties of the patriarchal Caballeros. Finally, in 1917 Granada became the new home of Jesuits recently expelled from Mexico. Deeply scarred by their encounter with revolutionary modernity, these foreigners played a key role in encouraging Granada's Conservative elites to band together as Caballeros Católicos and embrace the Vatican's incipient crusade against "modern conditions."[4]

From Granada, the Liga de Caballeros Católicos quickly spread to other major urban centers and became a fixture in the lives of many upper-class Nicaraguans. Meeting once a month, its members organized numerous religious activities, including processions, regular prayer meetings, and annual spiritual retreats. They also founded newspapers and civic organizations geared toward the lower classes. The Liga attracted some Liberals but the overwhelming majority of its members belonged to the ruling Conservative Party. In all likelihood, the Liga was an elite-dominated organization closed to poorer Nicaraguans. Why else was it widely known as an organization of "nobles and millionaires"?[5] According to the scant data available, the Liga's size in different communities varied from at least seventy-five members in Granada to about thirty in the smaller provincial town of Jinotepe in the department of Carazo.[6] Although the Liga represented a minority of elite Nicaraguans, it wielded enormous influence. Its members included not only some of the country's richest merchants and landlords but many leading Conservative politicians, such as President Emiliano Chamorro (1917–20) and his successor (and uncle) Diego Manuel Chamorro.

From the start, the Caballeros Católicos sought to achieve, as an anticlerical paper fearfully put it, "hegemony over Nicaragua's public sphere."[7] In addition to disseminating their views via newspapers like *El Católico*, they promoted Catholic practices within the populace by helping priests establish recreation centers, libraries, and schools (for children and for adults), by financing charity organizations like the Society of Saint Vincent de Paul, and by sponsoring Catholic lay groups such as women's Catholic social action (Acción Social Católica de Damas y Señoritas), the Hijas de María, and Catholic workers' circles (Círculo Católico de Obreros). The primary objectives of the Caballeros Católicos may be summed up as follows: first, to defend their country's "true," Catholic identity by curbing the spread of Protestantism and Freemasonry; second, to prevent Nicaraguans, particularly elite women, from falling prey to the vices of modernity; and third, to promote the material and spiritual conditions of the "poor," who were considered the principal victims of capitalism.

The formation of the Liga de Caballeros Católicos reveals how strongly elite Conservatives had turned against the ideal of a cosmopolitan nation-state. While some Caballeros Católicos were longstanding proclerical zealots, many others had only recently shed their anticlerical views. The Liga's ranks included numerous Conservative politicians who, in 1911, had opposed congressional attempts to declare Catholicism the state religion. By the time they joined the Liga, they obviously had switched sides on this volatile issue. Perhaps the most significant change of heart occurred with Carlos Cuadra Pasos, the country's second most important Conservative politician after Emiliano Chamorro. In the early 1910s Cuadra Pasos opposed Chamorro's proclerical agenda, fearing that it would block the country's political and economic modernization. But by 1918 his newly found proclerical credentials were so strong that Granada's Caballeros Católicos elected him their first president. Unfortunately, Conservatives like Cuadra Pasos never truly explained why they shed their liberal views. But we do know that he and other liberal Conservatives had become troubled by their country's alleged slide into what they viewed as a moral abyss. Initially, they believed that this moral decay was an outgrowth of the peculiar brand of political liberalism that had marked the lengthy dictatorship of José Santos Zelaya (1893–1909). But as Conservatives' rule wore on, they increasingly faulted the U.S.-derived "modern conditions" for corrupting Nicaragua's social fabric.[8]

Defending a Catholic Nicaragua

The growth of antiliberal cultural tendencies among an elite sector long renowned for its worldly views first manifested itself in the Caballeros Católicos' campaign against the most cosmopolitan association of the era, the Freemasons. Reflecting their liberal spirit, many upper-class Conservatives had become Freemasons during the late nineteenth century. In the early 1910s, prominent Conservatives such as President Adolfo Díaz (1911–16) still wore their Masonic affiliation proudly. But this was before the Caballeros Católicos began to blame Freemasons' cosmopolitan and secular spirit for producing society's moral ills.[9] By 1925 Freemasonry had become such a stigma that the newly elected Conservative President Carlos Solórzano frantically denied press accounts that he was a Freemason.[10] Anti-Masonic sentiments were not confined to Conservative politicians. In fact, they were so widespread that once the Masonic affiliation of a Granadan physician was exposed many of his clients refused to see him again for fear that "the devil dwelled in his clinic."[11]

However virulent their anti-Masonic campaign, the Caballeros Católicos' embrace of an inward-looking, antimodern nationality was more fundamentally shaped by the long and bitter crusade they waged against U.S. Protestant missionaries. Of course, nationalist opposition to U.S. Protestantism was hardly new to Nicaragua. It was already present in the era of William Walker. But anti-Protestantism gained strength in 1917, when U.S. Baptists started to missionize western Nicaragua, the country's most Hispanized and populated zone. The arrival of these U.S. missionaries was a direct result of the "Congress on Christian Work in Latin America," held in Panama in February 1916.[12] At this congress, the main U.S. Protestant denominations divided Latin America into different zones in order to facilitate its "evangelization." For no apparent reason, they allotted Nicaragua to the Northern Baptist Convention based in New York.

At first, U.S. missionaries of the all-male American Baptist Home Mission Society and the Women's American Baptist Home Mission Society lived and worked in Managua, the country's capital. They included not just ministers but also physicians, nurses, and schoolteachers. From Managua, the Baptist mission quickly expanded to other urban centers and the countryside, particularly the coffee fields in the southern uplands that stretched toward Carazo and Granada. While they built churches, these missionaries also founded schools and health clinics whose doors were open to all Nicaraguans, regardless of their faith, income, or social status. Within ten years, the Baptists became the largest Protestant denomination in western Nicaragua, surpassing another U.S. group—the Central American Mission—that had arrived in 1902.[13] Despite their success, U.S. Baptist missionaries hardly converted a large number of Nicaraguans to their faith; as late as 1933 only 735 Nicaraguans (about 0.1 percent of the total population) formally belonged to a Baptist church.[14]

Yet conversion was not what most perturbed the Caballeros Católicos. Instead, they feared the ecumenical institutions that Baptists were building throughout western Nicaragua. By most accounts, Baptist schools and clinics were quite popular among what U.S. missionaries called the "proletariat."[15] In 1923, for example, about eight hundred children attended Baptist day and Sunday schools.[16] To the Caballeros Católicos, such aggressive institution-building indicated that U.S. missionaries were bent less on "Protestantizing" Nicaragua than on "de-Catholicizing" it.[17] The Caballeros Católicos frequently identified "de-Catholization" with the spread of "immorality." To drive their point home, they stressed how the homeland of the U.S. mission-aries suffered high divorce rates and thus a profound crisis of what they considered to be society's most sacred institution, the family. With regard to their own country, the Caballeros Católicos were mainly troubled by the apparent ease with which Protestant-run schools and health clinics lured poorer Nicaraguans into adopting "modern" and anti-Catholic views. "The Fatherland can expect nothing," the Caballeros Católicos admonished, "from those citizens who . . . because of their urge to absorb everything new, and thus appear as modern and unconcerned men, commit the cowardly crime of abandoning the religion of their parents."[18]

The Caballeros Católicos' anti-Protestantism was not solely dictated by their concern for the moral state of their compatriots. To them, de-Catholization also represented an Anglo-Saxon attack on Nicaraguan sov-ereignty and on the "Latin race" more generally.[19] Accordingly, U.S. Protes-tant missionaries represented the "spiritual vanguard" of the U.S. "conquest" of Latin America. As a Caballero Católico from Granada stated, "The Yankees know very well . . . that it is extremely difficult to convert individuals of Spanish descent into sincere Protestants; what they are really trying to do is to de-Catholize the common folk in order to weaken the strength of our race [and] transform [Latin] Americans into a conquered people."[20] Of course, such claims were rejected by the few Nicaraguans who converted to Protes-tantism; their beliefs and practices, they countered, represented modernity and could thus only strengthen the Nicaraguan nation.[21] Yet however loudly Nicaraguan Protestants made their case, the Caballeros Católicos insisted that "to defend the Catholic religion is to defend the nationality."[22]

In developing their anti-U.S. outlook, the Caballeros Católicos capitalized on how U.S. missionaries represented themselves to the Nicaraguan public. They put to good use the deep anti-Catholic sentiments harbored by many if not most U.S. missionaries then active in western Nicaragua.[23] The Caba-lleros Católicos also exploited missionaries' self-portrayal as agents of mod-ernization. Whether active in a church, school, or health clinic, Protestant missionaries stood out for their zeal to transform Nicaraguans' customs.[24] Nowhere was this passion more noticeable than in their efforts to "uplift" Nicaraguan women, particularly by teaching them "modern" notions of cooking, personal hygiene, sanitation, and other aspects of household man-agement. As one female Baptist missionary put it, "the practical lessons in domestic science and home making [are] the most important part of our educational work" in Nicaragua.[25] For the Caballeros Católicos, this "educational work" represented nothing less than an attack on Nicaraguan nationality, since they "opened the doors of the Fatherland [*Patria*] to the enemy."[26] Indeed, U.S. missionaries' quest to "uplift" Nicaraguan women built on the nationalist campaign that their churches—together with government agencies, corporations, and labor organizations—were then waging in the United States to "Americanize" female immigrants, particularly those from eastern Europe and Mexico.[27] Such campaigns targeted women largely because Americanizers saw mothers as "primarily responsible for the transmission of values in the home."[28] Since the Caballeros Católicos also linked motherhood with nationhood, it is not surprising that they vehemently opposed U.S. missionaries' attempt to transform the values and practices of Nicaraguan women.

The Caballeros Católicos pursued their anti-Protestant crusade by various means. In Granada and elsewhere, they used proclerical newspapers to denounce the "de-Catholization" efforts of U.S. missionaries. They also organized boisterous demonstrations to shut down Protestant churches, schools, and health clinics, or to prevent them from opening in the first place. In addition, the Caballeros Católicos blacklisted native Protestants or Catholics who sold goods and services to U.S. missionaries. The Caballeros Católicos called on the local populace not just to boycott these merchants' businesses but to "completely isolate and eliminate them."[29] Many proclerical zealots took the Caballeros Católicos at their word and began to physically attack U.S. missionaries and their Nicaraguan followers. Such acts ranged from simple stone-throwing to fatal machete attacks and the destruction of Protestant-run institutions. By 1926 this violence became so widespread that it led the American Baptist Home Mission Society to brand Nicaragua as perhaps the most dangerous missionary field in Latin America.[30]

Much of Nicaragua's anti-Protestant violence occurred in the countryside and targeted Baptist missionaries. Yet the most celebrated attack took place in the city of Granada and involved U.S. appointees of the Central American Mission. This Dallas-based group first arrived in Granada in 1922 to open a day-school and a meeting place on the city's outskirts. From the start, the missionaries were constantly harassed by proclerical forces. But their troubles increased dramatically in June 1925 when they decided to move their headquarters to the center of the city—a space traditionally reserved for the local elite. Within a week, fifty Caballeros Católicos and upper-class women joined the city's bishop in writing a letter of protest to the mayor. They claimed that this "house of Protestant *evangelization*" so greatly insulted their religion and society that it obliged them to defend their "conscience unjustly attacked by a foreign enemy."[31] The Caballeros' main daily reinforced this threat when it published a letter in which the bishop warned the U.S. missionaries to leave Granada, "where in a scandalous fashion you have undertaken the despicable task of propagating your errors by means of money and thus of carrying out an immoral trade in souls."[32]

The U.S. missionaries failed to heed the bishop's threat. In consequence, the Caballeros Católicos and their female allies intensified the struggle against the Central American Mission. They were led by the fifty-nine-year-old matron Isabel Argüello de Cardenal. Widely known as "Isabel la Católica," Argüello was the wife of the extremely wealthy Caballero Católico Salvador Cardenal and mother of Julio Cardenal, then the vice mayor of Granada (in 1928 he would become the vice presidential candidate of the Conservative Party). Argüello and her oligarchic followers first sought to interrupt the Protestants' worship by congregating outside of their mission and singing religious hymns. Later, or so the mission's pastor charged, women of Granada's most prominent Conservative families started to hurl stones, "excrement and other filth" at the U.S. missionaries and their parishioners, while others hit them with "sticks."[33] Finally, on 19 July 1925, a Jesuit priest appeared at the doorsteps of the mission's chapel and publicly warned its U.S. members that if they did not leave Granada immediately "blood would surely flow in the streets."[34] The next day, at four in the morning, a bomb exploded at the door of the mission's building. Although the bomb damaged only the building, the missionaries were convinced that it had been intended to kill them.[35] When a subsequent mass demonstration once again turned violent, the Nicaraguan government finally sent troops from Managua to quell the conflict. But even this deployment failed to pacify Granada's Catholic zealots who continued to stone and smear human excrement on the mission's building. After four months of terror, the Central American Mission finally gave in and left Granada for good in September 1925. Proclerical forces throughout Nicaragua celebrated their departure as an important victory for the nation.

It was thus against this violent backdrop that the Caballeros Católicos embraced a religiously based anti-Americanism. Their newly found nationalist outlook reflected the efforts of other upper-class Latin Americans to collapse anti-Protestantism with anti-Americanism.[36] But the anti-Americanism of

Nicaragua's Caballeros stood out in two key ways. First, it was articulated by individuals most associated with U.S. imperial rule—a fact that often surprised newly arrived U.S. missionaries. Equally puzzling, the Caballeros Católicos belonged to the regional elite that had spearheaded Nicaragua's Americanization during the late nineteenth century. Their postwar evolution into critics of U.S. cultural intervention was therefore rather peculiar.

At the same time, the anti-Americanism of the Caballeros Católicos contrasted sharply with the anti-U.S. sentiments harbored by many other Nicaraguans. True, both forms of anti-Americanism targeted dollar diplomacy, then the main mode of U.S. intervention in Nicaragua. But most Nicaraguan nationalists tended to attack dollar diplomacy's economic impact. In particular, they maintained that the restrictive fiscal and financial policies of dollar diplomats inhibited the growth of Nicaragua's coffee industry and thus the country's march toward modernity. The Caballeros Católicos, by contrast, shared dollar diplomats' antistatist economic outlook but denounced them for spreading cultural practices that undermined Nicaragua's "spiritual" condition. Above all, they criticized dollar diplomats for promoting the work of U.S. Protestant proselytizers, whom they scorned as "dollar missionaries."[37] If most Nicaraguan nationalists embraced economic nationalism, the Caballeros Católicos espoused a cultural nationalism that stressed their country's need for a moral, not economic, regeneration.

Campaigning against the "Modern Woman"

In the eyes of the local populace, the most outstanding characteristic of the Caballeros Católicos was not their anti-Protestant crusade but their campaign against the modern lifestyles then so popular in elite circles. As elsewhere in Latin America, the postwar revolution in communications and the 1920s economic boom enabled elite Nicaraguans to consume a greater number of goods and leisure activities deemed "modern." Such goods ranged from automobiles, phonographs, and radios to silk stockings, sleeveless dresses, and lipstick, while "modern" forms of entertainment consisted largely of going to movie theaters and dance halls, playing or watching sports, and cruising in motorcars.[38] To be sure, the Caballeros Católicos adopted many of these goods and leisure pursuits during the Roaring Twenties. Still, they opposed the proliferation of modern lifestyles, for they believed that it drove many elites to moral ruin. And since these lifestyles emanated largely from the United States, the Caballeros' moralizing crusade only reinforced their nascent cultural anti-Americanism.

The Caballeros Católicos were so concerned about the alleged crisis of elite morality precisely because it seemed to accelerate the populace's waning respect for social hierarchy (*autoridad*). This fear is exemplified by the way the leading Conservative paper *El Diario Nicaragüense* reported Granada's reaction to the execution of a murderer in January 1920. Staged as a mass spectacle, this execution caused great consternation, for it was the first to be carried out in Granada since 1871. Many speculated that the assassin, a fifty-three-year-old bricklayer who had fatally stabbed a local moneylender, would not have been executed had he been "rich." For *El Diario Nicaragüense*, this popular belief "was the greatest criticism that could be made against the upper class," as it suggested that elites were in danger of losing their moralizing influence over the general populace. "The common folk measure and weigh," the paper warned, "the habits of the ruling classes, as they are the models to imitate."[39] And since the authority of the ruling Conservatives was already weak due to their association with U.S. imperial rule, it could only further erode if their members continued to make moral mistakes. This perception help explains why the Caballeros Católicos were so troubled about high society's alleged slide into a moral abyss. They were not just waging a moral crusade, they feared the decline of their power.

This equation was most apparent in the campaign the Caballeros Católicos waged against the "modern woman"—an image/identity of femininity that emerged throughout much of the world in the 1920s.[40] The Caballeros Católicos certainly associated the "modern woman" with feminist demands for greater political rights and economic independence.[41] But like most Nicaraguans, they identified her primarily with the new female consumption and leisure habits that appeared in the postwar era and were most strongly embraced by elite women (see figure 13). Such habits included daring new fashions, especially lower cut dresses, short skirts, and pants; short, bobbed haircuts; more sensual dance forms like the fox-trot; and sports that had hitherto been the exclusive domain of men.

According to the Caballeros, Nicaragua's "modern woman" emanated principally from the United States. And in many ways they were right, for the image of the "modern woman" was spread by the wives and daughters of dollar diplomats and U.S. businessmen as well as female U.S. missionaries. In addition, she was popularized by local merchants who imported women's

13. "Modern" Nicaraguan women, 1927. *Courtesy of U.S. National Archives.*

fashion from the United States, and by the many Nicaraguans who traveled to and from the United States. For example, basketball, which quickly became the leading women's sport in Nicaragua, was introduced in 1920 by Nicaraguans who had studied in the United States.[42]

For the most part, however, Nicaraguans learned about the U.S.-styled "modern woman" through two means of communication that boomed after World War I and helped transmit the "American way of life" throughout Latin America: the film and magazine industries. By the late 1920s, movie theaters had been established in most of Nicaragua's urban centers, while in smaller towns and some rural villages movies were mainly shown on outdoor screens. Moviegoers generally came from all social classes, though urban audiences were usually segregated, with the rich in the front and the poor seated at the very back of the theater in the section commonly known as the "chicken coop."[43] As in much of Latin America, nearly all films screened were U.S. productions. Magazines, by contrast, were mostly of Nicaraguan origin, but they frequently carried advertisements for Hollywood films and other U.S. products, as well as articles and photos originally published in the United States. These magazines and films so greatly helped spread the image of the "modern woman" that they became prime targets of the Caballeros Católicos' moralizing campaign. For example, in places where movies were shown outdoors, the Caballeros and their supporters sought to harass moviegoers by parading around the premises with lighted candles and singing hymns as loudly as possible.[44]

Elite men waged such a fierce battle over the "modern woman" largely because they felt that (elite) women embodied the nation's most essential values and were thus a barometer of its social and cultural condition. For her many defenders, the "modern woman" expressed the continuous viability of a cosmopolitan nationalist project.[45] To the Caballeros Católicos, however, she stood for the crisis of patriarchy then plaguing society, particularly high society. Like other conservative elites in Latin America, these Caballeros believed that the authority of high society hinged primarily on the "honorable" lifestyle of its women.[46] And in their eyes, the cultural practices of the "modern woman" undermined elite authority in two key ways. First, these practices accentuated elite women's sexuality and thus promoted female adultery ("free love") and other acts of "immorality." In addition, they masculinized elite women, in the process blurring the "natural" differences between male and female that the Caballeros Católicos deemed crucial to society's moral health.[47] But if the Caballeros launched their moralizing campaign against the "modern woman" as a battle to restore elite authority, they eventually transformed it into a crusade against U.S. cultural influence more broadly.

Their moralizing discourse notwithstanding, it is important to stress that the Caballeros Católicos were hardly models of propriety. On the contrary, many belonged to an oligarchy whose members were notorious for their predatory sexual practices. Not surprisingly, the hypocrisy of the Caballeros was gleefully denounced by their political opponents. Consider, for example, the Liberal Juan Manuel Mendoza's attack on the Caballero Católico Vicente Rappacciolli, an influential Conservative senator and rich coffee baron, as a "vulgar, brutal tyrant . . . who is cruel with women and cannot live without being caressed by them. But because people tolerate the transgressions [desaciertos] of the rich, many lead lives fatally marked by reprehensible acts and yet are considered to be good, impeccable men."[48] For Nicaraguans, nothing better evidenced such promiscuous practices than the numerous illegitimate children that oligarchs like Rappacciolli fathered but refused to recognize. Although most Nicaraguan towns had brothels, oligarchs tended to prey on poorer women who worked for them, either as domestic servants in their mansions or as laborers on their landed estates; once these women became pregnant they were usually fired.[49] Rarely did elites' predatory sexual practices find their way into official records. Still, they were anything but hidden. Elite men often boasted about their sexual "conquests."[50] This was not surprising in a society as patriarchal as U.S.-occupied Nicaragua, where male adultery was legally condoned but female adultery harshly penalized.[51] Indeed, as historian Jeffrey Gould has shown for the northwestern region of Chinandega, the ability of elite men to sexually coerce young, poorer women was a way for them to display their "class power."[52] The erosion of this power, not the putative spread of "licentious" sexual practices in which the Caballeros Católicos themselves participated, led Conservative oligarchs to combat so intensely the rise of the "modern woman."

The Caballeros Católicos attacked the U.S.-based "modern woman" on several fronts. At home, they tried to prevent their daughters and other female members of the household from embracing the habits of the "modern woman" by having them join religious associations, particularly the Hijas de María. They also prohibited them from committing "immoral" acts such as playing sports, reading "racy" novels, smoking cigarettes, drinking alcohol in public, attending dances where "modern" music (especially jazz) was played, wearing "sexy" dresses, or riding in cars with young men. As a Granadan Hija de María of the era recalled, her grandfather did "everything" to prevent her from becoming a "modern woman"; he even prohibited her from riding a bicycle for he did not want her to venture out into the streets alone.[53] In addition, the Caballeros Católicos railed in proclerical newspapers against women's enthusiastic embrace of new canons of fashion, dance, and physical fitness. Some also published prescriptive novels in order to cure, as one Caballero put it, "the countless ills that plague modern society."[54] Many more worked closely with Catholic priests and bishops, who not only used the pulpit to denounce the "modern woman" and her promoters, such as the movie industry, but refused to give the sacrament to women who went to church wearing sleeveless blouses and skirts that did not reach the ankles.[55] Moreover, as long as the U.S.-backed Conservatives governed, the Caballeros Católicos could count on local police forces to close down "indecent" dance halls and arrest (elite) women caught practicing such terrible "modern" habits as riding in cars late at night.[56] The Caballeros even took their moralizing crusade to Congress, where they passed laws designed to defend female honor. Such efforts included one law that sought to prohibit women and men, if not previously acquainted, from talking to each other on the streets. So notorious was this 1918 measure that it galvanized Nicaragua's nascent feminist movement and was quickly overturned by the Supreme Court.[57]

To their dismay, the anxiety the Caballeros Católicos expressed over women's "modern" lifestyles was not universally shared by their class. And since elite men had long upheld similar ideals of femininity, this disagreement reveals how high society had become culturally more divided during the U.S. occupation. In the 1911 debate over the religious question, for example, rival congressmen represented women in similar terms. Whether pro- or anticlerical, they generally believed that women were morally more "pure" and "innocent," and hence more pious than men. But they also deemed women more spiritual, emotional, and superstitious. Partly for these reasons men of all political hues denied women the vote.[58] The male consensus over femininity began to crack at the end of World War I. First in September 1916 a Liberal paper from León openly supported female suffrage. Then in December 1917 a small but prominent group of Liberals criticized their leaders for preventing women from voting in party elections.[59] By the mid-1920s the demand for female suffrage had become forceful enough that not only the Liberal Party but numerous dissident Conservatives openly supported it. In fact, in 1923 President Bartolomé Martínez, a Conservative, proclaimed himself a "feminist" and appointed the first woman ever to a Nicaraguan presidential cabinet: Juana Molina de Froeman (1894–1934), a graduate of New York's Columbia University, became Vice Minister of Education.[60]

Yet proclerical Conservatives stubbornly resisted the call for female suffrage. In a speech to female students, the prominent Conservative senator Carlos Cuadra Pasos explained why he and other proclerical oligarchs rejected feminists' political demands. He called feminism "one of the gravest problems troubling mankind" and maintained that women's intervention in the public sphere should be restricted to the cultural domain. Women's public mission, this Granadan oligarch sternly warned, was not to promote political and social change by exerting their rights of "citizenship." Instead, women should use their moral superiority to ensure that the world would become more "feminine" and hence more "cultured" and "civilized."[61] Not surprisingly, Nicaraguan feminists—much inspired by their U.S. colleagues— denounced the views of Cuadra Pasos and his like as "reactionary" and antagonistic to the "modern spirit" they believed was triumphantly advancing elsewhere in the "civilized" world.[62]

For many Nicaraguans, the clash between "modern" and "reactionary" ideals of femininity was most noticeable in the conflict triggered by women's growing participation in sports. Unheard of at the turn-of-the-century, female athleticism boomed in Nicaragua during the 1920s, with basketball quickly emerging as the most popular women's sport and tennis a distant second. Women of all social classes watched sports, but most female athletes came from the upper classes and were usually in their late teens or early twenties. To their many male supporters, women's sports were an important expression of Nicaragua's march to progress, as female athletes stood out for their modern ways: They were independent, worldly, strong, and healthy. As the magazine *El Gráfico* argued, sporting women represented a "head-on challenge" to the traditional notion that women were "weak," "tender," and "delicate."[63] So readily did prominent men accept women's sports that in 1924 a Liberal presidential candidate, Leonardo Argüello, included their promotion in his political platform. Believing that modernity meant greater gender equality, this future president of Nicaragua (1948) proclaimed that sports were not only for men but also for women, on whom "weigh false notions and prejudices . . . that greatly restrict their rights and prerogatives."[64]

No doubt, the "false notions and prejudices" that Argüello and other elite men criticized were those expressed by the Caballeros Católicos. As with "modern" fashion, the Caballeros claimed that physical recreation would masculinize women, transforming them into the deformed *marimacha* (a female cross between man and woman) and blurring gender differences.[65] "The day nears," a prominent Caballero Católico polemicized, "when all of us will need to carry a sign on our back, saying: I am a man, I am a woman."[66] If frightened by the alleged masculinity of athletic women, the Caballeros Católicos worried even more about their skimpy uniforms. In their view, any outfit exposing much of women's legs, arms, shoulders, chest, and so on, provoked "lustful glances" and, in the process, damaged their "soul with the mire of impurity."[67] According to a female basketball player from Granada, some Caballeros even shared the belief of the city's bishop that most men went to female sporting events solely to "look under the athletes' short skirts and peek at their underwear."[68] To these wardens of female purity, women as "scantly" dressed as female athletes could only worsen "the general corruption of morals" (see figure 14).[69]

Despite the Caballeros's attacks, women's participation in sports flourished during the 1920s. Even daughters and wives of proclerical moralizers joined

14. Female basketball
players, ca. 1927.
*Courtesy of U.S. National
Archives.*

the basketball teams then burgeoning in Nicaragua's urban centers. Evidently, many did so against the will of their fathers and husbands.[70] Such was the case of the Granadan Lola Vijil, an Hija de María and one of the best basketball players to emerge in the 1920s. Vijil played for the city's main basketball club, the mighty Flor de Lys, which competed regularly against Granada's two other clubs (5 Stars and Excelsior) as well as against teams from Managua, León, Masaya, Diriamba, and Corinto. Like most of her teammates, Vijil was of oligarchic origin (her great-grandfather was the famous pro-Walker priest Agustín Vijil). Still, the Flor de Lys was extremely popular and attracted to its games and practices numerous fans, male and female, rich and poor, young and old. In fact, so many spectators watched their games that bleachers had to be installed. Fans also celebrated the team's frequent victories at evening parties where young men and women danced the fox-trot. But even though Lola was the team's star (as its top scorer), every time she left the house to play basketball her father, Francisco, went "berserk." A prominent merchant and publicist, Francisco Vijil (1880–1940) also happened to be one of Granada's most vocal Caballeros Católicos. Out of principle, he thus opposed women's playing basketball. But what angered him most was that his daughter was famous not just for her basketball talents but for flaunting her "sex appeal" on the court. Vijil's inability to prevent his daughter from playing basketball was humiliating and only increased Lola's fame as a "free woman" in the eyes of her fans. The Vijil family was not alone. Countless other young elite women defied their fathers by joining the popular basketball teams.[71]

In the end, then, the Caballeros Católicos failed to prevent many elite women from embracing the "immoral" habits of the "modern woman." On the contrary, women's sports, modern fashion styles, and even "indecent" dance halls thrived during the U.S. occupation. In addition, numerous upper-class women, including Miss Nicaragua 1933, increased their independence by joining the labor market—a phenomenon hitherto limited to non-elite women. The remarkable rise of Nicaragua's "modern woman" in the face of many obstacles led the country's leading women's magazine to state: "The woman of yesterday is very different from that of today who, conscious of the right given to her by nature, thinks that she is an individual capable of working and supporting herself independently."[72] Echoing this conclusion, two women of Granada's Conservative oligarchy who played sports during the 1920s recall that they felt much more "liberated" than their mothers' generation.[73] In spite of the fierce moralizing campaign waged by the Caballeros Católicos and the Church, they had been able to embrace "everything new," socialize on their own, and become gainfully employed. Although they did not identify as "feminists," both firmly believed that they grew up as "modern" women.

Perhaps no one could better judge the successful rise of the "modern woman" than the Caballeros Católicos themselves: As their spokesman Pedro Joaquín Cuadra Chamorro (1887–1956) complained in a 1928 speech to female students, "whoever has even a little knowledge of the world . . . can with profound sadness say *adiós* to the old patriarchal customs, almost all of which are now gone forever."[74] For the Caballeros Católicos, the apparent erosion of "old patriarchal customs" was best exemplified by the triumphant rise of the U.S.-based "modern woman."

Redefining Elite Masculinity and the Nation

If the transformation of elite femininity troubled primarily a small but powerful group of oligarchs, dollar diplomacy's deleterious impact on elites' economic fortunes led not just the Caballeros Católicos but many other rich men to fret over their own, male identity. As we have seen, Liberal elites tended to counter these anxieties by identifying ever more strongly with "modern" economic values, particularly the culture of coffee. At the same time, they strove to represent their political rivals, the ruling Conservatives, as stalwarts of economic "backwardness." Oddly, many Conservative oligarchs reinforced this recasting of mythical elite divisions, for they also came to conceive of themselves as anything but what they truly were: the country's economic vanguard. No longer idealizing the coffee entrepreneur, they tended to celebrate instead the "backward" but "benevolent" cattle hacendado as the very definition of manliness. In the process, they more strongly embraced an inward-looking vision of the nation constructed against U.S. ideals of modernity.

Initially, this shift in elite outlook was most noticeable in the way the Caballeros Católicos began to attack the capitalist culture of coffee. If many elite Nicaraguans continued to celebrate the coffee finca as the symbol of progress, the Caballeros Católicos increasingly branded it a site of exploitation and immorality characteristic of modern, U.S.-style capitalism. Especially during the coffee harvest, proclerical Conservative newspapers published articles criticizing the living conditions on coffee fincas. While they did not neglect to stress the brutal exploitation of migrant coffee workers, they were more bent on representing coffee fincas as sites of "orgies" where male workers preyed on female workers. Pointing out that both male and female laborers were forced to sleep in the same crowded room, these proclerical papers castigated coffee barons for promoting the moral "degeneration" of Nicaragua's laboring classes.[75]

The Caballeros Católicos argued that the main problem facing Nicaragua under dollar diplomacy was not, as prominent Liberals proclaimed, the return of "feudalism" but, rather, "capitalism," the driving force behind modernity. In particular, they challenged the dominant elite view that capitalist entrepreneurs were promoting the well-being of the nation through their productive use of capital. Instead, the Caballeros Católicos claimed that "the unrestricted liberty of capital" was polarizing society into two opposing armies, "capitalism on the one hand and pauperism on the other."[76] However strident their anticapitalist views, the Caballeros were anything but social radicals. Indeed, they worried less about the growing income disparity than about the failure of "capitalists" to assume elites' traditional responsibility for the welfare of the "poor." As the editor of El Diario Nicaragüense stressed, "capitalism is not odious because it represents the accumulation of wealth in the hands of a few, but rather because its mechanism does not drive charity."[77] Still, it was a milestone for members of Nicaragua's most powerful elite sector to question openly the presumed link between material progress and moral well-being.

In a move that only further distanced them from the capitalist culture of coffee, the Caballeros Católicos began to valorize the cattle hacienda as the embodiment of egalitarianism, social justice, and Christian values. Many argued that the cattle industry was structurally the most democratic of economic sectors, both in terms of land tenure and income distribution.[78] Yet not all was structural. The Caballeros Católicos also mythologized the supposedly egalitarian culture of the cattle sector, particularly the values associated with the country's cowboys, the so-called *campistos*. To them, campistos were blissful ignorants who led a virtuous Christian life—"a mixture of gold and dirty mud," as one Caballero put it.[79]

Overlooking the "dirty mud" in the campisto, Conservative patricians strove to bond with this epitome of healthy individualism. According to the leading Caballero Católico Carlos Cuadra Pasos, Conservative oligarchs of Granada would spend much of their childhood living on cattle haciendas in Chontales, where they learned the skills of horsemanship from the campistos. From a young age, then, they allegedly shared a common notion of manliness with the campistos.[80] In addition, Cuadra Pasos suggested that this masculine culture was rooted in the common racial heritage linking Granada's "ladino" (i.e., white) elite with the campistos of Chontales. Although Indian communities in Chontales persisted well into the twentieth century, Cuadra Pasos stressed this rural region's ladino character, claiming that "the Chontaleño . . . is perhaps the most Spanish of all Nicaraguans."[81] Few events better underscore this attempt to identify with Chontales's cattle culture than the equestrian games elite Granadans organized at their city's patron-saint festival, the *fiestas agostinas*. As local newspapers stressed, many of the bulls and horses exhibited at this annual festival came from large cattle ranches owned by Granadans in Chontales. Even more important was the participation of Chontaleño campistos in the fiesta's most ritualized events—bullfights, rodeos, and horse races. By competing with the much-revered campistos, Conservative oligarchs hoped to show that both groups shared the same manly ideals.

Yet as much as the Caballeros Católicos sought to stress their "natural" affinity with the cattle culture of Chontales, this affinity was anything but innate. In fact, until recently most elite Conservatives had identified with coffee's culture of modernity and denigrated Nicaragua's main cattle region as a symbol of cultural "backwardness." Their contempt for the Chontaleño ran so deep that they had long used the term as an insult. A prominent woman from Chontales who moved to Granada in 1883 stated that already in the earliest stages of the country's first coffee boom "bumpkinish, ignorant, crude, or asocial people were generally called 'Chontaleño' in Granada."[82] By the 1920s, however, the self-imagery of upper-class Granadans had changed so profoundly that they now proudly associated themselves with the cattle culture of Chontales. Consider again the case of Carlos Cuadra Pasos, head of Granada's Caballeros Católicos. As late as 1912, Cuadra Pasos vehemently defended the extraordinary entrepreneurialism of Granada's Conservative oligarchs, pointing out that they had pioneered the country's highly dynamic export economies of coffee, sugar, and bananas.[83] A decade later, he had no qualms about representing his class as a cattle-based "Creole patriciate of colonial origins" that had become impoverished and subsequently been supplanted by a coffee-based "bourgeoisie of new rich" during the Liberal dictatorship of Zelaya (1893–1909).[84] Of course, Cuadra Pasos's representation of elite divisions hardly corresponded to economic reality. Granada's Conservative patricians were not only among the most dynamic coffee producers of the post-Zelaya era, but the economic basis of many "new rich" lay in the cattle sector. Still, these mythical elite divisions were crucial to the self-imagery then emerging among Caballeros Católicos like Cuadra Pasos.

The work that perhaps best illustrates how elite Conservatives of the 1920s sought to project themselves as the very antithesis of the modernizing capitalist is *Entre dos filos: Novela nicaragüense*, a romance written by Pedro Joaquín Chamorro Zelaya in the mid-1920s.[85] Born in 1891, Chamorro was a prominent Caballero Católico from Granada who wrote this "Nicaraguan novel" upon becoming a senator in 1925. Between 1926 and 1928, Chamorro served as vice minister of the interior in the Conservative government of President Adolfo Díaz; shortly thereafter he became editor of Managua's leading Conservative daily, *La Prensa*, a position he would hold until his death in 1952 (see figure 15). Despite the novel's anticapitalist and antimodern bent, Chamorro had vested interests in economic sectors mainly associated with capitalism and modernity: coffee, sugar, and bananas. In addition, his grandfather President Pedro Joaquín Chamorro Alfaro (1875–79) was the

15. President Adolfo Díaz (foreground) and Pedro Joaquín Chamorro Zelaya
(left), ca. 1927. *Courtesy of U.S. National Archives.*

politician most responsible for implementing the liberal reforms that facilitated the late-nineteenth-century takeoff of Nicaragua's agroexport economy.
In spite of these contradictions, or maybe precisely because of them, Chamorro's novel had a major impact when it came out in 1927. Prominent
Conservatives lauded it for accurately portraying "our customs" and for
having succeeded in "expressing and disseminating a perfect specimen of the
National [*lo Nacional*]."[86] Indeed, through his novel Chamorro attempted to
identify not only his class but the nation with the precapitalist values embodied in the country's cattle sector. Like other national romances, *Entre dos filos*
served as a "foundational fiction" for a new national project and helped
crystallize the anti-American and antibourgeois spirit then emerging among
elite Conservatives.[87]

First and foremost, Chamorro's novel portrays competing elite identities.
It contrasts the values and manly identities of long-established landed elites
with those of the "new rich." Accordingly, traditional ideals of manliness
center on the capacity to protect the weak, while the capitalist ideal solely
extols the capacity to conquer capital. Embodying such distinctions are the

novel's two main protagonists, both Granadans: the young Conservative estate owner (*hacendado*) Alvaro Carvajal, member of an old elite family, and the sixty-two-year-old Liberal loan shark and parvenu Robustiano Robles. Not coincidentally, Carvajal's main sources of income—cattle and cacao—derive from economic sectors most closely associated with Spanish colonialism. Robles's usurious activities, by contrast, are meant to reveal the odiousness of U.S.-styled capitalism. So if Carvajal comes across as the model of male honor, Robles symbolizes the unscrupulous and dishonest capitalist. And no matter how much new rich like Robles seek to become "important members of society," they lack its primary requisite: honor.

Chamorro's novel, however, also seeks to redefine "lo Nacional." To do so, it belittles the longstanding elite ideal of a cosmopolitan Nicaragua and instead represents the nation as a more inward-looking, traditional community with the extended hacienda (estate) family as its main building block. The novel goes to great lengths to mythologize the "sanctity of rural life" as practiced on Carvajal's hacienda and celebrated in rural festivals.[88] The novel's idyllic portrayal of rural society mirrors a strategy then deployed by antimodern writers elsewhere in the world. But if these writers tended to idealize the peasant or the cowboy as a symbol of a more authentic national identity, Chamorro followed his fellow Caballeros Católicos in extolling the cattle hacendado.[89] Carvajal's love for the countryside and its traditions in turn sets this deeply religious cattle hacendado apart from his main rivals, who tend to privilege things modern and North American. Typically, the person who most strongly embodies cosmopolitanism is a woman: Angelita, the daughter of the anticlerical and Freemason Robles. Educated in the United States, this English-speaking, car-driving "amazona" displays all the manly qualities supposedly characteristic of the U.S.-based "modern woman." When Carvajal's aunt catches Angelita riding a horse "like a man," the aunt exclaims, "It's fine that *Yancas* [female Yankees] and marimachas do it; but not girls educated in the Christian way. God save us from seeing you riding like a man."[90]

Since Carvajal and Angelita embody distinct nationalist visions, his ability to conquer her Americanized soul at the end of the novel holds great symbolic significance. To be sure, this conclusion may symbolize Nicaraguans' outright rejection of modern U.S. ideals. But it could also signify the absorption of such ideals into a community imagined around one of the most colonial of institutions: the hacienda family. Indeed, rather than evoking a simple return to the colonial past—a charge often hurled at Chamorro and other Caballeros Católicos—the novel celebrates a more hybrid national project that seems to accept the modern as long as it can be assimilated into the traditional patriarchal order upheld by Carvajal and other members of the cattle-based "Creole patriciate of colonial origin."

To Nicaragua's emerging antibourgeois elite, this patriarchal order preserved social peace and thus secured the nation's well-being precisely because it could both maintain stable social hierarchies and uphold a tradition of social solidarity.[91] In *Entre dos filos*, the tension between hierarchy and solidarity is most clearly represented by the patron-client relations reigning on (cattle) haciendas of colonial origin. As the novel's narrator emphasizes, such relations depend greatly on the strength of personal interactions that at once legitimize the patron's "divine" authority and affirm the common bonds of rural society:

> The families [of large cattle ranchers] used to live in contact with the people who came to farm the land; they did not stress class differences, nor did they interpose the profound chasm that separates people and at times turns them into enemies. They all came to form one large family that gave a patriarchal color to the social life then prevailing in the countryside. The patrons [*amos*] lived by honestly and peacefully enjoying what was theirs. . . . and those who worked for them, after earning their just salary, went home blessing the name of the good patron and giving thanks to God. . . . [The patrons] helped [the workers], acted as godfathers to their small children while teaching the older ones, and took in the younger, single women workers [*mozas*]. . . . When some of the older workers needed help, the patron came to their rescue. . . . In exchange they provided their patrons with labor . . . and treated them with respect while making sure that the latter fulfilled their obligations and treated them justly.[92]

As this passage illustrates, the myth of rural sanctity emerging among elite Conservatives like Chamorro centered primarily in their belief that the patriarchal hacienda family was a "positive social Christian organization" where "respect" and "justice" were naturally practiced.[93] To them, nothing threatened the idyllic social order of rural Nicaragua more than U.S.-style capitalist modernization, "the counterpoint to Christianity."[94]

In conjuring up this crisis of patriarchy, Chamorro's novel echoed the pessimistic sentiments shared by many upper-class Nicaraguans during the 1920s, whether Liberal or Conservative, pro- or anticlerical. But it also illustrates that such anxieties elicited a peculiar response from the Caballeros

Católicos. For most elite Nicaraguans, especially Liberals, their country's malaise resulted from dollar diplomacy's allegedly deleterious effect on capitalist development. To cope with dollar diplomacy's "antimodern" impact, they reinforced their identification with the culture of capitalism. Pedro Joaquín Chamorro Zelaya and his fellow Caballeros Católicos, by contrast, did not view dollar diplomats' economic policies as the main culprit. To them, Wall Street was anything but the all-powerful "diabolic machine" vividly portrayed in Hernán Robleto's *Los estrangulados*. Instead they claimed that the culprit was (U.S.) mass culture produced by the likes of Hollywood and its driving force, capitalism. Not too little but too much modernity and capitalism was the true cause of Nicaragua's malaise.

Little wonder, then, that the Caballeros Católicos so fiercely denounced the supposedly leveling impact of modern mass culture. This equalizing effect, they claimed, posed the greatest threat to the precarious balance between hierarchy and solidarity that the traditional patriarchal order had long upheld. Their paper *El Católico*, for example, complained that the growing commercialization of local patron-saint festivals created the dangerous illusion of social equality. "The lack of respect is so widespread in Nicaragua," *El Católico* criticized, "that it couldn't be greater: many strongly believe in equality, which they confuse with the most repugnant form of rudeness and vulgarity."[95] This proclerical newspaper even claimed that the key bourgeois ideal of promoting equality among the "popular masses" was nothing but a "real crime."[96] To counter this general decline in "respect," Caballeros Católicos like Pedro Joaquín Chamorro Zelaya strove to more strongly extol the (cattle-based) hacienda family of colonial origin.

While the Caballeros Católicos' ideal of rural sanctity cannot be dismissed as mere nostalgia, it was filled with contradictions. Landlords' charity work, intense personal interactions with their subordinates, and involvement in local festivals all lent much credibility to the Caballeros' celebration of rural sanctity. Still, patron-client relations on cattle ranches were often fraught with physical and verbal violence—even in Granada, the Caballeros Católicos' main stronghold.[97] Numerous court cases attest to the eruption of violent fights, and at times murder, when Granadan cattle barons refused to pay their employees. In the face of such refusals, moreover, peasants engaged in cattle rustling as a form of revenge. Workers on cattle haciendas also resented being politically manipulated by their employers, a feeling that perpetuated antielite violence in cattle-raising areas such as Malacatoya. And although far fewer women worked on cattle haciendas than on coffee estates, they too were sexually abused by their bosses. The violence that marked daily interactions among workers on cattle ranches also defied the harmonious idyll promoted by Conservative oligarchs. Further challenging this myth of rural sanctity, numerous peasants abandoned the countryside for the city because they were attracted, not repulsed, by its signs of modernity or, as one Caballero candidly admitted, "by the mirage of banks, shops [and], the life of movies, bars, dance halls, and so on."[98]

Yet the myth's greatest contradiction lay in the attempt by the Caballeros Católicos to represent themselves as the very opposite of what they truly were: they were Nicaragua's most entrepreneurial agroexport producers who had long stood out for their cosmopolitan, Americanized ways. This contradiction was especially evident at Granada's fiestas agostinas, where Conservative oligarchs sought to associate themselves with a more inward-looking vision of the nation. In this regard, their participation in highly ritualized equestrian events was particularly important, as these events allowed them to display the anticosmopolitan manly ideals they supposedly shared with the campistos. But the Caballeros Católicos and other elite Granadans did not celebrate their victories in popular *cantinas* where the campistos tended to go. Instead, they flocked to the exclusive restaurants that the common folk associated with cosmopolitanism. Not only did these "aristocratic centers" all have international names, such as *Versailles, París,* or *Turín,* they were privileged sites where Granada's "highlife" paraded foreign visitors and publicly displayed its knowledge of English.[99] When not engaged in equestrian events, the Caballeros Católicos dazzled the crowd by driving around in U.S.-made cars, then the prime symbol of modernity.[100] This gesture perhaps best illustrates the tension between modern and reactionary impulses that came to define the culture of Granada's Conservative oligarchy during the U.S. occupation.

Conclusion

How are we to explain the apparent paradox of a highly entrepreneurial and cosmopolitan upper class embracing antimodern ideals? This apparent contradiction, while unusual, was not without precedent. In the United States and Western Europe, for example, various industrial and agrarian elites strongly associated with capitalism also sought to identify themselves with antimodern values rooted in the myth of rural sanctity.[101] The prominent social scientist Barrington Moore has argued that such reactionary imageries "are liable to flourish in a landed upper class that manages to hang on to political power successfully although it is losing out economically or perhaps is threatened by a new and strange source of economic power." In particular, he claims that "where commercial relationships have begun to undermine a peasant economy, the conservative elements in society are likely to generate a rhetoric of extolling the peasant as the backbone of society."[102] To be sure, Nicaragua's Caballeros Católicos articulated such a reactionary rhetoric—called "Catonism" by Moore—as they blamed capitalism and modernity for the cultural and social crisis allegedly engulfing their country during the 1920s. But contrary to Moore's claim, they extolled the (cattle) hacendado, not the peasant, as the building block of society.

In U.S.-occupied Nicaragua, capitalist expansion was not the reason why the country's economic vanguard, Granada's Conservative oligarchy, turned against the U.S. road to modernity. Rather, its members were responding to the unintended ways that dollar diplomacy weakened elite power. To use Moore's framework, Nicaragua's economic vanguard indeed embraced "Catonism" at a time when this group managed to hang on to political power but was losing out economically. However, the main threat to its economic power did not come from a new and strange source ("modern conditions"), as the Caballeros Católicos asserted. Instead, it sprang from an old and very familiar one: small- and medium-scale producers who proved much more resilient in coping with the economic effects of dollar diplomacy than their anxious elite counterparts.

In addition, the Caballeros' embrace of cultural anti-Americanism responded to the indirect ways that dollar diplomats promoted the activities of U.S. Protestant missionaries and the diffusion of the U.S.-based "modern woman." Both trends, as well as the postwar rise of labor unions and leftist parties, challenged elite patriarchal authority. Ruling Conservatives responded to this challenge partly by seeking closer ties with popular sectors. In so doing, they more forcefully embraced social Catholicism and constructed a national image more attuned to local cultural practices than was the case with their previous ideal of a cosmopolitan Nicaragua. As we will see, this new, agrarian-based nationalism constructed against U.S. ways would underpin the surprisingly revolutionary response of Nicaragua's most entrenched elite sector to the post-1927 militarization of U.S. imperial rule.

8 Militarization via Democratization

The U.S. Attack on Caudillismo and the Rise of Authoritarian Corporatism

THE CIVIL WAR OF 1926–27 radically transformed U.S. imperial rule in Nicaragua. Ever since 1912, the United States had believed that financial stability was key to its control over Nicaragua. The civil war unambiguously exposed the limits of dollar diplomacy. Above all, it led U.S. officials to conclude that the main threat to stability now resided in Nicaragua's "backward" system of caudillismo, a form of political clientelism they believed inhibited peaceful change in government. After ending the civil war, the United States thus abandoned dollar diplomacy and instead sought to safeguard its hegemony by having the U.S. military impose on Nicaragua its version of a more democratic order based on "free and fair elections."

The United States sealed its "democratization" project in May 1927, when the U.S. envoy and future secretary of state (1929–33) Henry Stimson forced a peace treaty on the ruling Conservatives and the insurgent Liberals.[1] Through this treaty, the U.S. military secured the right not only to run Nicaraguan elections but to establish and lead a native armed force—the Guardia Nacional de Nicaragua—that was to become the main guarantor of the democratization process. Officially, the Guardia Nacional was to maintain "order," ensure clean elections, and, as one U.S. Guardia officer put it, "implement public liberties and democratic practices."[2] But U.S. policymakers also expected the Guardia Nacional to wrestle control of the countryside from caudillos, for they deemed these rural "bosses" the main obstacle to stability in Nicaragua. In addition, U.S. officials hoped that the Guardia's Nicaraguan members would become the "nucleus" of the native middle class and, therefore, the "bulwark" of democratic rule.[3] In short, the U.S. government trusted that its military would accomplish what dollar diplomats had failed to achieve: stability via the modernization of Nicaragua's political culture.

Nicaragua's Guardia Nacional was modeled after the constabularies the United States had established in its Caribbean protectorates of Haiti and the Dominican Republic.[4] Each of these centralized institutions functioned as both a military and a police force, with the officer corps dominated by U.S. Marines and the rank and file filled with native volunteers. To U.S. officials, the constabularies represented the very opposite of the caudillo armies they replaced; they were to be nonpartisan, professionalized forces based on bureaucratic ("scientific") principles, not personalism.[5] In all cases, the constabularies' main goal was to secure a stable, pro-U.S. political order. For good reasons, many scholars have characterized these constabularies as neocolonial armies or, to cite historian Louis Pérez, as "gendarmes of empire."[6] But in doing so, they have overlooked the important fact that in Nicaragua— and only there—a U.S.-led constabulary sought to defend the "empire" by promoting "democracy" rather than authoritarian rule.[7]

The post-1927 U.S. "democratization" campaign revolutionized Nicaraguan state-society relations but not in the ways envisioned by U.S. policymakers. Most palpably, the campaign facilitated the rise of Latin America's lengthiest dictatorship of the twentieth century: the Somoza regime of 1936– 79, whose main pillar of support was the Guardia Nacional. Yet this authoritarian outcome did not result from the failure of the U.S. military to implement its democratization campaign. On the contrary, the U.S. military ensured that Nicaraguan elections were more open than they had ever been. In fact, the U.S.-supervised elections of 1928 brought about the first peaceful regime change in Nicaraguan history. Perhaps more important, the U.S.-led Guardia crippled the power of caudillos in the countryside, where about three quarters of Nicaraguans resided. Yet the U.S. democratization campaign also militarized rural society and politics in fatal ways that have not been fully explored. In part, this militarization stemmed from the revolutionary war that Augusto Sandino's peasant-based guerrillas waged against U.S. and Guardia troops in the northern frontier region of the Segovias (see chapter 9). But in most of Nicaragua, society became more militarized primarily because of the U.S. electoral campaign and its attack on caudillismo. On the one hand, U.S. democratization efforts transformed the Guardia into the country's most powerful state institution. It also led the Guardia to take over the function of many rural authorities, thus allowing this U.S.-led military to become the main political force in the countryside. On the other hand, the U.S. democratization campaign deepened the anti-U.S. turn of Nicaragua's most entrenched elites, for it pushed many Conservative oligarchs to abandon their faith in U.S. political ideals and instead embrace authoritarian corporatism. In the end, U.S. efforts to impose democracy not only failed to produce deep and durable democratization, they actually paved the way for authoritarian rule.

Imposing Democracy

For Nicaraguans, the U.S. military's effort to impart what Henry Stimson called "the elementary lessons of democracy" represented a radical departure from the antidemocratic thrust that had characterized U.S. imperial rule since 1910.[8] In reality, however, this effort built on the various democracy campaigns that the United States had waged elsewhere in Latin America. Beginning with Cuba in 1906, the U.S. government intervened over the next two decades in sixteen Latin American nations in the name of promoting democracy.[9] For the most part, U.S. policymakers defined "democracy" as regimes that came to power through clean elections. Such regimes did not have to be mass democracies. On the contrary, U.S. officials willingly accepted "limited democracies with a narrow range of participation, contestation, and pluralism."[10] This acceptance underscores how strategic concerns drove the United States to promote the continent's democratization. Indeed, in Latin America the United States initiated what some scholars argue was the most peculiar feature of its foreign policy during the twentieth century: the defense of national security through the promotion of democracy abroad.[11] In early-twentieth-century Latin America, the United States tended to foster democracy through political pressure—mostly by withholding recognition of unconstitutional governments. In post-1927 Nicaragua, however, it used military means to impose its brand of democracy.

The U.S. military became so heavily involved in transforming Nicaragua's political system precisely because military leaders believed that promoting democracy meant more than simply ensuring free and fair elections. It also entailed the destruction of caudillismo. U.S. officers frequently compared caudillismo to medieval feudalism, where the rural poor were brutally exploited pawns of feuding elite families led by charismatic strongmen: caudillos. As one senior U.S. officer (Admiral Clark Woodward) put it, power in rural Nicaragua "has traditionally been administered . . . through 'caudillos'—members of the [Conservative] Party well known locally as important property holders, employers of labor and prominent in a social way." This system, he stressed, "partakes in many respects of the features of the feudal system of Europe in the Middle Ages in that it is based upon the dependence of the masses on the favor of the classes."[12] For many U.S. officers, elections thus represented nothing more than violent feuds among the "landed gentry" in which caudillos, as a U.S. lieutenant noted, drove the "gente sencilla [simple folk] . . . back and forth like sheep."[13] Little wonder that the U.S. military was bent on destroying a system that it considered to be "entirely out of harmony with the principles of democratic government."[14]

In reality, however, caudillismo and "democracy" were more closely linked. For example, U.S. officers overlooked how some caudillos effectively represented popular aspirations; this was even true for powerful Conservative caudillos like Emiliano Chamorro who belonged to the "landed gentry." In addition, they ignored how many peasants had enhanced their political rights by participating in insurgent movements led by caudillos. Above all, however, U.S. officers failed to see how elections represented the primary means through which rival patron-client networks vied for access to state power and control over an array of public resources.[15] This was particularly the case for municipal elections in the countryside, as such elections determined the distribution of political offices key to rural wealth and power. Caudillismo thus gave elections an element of competitiveness. Still, elections were hardly "free and fair." Not only were they controlled by Conservative caudillos, but they frequently excluded Liberals. Against this backdrop, the U.S. campaign to promote clean elections, for all its limits, represented a significant opening of Nicaragua's political system. Why else, then, would such a wide group of Nicaraguans—ranging from Liberal landlords to indigenous clients of Conservative caudillos to leftist labor activists—have openly embraced this campaign? Even the radical, anti-U.S. socialist leader Apolonio Palacios clamored loudly for U.S. military supervision of the 1928 elections: in his view, only such supervision would prevent Conservative landlords from manipulating the all-important rural vote.[16]

The U.S. military personnel chiefly responsible for the democratization of Nicaragua were members of the missions that managed the presidential and congressional elections of 1928, the congressional elections of 1930, and the presidential and congressional elections of 1932.[17] Each electoral mission consisted of about 50 officers and 550 to 900 enlisted men from the Army, the Navy, and the Marine Corps who arrived about four months before the elections. Most officers spoke Spanish and had served in U.S. military governments elsewhere in the Caribbean Basin and the Philippines. The enlisted men, in contrast, had rarely been stationed abroad. In consequence, they had to spend the first two months attending "Electoral School" where they practiced electoral supervision and received instruction in Spanish, local customs, and Nicaraguan electoral law.

16. Cantonal electoral board in rural Nicaragua, 1928.
Courtesy of U.S. National Archives.

These missions most effectively transformed Nicaragua's political system by controlling the electoral boards that existed at the national, departmental, and cantonal (precinct) levels (see figure 16). Every board consisted of a U.S. chairman and one representative each from the Conservative and Liberal parties. While U.S. officers headed the national and the 13 departmental boards, enlisted men presided over the 492 cantonal boards established for each urban and rural polling place.[18] At all three levels, the U.S. chairman exerted great power over his Nicaraguan colleagues, for he could nullify their decisions. The boards oversaw the five days of voter registration and the balloting on election day itself (eligible voters were Nicaraguan males over twenty-one, or over eighteen if married or able to read and write). Yet "the mechanical task of conducting an election," as one U.S. electoral monitor stressed, was "but part of the job. By far the greater effort went to maintaining a pre-election atmosphere of freedom and fairness for all parties and persons."[19]

As president of the national board, the chief of the U.S. electoral mission wielded sweeping powers that gave him a decisive role in shaping Nicaraguan politics. In addition to controlling all electoral boards, mission chiefs implemented key electoral reforms like the enactment of the secret franchise, arbitrated any conflict pertaining to the electoral process, and presided over the final vote count. To the chagrin of Nicaragua's leading caudillos, mission chiefs also exercised de facto veto power over the nomination of candidates for the nation's presidency. In 1928, for example, General Frank Ross McCoy blocked Emiliano Chamorro's nomination as the Conservative presidential candidate; and in 1932 Admiral Woodward crushed President José María Moncada's efforts to impose his candidate on the Liberal ticket.[20] Perhaps more important, mission heads limited electoral participation to the Liberals and Conservatives by essentially proscribing third-party challengers. This practice was initiated in 1928 by General McCoy, who feared that a multiparty system would prevent any party from obtaining a majority in national elections. For U.S. officials, such a scenario was unacceptable as it conjured up images of what they dreaded most: political instability.

Mission chiefs also weakened caudillismo by dismantling some of the clientelistic structures they believed stood in the way of more democratic elections. Their most important decision was to suspend thousands of rural sheriffs whom they viewed as political instruments of caudillos.[21] A similar fate befell indigenous authorities (*capitanes de cañada*) who could mobilize thousands of Indian votes on behalf of national caudillos.[22] Mission chiefs also enacted policies that sought to prevent political parties from using public resources to mobilize electoral support. For caudillos, the mission chiefs' harshest order was to have the Guardia seize all distilleries and depositories of liquor about three months prior to the elections. As a result of this measure, caudillos were deprived of a key means of obtaining votes.

However powerful the mission chiefs, the chairmen of the thirteen departmental boards played an even more decisive role in weakening caudillos' political authority. These U.S. officers usually set up their office in the departmental capital about four months before election day. After introducing themselves to the local elite, departmental chairmen's first major task was to inspect all rural polling places (*mesas*) located in their region. Such visits often entailed long, arduous journeys by horseback or on foot into extremely remote areas. In surveying the countryside, departmental chairmen clarified the boundaries of the electoral cantons, making sure that they each had about five hundred voters and that the mesas were accessible to all voters. But more important, departmental chairmen sought to identify rural "bosses" and their "henchmen" who could jeopardize the holding of clean elections by intimidating voters or buying their vote.[23]

Departmental chairmen made a special effort to interview those they deemed the main victims of caudillismo: the rural poor. One chairman thus stressed that he "frequently digressed from the regular itinerary and visited unfrequented spots in order to get the viewpoints of the peasant class."[24] But since these U.S. officers knew little about the countryside, they often depended on native guides to steer them through the outlying hamlets and explain the intricacies of rural politics. Not surprisingly, they usually chose as their guides the Nicaraguans with whom they most frequently socialized: U.S.-educated landlords who lived in the departmental capitals. Unbeknownst to them, some of their guides were powerful caudillos. For example, the 1928 chairman of Granada's departmental board, Colonel Cornelius Smith, inspected the countryside with the help of Francisco Granizo, a fifty-six-year-old Conservative who had attended Fordham College in New York.[25] Smith knew that Granizo owned several cattle haciendas. Yet he failed to grasp his guide's clientelistic ability to mobilize peasants, as in the 1912 civil war when Granizo helped lead the region's anti-U.S. revolutionary movement. Like Colonel Smith, many departmental chairmen inadvertently ended up seeing much of the countryside through the eyes of the very caudillos they sought to eliminate.

Still, departmental chairmen often overcame their dependency on caudillos and implemented measures that effectively weakened the power of rural powerbrokers. Many refused to accept uncritically the traditional sites of mesas, as they realized that caudillos often controlled the rural vote by placing these polling stations on their haciendas.[26] Some thus ordered the transfer of mesas to rural communities where caudillos exerted less clout over the local populace.[27] In addition, departmental chairmen strove to prevent caudillos from misusing public resources for electoral purposes. These abuses generally involved the bribing of voters through the illegal distribution of state resources such as public lands, funds, and liquor. They also centered on authorities' efforts to intimidate voters via the cancellation of commercial licenses, the expulsion of peasants from public lands, the unwarranted collection of taxes, arbitrary arrests, and physical violence. To curb these abuses, departmental chairmen often sought to dismiss officials they claimed were corrupt. In 1928, for example, Granada's departmental chairman, Colonel Smith, ordered the arrest of a rural mayor and his assistants, who were charged with abusing their offices for electoral ends. Smith claimed that the mayor had "trampled on the liberties of people" and was nothing but a "political boss . . . persecuting the lowly people and catering to the 'great.'"[28]

Of course, departmental chairmen could not do without the hundreds of lower-ranked U.S. troops who ran the cantonal electoral boards. In fact, one chairman admitted that these young North Americans "were the ones who really supervised the elections; they served on the front line where real difficulties and actual danger existed."[29] Most enlisted men arrived in their rural cantons about two months prior to election day in order to establish a political climate of "freedom and fairness." From the very start, they sought to curb abuses of public authority by monitoring local officials and political events. In regions with large plantations, they often intervened on behalf of rural workers who had been dismissed for political reasons. In 1928, for instance, one lowly U.S. ensign in rural Granada successfully prevented the manager of a sugar mill that belonged to the presidential candidate of the Conservative Party, Adolfo Benard Vivas, from discharging workers who "would not sign binding themselves to vote for Benard."[30] And as the elections neared, the enlisted men who ran the cantonal boards crisscrossed their cantons to "educate" the rural populace personally about the voting procedures, the location of the polling stations, and the candidates themselves.[31]

For many Nicaraguans, it was on election day itself that U.S. military personnel most noticeably strove to weaken caudillos' hold over rural voters. Always falling on a Sunday, the day began with about twenty-five airplanes and up to seven thousand ground troops patrolling the whole country to thwart caudillos and their minions from obstructing the voting process. In particular, the U.S. military tried to ensure that all voters could reach the polls safely and that none would be bribed with money, food, or liquor. At the polling stations, the U.S. chairmen sought to secure the secret franchise by having Guardia soldiers block party workers, employers, and others from instructing voters which way to vote. They also removed campaign signs from the vicinity of voting booths and ensured that voters received ballots from all participating parties. To prevent fraud, cantonal chairmen verified that voters were correctly registered and forced them to dip their fingers in ink. Once the polls closed, cantonal chairmen tallied the votes and sealed the ballot boxes in order to prevent local officials from stuffing or stealing them. U.S. troops then transported the sealed boxes to Managua by land, air, and

17. Transporting ballot boxes to Managua, 1928.
Courtesy of U.S. National Archives.

water, so that the chief of the electoral mission could certify the results (see figure 17).

After supervising its third election in 1932, the United States claimed that its efforts to secure Nicaragua's political stability by promoting democracy had been a complete success. According to the State Department, U.S. electoral missions had helped Nicaragua "lay the foundations for permanent peace" by ensuring democratic elections.[32] In particular, U.S. officials gloated that the 1928 elections had produced the first peaceful regime change in Nicaraguan history; nearly 60 percent of the electorate voted for the Liberal ticket headed by the fifty-seven-year old José María Moncada, the former military leader of the 1926–27 insurgents. This victory was significant, for it ended eighteen years of U.S.-sponsored Conservative rule and permitted a party long ostracized by the U.S. government to come to power. But U.S. officials also stressed how the electoral missions had promoted Nicaragua's democratization more generally by fatally weakening caudillismo.[33] For many mission members, nothing better symbolized the success of their anti-caudillo campaign than the inability of the "landed gentry" to win clean elections in their rural bastions. The most celebrated defeat occurred in

1930 when the Conservative Pedro Joaquín Chamorro Zelaya—editor of *La Prensa*—became the first member of Nicaragua's premier clan to lose an election in rural Granada. To U.S. electoral officers, Chamorro's humiliating loss illustrated just how effectively their democratization campaign had freed rural voters from what they deemed were the feudalistic clutches of powerful oligarchs.[34]

Of course the U.S. military's effort to democratize Nicaragua was not the unmitigated success that Washington claimed it to be. Even in 1932 U.S. electoral personnel confidentially admitted that they encountered "considerable difficulty" in attempting to prevent public officials from committing electoral fraud.[35] Nor could they completely stop landlords from dictating the voting behavior of their laborers. Many also lamented that they could not block the national leadership of the Liberal and Conservative parties from imposing congressional candidates against the wishes of local party members. U.S. electoral personnel further deplored that their government had allowed President Moncada (1929–32) to use the war against Sandino's army as a pretext to replace elected municipal officials in the country's five north-central departments with his cronies. As one U.S. officer confidentially complained, "It is futile to talk of . . . political freedom, free and fair elections or other high sounding phrases indicating political liberty so long as a large percentage of the people are deliberately being deprived of their basic constitutional right of local self-government in their municipalities."[36] But perhaps most important, the de facto U.S. proscription of third-party challengers such as the pro-Sandino Partido Autonomista significantly curbed Nicaragua's democratic opening. Indeed, the U.S. military did not hesitate to arrest and even deport leading Autonomistas, as well as censor the party's unofficial newspaper, *La Tribuna*.

Despite its clear limits, U.S. electoral supervision promoted the country's democratization in significant ways. As Liberal and Conservative party officials acknowledged, the elections of 1928–32 stood out for the absence of the brazen intimidation, bribery, and fraud that had marked past campaigns. For the first time ever, the political opposition trusted that the country's military and police forces would remain neutral. The rural populace, in particular, could appreciate how U.S. electoral supervision weakened caudillos' ability to dictate the electoral outcome. For instance, a 1930 handbill written by Liberal farmers from rural Estelí stressed that "fraud and all the other thousand stratagems used by the political 'caciques' to cheat the wish of the people no longer exist."[37] Moreover, despite the de facto proscription of third parties, voters could choose between two mass-based parties with distinct ideologies; hence the victory of the Liberal opposition in the 1928 elections did produce a significant regime change. Finally, participation in the U.S.-supervised elections was extremely high even though voting was not compulsory and pro-Sandino forces called for an election boycott. In fact, a higher percentage of the population (about 20 percent) participated in the elections of 1928 and 1932 than in any other presidential election held in Latin America up to that point.[38] The historical evidence thus suggests that Nicaragua's U.S.-managed elections were not simple charades.[39] However tentatively, they fostered political equality, participation, accountability, and contestation—outcomes that political scientists deem key to the creation of a democratic polity.[40]

Yet the U.S.-sponsored democratic opening came at an enormous cost to Nicaragua. True, in 1928 Nicaragua's leading Liberal politicians applauded the United States for finally living up to its reputation as the world's premier democracy. To show their appreciation, Liberals greeted U.S. president-elect Herbert Hoover when he stopped in the port of Corinto shortly after the 1928 elections and presented him with a young woman dressed up as the U.S. Statue of Liberty.[41] Over time, however, more and more Nicaraguans came to resent U.S. electoral supervision. Not only did this supervision suggest that they were incapable of promoting democratic rule on their own, it also deepened the U.S. military's control of their country. Typifying this ambivalence, a Liberal pharmacist from rural Masaya could be, as one U.S. officer reported in 1930, a "good friend of the Electoral Mission" and actively support its democratization efforts but nonetheless feel "humiliated" for the way the U.S. military "controlled" his country.[42] And Nicaraguans did pay dearly for the U.S. military's democratization campaign, for it militarized their country in unprecedented ways.

First and foremost, the campaign secured military control over elections. But it also enabled military personnel to become key arbiters of social conflicts. This was especially true in the countryside, where members of the U.S. electoral missions mediated an array of disputes, whether between or within communities, whether between rival caudillo networks, landlords, or peasants.[43] Mission members themselves observed that in remote areas where "people have a very vague and confused idea of government" they were viewed not just as electoral supervisors but as "general arbitrators."[44] Yet electoral missions' stay in Nicaragua—usually about six months—was too short for them to become truly embedded in local society. Instead, the U.S. military reached deeply into rural society mainly via the Guardia Nacional.

Militarization

The U.S. military founded the Guardia Nacional in May 1927, right after it had forced the Liberal insurgents and the ruling Conservatives to lay down their arms. In addition to restoring stability to war-torn Nicaragua, the Guardia was to help the United States secure a more democratic order by waging a full-scale assault against rural caudillismo. And it was under this banner of promoting democracy that the Guardia became a powerful political force in the countryside.

Immediately after its founding, however, the U.S.-led Guardia acquired another task that unexpectedly accelerated Nicaragua's militarization: the war against Sandino's guerrilla force. Waged between 1927 and 1933, this lengthy war ensured that the Guardia evolved into a larger and costlier state institution than originally planned. Designed to consist of six hundred men, the Guardia's ranks instead swelled to over three hundred officers and twenty-three hundred soldiers.[45]And the Guardia's budget quickly came to absorb about 25 percent of the total expenditures of the Nicaraguan government, not 10 percent as initially planned. Because of the war, Nicaragua's military budget was the only one in the region that did not shrink after the Great Depression broke out in 1929. Thanks to its lavish funds, the Guardia developed into a modern military organization whose members were well paid, trained, and outfitted.[46] More important, it had the necessary resources and autonomy to become Nicaragua's strongest state institution. Yet this militarization was not limited to the state apparatus, for the Guardia also developed into a major force in rural society.

Initially, the Guardia's tightening hold over the countryside was most noticeable in the Segovias, the region primarily affected by the Sandino Rebellion. Home to about 10 percent of the Nicaraguan population, this mountainous zone encompassed the northern departments of Nueva Segovia, Estelí, Jinotega, and Matagalpa. For six years, over one thousand Guardia troops battled the one thousand to two thousand guerrilleros and terrorized the Sandinistas' perceived sympathizers.[47] Backing the Guardia was a U.S. air squadron of twenty-four planes and, up to 1930, a combat force of about five

18. U.S. military distributing milk and smallpox vaccine, 1931.
Courtesy of U.S. National Archives.

thousand U.S. Marines. The brutal war waged in the Segovias attracted worldwide attention from the very start. Less known but just as fierce was the nonmilitary campaign that the Guardia carried out in this frontier region.[48] The Guardia created a dense web of social control by deploying spies, informers, paramilitary units, and more modern forms of surveillance, such as Nicaragua's first radio system. In addition, the Guardia carried out civic projects designed to gain the populace's political support. These projects ranged from the construction of rural roads and schools to the free provision of medical services, including smallpox vaccination (see figure 18). With the outbreak of the Great Depression in 1929, the Guardia also began to distribute food to the rural population; in extremely remote areas it even used planes to fly in food. Finally, the Guardia sponsored numerous leisure activities including social dances, festivals, movies, and baseball games.[49] Due to this wide-reaching counterinsurgency campaign, the Guardia became a powerful political force in the Segovias.

    In the rest of Nicaragua, however, the militarization of rural society stemmed primarily from the Guardia's efforts to dismantle the structures of caudillismo. So important was the Guardia's original mission to its leadership that even at the war's apex (mid-1932) about one thousand national guardsmen, and not just a handful as often assumed, remained stationed outside the war zone.[50] While many more were posted in towns than in rural villages, urban-based Guardia troops patrolled the countryside constantly (see figure 19). Moreover, rural patrols increased dramatically during election years, for Guardia troops were charged with protecting U.S. electoral supervisors and monitoring political activities. In the name of promoting democracy, then, the Guardia became heavily involved in policing the lives of rural Nicaraguans unaffected by the war. As in the Segovias, this U.S.-led force carried out civic projects and organized leisure activities that reinforced its clientelistic bond with the peasantry. Some U.S. officers even tried to form Boy Scout units in order to inculcate in the youth a "democratic and entrepreneurial spirit."[51] Many also collaborated with U.S. Protestant missionaries bent on expanding their work to outlying areas.

Yet what most affected rural people was the Guardia's takeover of police and judicial functions traditionally carried out by local officials. Such authorities included the much-feared rural sheriffs (*jueces de mesta*) and their assistants (*jefes de cantón*), as well as rural guards, contraband controllers (*inspectores de hacienda*), and police agents. At times, U.S. Guardia officers even dismissed rural mayors they deemed corrupt. So greatly did the Guardia come to dominate local governance that in some departments the main civil authority—the *jefe político*—was apparently rendered a "figurehead."[52] The Guardia emerged as the main link between the peasantry and the state precisely because U.S. officials believed that rural authorities were indispensable to the political system they strove to destroy: caudillismo.

But by displacing caudillos, the Guardia also became a key channel through which the rural poor could press their demands against the landed elite. True, some landlords wanted their workers to believe that this U.S.-led force was an instrument of the rich.[53] And the Guardia's U.S. officers reinforced this belief by socializing at elite clubs. Still, like their counterparts elsewhere in the Caribbean Basin, many U.S. Guardia officers despised native elites for callously exploiting the poor.[54] As the Guardia's chief of staff put it, "The wealth of [Nicaragua] is concentrated in the hands of the aristocraticos [*sic*], who . . . [have] reduced the poorer class to a condition of economic slavery." For this reason, he said, "we find in Nicaragua an oligarchical government masquerading in the guise of a Republic."[55] Driven by such antielite sentiments, U.S.

19. Typical Guardia Nacional infantry company, 1931.
Courtesy of U.S. National Archives.

Guardia officers sometimes subjected local elites to humiliating arrests for petty offenses. In Granada, for example, the U.S. Guardia commander harassed and insulted local notables so frequently that he became known among local elites as the "scourge" of their city.[56] More important, some U.S. Guardia officers supported popular mobilization against local elites. One of the earliest of such efforts occurred in July 1927, when the Guardia department commander of Chontales sought to help Indians recover lands they had lost to nonindigenous landlords.[57] Similar efforts occurred on the Atlantic coast.[58] Over time, U.S. Guardia officers went so far as to rally Nicaraguan workers against their U.S. employers. One U.S. mine owner complained that U.S. Guardia officers were "a source of . . . continuous trouble, inciting the workmen to their ideas, and allowing . . . disorder at their pleasure."[59]

The Guardia's antielite outlook was also shaped by its Nicaraguan members. This was hardly surprising, for the overwhelming majority of the Guardia's rank and file were of lower-class origin and, according to local newspapers, bent on undermining elite authority. Or as the newspaper of Granada's Conservative oligarchy put it, the Guardia consisted of "society's most uncivil elements," who were hardly capable of fulfilling the "great duties of social defense."[60] With the 1930 opening of the Military Academy in Managua, the Guardia's composition changed noticeably, since it led about 120 well-off Nicaraguans to enlist as junior officers. These young officers, however, also tended to embrace the institution's antielite identity. Even those who belonged to prominent elite families, such as the Cuadras from Granada, adopted a populist outlook.[61]

Why did these Nicaraguan officers espouse an antielite vision? No doubt, they assimilated much of the antielitism of their U.S. superiors through military training and practice. Yet they also reshaped it by socializing among themselves. Unlike Nicaraguan soldiers of the past, Guardia troops had their own social clubs, sports teams, and a journal. These men formed such a distinct corporate identity that, by the end of the U.S. occupation, elites feared less the Guardia's predominantly nonelite ("dishonorable") composition than its development into a powerful "military caste." Or as a Conservative oligarch complained, the "basic error in the institution of the Guardia consists in the binding of young men by contracts for several years, during which the daily routine of camp life, training, and campaigns creates . . . a spirit of group solidarity and restricted outlook." Such "a state within a state," he concluded, "will always be divorced from civil society and will be a danger for public liberty."[62]

The Guardia's evolution into the country's most powerful and cohesive state institution was clearly a double-edged sword. Many—and not just the rich—appreciated the greater security provided by the Guardia, particularly in the countryside.[63] Many rural people also welcomed the badly needed public improvements made by the Guardia, and the key social services it provided. On the other hand, this military force gravely endangered "public liberty." Yet the danger lay not in the Guardia's "divorce" from society, as frequently assumed.[64] On the contrary, it stemmed from the way the U.S. attack on caudillismo had enabled the Guardia to become deeply embedded in local society. The Guardia's efforts to cripple powerful caudillo networks were supported by many peasants, Indians, and rural laborers. But this assault also hurt numerous poor Nicaraguans, such as members of Matagalpa's indigenous community, who suffered noticeably from the Guardia's dismantlement of the network headed by Emiliano Chamorro.[65]

By the occupation's end, the U.S. democratization campaign had greatly reduced the lower classes' ability to exploit the competition that traditionally existed among rival caudillo networks. As a result, rural people became increasingly beholden to a single patron: the Guardia Nacional. And though this military institution channeled popular demands and aspirations, its main goal was to control, not mobilize, the countryside. Landlords too felt threatened by the Guardia's rise, as their fortunes and power rested heavily on the shoulders of beleaguered caudillos. Little wonder, then, that the U.S. drive to promote clean elections and destroy caudillismo helped push members of Nicaragua's most entrenched landed elite sector to embrace novel authoritarian notions of governance.

Embracing Authoritarian Corporatism

U.S. officials were hardly surprised that their democratization campaign spurred upper-class Nicaraguans to develop new conceptions of state-society relations. Many, in fact, gleefully observed that this ideological fervor affected primarily those most hurt by the U.S. military's assault against caudillismo: Conservative oligarchs. The chief of the 1932 electoral mission, Admiral Woodward, thus reported that more and more "nonconformist" Conservatives were revolting against "the efforts of caudillos to retain a strong domination over the voters and . . . the Party's activities."[66]

These "nonconformists" emerged after the U.S.-supervised elections of November 1928 ended eighteen years of Conservative rule. Conservatives' sudden loss of power caused pessimism to prevail among their ranks. But others seized the moment to break with the traditional system of caudillismo. For example, two days after the 1928 elections the son of a former president asked the great-nephew of another president to help him and like-minded Conservative oligarchs rid the country of caudillismo. In doing so, he claimed that "caudillismo, as a political system, has led us to the most significant of disasters." Moreover, he stressed, this "sad and nefarious legacy of an ill-fated epoch . . . [was] endangering the existence of our nationality and causing the moral and material decline of the Republic."[67] U.S. officials welcomed the rise of such anticaudillo sentiments. In the end, however, Conservative "nonconformists" did not embrace the U.S democratization campaign, even though they belonged to Nicaragua's most Americanized elite sector. Instead, they developed new, quasi-fascist notions of governance that contrasted sharply with U.S. political ideals.

The most prominent "nonconformist" Conservative oligarchs were the Granada-based *vanguardistas*. These oligarchs still enjoy much international fame, particularly for the literary works of José Coronel Urtecho (1906–94) and Pablo Antonio Cuadra Cardenal (1912–2002). In highlighting their broader significance, scholars have focused on the ways the vanguardistas challenged bourgeois culture and conventions and promoted an anti-U.S. national imagery that valorized the "traditional" values of rural society.[68] Yet as revolutionary as their aesthetic forms may have been, the vanguardistas' cultural project was not the novelty they claimed it was. Both their attack on Nicaragua's Americanization and their idealization of the cattle hacendado mirrored the "antibourgeois spirit" that the Caballeros Católicos had been developing since the end of the First World War. Instead, the vanguardistas were most revolutionary in the realm of political ideas, for they developed new, more authoritarian models of state-society relations.

The vanguardistas were not the only "nonconformist" Conservatives bent on radically transforming the existing political system. Indeed, they were joined by many other Caballeros Católicos. Among the most famous were Senator Carlos Cuadra Pasos (father of Pablo Antonio Cuadra); Pedro Joaquín Chamorro Zelaya and his fellow editor of La Prensa, Adolfo Ortega Díaz (nephew of President Adolfo Díaz); Pedro Joaquín Cuadra Chamorro, editor of El Diario Nicaragüense (and nephew of Carlos Cuadra Pasos); the influential Conservative ideologue and politician Diego Manuel Chamorro Bolaños (son of President Diego Manuel Chamorro, who died in 1923); Gabry Rivas, editor of La Nueva Prensa; and the renowned poet Azarías Pallais, a Catholic priest from León who has been characterized by some scholars as a forerunner of liberation theology.[69] In addition to these luminaries, the vanguardistas also enjoyed the support of many wealthy and politically well-connected Conservative Caballeros Católicos such as Dionisio Cuadra Benard and Salvador Cardenal Argüello, the nephew and son of the 1928 Conservative presidential and vice presidential candidates, respectively.

Although Conservative "nonconformists" shared U.S. officials' disdain for caudillismo, they believed that democracy was the root cause of Nicaragua's problems, not its panacea. Like true Caballeros Católicos, they criticized the ways in which the "democratization of leisure" had promoted the "dissolution" of Nicaraguan society.[70] But above all, these elite Conservatives claimed that political democracy, and electoral competition in particular, produced the divisions within the body politic that so gravely endangered Nicaraguan sovereignty. José Coronel Urtecho could thus claim that "the so miserable, so sad, so blind story of our independent life is the history of the epidemic of democracy, with its entourage of civil wars and foreign invasions."[71]

The depth of elites' newfound hostility toward liberal democracy was especially noticeable in the 1932 survey launched by the vanguardistas from the pages of the Granada newspaper *El Correo*.[72] Nicaraguans were not necessarily startled by the predictable responses of virulent antidemocrats like José Coronel Urtecho. Instead, the 1932 survey was so controversial because it showed that the vanguardistas' authoritarian outlook was shared by widely respected and seemingly apolitical elites throughout Nicaragua. Consider the case of Modesto Espinoza, a thirty-one-year-old merchant, industrialist, and landlord from León. According to U.S. officials, Espinoza was "generally looked upon by his fellow citizens with great respect because of his interest in the public welfare, his impartiality, and [for] not being a man given to cheap party antagonism."[73] In fact, his political activities were so low-key that the U.S. electoral personnel mistook this Conservative for a Liberal. Had they read his response to the survey, surely they would have been shocked to see how this businessman vehemently clamored for a radical, authoritarian form of governance. Espinoza was well aware that his response would stir up controversy. "If I were to tell you," he wrote, "that I would very much accept a dictatorship upheld by intellectuals, agricultural producers [*agricultores*], and artisans, I surely would be called a Bolshevik."[74] Like many other upper-class Nicaraguans, Espinoza concluded that only such a dictatorship could save the country.

This clamor for authoritarian rule was the most radical step elite Conservatives took in response to U.S. efforts to democratize Nicaragua. Traditionally, opposition to dictatorial rule had been a key tenet that united Conservatives. Abandoning this tenet thus entailed grave political risks for the Conservative Party, risks not all "nonconformist" Conservatives were willing to take. Among the latter was Pedro Joaquín Cuadra Chamorro, the influential editor of *El Diario Nicaragüense*. As opposed as he was to liberal democracy, Cuadra claimed that dictatorships were inherently a product of liberalism and could beget nothing but revolution and foreign intervention.[75] Yet these were precisely the outcomes that the vanguardistas and like-minded Conservatives hoped to block via dictatorial rule. They agreed with Cuadra that oligarchic rule was the most ideal form of governance, but they insisted that the deepening of U.S. intervention in Nicaragua demanded a radical break with the past. To them, only a dictatorship could stop the vicious cycle of foreign interventions that made Nicaragua "the disgrace of the whole continent."[76] This anti-imperialist impulse—coupled, of course, with the fear of eroding power—drove Conservative oligarchs to believe that "dictatorship is the natural regime of an independent Nicaragua."[77]

But what kind of dictatorship did "nonconformist" Conservatives envision? Their authoritarian project certainly smacked of fascism, as U.S. officials would later claim. Yet these elite Conservatives drew their main inspiration not so much from fascist Italy and Nazi Germany as from Catholic corporatist dictatorships such as Primo de Rivera's Spain (1923–30), Salazar's Portugal (1932–68), and Dollfuss's Austria (1932–34), as well as from Catholic-based movements like the Action Française and Argentina's Nationalists.[78] Nicaragua's Conservative oligarchs readily embraced Catholic, authoritarian corporatism largely because its principles of organizing state-society relations closely corresponded to those that underpinned their own antimodern vision of nation and society. Not only did they valorize the organic view of a hierarchically ordered, harmonious, morally correct society that defined most contemporary versions of authoritarian corporatism, they also shared the social reformist and anticapitalist bent of Catholic corporatism.[79] Further, Conservatives waging a moralizing crusade against U.S.-based visions of modernity were attracted to Catholic corporatist regimes' use of the state to pursue moral ends. Troubled by dollar diplomacy's attack on their economic power, they also came to embrace corporatists' vision that the state, not the free market, should regulate the economy.

To install authoritarian corporatism in Nicaragua, elite Conservatives generally envisioned two distinct avenues: one within and the other outside existing political structures. The former model was generally advocated by prominent, well-established Conservative politicians like Carlos Cuadra Pasos. Long a defender of liberal democracy, Cuadra Pasos had openly embraced Catholic corporatism by the early 1930s. His corporatist sympathies were particularly evident in the important speech he gave to law students at the University of Granada in January 1932. Breaking with the Conservative tradition of a laissez-faire state, this eminent Caballero Católico advocated a strong, interventionist state that would put an end to "one hundred years of political discord."[80] Cuadra Pasos most strongly betrayed his corporatist sentiments in his views on the organization of municipal government, which not coincidentally was the focus of post-1927 U.S. democratization efforts. Like Catholic corporatists elsewhere, he idealized preliberal forms of communal organization but recognized that republican rule made a return to the ancien régime "impossible." Still, Cuadra Pasos advocated a partial return to the antipolitical, corporatist tradition of the colonial *ayuntamiento* (city council) by demanding that control over the municipal governments be taken away from the Liberal and Conservative parties. Significantly, he believed the council members should represent what he deemed society's four principal occupational groups (*gremios*): merchants, agricultural producers, artisans, and professionals or intellectuals. In key ways, this municipal structure based on functional representation mirrored the one established in Spain by the dictatorship of Primo de Rivera.[81]

If Cuadra Pasos's vision of corporatist rule was ultimately evolutionary, with its main impetus coming from the municipality, many "nonconformist" Conservatives strove for the opposite—the revolutionary installation of a more centralized corporatist regime built on the ruins of the traditional parties. The leading advocate of such a regime was the vanguardista Luis Alberto Cabrales (1901–1974), nephew of the prominent Conservative politician and Caballero Católico Toribio Tijerino. While studying in France between 1922 and 1924, Cabrales became an ardent admirer of the right-wing nationalist Charles Maurras, leader of the pro-Catholic Action Française. Like Maurras, Cabrales was fervently antiliberal and hostile to representative electoral regimes. To him, liberal democracy was nothing but a "democracy that bred caudillos and deceived the people."[82] But if the militantly royalist Maurras advocated rule by one dictator, ideally the monarch, Cabrales envisioned a corporatist regime based on single-party rule. This corporatist party—the Partido Trabajador Nacionalista (Nationalist Worker's Party)—was to unite the country's "producers," that is, not only workers and peasants but also intellectuals, professionals, landlords, industrialists, and entrepreneurs. Its primary objective was also vaguely stated: "to destroy the old parties and expel all parasites from state offices." In Cabrales's polarized worldview, "parasites" were above all "professional politicians, bureaucrats, usurers, [and] hoarders of basic grains." In short, Cabrales championed an authoritarian corporatism that in its totalitarian traits tended toward fascism.

Despite their differences, the moderate and radical versions of authoritarian rule converged in important ways. Both indicted capitalism and liberal democracy for promoting class conflict instead of class harmony. As elitist as their traditional view of governance may have been, never before did elite Conservatives so strongly embrace authoritarian rule. In addition, their call for greater state intervention in the economic and social spheres represented an important break with their previous defense of a laissez-faire state. But Conservative corporatists, whether radical or moderate, most dramatically challenged political tradition by espousing a system of governance where access to power was regulated not by social origin or wealth, as traditionally the case, but by membership in occupational groups (gremios). In advocating for functional representation, they agreed that the gremios should group together agricultural producers, urban producers, and professionals. But if relative moderates like Cuadra Pasos envisioned gremios where labor and capital were more organically integrated, Cabrales and other radical corporatists tended to emphasize class differences. This was particularly evident in Cabrales's conception of a gremio grouping urban and rural popular sectors (*obreros y campesinos*) that was separate from the gremios of large rural and urban producers (*agricultores* and *industriales/empresarios*, respectively). Cuadra Pasos, by contrast, placed popular sectors into separate gremios, with "campesinos" subordinate to "agricultores" and "obreros" to "artesanos" (a gremio dominated by industriales/empresarios).

In practice, the definition of such occupational terms was highly problematic for social relations and identities were quite fluid and malleable. Not only were many upper-class Nicaraguans at once landlords, urban entrepreneurs, and merchants, but "campesino," "artesano," and "obrero" were categories that contemporaries defined in multiple and often contradictory ways. Further, the division between urban and rural laboring classes was anything but straightforward, as many urban workers left for the countryside during the lucrative coffee harvest, while peasants close to urban centers often supplemented subsistence production by working as urban wage laborers. This fluid social landscape gravely hindered elite Conservatives' efforts to promote a Catholic-based authoritarian project.

Speaking for the "People"

Following their loss of power in 1928, Conservative corporatists went to great lengths to rally the masses. Such efforts were largely geared toward winning the U.S.-supervised elections scheduled for November 1932. Despite their antidemocratic ideals, Conservative corporatists knew that as long as Nicaragua remained under U.S. control, elections represented their only viable path to political power.[83] And since the U.S. anticaudillo campaign had gravely undermined their ability to mobilize the rural populace via traditional means, Conservative oligarchs increasingly shifted their attention to urban sectors and to corporatist forms of political mobilization. But they also courted the urban populace because it was well organized. Indeed, there may not have been a better way to incorporate urban sectors into a Catholic-based corporatist regime than by building on the numerous artisan, women's, and charity organizations that Catholic priests and elite Conservatives had established after the fall of Zelaya's dictatorship. Of course, the mobilization efforts of elite Conservative corporatists also had a hegemonic aspiration. In particular, they hoped that their efforts to integrate urban sectors more fully into their own organizations would curb the social unrest that proliferated after the 1929 Wall Street crash wreaked havoc on Nicaragua's economy.[84] Their chief objective, however, was to gain control of the state.

Conservative corporatists mainly sought to mobilize popular support by reaching out to artisan organizations and other popular groups in Nicaragua's urban centers. In these encounters, they not only advocated corporatist rule but also attacked their main enemy, the Americanized "bourgeoisie." In December 1931, José Coronel Urtecho addressed Granadan artisans connected with Obrerismo Organizado, the country's largest labor group.[85] This leading vanguardista began by acknowledging that "nothing is as important for the future of Nicaragua . . . as Obrerismo." He then celebrated artisans' commitment to quality workmanship and equated artisanry with excellence. But Coronel Urtecho spent most of the rest of the evening attacking the "bourgeois." In particular, he criticized the "bourgeoisie" for brutally disrupting "social harmony" by exploiting "the poor workers." Coronel Urtecho also laced his attack with an anti-U.S. discourse, claiming that the present "merchant bourgeoisie" had secured its power by placing "political authority and foreign policy into the hands of the Yankee, thus sacrificing the nation's fate." Rejecting liberal democracy, Coronel Urtecho concluded that only a Catholic-based corporatist regime could "save" the artisan and the nation from misery and foreign rule.

Coronel Urtecho's speech echoed the radical corporatist principles espoused by his vanguardista colleague Luis Alberto Cabrales. In practice, however, Coronel Urtecho hesitated to make a radical break with existing political structures. Ignoring public pleas to the contrary, Coronel Urtecho first strove to realize his authoritarian-corporatist dreams by working within the Conservative Party. Coronel Urtecho's antibourgeois tirades were not those of an isolated political extremist. This outspoken oligarch was one of the many "nonconformist" elite Conservatives who struggled for the hearts and minds of popular sectors.

To win this battle, elite corporatists were well aware that they had to propose far-reaching social reforms. As the elections of November 1932 drew nearer, corporatists increasingly championed four major reforms: a massive distribution of state lands to "all who would like to devote themselves to agricultural work"; a moratorium on the foreclosure of indebted farms; a homestead law ensuring that urban dwellers would not lose their homes to foreclosure; and a law against what they indicted as the country's main "social cancer"—usury.[86] While some Conservative corporatists pushed for these reforms from their seats in Congress, others toured the country trying to mobilize popular support. One of the more active campaigners was Carlos Cuadra Pasos, then the country's foremost Catholic corporatist. In drumming up popular support for his reformist program, Cuadra Pasos beseeched his party to embrace the proposed social reforms so that it would return to power in the 1932 elections.

As moderate as these reforms may seem today, they were extremely threatening to upper-class Nicaraguans of the era. As Cuadra Pasos acknowledged, his call for social reforms "produced alarm because people seek to give them a socialist bent, when in reality they are nothing but the crystallization of profoundly Christian thoughts."[87] Of course, the oligarchic corporatist Cuadra Pasos was anything but a Marxist; he advocated a hierarchical, not classless, society that sanctified the principle of private property.[88] Still, his elite opponents were not completely off the mark, as his proposed reforms were about as radical as those put forth by organized labor and leftist parties.[89] Moreover, despite their concern for order and stability, Cuadra Pasos and other Catholic corporatists came to embrace the Marxist belief that radical social change carried out by a strong state was a legitimate and, at times, necessary means for achieving "social justice." His support for these ideas is just another indicator of how Caballeros Católicos like Cuadra Pasos had radicalized their views of state-society relations following the 1927 shift in U.S. imperial rule.

In the end, elite corporatists exerted more ideological influence than political power. Those working within the Conservative Party succeeded in stamping their reformist views on the party's program for the 1932 elections.[90] Yet they were unable to wrestle control of the party machinery from the old guard. This was especially evident in their failure to prevent the party from nominating Adolfo Díaz and Emiliano Chamorro as its presidential and vice presidential candidates. Both of these ex-presidents stood for what Conservative corporatists most struggled against: if Díaz symbolized the cosmopolitan, Americanized *vendepatria*, Chamorro epitomized caudillismo. Torn between reformist corporatists and traditional caudillos, the Conservative Party lost the 1932 elections to the governing Liberals by about the same margin as in 1928. Elite corporatists operating outside of the Conservative Party suffered a similar fate, as they generated little popular support for their new Partido Trabajador Nacionalista.

How are we to explain the failure of elite corporatists to capture power in the 1932 elections? No doubt their limited political influence resulted from the uneven impact of the post-1927 U.S. attack on caudillismo. While this attack effectively weakened caudillismo at the local level, it left intact caudillos' control over the Conservative Party's machinery at the national level. In addition, corporatists seeking a more radical break with the existing political order were stymied by the unwillingness of U.S. electoral officials to allow third parties to register for national elections. The United States thus played a decisive role in blocking the political rise of elite corporatists.

But these Conservative oligarchs also suffered from their blatant inability to rally the masses. Organized labor, for example, shared their frustration with capitalism and caudillismo.[91] Yet labor's main solution to these problems was a more thoroughgoing democratization of the existing system, not the antidemocratic and hierarchical order elite corporatists were calling for. Elite corporatists' attempt to bond culturally with popular sectors proved illusory as well. The class distinctions separating the two were simply too great to overcome. No matter how much these elites attacked the bourgeoisie and tried to speak "the language . . . of the people," in the eyes of most urbanites they remained "bourgeois."[92] Thus, even if a moderate Conservative corporatist like Carlos Cuadra Pasos was widely respected for his charitable work, his unwillingness to "mix with the people" ensured that the general populace viewed him as a snobbish "aristocrat."[93] Radical corporatists like Luis Alberto Cabrales faced similar difficulties in reaching out to popular sectors, largely because, as an artisan stressed, they "did not belong to the working class."[94]

In fact, many artisans were greatly angered by Conservative corporatists' attempts to speak for the "artesano" and the "obrero." A leader of Granada's artisans, Alfonso Castillo, fiercely criticized members of "the blue race" (aristocracy) for attempting to mobilize artisan support on behalf of their authoritarian project.[95] Castillo stressed that the interests of the "nobility" were inherently at odds with those of the "artisan class." But above all he attacked the populist image elite corporatists were desperately seeking to project. In particular, he criticized those "who have been born and have been raised with all of life's comfort" for acting as if they could feel "our pain and sorrow." Only "humble people," he claimed, could truly represent the masses since "pain can only be explained when one feels it." For Castillo, elite corporatists' efforts to mobilize popular support were nothing more than "a hypocritical smile on the lip, looking to obtain a preconceived end [and] pretending to surprise us humble people with fallacious and abolished theories that have been and will continue to be a disaster for the artisan and the proletariat more generally." According to Castillo, in the worldview of elite corporatists "we artisans do not have any rights other than to be beasts of burden and to lend them a hand so that their ilk can enter parliament . . . where all they do is pass laws detrimental to the interests of the artisan class."

By late 1932, Conservative corporatists realized that they could not mobilize necessary political support on their own. This inability to move the masses helped push them to seek a populist dictator who could realize their authoritarian project. As chapter 9 will show, they made what now seems an incomprehensible decision, turning to a revolutionary nationalist whom most elite Nicaraguans deemed a dangerous communist: Augusto Sandino.

Conclusion

In the end, U.S. efforts to impose "democracy" in Nicaragua only pushed elite Conservatives further away from the U.S. model of development they had once admired. Certainly their efforts to establish a corporatist dictatorship also reflected a broader trend, for elites throughout Latin America were then rejecting electoral politics in favor of new forms of authoritarian governance. In large part, these elites turned against electoralism with the rise of mass politics.[96] For decades, Latin American democracies had remained very elitist, as much of the population was excluded from elections. However, this system of "aristocratic republics" came crashing down when the 1929 Depression unleashed an unprecedented surge of social mobilization. Pressure from below clearly pushed Nicaragua's Conservative oligarchs to embrace authoritarian corporatism. Yet they felt this pressure already before the 1929 crash.

Indeed, the main catalyst for Conservatives' antidemocratic turn was not the Great Depression but the deepening of U.S. imperial rule during the 1920s.

Above all, Conservative oligarchs embraced authoritarian corporatism in response to the "democratizing" effects of the U.S. occupation. Their author-itarian turn sprang from the inadvertent ways that dollar diplomats strength-ened the economic power of small- and medium-scale producers while weakening that of landlords. Dollar diplomacy further eroded elite authority by spreading U.S.-style mass culture to Nicaragua—a culture that, in the eyes of Conservative oligarchs, promoted dangerous ideals of "equality." But what most weakened the political power of Nicaragua's wealthiest elite sector was the U.S. military's campaign to secure clean elections and eliminate rural caudillismo. These democratizing impulses of U.S. imperial rule led Conser-vative oligarchs to worry that they were, as one U.S. officer implied, "losing [their] grip" over society.[97] But Nicaragua's most entrenched elite sector apparently feared more than just the erosion of its authority. Time and again, Conservative oligarchs justified their embrace of authoritarian corporatism as a means to defend the nation against both imperial impositions and Americanization. For them, there was nothing irrational about courting Sandino. While right-wing elite corporatists elsewhere in Latin America ab-horred leftist revolutionaries like Sandino, for Nicaragua's Conservative corporatists this guerrillero could signify not just authoritarianism but also anti-Americanism.

9 Revolutionary Nationalism

Elite Conservatives, Sandino, and the Struggle
for a De-Americanized Nicaragua

WHEN GENERAL AUGUSTO SANDINO drove into the nation's capital on 19 May 1933, Conservative corporatists were among the few Nicaraguans eagerly awaiting the guerrillero's arrival. This was only the second time that Sandino had left his remote stronghold in the northern Segovias since the twenty-year U.S. occupation came to an end on 2 January. The world-famous guerrillero had first visited Managua on 2 February to sign the peace treaty that formally ended the six-year war his peasant-based army had waged against U.S. Marines and Nicaraguan troops from the Guardia Nacional. Back then, large crowds had celebrated the seasoned revolutionary for bringing peace to their war-torn country. But when Sandino returned in May to found a new political party, the capital's mood had chilled. Above all, Managuans feared that the true purpose of Sandino's visit was to organize a communist uprising like the one his former aide, Agustín Farabundo Martí, had vainly launched in neighboring El Salvador a year earlier. Although staunchly anticommunist, Sandino's sympathizers within the Granada-based Conservative oligarchy did not share the fears of most other elite Nicaraguans. On the contrary, they hoped to enlist the guerrillero in their quest to establish a corporatist dictatorship that would rid Nicaragua of the last vestiges of U.S. imperialism. Sandino's second trip to Managua, to launch his new party, would be the oligarchs' chance to finally meet with him.

Conservatives' efforts to forge an alliance with Sandino in 1933 might seem inscrutable, for the two came from opposite ends of the social and political spectrum. If Conservatives hailed from Nicaragua's most exclusive planter class, Sandino (1895–1934) was the illegitimate son of an Indian servant and a medium-scale coffee grower from a small village in rural Masaya (Niquinohomo).[1] And while Conservatives were widely considered Central America's foremost fascists, Sandino was viewed by many as a communist revolutionary. As early as 1925 elite Conservatives from Granada fretted that Mexican "bolsheviks" would bring to Central America the red-and-black banner that symbolized, in their eyes, "blood and extermination."[2] By 1927, their fears essentially came true as Sandino appropriated the *rojinegro* flag and the leftist

20. Captured Sandinista flag. *Courtesy of U.S. National Archives.*

ideals of the Mexican Revolution in his struggle for a "new Nicaragua" (see figure 20).

Why, then, did Conservatives' deep-seated horror of revolutionary upheaval not deter them from reaching out to Sandino in 1933? No doubt geographic distance helps explain why Granada-based oligarchs felt less threatened by Sandino than did northern elites who lived much closer to his base of operation in the Segovias (see map 5). In addition, elite Conservatives had a tradition of defending their political interests by forging alliances with popular movements, particularly indigenous ones.[3] One might thus be inclined to think it was simply short-lived political expediency that pushed Conservatives toward Sandino. Indeed, these oligarchs admitted that their inability to rally popular support for their authoritarian project was the main reason they decided to court the famous guerrillero.

Yet Conservative oligarchs were also attracted to Sandino because they identified with his brand of revolutionary nationalism. First and foremost, they shared the guerrillero's fierce opposition to the U.S. occupation and the Americanization of Nicaraguans' "way of life." They could also relate to Sandino's anticapitalist, antibourgeois sentiments, as well as his virulent,

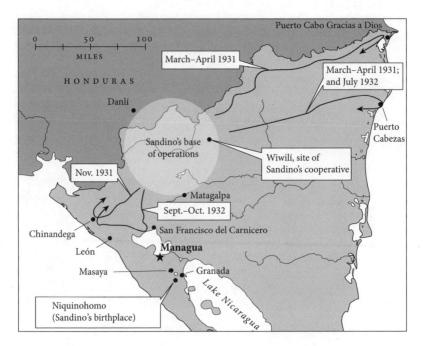

MAP 5 Sandino's base of operations and major Sandinista raids, 1927–33

agrarian-based nationalism that celebrated race-mixture (*mestizaje*). Finally, both firmly believed that the only way Nicaragua could resist U.S. imperial impositions was by establishing a corporatist dictatorship. In the end, Conservatives' ideological convergence with Sandino was anything but complete. If anti-Americanism helped bring self-proclaimed reactionaries closer to the continent's most celebrated popular revolutionary, competing visions of a "new Nicaragua" would ensure that Conservatives' efforts to forge an alliance with Sandino never bore fruit. When approached with an offer, the guer-rillero refused to formally join forces with reactionary oligarchs.

The fascinating if ambivalent ties that Conservative oligarchs forged with Sandino have eluded scholarly attention. Although the historiography on the Sandino Rebellion is immense, it has concentrated almost exclusively on the guerrilla war that Sandino's "Defending Army of the National Sovereignty of Nicaragua" (Ejército Defensor de la Soberanía Nacional de Nicaragua) waged against U.S. and Guardia troops in the Segovias. Initially, scholars tended to stress the anti-imperialist thrust of the Sandinista struggle.[4] Over time, however, the scholarly focus shifted toward the social objectives of the charismatic guerrillero and his followers. In general, scholars have emphasized Sandino's highly eclectic social vision, which drew on the wide range of ideologies and belief systems—including socialism, communism, anarcho-syndicalism, and spiritism—that he encountered while working in the oilfields of revolutionary Mexico between 1923 and 1926.[5] Charting new paths, more recent studies have explored the social outlook of the more than two thousand men and women who fought with Sandino.[6] These studies show that the Sandinistas consisted largely of Segovian mountain peasants who were waging a revolutionary struggle for political autonomy and social justice. And nowhere was the revolutionary nature of the Sandino Rebellion more apparent than in the new, military-based state that these insurgents created in the Segovias. Thanks to this bottom-up view, we have a clearer understanding of how the Sandinistas strove to remake local society. Yet due to the scholarship's regional focus, key aspects of what may be Latin America's most celebrated anti-U.S. insurgency remain unexplored. Above all, we know very little about how the Sandinista struggle for a "new Nicaragua" was viewed by the vast majority of Nicaraguans who lived outside of the Segovias.

If we look beyond the immediate war zone, the Sandino Rebellion takes on new meanings. On the one hand, this broader view shows that Sandino's popular support in the rest of Nicaragua was significantly weaker than it was in the Segovias. On the other, it indicates that Sandino enjoyed much stronger elite support than commonly assumed. And this support was not because Sandino, as a recent study posits, "tried to carry through in the name of the poor and oppressed a bourgeois nationalist revolution of the rich."[7] On the contrary, as one Sandinista put it, the guerrilleros saw their fight as a "struggle of us the poor against the rich."[8] Finally, a look beyond the Segovian war shows that Sandino did not give up his efforts to create a "new Nicaragua" once the U.S. occupation ended. He simply used different means. As Sandino promised his soldiers when they demobilized in February 1933, "This revolution that I am going to make is not with rifles nor with arms; it is going to be a political revolution."[9] It was in the course of this "political revolution" that Conservative oligarchs would seek an alliance with Sandino under the banner of anti-Americanism. But before they could reach out to the guerrillero, they first had to overcome a history of missed opportunities and mutual distrust.

Elite Conservatives' Shifting Relations with Sandinismo, 1927–1932

Sandino's revolutionary movement emerged with the U.S. intervention in the 1926–27 civil war between Liberal insurgents and the ruling Conservatives. Of the many Liberal generals, the thirty-two-year-old Augusto Sandino (see figure 21) was the only one to reject the U.S.-imposed peace treaty of May 1927. Instead, he and his troops retreated to the inaccessible mountains in the Segovias, where they began a protracted guerrilla war against U.S. Marines and Guardia troops. From early on, Sandino's struggle garnered worldwide support from a wide range of international organizations, particularly the Communist International, the Fellowship of Reconciliation, and Victor Raúl Haya de la Torre's American Popular Revolutionary Alliance (APRA). In addition, numerous Latin American communists and other leftist radicals trekked from as far as Mexico, the Dominican Republic, and Colombia to fight with Sandino's army; the most prominent was the Salvadoran communist leader Agustín Farabundo Martí, who served as Sandino's private secretary between 1928 and 1929. Thanks to this broad-based international support, Sandino became one of the world's leading anti-imperialist icons of the interwar era. Exemplifying his sudden rise to fame, Chinese nationalists celebrated their 1928 victory over a pro-Japanese regime by marching into Beijing with portraits of the Nicaraguan guerrillero.[10]

Yet as popular as Sandino was abroad, the Nicaraguan public long disregarded his anti-U.S. struggle. Of course, this was not the case in the Segovias, where Sandino's movement greatly polarized local society and was fiercely condemned by local elites, whether Liberal or Conservative. But Nicaraguans living beyond the Segovias first paid little attention to the Sandino Rebellion. Some of Sandino's urban supporters claimed that this apathy resulted from the government's censorship of news reports on Sandinista activities.[11] In reality, however, most Nicaraguan newspapers regularly published articles on the war. While the media often denounced the Sandinistas as bloodthirsty "bandits," it mostly portrayed the Sandino Rebellion as if it was occurring in a foreign country. Indeed, because the war was circumscribed to the remote Segovias until November 1931, many Nicaraguans perceived the Sandinista struggle not as their own but as a peculiarly "Segovian problem." And in many ways they were right, for the Sandinista struggle drew much of its force from this region's unique political-cultural milieu.[12] Even Sandino admitted that his cause suffered greatly from its "lack of friends in the principal cities."[13]

21. General Sandino *(center)* and two members of his general staff—Agustín Farabundo Martí of El Salvador *(right)* and José de Paredes of Mexico *(left)*—in El Salvador en route to Mexico, 1929. *Courtesy of U.S. National Archives.*

Sandinismo's limited appeal was not for lack of popular opposition to the U.S. occupiers. Time and again, urban dwellers openly demonstrated against the numerous offenses perpetrated by U.S. military personnel. Yet no matter how fiercely the demonstrators denounced the U.S. transgressors, few publicly sympathized with Sandino's cause. The largest anti-U.S. demonstration of the era is a good example: On 25 October 1931, over six thousand Nicaraguans took to the capital's streets to protest the inability of U.S. and Nicaraguan authorities to solve the country's deepening economic crisis. Many marchers carried colorful, anti-U.S. signs such as "Down with the oranges of California . . . and *viva* the oranges of Chinandega." In addition, student and labor leaders made speeches denouncing the U.S. occupation. Yet not one sign or speech mentioned the Sandinistas.[14]

Geographic distance and government repression help explain why such anti-U.S. sentiments did not necessarily translate into open support for the Sandinistas. But perhaps more important, many Nicaraguans simply did not share Sandino's brand of revolutionary nationalism. Above all, Sandino misjudged how few Nicaraguans would follow him in denouncing U.S. efforts to secure "free and fair" elections. Not only did many Liberal insurgents of 1926–27 vilify their former comrade-in-arms for refusing to accept their party's victory in the 1928 elections, they continued to valorize U.S. ideals of democracy, which Sandino violently rejected. The violence that the Sandinistas inflicted on their fellow citizens of course also alienated potential supporters. The guerrilleros were particularly infamous for their "vest cuts," by which they chopped off their victims' heads and arms. With good reason, then, Sandino warned his men that "most of the people of Nicaragua don't like us."[15]

Given this antipathy, it is ever more striking that influential Conservative oligarchs from Granada and other regions openly supported Sandino's anti-U.S. cause from early on. Already in 1927 leading Conservative newspapers of Managua and Granada endorsed Sandino's demand that U.S. troops leave Nicaragua immediately. Prominent Conservatives also attempted to gain the guerrillero's political support on the eve of the 1928 elections. The most important overture was instigated by the newly formed Partido Autonomista. Although this nationalist group included Liberals, it was dominated by Conservative corporatists such as Toribio Tijerino, Salvador Buitrago Díaz, Adolfo Ortega Díaz, and Gabry Rivas. In general, the Autonomistas adhered to social Catholic principles, believed in a strong state, rejected Wall Street's control of Nicaragua's public finances, and implored their compatriots to "liberate themselves from the old parties."[16] As good Caballeros Católicos, they also opposed the Americanization of Nicaraguan culture and society. Above all, however, Autonomistas resisted the post-1927 militarization of U.S. imperial rule. Yet because most Autonomistas were pacifists, they also implored Sandino to lay down his arms and join their peaceful struggle for national autonomy.

Despite their frantic efforts, the Autonomistas were consistently rebuffed by Sandino. Although the guerrillero left no records explaining his refusal to meet with them, we do know that he did not believe in confronting U.S. imperialism with pacifism. "One does not discuss the sovereignty of a people," Sandino famously told a U.S. admiral, "but rather defends it with weapons in hand."[17] Still, this did not prevent Sandino from reaching out to groups like the socialist Partido Laborista, which also used peaceful means to struggle against the U.S. occupation. And since these groups were dominated by dissident Liberals and artisans, Sandino likely rejected the Autonomistas for their Conservative and oligarchic background. Indeed, one can only speculate whether Sandino still resented the way he, as a child, was treated while working on coffee plantations owned by Conservative oligarchs from Granada.[18] Unable to move Sandino and banned from the 1928 elections, the Partido Autonomista fell apart, and most of its leaders were expelled from Nicaragua by the Liberal government that came to power in 1929. While some Autonomistas turned against Sandino, others continued to work on his behalf. The most active supporter was Toribio Tijerino (1888–1963), who had been President Emiliano Chamorro's private secretary between 1917 and 1920. From his Honduran exile, Tijerino supplied the Sandinistas with arms and distributed Sandinista propaganda, such as the journal *Sandino: Revista anti-imperialista*, which his brother published in Costa Rica. Despite the Autonomistas' political failure, their open courting of Sandino and the greater sympathy they elicited from Conservative papers led many Nicaraguans to believe that the Sandinistas enjoyed their greatest political support from those against whom they had rebelled in the first place: the Conservative "vendepatrias."[19]

Such public views were reinforced by the murky conspiracies hatched by former president Emiliano Chamorro, who together with Adolfo Díaz was one of the Conservative politicians Sandino most despised. At first, Chamorro provided the pro-Sandino Autonomistas with political and financial support. His support might have been ideologically motivated, as the Autonomista leader Toribio Tijerino would later insinuate.[20] But Chamorro himself admitted that it was primarily a Machiavellian scheme designed to sabotage the U.S.-supervised elections of 1928.[21] To further disrupt these elections, Chamorro's allies waged a terror campaign in the Nicaraguan countryside. And since much of this violence was centered in the Segovias, many Nicaraguans believed that Chamorro's followers and the Sandinistas were working hand-in-hand.[22] Even after his party lost the 1928 elections, Chamorro continued as if he supported Sandino's cause. Not only did he allegedly encourage Conservatives from as far south as Granada and Rivas to join the Sandinistas in the northern Segovias, but he was also accused by U.S. military intelligence of planning an anti-U.S. armed uprising.[23] In the end, such plans never materialized. Moreover, very few pro-Chamorro Conservatives joined the Sandinistas or provided them with arms and ammunition. Still, rumors that Sandino was in league with Chamorro proved hard to silence, as even the guerrillero was forced to acknowledge.[24]

Other elite Conservatives from Granada were more sincere than Chamorro in supporting the early stages of Sandino's anti-U.S. struggle. Much of this support came from the vanguardistas, who opposed the rule of caudillos like Chamorro. Although these corporatists were born into Americanized households, they identified with Sandino's anti-Americanism. The vanguardista José Coronel Urtecho later testified that he and other Granadan oligarchs were "supporters of Sandino because he was anti-Yanquista like us. Although we were rooted in North American culture . . . we opposed U.S. domination over [Latin] America and the things they sought to impose: commercialism, capitalist industrialism, capitalism."[25] The vanguardistas frequently met in a private home where, under a Sandino portrait and an altar dedicated to the guerrillero, they would hatch "imaginary war plans" against the U.S. occupiers.[26] But it was in the realm of propaganda that these Granadan Conservatives most effectively contributed to Sandino's cause. Exploiting their foreign contacts, they clandestinely distributed to the local populace large quantities of pro-Sandino handbills printed abroad. In addition, they often sneaked out at night to plaster prominent facades with slogans such as "To be Sandinista is to be Nicaraguan." One night they even victimized the sacrosanct facade of Granada's elite social club—"Leave your rocking chairs and follow Sandino" was the memorable message they chose for their fellow club members.[27] Like the Autonomistas, vanguardistas sought to meet with Sandino, but to no avail.

Sandino's repeated refusals to respond to Conservatives' overtures diminished their support for him. But their eventual turn against Sandino more fundamentally responded to two events that radicalized the Sandinista struggle in 1929. The first was Sandino's surprising decision to go to Mexico in June 1929 to obtain more military and financial aid. Although Sandino had envisioned this would be a brief visit, he stayed for nearly a year, leading most of his international supporters to conclude that the Sandinista struggle had fizzled out. In reality, the Sandinistas continued their war in the Segovias (see figure 22), bogging down about fifteen hundred U.S. and Guardia troops. But the absence of their charismatic leader greatly delegitimized their cause in the eyes of Sandino's Conservative supporters. In particular, elite Conservatives believed that foreign forces were transforming his nationalist struggle into full-blown class warfare. The formerly pro-Sandino *La Prensa*, for instance, claimed that the "Segovias are a bed of Bolshevik territory, a Russian island in the American continent."[28] Contrary to press reports, few foreigners joined

22. Sandinista soldiers in the Segovian mountains.
Courtesy of U.S. National Archives.

the Sandinistas during their leader's Mexican sojourn. Still, these reports were not completely wrong, as the guerrilleros exploited Sandino's absence to intensify their attacks against local merchants and landlords.[29] Compared to Sandino, who consistently emphasized the movement's anti-U.S. trajectory, many Sandinistas were more compelled by social grievances.[30] In all likelihood, then, Sandino's elite supporters were troubled not just by his prolonged absence but by the way it helped radicalize the war waged by Sandino's troops.

Such fears were reinforced by the Wall Street crash of October 1929. The crash cost many people their jobs, which in turn spawned "bandit" activity—particularly cattle rustling—throughout the country. With more outlaws marauding in their own backyard, elite Conservatives now began to fear that the whole country was becoming "Segovianized."[31] But perhaps more important, the crash spurred the "Nicaraguanization" of the war in the Segovias, for it pushed the United States to replace its combat troops with Nicaraguan soldiers from the Guardia Nacional. In addition, the crash led the Guardia to establish paramilitary forces that were subsidized by rich Segovian merchants and coffee growers. In response, the Sandinistas stepped up their attacks against local elites.[32] When Sandino finally returned to the Segovias in May 1930, many of his former Conservative sympathizers had already concluded that his "patriotic" struggle had irrevocably "degenerated" into simple "banditry."[33]

Still, these Conservative oligarchs remained less inclined than most upper-class Nicaraguans to view Sandinismo as a revolutionary threat to the nation. And their view did not change much even when the Sandinistas started to attack the coastal districts of western Nicaragua in November 1931 (see map 5). This was not the first time the Sandinistas had ventured out of the Segovias. Seven months earlier they raided U.S. banana and logging companies on the Atlantic coast. These attacks helped seal the U.S. government's decision to end the occupation after the elections of November 1932.[34] But urban Nicaraguans were not perturbed by raids in a region geographically and culturally removed from their lives. Their attitude changed radically when Sandino's men suddenly appeared in the densely populated departments of León and Chinandega. Although the insurgents retreated as soon as Guardia troops arrived, their first incursion into the Pacific coastal plain jolted the nation. Throughout 1932, the Sandinistas continued to raid this zone, going as far south as San Francisco del Carnicero, a town at the northern tip of Lake Managua.

These brazen raids deep into the country's center of power led many Nicaraguans and U.S. officials to believe that the Sandinista movement had assumed a "revolutionary character" that could spread nationwide.[35] Not surprisingly, they reinforced the Sandinistas' belief that they would eventually triumph. After one such raid, one Sandinista officer wrote to another: "I think that I will be writing to you soon from a city, perhaps Managua, because there is no doubt that people are now awakened and that they have been stirred by the combats near urban areas."[36] According to U.S. military intelligence, the Sandinistas gained much support in western Nicaragua, particularly among university students and the rural populace of the León/Chinandega region.[37] U.S. military officials worried that peasants and rural laborers believed the Sandinistas were better dressed and equipped than the Guardia's Nicaraguan troops, and thus more likely to win the war. Nicaraguan civil authorities, by contrast, were mainly concerned that the masses had "kindly" received the Sandinista message that "all goods were common property and that taking from the wealthy was not stealing."[38] Leading Conservatives also fretted over these Sandinista raids; yet few believed that they actually threatened the existing order.[39]

Conservatives' less perturbed view of Sandinismo was also apparent in their response to an event that greatly unnerved upper classes throughout Central America: El Salvador's popular uprising of January 1932, which ended with the state-sponsored massacre of over ten thousand peasants and Indians. Typically, the Nicaraguan press reduced this complex rebellion to a simple image—a "bloody" Communist revolution in which professional agitators had encouraged Indians to sow "Red terror" against innocent townsfolk and landowners.[40] Yet Nicaraguan papers differed sharply about whether their country was on the edge of a similar uprising. The Liberal press generally claimed that, because of Sandinismo, a communist revolution was a "real threat." And in their view, the Nicaraguans most susceptible to communist "infiltration" were precisely those who formed the social base of Sandinismo: the peasantry. The Salvadoran uprising thus pushed Liberal politicians to tour the Nicaraguan countryside and warn peasants not to embrace communism.[41] Most Conservative papers, by contrast, not only refused to collapse Sandinismo with communism, they downplayed the peasantry's vulnerability to communist agitation.

Conservatives' dismissal of the Sandinista/communist threat had much to do with the "myth of rural sanctity" that was so fundamental to their new nationalist imagination. Or as the Conservative daily *La Prensa* claimed, "Nicaragua is not a propitious land for communism, because it does not have the terrible and odious problems that emerge when social inequality oppresses a certain sector of the population."[42] And Nicaragua was allegedly free of such "odious problems" precisely because its rural masses benefited from a landed elite that was less capitalist and more benevolent than elsewhere in the isthmus. As discussed in chapter 7, this bucolic image fell far short of reality. Yet it powerfully molded Conservatives' views of the Sandinistas as "honest" if "primitive" peasants who became "bandits" not because of any affinity with communism but for the despair caused by capitalism and the wanton violence of U.S.-led forces.[43]

Leading Conservatives therefore openly advocated for a peaceful solution to the Sandinista Rebellion. Time and again, they implored that "pacification" could be achieved only via an armistice and the realization of "social-Catholic works" in the Segovias.[44] In addition, Conservative papers and politicians opposed government efforts to escalate the war. They remained unfazed even as the Sandinistas reached the apex of their military power in mid-1932. Indeed, in August 1932 the Conservative Party included the call for an armistice in its platform for the upcoming national elections.[45]

By 1932 many Conservative oligarchs had come to admire Sandino's ability to resist the U.S. occupiers. Still, most believed that once the armistice was established the guerrillero's influence would fade. For instance, the newspaper of Granada's Conservative oligarchy, *El Diario Nicaragüense*, stated that "Sandino with weapon in hand against the Yankee is of great merit in the Segovias" but that once the country returned to peace, he would "no longer wield any kind of political influence."[46] In reality, however, Sandino's political influence would rise, not sink, once peace was established following the U.S. troop withdrawal of January 1933. And elite Conservatives closely affiliated with *El Diario Nicaragüense* would be the ones who reached out to the guerrillero with the greatest enthusiasm.

Reembracing Sandino, 1932–1933

Conservative oligarchs made their first public overture to the guerrillero on 2 March 1932, when *El Diario Nicaragüense* published José Coronel Urtecho's response to Sandino's call for a boycott of the upcoming elections. While this influential Conservative corporatist reiterated Sandino's view that the Sandinista struggle concerned the nation as a whole, he opposed the proposed electoral boycott. Instead, Coronel Urtecho hoped to enlist the guerrillero's support for a nationalist movement that would seek to obtain power via the ballot box. In the months leading up to the November elections, more and more elite Conservatives followed Coronel Urtecho's lead in cautiously reaching out to Sandino. Conservatives hoped Sandino would be able to do what they had not: marshal popular support for their corporatist project.

Conservatives were fortunate that their reembrace of Sandino occurred just as the guerrillero mollified his own views of Nicaraguan elites. At the beginning of his anti-U.S. struggle, Sandino courted "patriotic" elites, particularly Liberal ones. But after he rejected the Liberal victory in the 1928 elections, he adopted a stridently antielite stance. By late 1931, the guerrillero again realized that he needed elite support in order to expand his political base beyond the Segovias. He thus accepted the offer of Liberal exiles in El Salvador to organize anti-U.S. elites in Nicaragua's urban centers on his behalf. This small group—the Comite Pro-Liberación de Nicaragua—was officially led by a Liberal general (Horacio Portocarrero) who had fought against the U.S. invaders of 1912. Unbeknownst to Sandino, the group's actual leader was the Conservative oligarch Toribio Tijerino.[47] And as U.S. spies noted, Tijerino mainly sought "to induce Sandino to sign a pact with Conservatives."[48]

Not coincidentally, the Conservatives who most ardently pursued Sandino hailed from the stronghold of elite corporatists: Granada. Throughout 1932, Granada's Conservatives clandestinely distributed leaflets defending Sandino's armed struggle and pasted the guerrillero's portrait all across the city.[49] Some also sought secretly to rally public support for their efforts to form a pro-Sandino nationalist party.[50] Others promoted the fleeting presidential candidacy of the Conservative Ernesto Bermúdez, who proclaimed his desire to rule in a loose coalition with the Sandinistas. This declaration stunned the political establishment, for it implied that the Sandinistas were to be considered, as one paper stated, "an indispensable element for the political organization of the country."[51] In reality, Bermúdez was simply anticipating the upcoming efforts of Portocarrero's group to have Granada-based Conservatives coordinate their 1932 electoral campaign with Sandino.[52] Although these efforts bore little fruit, they reinforced the widespread belief that prominent Conservatives were aiding Sandino. Such rumors only hardened when in October 1932 the Nicaraguan public found out that twenty-five young Conservative oligarchs composed the mounted group that had been roaming Granada's countryside at night, yelling the names of Sandino and his feared general Pedrón Altamirano.[53]

Conservatives' courting of Sandino dramatically intensified after their crushing defeat in the 1932 elections. This development surprised Sandino, who had only recently stated that, were the Conservatives to win, they would not "seek agreements with us, nor we with them, and that the matter will be resolved with bullets."[54] Yet scarcely a month after their electoral defeat, many elite Conservatives had moved so close to the guerrillero that the U.S. minister to Nicaragua, Matthew Hanna, accused them of espousing "the professed ideals of Sandino."[55] These Conservatives certainly hoped to exploit Sandino for their own political purposes. But they also came to support the guerrillero's main goal: to secure a Nicaragua free from any form of U.S. influence. These were not necessarily contradictory impulses. Many Conservatives shared the belief of La Prensa's editor, Pedro Joaquín Chamorro Zelaya, that they had lost the elections because voters continued to associate the Conservative Party with the "evil" banner of "Americanismo."[56] To them, this fateful association was a false one, particularly since leading Conservatives had consistently denounced the post-1927 militarization of U.S. imperial rule. But as Chamorro admitted, Conservatives' pre-1927 exaltation of "Americanismo" had led them to be etched in the public's mind as "shameful" Yanquistas.[57] By thus aligning themselves with Sandino, Conservative oligarchs did not pursue nationalist goals alone. They also sought to use the celebrated guerrillero to shake their *Americanista* infamy.

Prospects for a peace treaty had never been better than after the 1932 elections. Not only were U.S. troops about to leave Nicaragua, but Sandino had instigated his rebellion on behalf of the newly elected president, Juan Bautista Sacasa, who had been the civilian leader of the 1926–27 insurgents. Moreover, with no economic recovery in sight, the distressed populace wished for nothing more than an end to the costly six-year war, which had already cost the lives of over one thousand Sandinistas and a large but unknown number of civilians.[58] Sandino's war-weary troops also longed for peace.[59] The Sandinistas had been discouraged by their inability to disrupt the 1932 elections beyond the Segovias. They also had been greatly affected by the civil war that broke out in neighboring Honduras in November 1932, for the war shut down their principal supply line and deprived them of their main safe haven.

But only after U.S. troops left on 2 January 1933 did Sandino agree to lay down his arms. The guerrillero paved the path for peace when he met with twelve prominent Liberal and Conservative politicians who had trekked to the Segovias in late January.[60] This peace mission of the so-called Grupo Patriótico was bitterly opposed by the Guardia's native officer corps, the Segovian elite, leading Liberals, and much of the Liberal press. Managua's leading Liberal paper, for example, claimed that the Sandinistas were nothing but bloodthirsty savages bent on carrying out a "chaotic communist socialist-sandinista revolution."[61] In its eyes, "peace should be made by shooting Sandino." Most Conservative politicians and papers, by contrast, supported the peace talks and stressed that Sandino's armed struggle had been legitimate. For them, the question was not whether Sandino was a devious communist, but whether he wanted to become a legitimate political actor by laying down his arms now that the U.S. troops were gone, or whether he would regress into a simple "bandit."[62] To their joy, Sandino

23. Sandino and the signers of the peace treaty of 2 February 1933. Sitting in
the front are the signers *(from left to right):* David Stadthagen (representative
of the Conservative Party), President Juan Bautista Sacasa, Augusto Sandino,
Crisanto Sacasa (representative of the Liberal Party). Standing in the rear are
members of Sandino's delegation *(from left to right):* Horacio Portocarrero,
Sofonías Salvatierra, Pedro José Zepeda, and Salvador Calderón Ramírez.
Courtesy of Instituto de Historia de Nicaragua y de Centroamérica.

accepted the peace treaty on 2 February after flying into Managua earlier that
day to confer with President Sacasa (see figure 23). While Sandino agreed to
demobilize his army of about eighteen hundred soldiers, Sacasa promised to
give amnesty to the Sandinistas, help them build an extensive agricultural
cooperative in the eastern Segovias, and allow them to maintain a force of
one hundred troops for at least one year. The signing of the peace treaty
triggered celebrations nationwide. In Managua, thousands streamed into the
streets shouting *vivas* for Nicaragua, peace, and Sandino. When the guerrillero left for the Segovias the next day, he received an unprecedented send-
off from the capital's populace.

This immense support for peace emboldened elite Conservatives to publicize even more strongly their affinity with Sandino. Conservative newspapers

drew particular pleasure in reiterating Sandino's claim that he and his compatriots had achieved something that had always eluded the United States: they had restored political stability to Nicaragua. Or as *La Prensa* editorialized, "The Nicaraguan people now know well that it is a great lie that this country can be peaceful only under the dominating boot of intervention."[63] In addition, Conservative journalists went to the Segovias to report on the enigmatic Sandinistas. So anti-U.S. were their press accounts that U.S. Minister Hanna demanded "an end to the publication of such defamatory articles."[64] Conservatives also staged rallies to honor visiting members of the Sandinista movement. Perhaps the largest one occurred in their bastion of Granada, where a huge crowd feted Sandino's parents, his brother Sócrates (also a Sandinista officer), and Juan Ferretti, the only Granadan to serve as an officer in Sandino's army.[65]

Conservatives further underscored their newly found ties with Sandino when the Nicaraguan Congress debated the amnesty promised by President Sacasa. Much of this debate centered on how to label Sandino, an issue of special concern to the guerrilla leader himself.[66] Many Liberal congressmen insisted on calling Sandino a bandit, not a general. Conservatives countered by claiming that Sandino deserved to be named a general as a result of his "patriotic" struggle against the U.S. occupiers. One Conservative deputy (Gustavo Manzanares) went as far as to valorize Sandino as "the Continent's leading figure."[67] In the end, Conservatives prevailed and Congress passed an amnesty decree that identified Sandino as a general.

The main way Conservatives spearheaded Sandino's political rehabilitation was by supporting the guerrillero's quest to establish a new "Autonomist" party. Liberals in unison opposed the creation of a Sandino-led party, with most fearing that it was either a front for the expansion of "Sovietism" or, conversely, a Conservative scheme to siphon off Liberal votes. Sandino's political call certainly also concerned many elite Conservatives, but they tended to react with greater sympathy. Some Conservative corporatists even proclaimed their desire to join Sandino's party. It was these oligarchs whose support Sandino would eventually enlist in his political struggle for a "new Nicaragua."

Sandino's decision to reach out to Conservative corporatists had much to do with the dearth of political allies he could choose from. While he was popular among the approximately three hundred university students in western Nicaragua and the few thousand Spanish-speaking enclave workers on

the Atlantic coast, both groups were politically too weak. Peasants, a seemingly natural ally, were hardly a viable alternative. Not only did they lack their
own organizations, many had become clients of Sandino's main enemy: the
Guardia Nacional. Yet what most hurt the guerrillero was how little support
he now enjoyed from his earliest urban allies: leftist, artisan-based groups.
Sandino's 1930 break with the Communist International greatly tainted his
relations with Nicaragua's fledgling communist movement, particularly the
Partido Trabajador Nicaragüense (Nicaraguan Worker's Party), founded in
1931.[68] But more important, the guerrillero had alienated noncommunist
labor groups as well. Above all, his relations with Nicaragua's largest artisan
organization, the Liberal-based Obrerismo Organizado, deteriorated significantly after he rejected the Liberal victory in the 1928 elections.

Sandino's relentless opposition to U.S. democratization efforts only heightened the fears of many artisans that the guerrillero was just another authoritarian caudillo—the very kind of politician they most despised.[69] Sandino's
vague socioeconomic program also pleased few artisans. Obreristas especially
took offense at his proposal to solve unemployment by sending the urban
poor to till the land.[70] In November 1932, Sandino further shocked many
artisans when he had the popular labor leader Arturo Vega executed. An early
supporter of Sandino, Vega had repeatedly risked his life to distribute pro-
Sandino handbills among the urban populace. After being exiled to El Salvador in December 1930, Vega helped found Sandino's main political front,
the Comite Pro-Liberación de Nicaragua. On the eve of the 1932 elections,
Vega was back in the Segovias. It was there that he encouraged the Sandinista
general Juan Gregorio Colindres to proclaim himself the country's provisional president. This proclamation so infuriated Sandino that he ordered
Vega's execution. In doing so, Sandino only reinforced artisans' fear that he
and his men were, as Managua's militant printers union exclaimed, "bandits."[71] Sandinista violence, not just political differences, thus drove many
artisans to oppose an alliance with Sandino in 1933.

In consequence, the guerrillero warily considered Conservatives' overtures. The first clear sign of their growing rapport came in late February 1933,
when Sandino selected as his medium of communication Managua's *La
Nueva Prensa*, then the main platform of Conservative corporatists. This
selection hardly surprised U.S. officials, who deemed *La Nueva Prensa* the
country's most anti-U.S. and pro-Sandino daily.[72] Yet its editor, the forty-
three-year-old Conservative landlord Gabry Rivas, shared a tense history

with Sandino. For long, Rivas had been a stalwart of the Conservative Party. Not only did he participate in the 1925 coup by Emiliano Chamorro, he also helped organize the 1928 campaign of the Conservative ticket headed by two Granadan oligarchs, the "Sugar King" Adolfo Benard Vivas and Julio Cardenal Argüello (see figure 24). After the Conservative defeat in the 1928 elections, Rivas joined the pro-Sandino Partido Autonomista. He became such an ardent Sandino supporter that he was among the Autonomistas expelled from Nicaragua in October 1929. Like other Autonomistas, Rivas turned against Sandino during the guerrillero's lengthy stay in Mexico. At one point he even proclaimed that the Sandinistas should be "destroyed" if they refused to disarm peacefully.[73] In part because of his anti-Sandino stance, Rivas was allowed to return to Nicaragua on the eve of the 1932 elections. But after the Conservative Party lost these elections, Rivas followed other Conservatives in reembracing Sandino. And once the guerrillero laid down his arms, few more vociferously celebrated Sandinismo than Rivas. In selecting *La Nueva Prensa* as his mouthpiece, Sandino showed his gratitude for Rivas's change of heart.[74] Of course political opportunism shaped the guerrillero's decision. Just as Conservative corporatists viewed Sandino as an "instrument" to gain political power, Sandino sought to use Conservatives to establish his new political party.[75] Still, both were drawn to each other for ideological reasons as well. As U.S. Minister Hanna fretted, "a community of interests and ideas" had brought Sandino and Conservative oligarchs together.[76]

"A Community of Interests and Ideas"

Elite Conservatives and Sandino converged mainly in their insistence that the end of the military occupation had not terminated Nicaragua's struggle against U.S. imperialism. Such an anti-U.S. stance stood out because it was shared by few Nicaraguans. Even the ever optimistic Sandino observed that "the disappearance of the armed intervention . . . cooled the spirits of the people because they tolerate the political and economic intervention. They don't see it, and worse than that, they don't believe it."[77] To counter this complacency, Sandino issued a manifesto that outlined his struggle to restore Nicaragua's full national autonomy.[78] Underscoring his close ties with Conservative oligarchs, Sandino had Pedro Joaquín Chamorro Zelaya's print shop publish this lengthy document in pamphlet form. Chamorro's *La Prensa* was also the only newspaper to put out the entire manifesto in serial installments.

24. Gabry Rivas *(second from left)* with a U.S. naval officer and
the Conservative presidential and vice presidential candidates,
Adolfo Benard Vivas *(second from right)* and Julio Cardenal
Argüello, in Granada on the eve of the 1928 elections. *Courtesy of
Instituto de Historia de Nicaragua y de Centroamérica.*

Sandino's manifesto enraged the Guardia's officer corps as well as most Liberal politicians and papers, for they believed that it called for nothing less
than the overthrow of the Sacasa government.[79] Conservative papers, by
contrast, loudly endorsed Sandino's "patriotic" efforts to eradicate all vestiges
of U.S. influence in Nicaragua. Conservative corporatists especially appreciated Sandino's insistence that Nicaragua could obtain its full political and
economic independence only by destroying the current, U.S.-styled mode of
governance.[80] Yet as much as Sandino and his Conservative supporters
sought to construct a new political and economic order, initially their "community of interests and ideas" was most noticeable in their crusade against
the Americanization of Nicaraguan culture.

The peaceful struggle began in mid-February 1933, when Sandino and his
Conservative supporters campaigned against the efforts of Paramount Pic-
tures to film the imminent disarmament of the Sandinistas in their Segovian

25. Sandinista soldiers at their disarmament in the Segovias, February 1933.
Courtesy of Instituto de Historia de Nicaragua y de Centroamérica.

camps (see figure 25).[81] This was not the first time that Hollywood had approached Sandino; its interest in the Nicaraguan guerrillero dates as early as January 1928.[82] Sandino certainly could have benefited from Hollywood's lavish funds and global reach. Yet he steadfastly rejected its offers for fear that his nationalist struggle would be "ridiculed" on the silver screen.[83]

Sandino's fears were hardly misplaced. By 1933, Hollywood had produced several box-office hits that glorified the U.S. Marines in Nicaragua while denigrating the Sandinistas as savage bandits. In Frank Capra's celebrated *Flight* of 1929, for instance, the commander of the U.S. aircraft squadron in Nicaragua typically warned his pilots that "the first time you see them bandits you'll be inclined to laugh at them. Don't underestimate them. They cut your heart out at the first opportunity. Now, we've been sent down here to bring peace to Nicaragua. But we can't have any peace until we capture this bandit Lobo [i.e., Sandino]."[84] Further distorting historical reality, Hollywood depicted the outmanned U.S. Marines as easily vanquishing the Nicaraguan "bandits." And when other Nicaraguans appeared on the screen, they were usually female prostitutes willing to betray any cause, or highly Americanized landlords who slavishly supported the U.S. occupation. Mostly, however, U.S. films about the Sandino Rebellion depicted Nicaragua as a jungle land that lacked an urban populace, large buildings, commercial establishments, roads, electricity, or other markers of modernity. Due to such "cruel" misrepresentations, the pro-Sandino *La Nueva Prensa* worried that foreign audiences had come to view Nicaragua as a "wild, uncultured, and uncivilized" country that could "progress" only with the aid of U.S. troops and companies.[85]

Sandino and his Conservative sympathizers had every reason to believe that Hollywood's caricature of U.S.-occupied Nicaragua served U.S. nationalist objectives. In fact, ever since the United States invaded Cuba and Puerto Rico in 1898, Hollywood films tried to justify U.S. intervention in the Caribbean Basin by lampooning the alleged inability of the region's peoples to govern themselves.[86] Such films also reflected Hollywood's more general portrayal of Latin America as a "primitive" and "backward" continent.[87] If Hollywood's products thus enabled North Americans to celebrate their nationalist aspirations, in Latin America they became a focal point for nationalist protest.[88] The pan-Latin American crusade to ban U.S. films deemed offensive to local cultures informed the anti-Hollywood campaign waged by Sandino and his Conservative allies in 1933. Yet Nicaragua's campaign was about more than just defending a "civilized" nationality. Above all, it challenged Hollywood's efforts to deny Sandino and other Nicaraguans the right to advance a nationality separate from that of the United States.

Ultimately, however, Sandino and his Conservative supporters believed that the main obstacle to creating a stronger nationality lay much closer to home: in Nicaraguans' embrace of U.S. customs. At first, Sandino blamed his compatriots' infatuation with "Americanism" on the Wall Street bankers who, he claimed, had introduced "the corrupting influence of the dollar into Nicaragua."[89] Then, as the Guardia Nacional became more powerful, Sandino increasingly attributed Nicaraguans' "denationalization" to this Americanized institution. Pro-Sandino Conservative oligarchs shared the guerrillero's view that "the fiendish dollar" and the "renegade" Guardia were gravely undermining Nicaraguan nationality. But to them, the principal cause of Americanization lay in Nicaraguans' valorization of U.S. culture. In particular, they targeted the "modern woman," whose Americanized lifestyle Caballeros Católicos had been attacking since the early 1920s. With the post-1927 militarization of the U.S. intervention, they further condemned

Nicaraguan (usually elite) women for fraternizing with U.S. troops. While the more frequent attacks occurred via newspapers, the most notorious were carried out from the pulpit and at anti-U.S. demonstrations where Conservatives marched with signs such as "Death to the Nicaraguan women married to *Yanquis*."[90]

Nationalist concerns were not the only reasons why Conservative oligarchs fiercely objected to elite women's mixing with U.S. troops. More important still, these "Yankized" women represented a direct challenge to their own patriarchal authority. Consider, for example, a U.S. officer's observation that a priest did "not approve of the manner and customs the Marines have brought. The magazines they take have taught the girls to wear short dresses and bob their hair. He therefore feels as if he were losing his grip."[91] Conservative oligarchs particularly feared the sexual relations that many young, unmarried elite women maintained with U.S. officers and enlisted men. So great were these fears that Conservative oligarchs ostracized daughters who married U.S. military personnel.[92]

If Sandino and his Conservative supporters disagreed about who the most nefarious agents of Americanization were, they agreed that a "new Nicaragua" could be forged only by expelling, as one Conservative proclaimed, "the contagious American way of life from the popular spirit."[93] In consequence, they promoted campaigns that called on their compatriots to re-embrace cultural practices considered authentically Nicaraguan. Both, for example, adamantly defended Nicaragua's "traditional" music against the more "sensuous" and highly popular U.S. styles of dance music, such as jazz and the Charleston.[94] This well-publicized effort to de-Americanize Nicaragua's "popular spirit" provided perhaps the strongest ideological foundation to the alliance that Sandino and Conservative oligarchs started to form in early 1933.

Yet the two shared more than just simple anti-Americanism. Just as important, both insisted that Nicaraguans must break with the liberal, cosmopolitan model of national development that had prevailed since the Walker era. In its place, Sandino and his Conservative supporters advanced corporatist ideals. Both also extolled an agrarian-based and highly moralistic, religious vision of the nation that emphasized class harmony. They thus contrasted what they considered to be the autochthonous and healthier ways of the country folk with the Americanized, cosmopolitan hedonism of urban Nicaraguans. Homosexuality, for example, was an "urban degeneration" that the guerrillero claimed did not exist in the countryside.[95] In addition, the agrarian nationalism of Sandino and Conservative oligarchs had a strong anticapitalist and social reformist impulse, as evident in their call for a significant redistribution of state-owned land to peasants. Unlike previous generations of Nicaraguan nationalists, Sandino and his Conservative supporters looked inward, not abroad, to create a nation capable of resisting U.S. imperial pretensions.

Of course Sandino's nationalist project differed significantly from that of his Conservative supporters. While both embraced corporatism as a preferred form of governance, Sandino's model was obviously much more inclusive, for he believed that the reins of government should be in the hands of popular sectors, not the upper classes.[96] And if the religious overtones of the guerrillero's nationalism reflected his own anticlerical spiritism and the popular Catholicism of his followers, pro-Sandino Conservatives identified with a highly elitist and Church-centered form of social Catholicism. Both also attacked the economic basis of the liberal nation-state from very different angles. Whereas Sandino's anticapitalism was steeped in Marxist tradition, Conservatives echoed a religious-based critique then commonplace among fascistic, Catholic corporatists elsewhere in the Americas and in Europe. But perhaps the main difference was that Sandino championed the egalitarian, futuristic peasant cooperative as the nation's building block, while Conservatives valorized the hierarchical cattle-based hacienda of colonial origin as the backbone of society.[97] As much as Sandino's evocation of a pastoral utopia clashed with Conservatives' reactionary agrarianism, however, this did not prevent the two from jointly seeking to transform the Nicaraguan nation-state.[98]

Embracing *Mestizaje*

The cultural nationalism that brought Conservative oligarchs closer to Sandino mirrored the "antibourgeois spirit" they and other Caballeros Católicos had developed a decade earlier. Yet there was one crucial difference: pro-Sandino Conservatives valorized a nation based on the mestizo or, to use Sandino's term, on the "Indo-Hispanic" race. Conservatives' embrace of a mixed-race nationality—*mestizaje*—could not go unnoticed, since they had long been the Nicaraguans most identified with whiteness. In the 1920s some oligarchs still championed the "Spanishness" of rural Chontales and denounced the mixed "Indo-Latin race" for its "indolence."[99] But by 1933 more and more Conservatives were extolling "the union of the Spanish and the Indian" within the nation's soul.[100] Over time, Conservative oligarchs even came to celebrate their own mestizo identity—a shift perhaps most noticeable in the case of Senator Carlos Cuadra Pasos.[101] In fact, so firmly did they change their racial ideals that by the 1940s these oligarchs had become the country's leading proponents of mestizaje, with Cuadra Pasos's son (Pablo Antonio) its standard-bearer.

Since mestizaje has many meanings, it is significant that this nationalist ideology was viewed by Conservative oligarchs and Sandino in much the same light.[102] For instance, neither embraced race mixture in order to "whiten" the nation, nor did either claim to construct a mestizo nation against local groups such as "Indians," "blacks," or "whites." Rather, their main foil was a United States embodied by "blond beasts." For Conservative oligarchs, then, the conflict between U.S. and Nicaraguan nationalities came to involve more than just distinct cultural and religious practices. It now centered on purported racial differences as well. As the arch-Catholic Pablo Antonio Cuadra insisted, "We have been subject to the intervention of a different race. We want . . . to conserve our own . . . Indo-Spanish [*indo-español*] spirit."[103] Furthermore, Conservatives and Sandino similarly imagined "Indo-Hispanic" Nicaragua as a racially homogenous nation—not the diverse nation of "inditos, zambos, mulatos, and mestizos" so loudly celebrated by the Menistas of 1912.

If Sandino's mestizaje project converged to some degree with that of his elite supporters, the two views were not fully congruent. Conservatives, for example, had a far more benevolent view of mestizaje's roots in Spanish colonialism. They claimed that Nicaragua's mestizo nationality emerged from the peaceful encounter of Spanish colonizers and Indians.[104] Sandino, by contrast, stressed the violence of colonization. More important still, his mestizaje project strove to democratize social hierarchies. Yet the greatest difference stemmed from the fact that Sandino, at the beginning of his struggle, identified Conservative oligarchs with U.S. imperialism. As a result, his "Indo-Hispanic" nation initially excluded those who, in 1933, became his strongest elite supporters.

The metamorphosis of the "whitest" Nicaraguans into leading proponents of mestizaje clearly resulted from the Sandinistas' success in resisting the U.S. occupiers. Just a few weeks after Sandino launched his anti-U.S. struggle in

July 1927, a handbill distributed by pro-Sandino urban artisans complained that Nicaraguans' general unwillingness to resist the U.S. occupiers indicated "to what level of . . . degeneration our [Indo-Hispanic] race has sunk."[105] Within a year, however, the Sandinistas had apparently pushed many to view the "Indo-Hispanic race" in much more positive terms. As a German resident noted in July 1928, the "fact that the United States was strong enough to defeat Germany [in World War I] and cannot defeat a lone man like Sandino means to the people that being an Indio-Latin is better than being of the white race."[106] If Sandino's struggle did lead Nicaraguans to believe in the superiority of "Indio-Latins" over "whites," Conservative oligarchs bent on expanding their political base had good reason to tap into his brand of mestizaje. Moreover, with *indohispanismo* so dear to Sandino, Conservatives' adoption of mestizaje only facilitated their 1933 rapprochement.

Yet political opportunism alone hardly explains why Sandino's Conservative supporters transformed their racial image of the nation. The evolution in their position was also a response to the unabashed racism of the U.S. occupiers. The all-white U.S. force typically considered all native Nicaraguans to be nonwhite (usually of mixed race) and thus culturally inferior. Or as the Guardia's U.S. commander claimed, "Being of a mixture of latin and Indian blood, [Nicaraguans] are rather tumultuous, and they seem to enjoy . . . civil disorder in much the same spirit as we take football."[107] Such views particularly antagonized Conservative oligarchs, for they had long used the ideology of whiteness to legitimate their elite status. Moreover, as the country's main rural powerbrokers, they seethed at the racial paternalism underpinning the U.S. military's anticaudillo crusade. Conservative oligarchs especially felt that U.S. racism led to the humiliating arrest of many of their kind by U.S. Guardia officers.

These oligarchs also resented being represented as "primitives" in articles that U.S. officers wrote for North American journals. The most infamous piece was published in *National Geographic Magazine* by Lieutenant Colonel Dan Sultan.[108] According to *El Diario Nicaragüense*, Sultan consciously misrepresented the cultural practices of Granada's Conservative elite in order to show that Nicaragua was "a completely savage country full of . . . exotic practices [*cultos*]."[109] In particular, this mouthpiece of Granada's Conservative oligarchy objected to Sulton's claim that a photo illustrated how "Granadinos don fantastic garb to exorcise evil spirits on Christmas Eve," when the image actually displayed local elites participating in the Dance of the

26. This photo, which appeared in the May 1932 issue of the *National Geographic Magazine*, was bitterly criticized by Conservative oligarchs from Granada for its blatant misrepresentation of their cultural practices. The photo's original caption stated: "GRANADINOS DON FANTASTIC GARB TO EXORCISE EVIL SPIRITS ON CHRISTMAS EVE. Wearing fearsome masks and carrying a huge effigy of a saint, they march to inns and *cantinas*, pretending to seek a place for the birth of the Christ Child; but their search is never successful, though they affect to drive out devils wherever they go." In *National Geographic Magazine* 61.5 (1932): 604.

Gigantona, a secular celebration of mestizo culture that occurs on 7 December (see figure 26). By extolling mestizaje, pro-Sandino Conservatives openly contested U.S. claims about the inferiority of, as Sultan put it, "badly mixed" races.

Ultimately, however, Conservative oligarchs and Sandino valorized the homogenizing ideology of indohispanismo primarily as a means to heal the nation's divisions. This quest for national unity also helps explain why both advanced corporatist modes of governance. Their belief that corporatism and mestizaje went hand in hand was certainly shared by many Latin American nationalists of the Depression era.[110] Yet Sandino and his Conservative supporters embraced both ideologies not for fear that social conflicts were tearing the nation apart but because political divisions allegedly made Nicaragua the continent's main victim of U.S. intervention. Tellingly, pro-Sandino Conservatives implored Nicaraguans to support the guerrillero's political plans by imitating their forefathers, who joined together, overcoming grave political differences, to expel William Walker and his filibuster army in 1857.[111]

This historical analogy had a powerful allure. Still, it was not quite accurate, for the national reconciliation envisioned by pro-Sandino Conservatives differed from that of 1857 in two key respects. First, Conservative oligarchs now believed that the emulation of U.S. ways imperiled, rather than enhanced, Nicaraguan nationality. In consequence, their call for national unity invoked ideologies—authoritarian Catholic corporatism and mestizaje—that challenged the liberal U.S. ideals their forefathers had so fiercely defended. Second, pro-Sandino Conservatives strove for a different kind of national unity: rather than replicating the elite convergence of the Walker era, they sought to bring together entrenched oligarchs and popular revolutionaries. With great interest, then, these Conservatives welcomed the opportunity to meet with the guerrillero on 21 May 1933 in order to launch his new party.

The Puzzling Nonencounter

Sandino's convocation of the May meeting represented his first concrete effort to reshape Nicaraguan politics in the postoccupation era. In convoking the meeting, Sandino surely believed he could exploit the "revolutionary spirit" that, according to U.S. Minister Hanna, was then spreading among the country's populace.[112] Why else would a Sandinista officer report from the Segovias that his *jefe supremo* had gone to Managua in order to create a new party that would integrate the many "workers, students, and the great mass of peasants" who were fed up with all the political "garbage" of the past?[113] But Sandino was well aware that he could not found a mass movement alone. He thus wanted to use the May meeting to recruit political activists who could help him create a nationally based party.

Sandino invited a motley group of followers to the meeting. Some represented leftist, labor-based groups. Others were prominent student leaders. Yet to the Nicaraguan press, the most important invitees were Conservative corporatists, for they were seen as the masterminds behind Sandino's meeting.[114] The nation's leading newspaper, for example, published a cartoon that depicted the hand of "Conservatismo" grasping the "Third [i.e., Autonomist] Party" ax, with the comment that the ax was to be used to cut the Liberal Party to pieces.[115] Already before the May meeting, elite Conservatives like Luis Alberto Cabrales had traveled to the Segovias to meet with the guerrillero. However, the Guardia Nacional prevented them from approaching Sandino's camp.[116] Rank-and-file Conservatives also tried to hook up with Sandino in the Segovias. Ironically, one such individual was the young Granadan accountant Daniel Ortega Cerda, whose sons Daniel and Humberto would later lead the Sandinista Revolution of 1979.[117] On the eve of the 21 May meeting, Ortega wrote to Sandino stating "I ardently desire to be at your side and fight for . . . liberty and the nation's honor."[118] Not surprisingly, such sentiments only strengthened the widespread view that Sandino's closest allies were Conservatives.

But perhaps most important, Sandino convoked the May meeting less than a month after Conservative corporatists established the Partido Trabajador Nacionalista (not to be confused with the communistic Partido Trabajador Nicaragüense). And it was this party's program that Conservatives hoped Sandino would embrace at their planned meeting. Published in local newspapers, the program revealed that prominent Conservatives had come to embrace key aspects of Sandinismo. Although the program never mentioned Sandino by name, it indicated that Conservative corporatists shared much of his anti-Americanism; his demand for wide-reaching social reforms, such as the redistribution of state-owned land; his moralistic concern over the "degenerate" lifestyle of the urban masses; and his disdain for liberal modes of governance. At the same time, however, the party's program publicized the fact that Conservative corporatists had developed a more comprehensive plan for transforming state-society relations.

The program of the Partido Trabajador Nacionalista called for the establishment of an authoritarian corporatist ("national-socialist") state.[119] Not only did it demand that the "current legislative chambers of senators and representatives be destroyed and replaced with chambers of trades and professions," but that the country be governed by an elitist dictatorship. "The dictatorship of selected men," it proclaimed, "is not only desirable but urgent. That is where we are heading to. The Dictatorship is the indispensable instrument for all thoroughgoing renovations, and with it we will create the 'New Nicaragua.'" This emphasis on dictatorship and the need for a thoroughgoing moral and political renovation was intrinsic to the corporatist project elite Conservatives had been developing in response to the 1927 shift in U.S. imperial rule. New, however, was the program's stress on the need to militarize local society. "Not only should high schools be placed under a military regime," it declared, "but also the whole nation." More specifically, it called for "the Republic to be organized like an army of work, ready to be transformed into an Army of War whenever the National Defense demands it." This was the first time that Nicaraguan elite corporatists openly espoused a military regime. And as these Conservatives stated elsewhere, they wanted Sandino to head their dictatorship.[120]

Whether or not Sandino knew about the Conservatives' plan, he essentially nixed it when he called off the 21 May meeting a few hours before it was to take place. To the national press, Sandino curtly declared that he had canceled the much-awaited meeting because President Sacasa "deemed it inconvenient."[121] Sandino then quickly returned to his agricultural cooperative in the Segovias. Never again did he try to establish a nationally based party. The nonencounter of 21 May was thus an important turning point, for it marked the beginning of Sandinismo's end as a political force.

Sandino's fateful decision to abandon national politics baffled many Nicaraguans. It hardened widespread views that the seasoned guerrillero was either an inept politician, a Segovian regionalist uninterested in national politics, or a revolutionary bent on gaining power via military not democratic means.[122] While the last view was reasonable, the first two were hardly justified. Not only had Sandino shown much political skill in waging the most successful anti-U.S. guerrilla campaign in Latin American history, he was a fervent nationalist bent on creating a strong central state. Indeed, the day he cancelled the planned meeting, Sandino gave a second, little-publicized interview where he justified his decision by stating that "I could never be president of Nicaragua because I would immediately become a dictator." But he also added that a dictatorship "is what this country needs."[123] This statement echoed an earlier declaration in which Sandino asserted that Nicaragua needed a dictatorial regime to free itself completely from the chains of U.S. imperialism.[124]

In all likelihood Sandino cancelled the 21 May meeting for fear that he lacked the popular support necessary for his political project. As long as the guerrillero was ensconced in the Segovias, it was easy for him to believe that he could harness the "revolutionary spirit" of urban artisans and workers to his own "political revolution." But when the guerrillero arrived in the capital on 19 May and received a cold reception, he must have realized just how strongly popular sentiment had turned against him. Sandino, therefore, had good reason to delay the founding of his new party, hoping first to increase his popular support. Or as he stated shortly after canceling the meeting, "I have not renounced my rights as a citizen, and my program is still alive and not liquidated." But Sandino also maintained that "I will not commit suicide out of stubbornness."[125]

The Final Break

No matter how reasonable his motives, Sandino's failure to create a new party greatly diminished his political appeal to Conservative corporatists. Still, the main reason they ultimately broke with him was his ambivalent stance toward communism. Ever since 1927, Conservatives had defended Sandino against charges that he was a communist masquerading as a nationalist. After 7 June 1933, this was no longer possible. On that day Nicaragua's major newspapers published a private letter in which Sandino proclaimed "to the entire universe, with all the power of my being, that I am a rationalist communist."[126] Falling like a bombshell, this declaration was seen by many Nicaraguans as the definitive proof that Sandino had been a communist all along.

Sandino's declaration caused such a stir precisely because it came at a time when the guerrillero was ostracized by the communist movement. True, Sandino initially enjoyed much support from the Communist International (Comintern).[127] In 1930, however, he broke with this Moscow-led organization when it both refused to provide him with much-needed aid and demanded that he sever ties with his "petit bourgeois" and "bourgeois" allies.[128] As a result of this break, many of Sandino's foreign comrades, including Farabundo Martí, left his army or were expelled from it. In addition, Sandino came to be vilified by communists throughout the region as a "petit bourgeois caudillo." And when the guerrillero laid down his arms in February 1933, he was charged with having "gone over to the camp of the Nicaraguan bourgeoisie and landlords."[129] The rift had grown so large, U.S. officials reported, that "the general impression in Nicaragua" became "that Sandino never ha[d] been, or never would be, sympathetic to any communistic activities."[130]

Why then did Sandino suddenly insist that he was a "rationalist communist"? Some Conservative corporatists speculated that Sandino advocated a form of communism that was very different from the Marxism-Leninism espoused by the Comintern. Or, as one Conservative wondered, could the guerrillero's communism have echoed not the "cry of Soviet Russia" but "the love for the whole community, the fraternal embrace of men that would make him similar to the great revolutionary [*revolucionedor*] of all times, the magnificent Christ?"[131] While Sandino had once stated that he was a communist because Jesus Christ had been one, his communism was hardly an incipient form of liberation theology. Rather, it represented the doctrine of the "Magnetic-Spiritual School of the Universal Commune" (Escuela Magnético-Espiritual de la Comuna Universal), a spiritist group that Sandino joined during his 1929–30 trip to Mexico. Founded in Argentina in 1911, this school embraced the philosophy of rationalism in its quest to "communize" the world.[132] Hence its approximately five thousand members called themselves "rationalist communists."

The Magnetic-Spiritual School embraced some Marxist tenets, especially the ideal of a classless society. Still its communism differed sharply from Marxism-Leninism. For example, the school believed in the reincarnation of spirits, and thus privileged a spiritual over a materialist interpretation of history. But above all it sought to "communize" the world via the peaceful spread of futuristic communes, such as Sandino's peasant cooperative, rather than through class struggle.[133] And, in the school's eyes, the vanguard for "communization" was not the world's proletariat but the "Hispanic race." Yet since the Magnetic-Spiritual School remained little-known outside of Mexico and Argentina, few Nicaraguans grasped how greatly its brand of communism diverged from Marxism-Leninism. Small wonder that Sandino's embrace of "rational communism" led many of his compatriots to view him as a "Nicaraguan Lenin."[134] Oddly, the guerrillero did nothing to correct such ominous misconceptions.

As Sandino knew too well, his main political allies—elite Conservative corporatists—staunchly opposed communism. Moreover, their fear of communism grew in 1933 as Nicaragua's economic crisis hit its nadir and social conflict engulfed the country. Reinforcing such fears, Nicaraguan newspapers reported that revolutionary turmoil was spreading throughout Latin America, from Chile to Cuba. As a result, even the Conservative press began to revise its previous stance and express fear that Nicaragua might experience a "communist" uprising analogous to the one that erupted in El Salvador in

1932. To his Conservative sympathizers, Sandino could not have chosen a worse moment to declare himself a communist. As *La Prensa* put it, declaring oneself communist in this context was equivalent to committing political "suicide."[135]

Once convinced of Sandino's communist leanings, Conservative corporatists treated the guerrillero as a persona non grata. In particular, they refused to come to his aid in early 1934 when tensions between the Sandinistas and the Guardia Nacional pushed Nicaragua to the brink of another civil war. The crisis began when General Anastasio Somoza García, who had become head of the Guardia Nacional following the pullout of U.S. troops, demanded that Sandino disarm the one hundred men guarding his cooperative in the Segovias. The guerrillero responded by publicly challenging the constitutionality of this U.S.-founded institution. He further antagonized the Guardia by claiming in a well-publicized interview that there were three "powers" in Nicaragua: "the power of the president of the Republic, that of the Guardia Nacional, and mine."[136] Yet what most troubled the Guardia's officer corps was the compromise Sandino and President Sacasa achieved on 21 February: Sacasa promised to reform the Guardia within the next six months in exchange for Sandino's acceptance of a presidential delegate to oversee his troops.[137] To the corps' outrage, Sacasa selected one of Sandino's closest advisors as the presidential delegate.

Firmly believing that President Sacasa and Sandino were bent on destroying their institution, Guardia officers went ahead with their longstanding plan to "eliminate" Sandino and Sandinismo.[138] On the night of 21 February 1934, a Guardia patrol executed Sandino and four of his generals shortly after they left the Presidential Palace, where they had dined with President Sacasa. The next day, Guardia troops attacked Sandino's cooperative in the Segovias, killing over three hundred men, women, and children. With this massacre, the Guardia purged Sandinismo from the body politic.

Many Nicaraguans—rich and poor—welcomed the "annihilation" of the Sandinistas, hoping that Sandinismo's demise would solve the country's political and economic crisis.[139] Sandino's former Conservative supporters, in contrast, greeted this dramatic turn of events with silence, perhaps out of shame for having abandoned their erstwhile hero. They only explicitly endorsed Sandino's murder after 10 March, when the Guardia announced the sudden discovery of secret documents that allegedly proved Sandino had been planning a "communist" uprising all along. Like other Conservative oligarchs, the Granadan Manolo Cuadra, who was then writing a pro-Sandino account of the war waged between the U.S.-led Guardia and the Sandinistas, was deeply troubled by the discovery of Sandino's revolutionary plan. In a letter to a brother living in New York, Cuadra stated that "the acts of admiration for Sandino decreased . . . as soon as they found documents on him that attested [to his plans for] a revolutionary movement." He thus declared that "I can no longer write a book on behalf of Sandino; but I will definitively write one against the Yankees."[140] Even after his death, Sandino's apparently ambivalent stance toward "communism" haunted his former elite supporters. Yet it did little to weaken their anti-Americanism.

Conclusion

Sandino's murder marked the definitive end of Conservatives' historic efforts to join forces with Central America's foremost revolutionary movement. Ideological affinity, not simple political expediency, led Conservative oligarchs to seek the unexpected: an alliance with the region's most powerful revolutionary nationalist. Despite their concerted efforts, Conservatives never succeeded in winning over Sandino. This is hardly surprising, as various scholars have shown that elite and peasant groups opposed to a U.S. occupation elsewhere in Latin America were unable to overcome class differences to forge a durable alliance.[141] But it remains unclear precisely how class differences actually impeded Conservatives' rapprochement with Sandino. True, Conservative oligarchs broke with Sandino once he proclaimed to be a "communist." Yet they had no qualms about reaching out to the Sandinistas at the very moment—1932—when many Nicaraguans deemed the peasant rebels an unprecedented revolutionary threat to the existing social order. On the other hand, there is little doubt that Conservatives' attempt to forge an alliance with Sandino suffered from its lack of popular support. No matter how strongly Nicaraguans opposed U.S. imperial rule, few shared the belief of Conservative corporatists—and apparently of Sandino as well—that the only way Nicaragua could defend its sovereignty was via dictatorial rule.

In the end, however, what most doomed Conservatives' proposed alliance with Sandino were ideological differences. True, they converged on key points. But it was a deceptive sense of connection, for Conservatives overlooked or misunderstood key aspects of Sandinismo, particularly its ties with spiritual communism. The main difference between Conservative corporatists and Sandino was not, as Conservatives claimed, his Marxist-Leninist leanings. Rather, it was the fact that the guerrillero embraced a utopian form of anti-Americanism while their brand was profoundly reactionary. Conservatives' attempt to ally themselves with Sandino was therefore an extremely difficult proposition. Ironically, just as their extraordinary venture looked more and more viable to their political enemies, tensions between Conservatives' anti-Americanism and that of Sandino intensified and reached, by July 1933, the breaking point. Or as José Cornel Urtecho admitted shortly after Sandino's murder, the closer he and other Conservative oligarchs came to know the guerrillero, the less they identified with his political project.[142] This was certainly an accurate statement. But the very fact that that they tried to join forces with the region's foremost anti-U.S. revolutionary also underscores just how strongly U.S. imperial rule had pushed Conservative oligarchs to turn against the American dream that they had valorized for so long.

Indeed, as much as Conservative oligarchs turned their backs on Sandino, they did not reembrace Americanization. On the contrary, they continued to struggle for a "de-Americanized" Nicaragua. And after a decade or so, they would once again invoke the figure of Sandino. As the epilogue will show, Coronel Urtecho and other Conservative oligarchs had to wait until the triumph of the Sandinista Revolution in 1979 before they had the capacity to expunge "the contagious American way of life from the popular spirit" and thus "liberate" Nicaragua from the thing they considered the most enduring vestige of U.S. imperial rule. To be successful, however, they would have to overcome the tension between the reactionary and utopian forms of anti-Americanism that doomed their efforts to forge an alliance with Sandino.

EPILOGUE · Imperial Legacies

Dictatorship and Revolution

ON 19 JULY 1979, a massive and particularly bloody insurrection led by the Sandinista National Liberation Front (Frente Sandinista de Liberación Nacional, or FSLN) ousted the Somoza family dictatorship established in 1936 by the Guardia Nacional's first native leader. The next day, over one hundred thousand Nicaraguans packed Managua's main square to cheer the FSLN's leadership as it solemnly vowed to liberate the nation from "Yankee imperialism." Foreign observers could be forgiven if they wondered why this anti-U.S. discourse rang so loudly in a country with such minimal U.S. presence. Unlike prerevolutionary Cuba, Nicaragua had no U.S. military base on its territory. Neither had it become a Mafia-controlled playground for U.S. tourists. Nor was its economy dominated by U.S. corporations. Moreover, nearly half a century had passed since the U.S. occupation had ended. Many Nicaraguans nevertheless insisted that their country had remained a quasi-U.S. colony while it was ruled by the Somozas and the Guardia Nacional. In fact, so strongly did Nicaraguans identify the three Somoza dictators— Anastasio Somoza García (1936–56) and his sons Luis (1956–67) and Anastasio Somoza Debayle (1967–79)—with U.S. imperial rule that they called them "the last Yankee Marines." No doubt the downfall of the lengthiest dictatorship in twentieth-century Latin America liberated Nicaragua from the most nefarious legacy of the U.S. occupation. But what many Sandinistas failed to grasp in those heady moments of triumph was that other legacies of U.S. imperial rule would critically shape the peculiar course of their revolution.

For many foreign analysts, one of the revolution's most striking features was the support it received from elite Nicaraguans.[1] This support was especially surprising, since the revolutionary regime was striving to promote political and social equality by disempowering native elites. True, the Sandinistas first prosecuted only loyalists of the Somoza dictatorship. But within a year, the revolutionary regime began to attack the interests of non-Somocista elites as well. This attack notwithstanding, many wealthy landlords and industrialists continued to serve the revolution as "patriotic producers." Moreover, scores of upper-class Nicaraguans occupied key positions in the Sandinista regime. Of course, this was not the first time that elites had supported revolutionary change in Latin America. Still, since the Cuban Revolution's turn toward communism, Latin American elites have tended to oppose Marxist-inspired revolutionary movements like the FSLN with a vengeance.[2] And in few places has this opposition been more fierce than in Central America, a region not coincidentally marked by extreme social inequalities.

Why then did many elite Nicaraguans come to support one of Latin America's most radical social revolutions? Social scientists have typically explored this peculiar elite affinity for revolutionary change by focusing on its historical roots. Initially, most emphasized how two events of the 1970s so alienated elite Nicaraguans from the Somoza dictatorship that they were willing to embrace any kind of regime change.[3] The first was the 1972 earthquake that destroyed Managua and led the international community to provide Nicaragua with massive relief funds. To the horror of many, the Somozas and their cronies shamelessly exploited this natural disaster to expand their own economic power. Non-Somocista elites responded to this state-sponsored pillage by mounting a civic campaign against the Somoza regime. Their campaign received a tragic boost in January 1978 when Somoza's henchmen gunned down the dictatorship's main elite opponent, the fifty-one-year-old Pedro Joaquín Chamorro Cardenal (publisher of *La Prensa* since the 1952 death of his father, the Caballero Católico Pedro Joaquín Chamorro Zelaya). So shocking was the murder of this prominent Conservative oligarch that it pushed many elites to support the guerrilla struggle that the FSLN had been waging against the Somoza regime since 1962. The 1972 earthquake and Chamorro's assassination certainly facilitated the Sandinista triumph of July 1979. Yet scholars soon realized that both events did little to explain two peculiarities of the revolutionary process itself: the anti-Somoza elites' failure to control the youthful Sandinistas and, once the Sandinistas consolidated their power, these elites' active participation in the revolution.[4]

To better grasp the source of elites' weakness and progressive outlook, scholars began to dig deeper into Nicaraguan history. Some stopped in the 1950s and 1960s, when another agroexport boom transformed Nicaragua.[5] For these scholars, the boom created reformist but divided elites who came to back the FSLN.[6] Most analysts, however, took their cue from Sandinista ideologues and focused on the U.S. occupation.[7] Like the Sandinistas, they concluded that elite support for the Sandinista Revolution stemmed from the fact that U.S. imperial rule had thwarted the rise of a cohesive and powerful agrarian bourgeoisie.[8] This explanation has found its latest expression in

Jeffrey Paige's comparative study of the distinct role agrarian elites played in the Central American civil wars of the 1980s. In the case of Nicaragua, Paige claims that ever since the U.S. intervention of 1910 the native elite remained not only a "frustrated, fragmented bourgeoisie in the making" but the only one in the region still seeking to carry out a "bourgeois revolution."[9] According to this logic, elite Nicaraguans hoped to use the Sandinista regime to complete the liberal revolution that had been interrupted by the U.S. occupation.

Scholars like Paige are right to argue that elite support for the Sandinista Revolution was a key legacy of U.S. imperial rule. But in doing so, most inadvertently reproduce four powerful myths about the U.S. occupation. The first myth is that the U.S. occupiers privileged the economic interests of a backward, cattle-based Conservative oligarchy centered in Granada over those of a modern, Liberal coffee bourgeoisie based in León. As we have seen, the volatile nature of political conflicts plaguing the Nicaraguan elite actually superseded divisions by region or party affiliation. Moreover, elites were highly diversified economically, with Conservative oligarchs pioneering the country's dynamic agroexport economy. And if U.S. economic policies hurt many coffee planters, they did not discriminate against elites of a particular political stripe. This brings us to the second myth, that dollar diplomacy hurt Nicaragua's agroexport economy. In reality, Nicaragua's rural economy boomed under dollar diplomacy. More important still, this boom was driven by nonelite producers, who more easily adapted to changing market conditions and the credit crunch created by U.S. officials in charge of Nicaragua's public finances. If the economic power of large agroexporters indeed declined under dollar diplomacy, it was the work not only of "Wall Street" but of peasant producers as well. The third myth is that Sandinismo lacked meaningful elite support. True, many if not most Sandinistas believed they were waging a revolutionary struggle "of the poor against the rich." Yet this did not preclude their leader from being fervently courted by the country's wealthiest and most exclusive elite sector, the Granada-based Conservative oligarchy, whose members were also deemed to be fascistic and pro-U.S. *vendepatrias*. The final myth is that the U.S. occupiers actively promoted the rise of the Somoza dictatorship. When it imposed the Guardia Nacional on Nicaragua in 1927, the U.S. government certainly hoped that this force would become the country's most powerful state institution. And in 1936 it openly supported the Guardia's overthrow of a freely elected government. Still

Washington did not set up the Guardia to become, as is often alleged, a pillar of authoritarian rule. On the contrary, this force was critical to the democratization campaign waged by the U.S. military during the last years of the U.S. occupation. In the following pages, I consider how the revised account of the U.S. occupation developed in this book more fully explains the legacies of U.S. imperial rule. These lasting effects were indeed dictatorship and elite support for revolutionary change, as other scholars have recognized, but not for the reasons they propose.

Dictatorship

The rise of a military-based dictatorship scarcely three years after the occupation's end surely did not surprise many U.S. troops who had worked to "democratize" Nicaragua between 1927 and 1932. Even members of the U.S. electoral missions privately disagreed with their superiors in Washington, claiming that "backward" Nicaragua was not "ready" for democratic rule. As a U.S. officer supervising the 1930 elections in León confidentially stated, "poverty and ignorance have reduced [the local populace] to such a primitive state that abstractions such as democratic government, the free ballot, etc., have no meaning for them. They lack even the most primitive conception of law and justice, and I doubt if, beyond following some local leader or other they have any clear idea of what is going on in Nicaragua today."[10] The U.S. military was hardly alone in claiming that "primitive" structures and habits stymied Nicaragua's democratization. Such claims have also been forwarded by present-day U.S. scholars who take seriously their country's efforts to promote democracy by force. This is particularly true for those trying to explain why these efforts were more successful in industrialized countries, such as U.S.-occupied Germany and Japan, than in the "underdeveloped," predominantly agrarian societies of the Caribbean Basin, where U.S. hegemony was far greater. In perhaps the most important study on this topic, Tony Smith argues that entrenched inequalities in land distribution and the traditions of caudillismo doomed the U.S. "mission" to impose democratic rule in Central America and the Caribbean.[11]

In Nicaragua, however, "underdevelopment" hardly explains why the post-1927 U.S. democratization campaign facilitated authoritarian rule. Instead, this outcome had much more to do with two decisive changes wrought by the campaign itself. Most notably, it enabled the Guardia Nacional to become the strongest and best-organized institution in the country. The Guardia-based dictatorship of the Somozas of course culminated in a brutal regime divorced from civil society. In its first decades, however, the dictatorship enjoyed much popular support, largely because the Guardia carried out a populist project that promoted peasant interests at the expense of anti-Somoza landlords.[12] This project originated during the U.S. occupation when the Guardia gradually displaced caudillos as the main powerbrokers in the all-important countryside. And because the U.S. democratization campaign gravely weakened competition among rival patron-client networks, the rural populace became even more beholden to the Guardia. Finally, at a time when new, populist parties were emerging throughout Latin America, their rise was hampered in Nicaragua by the de facto U.S. proscription against third parties. In fact, the proscription only increased the political space for the Guardia to function as a channel for popular demands and aspirations. As a result, the Guardia became the most effective instrument through which the Nicaraguan state could not just repress popular sectors but also mobilize and control them politically. Scholars are certainly correct to argue that the U.S. occupation facilitated the rise of the Somoza dictatorship. But it is important to stress that this outcome was unintended. Only if we take the occupation's democratizing impulse seriously can we truly understand its perils.

The rise of authoritarian rule in Nicaragua cannot be comprehended, however, without understanding a second key legacy of U.S. democratization efforts: these efforts pushed the country's most entrenched landed elites—Conservative oligarchs based in Granada—to develop a new form of governance that eventually became the main ideological foundation for the Somoza regime. To be sure, the Somoza dictatorship drew much force by co-opting *obrerismo*, an ideology of worker affirmation and antielitism that urban artisans had developed prior to the U.S. occupation.[13] But it was above all Conservative oligarchs' model of authoritarian corporatism that Somoza appropriated in his quest to transform state-society relations from above.[14] Conservative corporatists also provided the general with crucial political support. For example, newspapers such as Gabry Rivas's *La Nueva Prensa* and José Coronel Urtecho's *La Reacción* emerged as key propaganda organs for the Somoza regime.[15] In addition, Conservative corporatists founded a paramilitary organization—the Camisas Azules (Blue Shirts) modeled after Mussolini's Black Shirts—that worked together with the Guardia Nacional to mobilize popular support for the dictator. Their support was so critical that decades later the FSLN founder Carlos Fonseca accused José Coronel Urtecho and other Conservative oligarchs of being, after Somoza García, the Nicaraguans most responsible for the rise of the dictatorship.[16]

That oligarchs like Coronel Urtecho could so seamlessly transfer their support from Sandino to Somoza has puzzled even some of their descendants.[17] Yet for Coronel Urtecho and his group, the embrace of Somoza was anything but illogical. True, Somoza frequently portrayed himself as a Liberal parvenu of nonelite origins. In reality, however, this Guardia general not only shared corporatists' disdain for a liberal political system, his father was a Conservative coffee baron who socialized with Conservative oligarchs from Granada. Little wonder that Conservative corporatists viewed Somoza as one of their own.[18] And even though the general often wrapped himself in the U.S. flag, Conservative corporatists believed that he shared some of their anti-Americanism. In particular, they knew that Somoza greatly resented U.S. Minister to Nicaragua Arthur Bliss Lane (1933–36) for impeding his efforts to establish a military dictatorship.[19] Moreover, they had a close-up view of how the general idealized the two leaders who then represented the greatest threat to the United States and its way of life: Hitler and Mussolini. But perhaps most important, Conservative corporatists felt that Somoza was expendable, for all they really needed was the support of the Guardia officer corps. And in their view, this officer corps not only shared their sympathies for fascism but controlled Somoza, not vice versa.[20] Only when it was too late did Conservative corporatists realize that Somoza was not so pliable. Not coincidentally, they broke with Somoza when the outbreak of World War II pushed the dictator to side definitively with the United States in its struggle against fascist Germany and Italy. To Conservatives' dismay, their turn against Somoza did the dictator little political harm, largely because his main pillar of support, the Guardia, maintained its hold over rural folk.

The dictatorship's control of the countryside was also rooted in a third legacy of U.S. imperial rule: dollar diplomacy's unexpected "democratization" of rural class structures. As historian Jeffrey Gould has shown, the regime of Somoza García enjoyed strong support from medium-scale farmers, the very rural sector that thrived under dollar diplomacy.[21] Together with the Guardia, these middling sectors mobilized peasants on Somoza's behalf and helped them wage land struggles against anti-Somoza landlords, particularly Conservative oligarchs. In exchange, they received from the Somoza regime key political support and generous economic aid like agricultural credit.[22] Had dollar diplomacy not inadvertently strengthened the power of medium-scale producers vis-à-vis local landlords, Somoza's populist project probably would not have succeeded in the countryside.

In the case of Nicaragua, then, we ought to contextualize Barrington Moore's influential thesis that rural authoritarianism in the modern world stems primarily from landlord efforts to secure cheap labor through political coercion.[23] This thesis has profoundly shaped scholarly analysis of why Central America's coffee nations traveled down such distinct political paths during the twentieth century. In particular, scholars have argued that brutal military regimes prevailed in Guatemala and El Salvador precisely because landlord power was the greatest in those countries, while a long-term democracy could develop only in Costa Rica because coffee production there was dominated not by labor-repressive landlords but by small- and medium-scale farmers.[24] Yet the case of the Somoza regime complicates the application of the Moore thesis to Central America in two ways. First, the rural base of the region's lengthiest dictatorship consisted of medium-scale farmers rather than large landlords. Second, these farmers sought the support of the Somoza regime not to satisfy their labor needs but to weaken the power of the country's most entrenched landed oligarchs.[25] So even if many analysts—as well as generations of U.S. officials—have assumed that middling sectors inherently crusade for liberal democracy, such groups can actually be crucial supporters of authoritarian rule.[26]

The Somoza dictatorship began to unravel once it abandoned rural populism. This anti-populist turn was certainly fueled by the transfer of power from Anastasio Somoza García to his sons, Luis and Anastasio Somoza Debayle, following the general's assassination in 1956. Although the slain dictator's sons had very different governing styles—Luis embodied the technocratic autocrat, while Anastasio epitomized the brutal despot—neither possessed their father's populist skills. In the end, however, the regime's antipopulist turn stemmed primarily from the way the agroexport boom of the late 1950s and 1960s transformed the Guardia's relationship with rural society. During this boom, Guardia officers of all ranks acquired significant amounts of land in the cotton-, coffee-, and beef-export industries.[27] If some officers bought their farms by misappropriating state funds and U.S. economic aid, others simply stole land from defenseless peasants. As a result, more and more peasants could no longer regard Guardia officers as legitimate mediators of their interests; instead they came to consider them as parvenu landlords who were threatening their livelihoods. The Guardia's evolution into a major entrepreneurial force triggered the rise of more autonomous peasant movements that eventually helped bring about the demise of the Somoza regime.[28] At the same time, it led landed oligarchs to view Guardia officers increasingly as a major threat to their economic interests. So greatly did the post-1960 rise of a quasi-military bourgeoisie antagonize native landlords that many adamantly opposed the 1978–79 efforts of the U.S. government to preserve the Guardia at all costs.[29] This unusual elite support for the military's destruction proved key to the revolutionary triumph of 1979.

Revolution

Once in power, the Sandinistas pursued a famously contradictory policy toward local elite groups. Committed to creating a socialist society, they forcefully attacked the political and economic basis of elite power. Not only did the revolutionary regime restrict the activities of various elite-led organizations and harass their leaders, it also confiscated numerous landed estates, industries, and commercial establishments. Yet however much the Sandinista leaders idealized communist Cuba, they did not seek to expunge all elite producers from the body politic. Instead, they strove to create a prorevolutionary "patriotic bourgeoisie" that would contribute economically to the revolution but be incapable of functioning as a dominant class. And according to Sandinista ideology, this "patriotic bourgeoisie" would consist largely of mestizo, medium-scale capitalists of plebian (*chapiollo*) origins who produced primarily for the domestic market.[30] This Sandinista construct built on the concept of a "national bourgeoisie" that has long been dear to Latin American populists and revolutionaries seeking the support of "progressive" elites. The search for the elusive "national bourgeoisie" has also preoccupied many Latin Americanist academics, particularly proponents of dependency theory.[31] Small wonder, then, that most scholars of the Nicaraguan revolution have taken the Sandinista definition of the "patriotic bourgeoisie" at face value. But in doing so, they have overlooked the fact that elites who actually came the closest to functioning as "bourgeois patriots" were not so much the acclaimed chapiollos but their antithesis: members of the Granada-based Conservative oligarchy. While some elite Conservatives, like the octogenarian José Coronel Urtecho, had championed the original Sandinistas of 1927–34, most were of a younger generation. Since these oligarchs hailed from the elite sector that most strongly backed Sandino's anti-U.S. struggle, should we deem their support for the Sandinista Revolution another surprising legacy of U.S. imperial rule?

Before addressing this question, let me first delineate the still obscure ties forged between the Sandinista regime and members of Conservative oligarchic families such as the Cuadras, Chamorros, Cardenals, Vivas, Argüellos, Arellanos, Guzmáns, and Lacayos. Granted, many of these pro-Sandinista elites were quite young when the revolution triumphed in 1979. Perhaps the most famous of these "youngsters" was General Joaquín Cuadra Lacayo (born in 1951), who in the 1980s served as the chief of staff of the Sandinista People's Army (Ejército Popular Sandinista). But many others were of an older generation and included oligarchs like Cuadra Lacayo's father, Joaquín Cuadra Chamorro, who in 1943 was deemed by U.S. military intelligence to be a leading fascist.[32] These older oligarchs most noticeably served the Sandinista regime by heading the Ministries of Finance, Domestic Commerce, Foreign Trade, Industry, Budget and Planning, Culture, and Education, as well as the Central Bank, the National Development Bank, and the Supreme Court.[33] In addition, elite Conservatives were appointed as vice ministers of the interior, finance, foreign affairs, and agricultural development and agrarian reform. Nearly all of these high-ranking officials remained loyal to the Sandinista Revolution until the bitter end, that is, until the FSLN's surprising loss in the 1990 elections. Elite Conservatives also secured many mid-level positions within the revolutionary state apparatus, particularly in the all-important Ministry of Agricultural Development and Agrarian Reform. In addition, scions of Conservative oligarchs helped direct the Sandinista People's Army, the FSLN's ideological institute (Instituto de Estudio del Sandinismo), and the party's official newspaper (Barricada).

At the same time, numerous Conservative oligarchs benefited economically from the Sandinista Revolution, especially its agrarian reform.[34] In addition to protecting their estates, the Sandinista state provided them with much economic aid, particularly subsidized agricultural credit. Conservative landlords appeared to have so greatly profited from the Sandinista agrarian reform that some Nicaraguan analysts have recently argued that the revolution resulted in an oligarchic restoration.[35] These revisionist views are incorrect, for even in the elite bastion of Granada peasant mobilization ensured that the overall thrust of the agrarian reform was indeed antioligarchic.[36]

Still, there is little doubt that in practice, if not in spirit, the Sandinistas stood their "patriotic bourgeoisie" on the shoulders of Conservative oligarchs.

Why then did the Sandinista Revolution apparently revive the original Conservative-Sandinista connection? No doubt political opportunism once again helped push oligarchs and revolutionaries to join forces at a critical juncture. In this instance, the FSLN sought to capitalize on Conservatives' technical and financial expertise as well as their international connections and economic resources, while the latter hoped to use the Sandinista state to defend their vested interests against revolutionary upheaval. The 1980s alliance also drew much strength from the integration of numerous sons and daughters of Conservative oligarchs into the Sandinista guerrilla well before the revolutionary triumph of 1979. The complete absence of such kinship ties from Conservatives' first association with Sandinismo helps explain its quicker demise. It also underscores how sharply the social profile of the original Sandinistas differed from that of their more recent namesakes. Finally, Conservative oligarchs shared a strong sense of ideological affinity with the latter-day Sandinistas. And it was in this realm of ideology that the legacy of U.S. imperial rule seems to have contributed most effectively to a revival of a Conservative-Sandinista alliance.

Conservative oligarchs so readily embraced the Sandinista Revolution precisely because they could see in the revolution the "antibourgeois spirit" developed by their forefathers during the U.S. occupation. Their conception of this spirit was no longer exactly the same as in the 1930s, however. For instance, in the 1940s its proponents had distanced themselves from fascism, largely because of the defeat of Germany and Italy in World War II. On the other hand, they had also tempered their anticommunist stance by the 1970s, with some, like the famous poet-priest Ernesto Cardenal (Sandinista minister of culture), even seeking to synthesize Marxist and Catholic principles under the rubric of liberation theology.[37] Nevertheless, key principles of the original "antibourgeois spirit" remained intact on the eve of the Sandinista Revolution.[38] Not only did many Conservative oligarchs steadfastly espouse anticapitalist sentiments rooted in Catholic social thought, they also advocated the corporatist forms of governance that had attracted the attention of Sandino. But above all, Conservative oligarchs continued to valorize an inward-looking, agrarian-based nationalism constructed against U.S. domination and Americanization. This valorization perhaps explains why, in the 1950s, elite Conservatives responded to the deepening of U.S. influence in their country's affairs by reembracing the figure of Sandino. In doing so, however, they made sure to champion a sanitized (i.e., anticommunist) image of the nationalist martyr.[39]

How and why the Caballeros Católicos' "antibourgeois spirit" reproduced itself over not just one but two successive generations of Conservative oligarchs remains an open question. But it was clearly not due to family bonds alone. Indeed, the Caballeros Católicos had developed the "antibourgeois spirit" against the Americanization project of their own parents. And what most upheld their anti-Americanism in the subsequent decades was the U.S. government's unwavering support for the Somoza dictatorship.[40] During these decades, the transmission of the "antibourgeois spirit" to the next generation occurred largely through civic institutions such as the Jesuit-run Colegio Centroamericano (Nicaragua's premier high school), the Acción Católica (the Catholic Church's social action organization), the Cofradía del Taller San Lucas (a cultural group based in Granada), and the Juventud Conservadora (the Conservative Party's youth organization).[41] In addition, the "antibourgeois spirit" infused leading Conservative journals like *Cuadernos del Taller San Lucas* and *Revista Conservadora*, as well as *La Prensa*, the country's main opposition newspaper. Together, these venues helped to transmit the Catholic social reformism and anti-Americanism of the original Caballeros Católicos to young Conservative oligarchs who came of age during the lengthy Somoza dictatorship. More generally, they helped to maintain the historical memory of Sandino within Nicaragua. This was particularly the case with *La Prensa*, which from the early 1950s onward commemorated Sandino's murder annually by publishing his portrait and paying homage to his nationalist struggle.

Yet the Conservative oligarchs who probably played the greatest role in promulgating Sandino's legacy and the "antibourgeois spirit" were those who lived long enough to have been allied with both the original and modern-day Sandinistas. The most prominent was José Coronel Urtecho, who after abandoning fascism and Somocismo became one of the FSLN's strongest elite supporters—a support he maintained up to his death in 1994 at the age of eighty-eight. In defending the Sandinista Revolution, Coronel Urtecho typically stressed his support for its nationalist struggle not just against "Yankee imperialism" but above all against the "Americanization" efforts of the "vendepatria bourgeoisie."[42]

Contrary to conventional wisdom, then, elites who most strongly supported the Sandinista Revolution did not seek to complete the liberal revolution that had been disrupted by the U.S. occupation of 1912–33. Instead, they were the descendants of the Caballeros Católicos who so fiercely turned against the liberalizing effects of U.S. imperial rule. Whether as government officials, military officers, or "patriotic producers," these Conservative oligarchs played a critical but contradictory role in the Sandinista Revolution. On the one hand, they helped the Sandinista regime defend itself against the U.S. government's relentless campaign to destroy the revolution. But just as important, these oligarchs gravely undermined the revolution's emancipatory impulses by seeking to impose a modern-day version of the Caballeros Católicos' myth of rural sanctity on a peasantry fighting for a very different social order. Once again, then, Conservatives' efforts to create a new Nicaragua by joining forces with Sandinista revolutionaries were plagued by tensions between reactionary and utopian forms of anti-Americanism. This time the tensions were not strong enough to preclude the formation of a Conservative-Sandinista alliance. But since the pull between utopian and reactionary impulses fundamentally shaped the Sandinista agrarian reform, which drove many peasants to join the counterrevolution, the tensions helped precipitate the revolution's surprising demise.[43]

The Price of Empire

Within Latin America, Conservative oligarchs' participation in the Sandinista Revolution struck an odd chord. But in the broader history of U.S. intervention, this involvement represented just one of the many "blowbacks" that the United States has experienced throughout the world. The term "blowback" was coined by the CIA and refers to the unintended consequences the United States incurs for its intervention abroad.[44] In many instances, the United States quickly reaps what it sows. Some sources of blowback, however, are more deeply rooted. This was the case with the crucial support that Nicaragua's Conservative oligarchs lent the Sandinista Revolution. As we have seen, the U.S. occupation of 1912–33 initially depended on the support of Conservative oligarchs. Yet the occupation eventually pushed the country's most Americanized elites to embrace an anti-U.S. outlook. And it was this anti-Americanism that would later underpin the Sandinista Revolution's powerful challenge to U.S. hegemony.[45]

The history of blowback, however, has not deterred contemporary U.S.-

based public intellectuals across the conservative-liberal spectrum from clamoring for the extension of an "American empire" to all corners of the world.[46] Their imperial vision has significantly shaped the interventionist impulses of U.S. foreign policy in the post–Cold War era, especially after the terror attacks of September 2001.[47] Some want the United States to spread its power simply in the name of national security. But there are many others who insist that U.S. imperial rule will make the world not just safer but better. In particular, they claim that poor and repressive countries—so-called failed states and rogue regimes—can become prosperous and democratic only by sacrificing their national sovereignty to a lengthy U.S. occupation. In making their case, proponents of such a "liberal empire" typically invoke the two instances—post–World War II Japan and Germany—where U.S. occupation helped develop political democracy and economic prosperity. Rarely do they acknowledge that past U.S. interventions in the Caribbean Basin—the center of the first U.S. overseas empire—failed to produce similar outcomes. And when they do, they simply state that this failure resulted from the "spasmodic" nature of such interventions.[48] In reality, U.S. interventions in the Caribbean Basin produced distinct results not because they were spasmodic. In fact, the U.S. protectorate system lasted far longer in Cuba (1898–1934), Haiti (1915–34), the Dominican Republic (1903–24), Panama (1903–38), and Nicaragua (1910–33) than in Japan (1945–52) and Germany (1945–55).

More important, U.S. imperial rule in the Caribbean Basin did not just fail to make things better; it made things worse. Consider, for example, the illiberal effects the U.S. occupation had on Nicaragua. In trying to remake Nicaragua into a "little United States," the occupiers not only cut short the country's first major democratic opening and helped produce three devastating wars, they also undermined the rule of law by politicizing state institutions; stymied economic development by blocking much-needed public improvements; and fatally militarized state-society relations by seeking to impose democracy via force. As this and other case studies suggest, the peoples of the Caribbean Basin paid a high price for U.S. imperial rule.[49] In fact, some prominent scholars argue that it is precisely because of U.S. dominance that "America's backyard" suffered unusually high levels of social inequality, political violence, and authoritarian rule during much of the twentieth century.[50]

The history of the first U.S overseas empire thus serves as a powerful reminder of the limits and perils of liberal imperialism. However much contemporary promoters of a U.S. "empire of liberty" showcase the U.S. occupations of Japan and Germany as models of U.S. liberal imperial rule, its more typical examples were the string of protectorates that the United States established in the Caribbean Basin during the early twentieth century.[51] And the tragic fate of these protectorates not only underscores the grave challenges that an imperial power faces in reshaping weaker nations, it also exposes the devastating, illiberal effects of liberal imperialism. At the same time, this history reminds us that imperial rule can rarely contend with subject peoples' desire for self-determination. While present-day advocates of liberal imperialism claim that the first U.S. overseas empire was doomed mainly because the U.S. public lacked the necessary imperial mindset, in reality it fell largely because the political and economic costs incurred to smother local opposition to U.S. imperial rule proved to be too high. To be sure, the Caribbean Basin has been home to some of the world's peoples who have most strongly adopted U.S. ways. But as we have seen, emulation of the United States should not be mistaken for an invitation to U.S. imperial rule.

The even greater mistake, however, is the tendency of the United States to equate all forms of foreign resistance to the spread of its influence with the rejection of "freedom." Of course, not all anti-U.S. movements have been democratic, and some U.S. interventions have actually promoted democratic rule. Still, the nearly two-hundred-year-history of U.S. intervention in its "backyard" highlights the powerful anti-democratic effects of, to quote President George W. Bush's 2005 inaugural address, "the great liberating tradition" of the United States.[52] No public debate about the wisdom of a contemporary U.S. "empire of liberty" will be very meaningful if it ignores Latin America's extensive experience with U.S. intervention. After all, few better foresaw the perils of such an empire than Latin America's independence hero Simón Bolívar, who in 1829 prophesied that the United States would "plague [Latin] America with torments in the name of freedom."[53]

Notes

INTRODUCTION

1 Mack, *Land Divided*, 101.
2 Cited in Burns, *Patriarch and Folk*, 162.
3 More generally, see Rosenberg, *Spreading the American Dream*.
4 U.S. Senate, "Instances of Use of United States Armed Forces Abroad."
5 While the U.S. military controlled Panama's Canal Zone for much of the twentieth century, it occupied the rest of the nation only between 1903–14 and 1918–20.
6 Denny, *Dollars for Bullets*, 384.
7 See esp. Wheelock, *Imperialismo y dictadura*, a pioneering study from 1975 that was written by a Sandinista guerrillero who later became minister of agrarian reform during the Sandinista Revolution. Other influential studies include Bermann, *Under the Big Stick*; Burns, *Patriarch and Folk*; Macaulay, *Sandino Affair*; Millett, *Guardians of the Dynasty*; Quijano, *Nicaragua*; Selser, *Sandino*; and Vargas, *Intervención norteamericana*.
8 Manolo Cuadra in Calatayud Bernabeu, *Manolo Cuadra*, 19.
9 This paragraph draws heavily on Fehrenbach and Poiger, "Introduction."
10 For recent examples by Latin Americanist historians, see Louis Pérez, *On Becoming Cuban*; Joseph, LeGrand, and Salvatore, *Close Encounters of Empire*; and Moreno, *Yankee Don't Go Home*. For case studies beyond Latin America, see Wagnleitner, *Coca-Colonization*; Kuisel, *Seducing the French*; Nolan, *Visions of Modernity*; and Fehrenbach and Poiger, *Transactions, Transgressions, Transformations*.
11 On how, e.g., Cuban nationalists appropriated U.S. ways in their struggle against Spanish colonial rule, see Louis Pérez, *On Becoming Cuban*. See also Hale, *Resistance and Contradiction*, on the ways that Miskitu people on Nicaragua's Atlantic coast used their "affinity" with Anglo-U.S. institutions and cultural practices to resist the Hispanization efforts of the Nicaraguan state.
12 On the use of this term in the Latin American context, see Roseberry, "Americanization in the Americas"; and Cabán, *Constructing a Colonial People*. For Europe and Japan, see, e.g., Zeitlin and Herrigel, *Americanization and Its Limits*.
13 For recent examples that define anti-Americanism as the rejection of U.S. influence, see McPherson, *Yankee No!*; Hertsgaard, *Eagle's Shadow*; and most of the essays in Ross and Ross, *Anti-Americanism* (key exceptions include the articles by Ana María Dopico and Mary Nolan, both of whom

stress anti-Americanism's complex link with Americanization). For some scholars' view that anti-Americanism is an attack on modernity more generally, see Hollander, *Understanding Anti-Americanism*.

14 Belausteguigoitia, *Con Sandino en Nicaragua*, 216.

15 Rodó, *Ariel*, 35.

16 Dorfman and Mattelart, *How to Read Donald Duck*, 95.

17 Mendieta, *Enfermedad de Centro-América*, 2:358.

18 On how a range of nationalist movements appropriated U.S. ideals of material prosperity, social mobility, and political democracy to challenge the dominance of U.S. corporations during the Great Depression, see O'Brien, *Revolutionary Mission*.

19 E.g., Rangel, *Latin Americans*.

20 Joseph, "Close Encounters," 5–6.

21 For a recent historiographical overview, see Ninkovich, "United States and Imperialism."

22 Here I follow Michael Doyle, who defines imperialism as "the process or policy of establishing or maintaining an empire," with empire being "a relationship, formal or informal, in which one state controls the effective political sovereignty of another political society." Doyle, *Empires*, 45.

23 For a critique of such views, see Louis Pérez, "1898 and Beyond."

24 E.g., Stephanson, *Manifest Destiny*.

25 Rosenberg, *Spreading the American Dream*, 234.

26 For a general overview, see Patrick Wolfe, "Imperialism and History."

27 E.g., Coronil; and Stoler and Cooper, "Between Metropole and Colony."

28 Club de Granada, *Memoria anual de la junta directiva del Club de Granada*, 1917, 1934 in Archivo Héctor Mena Guerrero (Granada); Oficina Central del Censo, *Censo general de 1920*, Managua: Tipografía Nacional, 1920.

29 For a list of the most important works, see Ninkovich, "United States and Imperialism," 86–87. Recent exceptions include Louis Pérez, *On Becoming Cuban*; and Findlay, *Imposing Decency*. For more on the historiography of U.S. intervention in Latin America, see Louis Pérez, "Intervention, Hegemony, and Dependency"; and Joseph, "Close Encounters."

30 See *Catálogo del Archivo Histórico de la Prefectura y Municipalidad de Granada*, Managua: Fundación Casa de los Tres Mundos, 2000.

1 · AMERICANIZATION THROUGH VIOLENCE

1 This paragraph is based on Walker, *War in Nicaragua*; Doubleday, *Reminiscences*; Bolaños Geyer, *William Walker*; and Jéronimo Pérez, *Obras históricas*, 226.

2   Jéronimo Pérez, *Obras históricas*, 226.

3   E.g., Burns, *Patriarch and Folk*, 197–218.

4   Manning, *Diplomatic Correspondence*, 4:409.

5   Walker, *War in Nicaragua*, 430.

6   For more on the United States' longstanding interest in the Nicaraguan canal project, see Mack, *Land Divided*.

7   Wilkins, *Emergence of Multinational Enterprise*, 28.

8   Folkman, *Nicaragua Route*, 163.

9   Herrera, *Bongos*, 44–70.

10 Conclusion based on ibid.

11 Burns, *Patriarch and Folk*, 184.

12 Ortega Arancibia, *Cuarenta años*, 116.

13 Herrera, *Bongos*, 77–108.

14 E.g., Dolores Gámez, "Granada que yo conocí."

15 Kinloch Tijerino, *Nicaragua*, 201–20.

16 "Noticias sobre la jeografía y estadística del Departamento Oriental," *El Nicaragüense*, 15 December 1855.

17 Herrera, *Bongos*, 175–207.

18 Texas State Library, *Papers of Lamar*, 4:1, 83.

19 For more on these struggles, see Burns, *Patriarch and Folk*.

20 For a succinct discussion of liberalism in mid-nineteenth-century Central America, see Mahoney, *Legacies of Liberalism*, 31–35.

21 Burns, *Patriarch and Folk*, 23. For how this struggle was waged elsewhere in Central America, see Gudmundson and Lindo-Fuentes, *Central America*, 93–120.

22 Kinloch Tijerino, *Nicaragua*, 101–41; Burns, *Patriarch and Folk*, 145–59; Casanova Fuertes, "Hacia una nueva valorización."

23 Burns, *Patriarch and Folk*, 151.

24 For more on Walker's Mexican expedition, see Brown, *Agents of Manifest Destiny*, 194–218.

25 See, e.g., Heine, *Wanderbilder*, 146; and Kinloch Tijerino, *Nicaragua*, 220.

26 On filibusterism more generally, see May, *Manifest Destiny's Underworld*.

27 "Speech of Gen. Walker," *El Nicaragüense*, 7 June 1856.

28 See, e.g., the following personal accounts: Doubleday, *Reminiscences*; "Experience of Samuel Absalom"; Jamison, *With Walker*; and Wells, *Walker's Expedition*.

29 May, *Southern Dream*, 77–135.

30 For Walker's German followers, see Houwald, *Alemanes en Nicaragua*, 141–47.

31 For an alternative view, see Brown, *Agents of Manifest Destiny*, 267.

32 Jéronimo Pérez, *Obras históricas*, 226, 235.

33 Kinloch Tijerino, *Nicaragua*, 207.

34 *Boletín Oficial*, 5 July 1849.

35 Squier, *Nicaragua*, 1:247.

36 E.g., Stout, *Nicaragua*, 145; Heine, *Wanderbilder*, 52; and Marr, *Reise nach Central Amerika*, 45.

37 Manning, *Diplomatic Correspondence*, 3:248–49, 262–64, 270–72, 409; 4:196–97, 278, 299, 339–40, 369, 379.

38 Cited in Dunkerley, *Americana*, 560.

39 Kinloch Tijerino, *Nicaragua*, 201–79.

40 Frutos Chamorro as cited in Burns, *Patriarch and Folk*, 12.

41 Manning, *Diplomatic Correspondence*, 3:266, 324–26; 4:369–70.

42 Ibid., 4:349–56.

43 Gámez, *Historia moderna*, 672.

44 Manning, *Diplomatic Correspondence*, 4:243.

45 Ibid., 4:369–70.

46 Ibid., 4:297.

47 Jéronimo Pérez, *Obras históricas*, 226.

48 Walker, *War in Nicaragua*, 73–75.

49 Petitions reproduced in Vijil, *Padre Vijil*, 159–62.

50 The transit company claims to have sent twelve thousand soldier-colonists to Nicaragua. See Bolaños Geyer, *Testimonio de Joseph N. Scott*, 141–42.

51 Manning, *Diplomatic Correspondence*, 4:518–21.

52 The sermon is reprinted in Vijil, *Padre Vijil*, 151–55.

53 Manning, *Diplomatic Correspondence*, 4:521.

54 Bolaños Geyer, *William Walker*, 4:16–17.

55 Petition sent by Terencio Mercado, Anastacio Hernández, Matilde Mercado, and María Calderón to William Walker on 24 December 1855, Callander Fayssoux Collection of William Walker Papers, catalog no. 118, reel 3.

56 *Boletín de Noticias*, no. 3 (22 April 1855). For how Walker's chief Nicaraguan foe acknowledged "the preaching of some of the ministers of religion in favor of the filibusters," see Manning, *Diplomatic Correspondence*, 4:519.

57 Doubleday, *Reminiscences*, 165–67.

58 Jéronimo Pérez, *Obras históricas*, 67, 273–74; Jamison, *With Walker*, 37–38, 42.

59 See the playbill reproduced in Rosengarten, *William Walker*, 201.

60 "El Coronel Valle de la fuersa expedicionariá del Medio Día a los pueblos del Estado," *El Nicaragüense*, 27 October 1855. For how a similar explanation was provided by another popular caudillo, see "El Coronel Méndez a sus amigos los Leoneses," *El Nicaragüense*, 8 March 1856.

61 Ortega Arancibia, *Cuarenta años*, 75.

62   For how Valle's former comrade-in-arms Bernabé Somoza (who was captured and executed in 1849) apparently admired the United States, see Stout, *Nicaragua*, 153.

63   Walker, *War in Nicaragua*, 250.

64   Burns, *Patriarch and Folk*, 209.

65   Walker, *War in Nicaragua*, 262–63.

66   Horsman, *Race and Manifest Destiny*, 208–97.

67   Slotkin, *Fatal Environment*, 256–57.

68   Burns, *Patriarch and Folk*, 66–109.

69   Slotkin, *Regeneration through Violence*.

70   Doubleday, *Reminiscences*, iii; "General Frederick Henningsen," 172.

71   On the ways that such competing notions of the "mission of regeneration" shaped U.S. expansion into Mexico, see Weinberg, *Manifest Destiny*, 160–89.

72   "General Frederick Henningsen," 171–73; Bolaños Geyer, *William Walker*, 5:381.

73   "Election in Nicaragua," *El Nicaragüense*, 3 April 1856, cited in Bolaños Geyer, *William Walker*, 4:40–41.

74   Jéronimo Pérez, *Obras históricas*, 223. Costa Rica, widely viewed as the Central American nation with the strongest democratic tradition, did not establish direct elections until 1913. See Lehoucq and Molina, *Stuffing the Ballot Box*, 2.

75   See "Efemérides," *Boletín Oficial*, 8 August 1856, reproduced in Jéronimo Pérez, *Obras históricas*, 405.

76   Walker, *War in Nicaragua*, 252–54; *El Nicaragüense*, 28 June 1856.

77   E.g., Jamison, *With Walker*, 42; and Archivo de la Municipalidad y de la Prefectura de Granada (hereafter AMPG), 1869, legajo (hereafter leg.) 229, caja 66, "Solicitud de reclamo al Supremo Gobierno por pérdidas sufridas por Francisco Cornelio Argüello en 1856," Granada, November 1869.

78   Bolaños Geyer, *William Walker*, 4:65–69.

79   For how this fear was recognized by some U.S. filibusters, see "Experience of Samuel Absalom," 664.

80   Manning, *Diplomatic Correspondence*, 4:540.

81   E.g., Carroll, *Star of the West*, 345–91.

82   Walker to Heiss, 29 June 1856, in "Walker-Heiss Papers," *Tennessee Historical Magazine* 1 (1915): 335. On how Walker's officers stressed the strength of popular Catholicism, see Whelpley, "Ranger's Life in Nicaragua," 39–40; and Jamison, *With Walker*, 68–69.

83   Burns, *Patriarch and Folk*, 164.

84   Coto, *Documentos históricos*, 65.

85 See the section "Proclamas y mensajes" in Coto, *Documentos históricos*.

86 For more on the war's course, see Brown, *Agents of Manifest Destiny*, 359–409; and Bolaños Geyer, *William Walker*, vol. 4.

87 Walker, *War in Nicaragua*, 340.

88 For an eyewitness account, see "Incendio y saqueo de Granada," *Boletín Oficial*, 15 and 22 April 1857, in *Revista de la Academia de Geografía e Historia de Nicaragua* 44 (1978–79): 221–25, 235–39.

89 Walker, *War in Nicaragua*, 195.

90 Ibid., 288.

91 E.g., Ratterman, "With Walker in Nicaragua"; and Whepley, "Ranger's Life."

92 Whepley, "Ranger's Life," 41. See also the 24 May 1857 letter by José Miguel Cárdenas in Arellano, *Historia básica*, 114.

93 Jéronimo Pérez, *Obras históricas*, 215–16; Jamison, *With Walker*, 67.

94 The Allied army consisted of about 3,500 Costa Ricans, 1,500 Guatemalans, 1,700 Salvadorans, 600 Hondurans, and 1,100 Nicaraguans. Figures taken from Bolaños Geyer, *William Walker*, 4:159, 228, 247; and Palma Martínez, *Guerra Nacional*, 416.

95 Lane, *Commodore Vanderbilt*, 108–38.

2 · AMERICANIZATION FROM WITHIN

1 For a recent critique of the widespread belief that cosmopolitanism and nationalism are incompatible, see Heater, *World Citizenship*.

2 Salomon, "Cosmopolitanism and Internationalism." For a recent case study that explores how, in late nineteenth-century Argentina, cosmopolitanism competed with other visions of nationhood that were more essentialist and exclusivist, see Bertoni, *Patriotas, cosmopolitas y nacionalistas*.

3 Barcia, *Escritos dispersos de Rubén Darío*, 1:125.

4 Charles A. Hale, "Political and Social Ideas," 225–26.

5 E.g., Burns, *Patriarch and Folk*, 213–18.

6 AMPG, 1856–57, leg. 139, Ministro de Gobernación to Prefecto del Departamento Oriental, 13 September 1857.

7 Manning, *Diplomatic Correspondence*, 4:650.

8 Ibid., 820.

9 Ibid., 685.

10 Ibid., 649.

11 Cole to Lamar, León, 8 May 1858, in Texas State Library, *Papers of Lamar*, 4.2:140.

12 Phelan, "Pan-Latinism"; and Ibold, "Erfindung Lateinamerikas."

13 On this phenomenon in Mexico, see Charles A. Hale, *Mexican Liberalism*, 203–6.

14 This conclusion is based largely on Kinloch Tijerino, *Nicaragua*, 299–310.

15 E.g., "Nacionalidad," *El Nacional*, 31 July 1858, in Texas State Library, *Papers of Lamar*, 6:382–84.

16 Kinloch Tijerino, *Nicaragua*.

17 Ibid., 304.

18 Charles A. Hale, *Mexican Liberalism*, 208–14.

19 Kinloch Tijerino, *Nicaragua*, 308.

20 See the pioneering work of Kinloch Tijerino, "Canal interoceánico."

21 Kinloch Tijerino, "Canal interoceánico," 43.

22 See the *actas municipales* in Pedro Ramírez, *Canal interoceánico*.

23 For Granada, see Guzmán, "Diario íntimo," esp. 52–96.

24 Tenorio-Trillo, *Mexico at the World's Fairs*, 8.

25 *Exposition de 1889: Guide bleu du "Figaro" et du "Petit Journal,"* Paris, 1889, 209.

26 Tenorio, *Mexico at the World's Fairs*, 19, 64–80, 97.

27 Pletcher, *Diplomacy of Trade and Investment*, 114–47, 280–98.

28 Mahan, *Interest of America in Sea Power*.

29 Pletcher, *Diplomacy of Trade and Investment*, 283.

30 Bermann, *Under the Big Stick*, 109–16.

31 Joseph Smith, *Illusions of Conflict*, 35–38, 81–116.

32 Crowell, "United States and Central American Canal."

33 For a perceptive contemporary account, see Ortega Arancibia, *Cuarenta años*. See also Cruz, *Nicaragua's Conservative Republic*.

34 This discussion draws heavily on Justin Wolfe, "Rising from the Ashes."

35 See also Charlip, *Cultivating Coffee*.

36 Madrigal Mendieta, *Evolución de las ideas*; Arellano, *Historia básica*, 148–59; Fumero Vargas, "De la iniciativa individual"; Whisnant, *Rascally Signs in Sacred Places*, 58–89.

37 For elites' valorization of the "spirit of association" that allegedly characterized U.S. civil society, see *La Tertulia*, 15 November 1875.

38 AMPG, 1883, leg. 508, Rodríguez to Inspector de Instrucción primaria de Granada, 9 May 1883.

39 For a contrasting view, see Mahoney, *Legacies of Liberalism*, esp. 99–104.

40 On the ways that Conservative elites elsewhere in Central America also embraced key liberal tenets, see Gudmundson and Lindo-Fuentes, *Central America*.

41 Guzmán, *Huellas de su pensamiento*, 10. Guzmán made this quip in 1876, well before he abandoned his radical views.

42 Cited in Buitrago Matus, *León*, 196–97.

43 For the claim that the expansion of agroexport (esp. coffee) production triggered the 1881 uprisings in Matagalpa, see, e.g., Wheelock, *Raíces indígenas*.

44 Gould, *To Die in This Way*, 26–38; Téllez, *¡Muera la gobierna!*, 293–305.

45 Gould, *To Die in This Way*, 35–37.

46 Justin Wolfe, "Rising from the Ashes," chap. 5.

47 Gould, *To Die in This Way*, 33.

48 Crispolti, *Mensaje de 24 de enero*, 68.

49 My analysis of these urban revolts is based largely on documents in Crispolti, *Mensaje de 24 de enero*; Buitrago Matus, *León*, 149–208; and AMPG, 1881, leg. 447.

50 For Granada, see AMPG, 1881, leg. 457, fols. 55–59.

51 "Nicaragua i la inmigración," *La Gaceta de Nicaragua*, 31 August 1867, 276.

52 "El Legislador de Nicaragua," *La Juventud*, 1 July 1868.

53 E.g., "El espíritu de imitación en el redactor de *La Gaceta*," *La Tertulia*, 15 July 1876, 122.

54 Zúñiga, *Historia eclesiástica*, 357–444. My analysis of this clash draws much inspiration from Ivereigh, *Politics of Religion*.

55 See, e.g., the conflict between Hijas de María and the (secular) Sociedad de Socorro as reported by *La Tertulia*, 28 December 1878 and 4 January 1879.

56 For a distinct interpretation that stresses the antimodern bent of Nicaragua's proclerical forces, see Pérez-Baltodano, *Entre el Estado*.

57 E.g., the manifesto of León's *iglesieros* in Buitrago Matus, *León*, 321–23.

58 President Chamorro, quoted in Buitrago Matus, *León*, 227; "El telégrafo," *La Tertulia*, 15 June 1876.

59 Justin Wolfe, "Rising from the Ashes," 250–51.

60 Guzmán, *Huellas de su pensamiento*, 159.

61 AMPG, 1881, leg. 453, Ministro de Educación to Sr. Inspector de Instrucción primaria del Departamento de Granada, 19 April 1881.

62 See, respectively, AMPG, 1881, leg. 457, fols. 55–59, and Justin Wolfe, "Rising from the Ashes," 164.

63 Bulmer-Thomas, *Economic History*, 65.

64 For more on the rise of Nicaragua's coffee industry, see Charlip, *Cultivating Coffee*.

65 Boyle, *Ride across a Continent*, 99.

66 Reyes, *Granada*, 78–86.

67 See esp. Wheelock, *Imperialismo y dictadura*.

68 Gould, "Café, trabajo y comunidad indígena." On the ways that elite and peasant patriarchalism help explain why so many debt peons were women and children, see Dore, "Patriarchy from Above, Below."

69   E.g., Dore, "Land Privatization"; and Charlip, *Cultivating Coffee*.

70   Dore, "Land Privatization." For a contemporary denunciation of how the politics of patronage enabled "antientrepreneurial" Conservatives to profit from the post-1870s coffee boom, see Mendoza, *Historia de Diriamba*.

71   Analysis based on agricultural censes taken in 1893, 1894, 1903, and 1907, and held in AMPG, books 169, 172, 186, and 189. See also Justin Wolfe, "Rising from the Ashes," 113–65.

72   For more on the privatization of Diriomo's common lands, see Dore, "Land Privatization."

73   E.g., see the list of coffee pickers for the 1904 harvest in AMPG, box 299, leg. s/n, Documentos varios, 1904.

74   Figures calculated on the basis of table 1 in Dore, "Debt Peonage in Granada," 529.

75   On the establishment by Diriomeños of a number of small coffee farms on the Mombacho, see Diriomo's coffee census of 5 November 1882 in AMPG, 1882, box 182, leg. 490 bis. For a sample of elite conflicts over land, see AMPG, 1889, box 241, leg. Denuncias de tierras; and 1889, box 245, leg. Denuncias de tierras baldías.

76   For Latin America, see Bauer, *Goods, Power, History*, 129–64.

77   José Coronel Urtecho, "Contra el espíritu burgués," *El Diario Nicaragüense*, 22 March 1931. On traditional elites' patriarchal ideals, see Burns, *Patriarch and Folk*, 66–109.

78   See, in particular, Bolaños, *Obras*, 149–431, which details the evolution of elite culture in Granada during the late nineteenth century.

79   See Guzmán, "Diario íntimo" (entries for 1882–83).

80   Ortega Arancibia, *Cuarenta años*, 297.

81   Cited in Buitrago Matus, *León*, 244.

82   In 1889 about half of the eighty-four prize-winning Nicaraguan coffee growers were from Granada. See Ministère du Commerce, de l'Industrie et des Colonies, *Exposition Universelle de 1889 à Paris: Liste des récompenses*, Paris, 1889, 567–79.

83   Mendieta, *Enfermedad de Centro-América*, 1:144.

84   See AMPG, 1882, box 182, leg. 490 bis, for the range of goods that elite Granadans imported in 1882 via the Nicaraguan Mail Steam Navigation Co.

85   Bolaños, *Obras*, 294.

86   On cosmopolitan nationality and import consumption, see Orlove and Bauer, "Giving Importance to Imports"; and Hoganson, "Cosmopolitan Domesticity." For a contrasting view, see Needell, *Tropical Belle Epoque*.

87   For the spread of places of entertainment in Granada, see Bolaños, *Obras*, 293–350.

88   Sheldon, *Notes on the Nicaraguan Canal*, 191.

89   E.g., Gunn, *Public Culture of the Victorian Middle Class*, 24–30.

90   *Memoria anual de la junta directiva del Club de Granada aprobada en junta general el 24 de diciembre de 1934*, 17, in Archivo Héctor Mena Guerrero (Granada).

91   Ortega Arancibia, *Cuarenta años*, 358.

92   See Gobat, "Against the Bourgeois Spirit," 74–75.

93   Analysis based on *Memoria presentada a la Asamblea Nacional Legislativa en su VIII periodo constitucional por el Señor Dr. don Fernando Sánchez, Ministro de Instrucción Pública*, Managua: Tipografía Nacional, 1901; *Memoria de la Secretaria de Instrucción Pública Presentada a la Asamblea Nacional por el Sr. Ministro José D. Gámez, 1906–1907*, Managua: Tipografía Nacional, 1907; and Toledo de Aguerri, *Enciclopedia nicaragüense*. For how U.S. schools Americanized Latin American immigrants, see Louis Pérez, *On Becoming Cuban*, 34.

94   Arellano, *Historia básica*, 156.

95   Stump, "Primer club de base-ball."

96   On the transformation of baseball into the U.S. pastime, see Goldstein, *Playing for Keeps*.

97   *El Periódico*, 18 March 1912; "Los gallos en el Congreso," *La Noticia*, 10 January 1918; and the February–March 1918 editions of *La Gaceta* on congressional debates that led to the banning of cockfights.

98   For a similar use of baseball in Cuba, see Louis Pérez, "Between Baseball and Bullfighting."

99   On baseball and social control, see Joseph, "Forging a Regional Pastime."

100   Coronel Urtecho, "Americanismo," 26–27.

101   Arellano, *Doctor David Arellano*, 51–52.

102   Coronel Urtecho, "Americanismo," 30–31.

103   Ibid., 27.

104   Wallace Thompson, *Rainbow Countries*, 46.

105   Ruhl, *Central Americans*, 118.

106   Darío, *Viaje a Nicaragua*, 210–11.

107   Bolaños, *Obras*, 293–94. For the Europeanization trend in Latin America, see Bauer, *Goods, Power, History*, 150–64.

108   E.g., Williams, *States and Social Evolution*, 194.

109   Seager and Maguire, *Letters and Papers of Mahan*, 9.

110   Keaseby, *Nicaragua Canal*, 1.

111   See the U.S. newspaper clippings in "Nicaraguan Canal, Scrapbooks, 1898–1900," box 100, W. R. Grace and Co. Papers, Butler Library, Columbia University.

112 McCullough, *Path between the Seas*, 259.

113 E.g., Dozier, *Nicaragua's Mosquito Shore*, 181; and Kinloch Tijerino, "Formación del Estado Nacional."

114 Jéronimo Pérez, *Obras históricas*, 187–88.

115 Pérez-Baltodano, *Entre el Estado*, 326.

116 E.g., "El ciudadano de los Estados Unidos," *Diario de Nicaragua*, 19–21 February 1895.

117 For the treaty's text, see Library of Congress, Congressional Research Service, *Background Documents Relating to the Panama Canal*, Washington, DC: Government Printing Office, 1977, 169–75.

118 Schoonover, *United States in Central America*, 136.

119 E.g., Healy, *Drive to Hegemony*, 82–83; and LaFeber, *Panama Canal*, 15–18.

120 McCullough, *Path between the Seas*, 325; Collin, *Roosevelt's Caribbean*, 177–79.

121 McCullough, *Path between the Seas*, 262.

122 Schoonover, *United States in Central America*, 142–45.

123 Ministerio de Instrucción Pública, *Memoria de la Secretaría de Instrucción Pública, 1906–1907*. Managua: Tipografía Nacional, 1907.

124 For the most infamous case involving a subsidiary of the United Fruit Company, see O'Brien, *Revolutionary Mission*, 62–65.

125 Gámez, "Canal anglo-japonés"; Schoonover, *Germany in Central America*, 118–33.

126 The note is reprinted in U.S. Department of State, *Papers Relating to the Foreign Relations of the United States, 1909*, Washington, DC: Government Printing Office, 1914, 455–57.

127 Schoultz, *Beneath the United States*, 210.

128 "Taking the 'Big Stick' to Zelaya," *Literary Digest*, 11 December 1909, 1047.

129 Cuadra Pasos, *Obras 1*, 277–78; Chamorro, "Autobiografía," 43; Alvarez Lejarza, *Impresiones y recuerdos*, 245.

130 Schoonover, *United States in Central America*, 147.

131 Quoted in Katz, *Secret War in Mexico*, 23.

3 · CHALLENGING IMPERIAL EXCLUSIONS

1 E.g., Moncada, *Influence of the United States*.

2 For the text of the Dawson Pact, see U.S. National Archives (hereafter USNA), Record Group (hereafter RG) 59, 817.00/1469½.

3 USNA, RG 59, 817.00/1445, Dawson to the Secretary of State, 28 October 1910.

4 Cuadra Pasos, *Obras 1*, 601.

5   For an overview, see Ninkovich, *United States and Imperialism.*

6   I take this term from Rosenberg, *Spreading the American Dream.*

7   Schoultz, *Beneath the United States*, 192.

8   Alvarez Lejarza, *Impresiones y recuerdos*, 400–401.

9   Pro- and anticlerical deputies are listed in *Boletín de la Asamblea*, 18 February 1911.

10 Ibid., 18 March 1911, 1.

11 Mendieta, *Enfermedad de Centro-América*, 2:359.

12 Lynch, "Catholic Church," 358–68.

13 For a transcript of these debates, see Diego Manuel Chamorro, *Discursos*, 9–17.

14 Cuadra Pasos, *Obras 1*, 572.

15 Diego Manuel Chamorro, *Discursos*, 9–17.

16 Cuadra Pasos, *Obras 1*, 364–65.

17 *Boletín de la Asamblea*, 10 and 18 February 1911.

18 Ibid., 25 February 1911.

19 For an exemplary case, see Arellano, *Laica apostólica.*

20 *Boletín de la Asamblea*, 31 January 1911.

21 On artisan ideology during the Zelaya era, see Rice, "Nicaragua and the U.S.," 112–15, 340–51.

22 Teplitz, "Political and Economic Foundations," 276–94.

23 E.g., the first article of "Estatutos de la Sociedad de Obreros y Socorros Mutuos de Granada," *Gaceta Oficial*, 12 February 1911.

24 *El Centinela*, 11 and 19 November 1910; *Diario de Nicaragua*, 19 September 1910.

25 For an eyewitness account, see Huezo, "Caída de un presidente."

26 For the treaty's text, see U.S. Department of State, *Papers Relating to the Foreign Relations of the United States, 1912*, Washington, DC: Government Printing Office, 1919, 1074–76.

27 For more on these conventions, see Hill, *Fiscal Intervention.*

28 William B. Hale, "With the Knox Mission," 186.

29 *El Periódico*, 8 March 1911.

30 USNA, RG 59, 817.00/1698, Gunther to Secretary of State, 29 September 1911.

31 USNA, RG 59, 817.00/1774, Division of Latin American Affairs, Memorandum, 13 March 1912.

32 Arellano, *Doctor David Arellano*, 69.

33 Ibid., 50.

34 *El Periódico*, 8 May 1912.

35 E.g., *La Información*, 26 September 1912.

36 This interview was also published in *El Diario Nicaragüense*, 10 April 1912.

37   *Diario de Nicaragua*, 22 January 1912.

38   For the U.S. arguments, see Rosenberg, *Financial Missionaries*, 14.

39   *El Diario Nicaragüense*, 27 February 1912.

40   Young, *Central American Currency*, 119–46.

41   E.g., *El Diario Nicaragüense*, 18 August, and 2 December 1911; and *Diario de Nicaragua*, 23 January and 13 February 1912.

42   The following analysis draws largely on articles appearing between January and July 1912 in Granada's pro-Mena Conservative daily *El Periódico* and Managua's Liberal daily *Diario Moderno*.

43   *El Periódico*, 15 March 1912. "Inditos" means literally small Indians (indios), while the term "zambo" was used to refer to people of mixed black and Indian ancestry.

44   Pasos Arana, "Granada y sus arroyos." *Revista de la Academia de Geografía e Historia de Nicaragua*, 6:1 (1944), 118.

45   Barcia, *Escritos dispersos de Rubén Darío*, 2:263.

46   According to a report made by the U.S. minister to Nicaragua in January 1912, Mena had received at least eighty thousand U.S. dollars from the national treasury. Shortly thereafter, Mena bought five thousand manzanas in the important cattle region of Malacatoya; this proved to be the largest land purchase Mena would ever undertake in his native region of Granada. See U.S. Congress, Senate, *Hearing before the Committee on Foreign Relations United States Senate, Sixty-Third Congress, Second Session on Convention between the United States and Nicaragua*, Washington, DC: Government Printing Office, 1913, 121; and Registro Público de la Propiedad de Granada (hereafter RPPG), *Libro de propiedades*, vol. 23, fol. 245.

47   Archivo del Instituto de Historia de Nicaragua y Centroamérica (hereafter AIHNCA), Fondo Díaz, 1904–1912, 107 hojas, Correspondencia de y para José Arambura, La Luz and Los Angeles Mining Co, Prinzapolka desde EE.UU. y Nicaragua, 17 February 1896.

48   Reinaldo Chamorro to Emiliano Chamorro and Adolfo Díaz in Correspondencia privada escrita y recibida por el General Emilano Chamorro E. en los años 1904–1929 (hereafter CPEC), 14 February 1912; AIHNCA, Fondo Díaz, folder: 3191, 1 February 1912.

49   My understanding of Nicaraguan mestizaje draws mostly on Gould, *To Die in This Way*.

50   *El Periódico*, 21 March 1912.

51   *El Diario Nicaragüense*, 2 April 1912.

52   *El Periódico*, 16 April 1912.

53   For the sources on which this paragraph is based, see Gobat, "Against the Bourgeois Spirit," 61–63.

54 *Diario Moderno*, 28 April 1912.

55 This song, "El Nandaime," was popular during the early twentieth century but has since faded from popular memory. I would like to thank Sra. Leypon de Talavera and Angel Márquez Leypon for bringing it to my attention.

56 *Diario Moderno*, 28 April 1912.

57 *El Periódico*, 28 June 1912.

58 Ibid., 16 April 1912.

59 Such papers included *Diario de Nicaragua*, *El 8 de Mayo*, and *Diario Moderno*.

60 For attendance at the Arauz-Chamorro wedding by the Cuadras, Pasos, and other "aristocratic" families, see *El Diario Nicaragüense*, 23 July 1912.

61 *El Diario Nicaragüense*, 16–18 April 1912.

62 Ibid., 17 April 1912.

63 Ibid., 16 April 1912.

64 Cuadra Pasos, *Obras 1*, 573.

65 For a list of club members, see Club de Granada, *Memoria anual de la junta directiva del Club de Granada, 1917*, Granada, Nicaragua, n.p., n.d.; and Club de Granada, *Memoria anual de la junta directiva del Club de Granada, 1934*. For the criteria I used to define elite membership, see Gobat, "Against the Bourgeois Spirit," 74–75.

66 Bourdieu, *Distinction*, 479.

67 *El Diario Nicaragüense*, 26 June 1912.

68 *Diario Moderno*, 22 and 24 May 1912.

69 For the case of Granada, see the numerous documents held in AMPG, 1912, leg. Notas y Telegrama, 189 fols., s.n.

70 *El Diario Nicaragüense*, 29 March 1912.

71 *Diario Moderno*, 22 May 1912.

72 CPEC, Bartolomé Martínez to Emiliano Chamorro, 11 April 1912.

73 E.g., *Diario Moderno*, 12 June 1912.

74 Ibid., 11 July 1912.

75 Ibid., 17 July 1912.

76 AMPG, 1912, leg. Notas y Telegrama, 189 fols., Emiliano Chamorro to Alcalde de Granada, 20 July 1912.

77 On the ways that the expansion of sugar and cattle haciendas weakened the grain economy, see Gould, *To Lead as Equals*, 26; and Edelman, *Logic of the Latifundio*, 53 and 62.

78 *El Diario Nicaragüense*, 25 July 1912.

79 This discussion draws largely on RPPG, Protocolo notarial del Dr. Ignacio Moreira, 1914, no. 68, fols. 93–96, "La Junta Directiva de la Comunidad de Indígenas de Masaya dan un terreno al Dr. José León Sandino en pago de sus

honorarios," 15 July 1914; and "La comunidad de indígenas y sus derechos en los terrenos ejidales," *El 11 de Octubre*, 27 January 1911.

80 Cuadra Pasos, *Obras 1*, 487–88.

81 *El Diario Nicaragüense*, 15 March 1912.

82 For example, Masaya's Indians attacked a cattle estate owned by the Liberal politician Felix Romero, who was then waging a bitter land dispute with two cattle barons of Granada, the Conservative Felipe María Arellano and the Liberal Coronado Urbina. See *Gaceta Oficial*, 28 June 1912, 1129–30; and *El Periódico*, 3 February 1912.

83 AMPG, 1912, leg. Notas y varias, 170 fols., Jefe Político de Granada to Alcalde de Granada, 11 June 1912.

84 *Diario Moderno*, 21 April 1912.

85 AMPG, 1912, leg. Notas y Telegrama, 189 fols., Police Agent Gustavo Rocha A. to Alcalde de Granada, 24 July 1912; *El Periódico*, 7 June 1912.

86 CPEC, Bartolomé Martinez to Emiliano Chamorro, 11 April and 23 May 1912.

87 This paragraph is based largely on the April–July 1912 issues of *El Diario Nicaragüense*, *El Periódico*, *Diario de Nicaragua*, and *Diario Moderno*.

88 For Granada, see AMPG, 1912, files on Demandas civiles.

89 LaFeber, *Inevitable Revolutions*.

90 Katz, *Life and Times of Pancho Villa*, 54–56; Crahan and Smith, "State of Revolution."

4 · BOURGEOIS REVOLUTION DENIED

1 Borge, *Patient Impatience*, 62.

2 Silva, *Jacinta*, 165.

3 USNA, RG 59, 817.00/2330, Diego Manuel Chamorro's speech, 15 January 1914.

4 USNA, RG 59, 817.00/2166, Weitzel to Knox, 31 July 1912.

5 E.g., USNA, RG 59, 817.00/2168, enclosure no.1.

6 E.g., the testimonies of the war veteran Adolfo Calvo Díaz in *Barricada*, 4 October 1980, and *Ventana*, 27 June 1981.

7 1 August entry of Benjamín Zeledón in his "Libro de guerra," reprinted in Gutiérrez, *Partes de guerra*.

8 USNA, RG, 817.00/2179, enclosure no. 4, Mena to Weitzel, 17 August 1912.

9 USNA, RG 59, 817.00/2167, enclosure no. 2.

10 *La Información*, 17 August 1912.

11 See the testimony of a former rebel soldier in *Ventana*, 27 June 1981.

12 *La Información*, 3 August 1912.

13 Zeledón's entry of 10 August 1912 in Gutiérrez, *Partes de guerra*.

14 E.g., USNA, RG 59, 817.00/2201, enclosure no. 1, Salvadoran Legation to Salvadoran Government, 5 August 1912; and *La Información*, 2 August 1912.

15 USNA, RG 59, 817.00/1821, Secretary of State to President, 5 August 1912.

16 USNA, RG 59, 817.00/1868, Weitzel to Knox, 17 August 1912.

17 *La Información*, 10 September 1912.

18 USNA, RG 59, 817.00/2205, enclosure no. 1, Diego Manuel Chamorro to the Salvadoran Minister, 10 December 1912, 7.

19 E.g., USNA, RG 59, 817.00/2131, Club de Granada to Southerland, 9 October 1912; 817.00/2134; *La Información*, 28 October 1912; and Ham, "Revolution in Nicaragua," 575.

20 My analysis of Granada's revolutionary violence is based largely on testimonies submitted by its victims to the Mixed Claim Commission held in AMPG in the following files: 1912, Demandas civiles; 1913, Notas municipales, 155 fols.; 1913, Asuntos civiles; and 1913, Documentos varios, 180 fols.

21 E.g., Joaquín, Guillermo, Carlos, and Mariano Argüello Vargas; José Miguel Gómez and his sons Joaquín and Pedro Gómez Rouhaud; Eduardo and Fulgencio Montiel; David and Francisco Osorno Rojas; Ernesto Selva; Narciso Arellano; Enrique G. Gutiérrez; Salvador Jiménez; and Manuel Zavala Chamorro.

22 See, e.g., the revolutionary oligarch Manuel Zavala Chamorro's kinship to various antirevolutionary members of the Chamorro family; and the fact that the revolutionary oligarchs David and Francisco Osorno lived next door to Mariano Zelaya Bolaños, one of the main victims of the antielite violence of 1912.

23 For a list of their names, see Gobat, "Against the Bourgeois Spirit," 109–11.

24 USNA, 817.00/1925, Weitzel to Knox, 31 August 1912.

25 See, e.g., the membership of rebel leaders Samuel Talavera and Rafael Monterrey on Nandaime's municipal council in 1911 (AMPG, 1911, leg. Notas varias, 197 fols., 18 July 1911). For the Talavera and the Monterrey families' dominance of the Club Conservador de Nandaime, see *El Centinela*, 22 November 1910.

26 For Chavarría's status as mayordomo, see AMPG, 1913, leg. Notas municipales, 155 fols., 18 April 1913.

27 For a list of the principal victims, see Gobat, "Against the Bourgeois Spirit," 114.

28 Held in USNA, RG 84, vol. 26, enclosures nos. 3–14 with dispatch no. 76 of 10 October 1912.

29 *La Información*, 28 October 1912.

30 USNA, RG 84, vol. 26, enclosure no. 13 with dispatch no. 76 of 10 October 1912.

31 E.g., ibid., enclosures nos. 5 and 10.

32 Ibid., enclosure no. 13.

33 Ibid.

34 Outram, *Body and French Revolution*, 1.

35 In addition to the cited testimonies, see USNA, RG 84, vol. 26, file 800, no. 74, enclosure no. 6.

36 USNA, RG 59, 817.00/2134, "ladies of Granada" to Admiral Southerland, 11 October 1912.

37 For how female honor upheld elite authority, see Dore, "Patriarchy and Private Property," 67–68.

38 For the relevant sources, see Gobat, "Against the Bourgeois Spirit," 122–25.

39 USNA, RG 84, vol. 26, enclosure no. 8 with dispatch no. 76 of 10 October 1912.

40 USNA, RG 59, 817.00/2198, enclosure no. 4, Labern to Thompson, 4 September 1912.

41 USNA, RG 84, vol. 26, enclosure no. 13 with dispatch no. 76 of 10 October 1912.

42 For specific examples, see Gobat, "Against the Bourgeois Spirit," 125.

43 USNA, RG 59, 817.00/2191, enclosure no. 19, 26 September 1912.

44 USNA, RG 59, 817.00/2119, Southerland to Secretary of the Navy, 27 September 1912.

45 USNA, RG 127, entry 43, box 2, folder NICA, 1912—Relations with Nicaraguan Officials, Summary of Argüello's interview with Lt. Col. Long, 10 October 1912.

46 Coronil and Skurski, "Dismembering and Remembering the Nation," 289.

47 E.g., Dore, "Patriarchy from Above, Below," 225.

48 See also Gould, "Café, trabajo y comunidad indígena."

49 E.g., USNA, RG 59, 817.00/1811, Weitzel to Secretary of State, 2 August 1912. More generally, see Nancy Mitchell, *Danger of Dreams*.

50 USNA, RG 59, 817.00/1940a, Huntington Wilson to President Taft, 30 August 1912.

51 Challener, *Admirals, Generals*, 302–8.

52 Schmidt, *Maverick Marine*, 54. For the opposition of the highest-ranking U.S. military officer in Nicaragua to a full-scale invasion, see USNA, RG 59, 817.00/1898, Terhune to Secretary of Navy, 3 August 1912.

53 USNA, RG 127, entry 43, file Nicaragua 1912—Reports of Operations, box 3, Long to Pendleton, 18 November 1912.

54 USNA, RG 59, 817.00/2183, Transcript of Miscellaneous Record Book of American Consulate, Corinto.

55 Venzon, *General Smedley Darlington Butler*, 103; Butler, *Old Gimlet Eye*, 141–43.

56 Ham, "Revolution in Nicaragua," 576.

57 *La Información*, 10 September 1912.

58 Leonardo Argüello's letter of 3 September 1912 to Southerland in Montalván, *Hace medio siglo*, 91–98.

59 Ramírez Delgado, *Narraciones históricas*, 85–87.

60 USNA, RG 59, 817.00/2013, Southerland to Secretary of the Navy, 3 September 1912.

61 USNA, RG 59, 817.00/2183 (esp. 3 September).

62 USNA, RG 59, 817.00/1940b, Huntington Wilson to Weitzel, 4 September 1912.

63 USNA, RG 59, 817.00/1944, Weitzel to Secretary of State, 4 September 1912; 817.00/2183; RG 127, entry 43, box 3, file Nicaragua 1912—Reports of Operations, Long to Pendleton, 18 November 1912.

64 USNA, RG 59, 817.51/504, Díaz to Mallet-Prevost, 23 September 1912.

65 *La Información*, 10, 21, 22, 24 September 1912.

66 Butler, *Old Gimlet Eye*, 160–61; testimonies in *El Centroamericano*, 26 October 1924.

67 USNA, RG 59, 817.00/2129, Memorandum of General Luis Mena, 10 October 1912.

68 USNA, RG 127, entry 43, file 1912 Nicaragua, box 3, Pendleton to Southerland, 11 October 1912.

69 E.g., Challener, *Admirals, Generals*, 306–7; and Schmidt, *Maverick Marine*, 52–53.

70 USNA, RG 59, 817.011/16, 15 January 1912; Lacayo's circular "Nicaraguenses, jefes, oficiales y soldados, centroamericanos," in USNA, RG 84, vol. 26.

71 USNA, RG 59, 817.00/2191, enclosure no. 14.

72 See Mena's statement in *La Información*, 12 October 1912.

73 USNA, RG 59, 817.00/1998, Weitzel to Secretary of State, 20 September 1912; 817.00/2191, enclosure no. 16.

74 Butler, *Old Gimlet Eye*, 157–58.

75 *La Información*, 2 October 1912.

76 USNA, RG 127, entry 43, file 1912 Nicaragua, box 3, Pendleton to Southerland, 11 October 1912.

77 USNA, RG 59, 817.00/2191, enclosure no. 18.

78 E.g., Valle Castillo, "Zeledón."

79 For more on Zeledón's upbringing, see Ediciones Ministerio de Educación, *Doctor y General*.

80 E.g., Instituto de Estudio del Sandinismo, *Pensamiento Antimperialista*, 147–49 and 153.

81 Marine Corps University Research Archives, U.S. Marine Corps, Gray Research Center (hereafter MCURA), Pendleton Papers, folder 7, Pendleton to Long, 2 October 1912.

82 USNA, RG 59, 817.00/2198, enclosure no. 2.

83 Testimony of Zeledón's father-in-law reproduced in Matus, *Estudio crítico*, 47.

84 Robleto, *Nido de memorias*, 242.

85 Ramírez's testimony in *Barricada*, 4 October 1980.

86 Matus, *Estudio crítico*, 44–49; *Barricada*, 4 October 1980; Robleto, *Nido de memorias*, 244.

87 MCURA, Pendleton Papers, folder 7, Butler to Southerland, 4 October 1912; USNA, RG 127, entry 43, box 2, folder NICA, 1912—Intelligence.

88 See the testimony of Carlos Muñoz in *Barricada*, 4 October 1981.

89 Conrad, *Sandino*, 63.

90 MCURA, Pendleton Papers, folder 7, Long to Pendleton, 1 October 1912; USNA, RG 84, vol. 26, General Francisco Baca to Weitzel, 29 September 1912.

91 USNA, RG 59, 817.00/2198, enclosure no. 77, E. Viggh to Weitzel, 3 October 1912.

92 USNA, RG 59, 817.00/2126, Southerland to Secretary of the Navy, 5 October 1912. For local claims, see Gould, *To Lead as Equals*, 25–26.

93 USNA, RG 127, entry 43, file Nicaragua 1912—Reports of Operations, Long to Pendleton, 18 November 1912.

94 USNA, RG 59, 817.00/2128, Southerland to Secretary of Navy, 10 October 1912.

95 USNA, RG 84, vol. 26, Southerland to Weitzel, 8 October 1912.

96 USNA, RG 127, entry 43, box 2, folder NICA, 1912—Relations with Nicaragua Officials, Long's interview with Argüello, 10 October 1912.

97 USNA, RG 59, 817.00/2160, Southerland to Secretary of Navy, 4 November 1912.

98 E.g., Venzon, *General Smedley Darlington Butler*, 127 and 130–32; USNA, RG 84, vol. 25, Martínez to Weitzel, 12 November 1912; and USNA, RG 59, 817.00/2164, Southerland to Secretary of Navy, 14 November 1912.

99 Montiel, "Tierra del no vivir."

100 For the higher estimate, see USNA, RG 59, 817.00/2264, enclosure no. 4.

101 For instance, Armando Benard Lacayo claims to have never heard of the 1912 revolutionaries' mistreatment of his father, Martin Benard. Interview with José Joaquín Quadra, Granada, 1 August 1996.

102 Quote is from USNA, RG 59, 817.00/2205, enclosure no. 1, Chamorro to Salvadoran Minister, 10 December 1912, 7.

103 Editorial, *Nation*, 112.2903 (1921): 278.

5 · ECONOMIC NATIONALISM

1   *New York Times*, 4 December 1912.

2   Tulchin, *Aftermath of War*.

3   E.g., Conant, "Our Mission in Nicaragua."

4   For a classic critique of dollar diplomacy's serving U.S. business interests, see Nearing and Freeman, *Dollar Diplomacy*.

5   Rosenberg, *Financial Missionaries*.

6   Rosenberg and Rosenberg, "Colonialism to Professionalism," 65.

7   For more on the dollar diplomacy–induced export of U.S. corporate culture to Latin America, see O'Brien, *Revolutionary Mission*.

8   E.g., USNA, RG 59, 817.00/2078, José María Moncada to State Department, 8 October 1912; and AIHNCA, Fondo Díaz, folder 4588, Salvador Castrillo to Adolfo Díaz, 4 October 1913.

9   For dollar diplomacy's discourse of "primitivism," see Rosenberg, *Financial Missionaries*, 198–218.

10 E.g., Drake, *Money Doctor*.

11 E.g., Kutzinski, *Sugar's Secrets*; Díaz Quiñones, "Enemigo íntimo"; and Reid, *Spanish American Images*, 153–62.

12 In Nicaragua, dollar diplomats consisted of the two U.S. members of the mixed commission (after 1917 one served as resident high commissioner, the other as examiner for the Nicaraguan National Bank); customs collectors in the main urban centers; managers of the National Bank in Managua and its branches in Granada, León, and Bluefields; and the manager of the Pacific Railway.

13 Arthur Thompson, "Renovating Nicaragua."

14 Otto Schoenrich (the commission's first president), "Nicaraguan Mixed Claims Commission," 868.

15 Analysis based on the 1913–14 editions of *La Gaceta*, which publicized all approved claims.

16 E.g., Argüello, *Por el honor*.

17 Archivo Nacional de Nicaragua (hereafter ANN), Fondo Díaz, box 15, folder 5.1-C11/E121, José León Román y Reyes to Adolfo Díaz, 30 January 1918.

18 F. Bartolomé Ibarra, *Memorias y episodios*, 93–102.

19 E.g., CPEC, Juan José Martínez to Emiliano Chamorro, 4 February 1914.

20 AIHNCA, Fondo Díaz, folder 3534, Schoenrich and Thompson to U.S. Secretary of State Bryan, June 1913.

21 CPEC, Emiliano Chamorro to U.S. Secretary of State, 18 August 1913.

22 Cumberland, *Nicaragua*, 126.

23 Hill, *Fiscal Intervention*, 32.

24 AIHNCA, Fondo Díaz, folder 3534, Schoenrich and Thompson to Secretary of State, June 1913. See also Hill, *Fiscal Intervention*, 92.

25 USNA, RG 59, 817.00/2428, Wicker to Secretary of State, 15 December 1915.

26 Salisbury, *Anti-Imperialism*, 23–65.

27 Hill, *Fiscal Intervention*, 34–41.

28 *El Comercio*, 27 November 1917.

29 Ibid., 3 November 1917.

30 Munro, *Intervention and Dollar Diplomacy*, 407.

31 Barrios de Chamorro, *Dreams of the Heart*, 75.

32 E.g., Berrios, *Réplica*.

33 Thorp, "Economy, 1914–1929," 57–81.

34 *Encuesta económica propuesta a la consideración nacional por el Señor Presidente de la República Don Bartolomé Martínez*. Thanks to Jeffrey Gould for providing me with a copy of this survey.

35 *Encuesta económica*, 115.

36 Greer, "Hughes and Nicaragua," 102.

37 *Encuesta económica*, 57.

38 See also Silva, *Jacinta*; Chamorro Zelaya, *Entre dos filos*; Toruño, *Mariposa negra*; and Aguilar Cortés, *Ramón Díaz*.

39 Robleto, *Estrangulados*, 29.

40 Ibid., 30–31.

41 Ibid., 75.

42 Berrios, *Réplica*, 14.

43 Mendieta, *Enfermedad de Centro-América*, 1:319.

44 "Crisis de hombres," *El Correo*, 11 April 1933.

45 Tijerino, "Apuntes," 58.

46 As this support suggests, U.S. opposition to Latin American economic nationalism of the 1920s was less rigid than often claimed. For a contrasting view, see Krenn, *U.S. Policy toward Economic Nationalism*.

47 USNA, RG 59, 817.00/3161, Playter to Secretary of State, 2 September 1924.

48 *La Noticia*, 3 April 1925 (cited in Kamman, *Search for Stability*, 108).

49 See also Canton, *Banco y ferrocarril*, vi.

50 Rosenberg, *Financial Missionaries*, 148–49.

51 Munro, *United States and Caribbean Republics*, 157–86.

52 USNA, RG 59, 817.00/3136, Gustavo Alemán Bolaños to Department of State, 25 July 1924.

53 *El Centroamericano*, 2 February 1924.

54 E.g., Tijerino, "Apuntes."

55 USNA, RG 59, 817.00/3055, Ramer to Hughes, 3 March 1924.

56 See esp. the newspaper's editions of August 1924.

57 Borgen, *Vida a la orilla*, 133.

58 Edelman, *Logic of the Latifundio*, 90–92.

59 Mendoza, *Historia de Diriamba*, 79–81. For Mendoza's valorization of mestizos as a common feature of elite discourse, see Gould, *To Die in This Way*, 134–39.

60 E.g., USNA, RG 59, 817.516/39, Hill (high commissioner) to Jenks, 18 August 1924; and 817.51/1513, Ham to Secretary of State, 29 August 1924.

61 Tijerino, "Apuntes," 57.

62 USNA, RG 59, 817.516/35, Anderson to Secretary of State, 21 August 1924.

63 E.g., Tijerino, "Apuntes," 60; and Huete Abella, *Banqueros*, 108.

64 Kamman, *Search for Stability*, 44–54.

65 *New York Times*, 5 January 1927.

66 USNA, RG 59, 817.516/103, Loree to Secretary of State, 10 May 1926.

67 Salisbury, *Anti-Imperialism*, 99–113.

68 Rosenberg, *Financial Missionaries*, 122–50.

69 *New York Times*, 11 January 1927, 1–2.

70 Ibid., 5 January 1927, 1.

71 USNA, RG 59, 817.00/5824, Robert Olds, "Confidential Memorandum on the Nicaraguan Situation," January 1927.

72 E.g., U.S. Senator Wheeler in *Literary Digest*, 22 January 1927, 5.

73 E.g., Moncada, "Estados Unidos en Nicaragua," 14; and Daniel Mena to *New York Times*, 18 January 1927.

74 Stimson, *American Policy in Nicaragua*, 55–56.

75 *Literary Digest*, 29 January 1927: 6.

76 E.g., José María Moncada's remarks to Stimson in Henry Stimson, "Report on Mission to Nicaragua (May 1927)," in Henry L. Stimson Papers, microfilm reel 144.

77 Aguado, *Nuevos rumbos*.

78 Binder, "On the Nicaraguan Front," 89.

79 Denny, *Dollars for Bullets*, 336.

80 *New York Times*, 15 December 1926.

81 Gould, *To Die in This Way*, 43–47, 88–89. See also USNA, RG 43, E1004, box 6, folder Chontales (Intell.), 20 September 1930, for the post-1928 Liberal regime's similar efforts to shore up its support among the rural populace by distributing public land.

82 Gould, *To Die in This Way*, 147–48.

83 Bendaña, *Mística de Sandino*, 18.

84 For the total number of enclave workers, see MCURA, Julian Smith Papers, box 6, folder 115, Stafford to Central Area Commander, 18 December 1930.

For the size of Nicaragua's labor force, see Oficina Central del Censo, *Censo general de 1920*, Managua: Tipografía Nacional, 1920, 6.

85 Schroeder, "Sandino Rebellion Revisited," 219.

86 On economic anti-Americanism's rise in Latin America, see O'Brien, *Revolutionary Mission*.

87 E.g., ANN, Fondo Díaz, box 16, folder 4.9-C9/E98, Ernesto Solórzano Díaz to Adolfo Díaz, 21 November 1922. See also Brooks, "Rebellion from Without," 149–51.

88 Charles R. Hale, *Resistance*, 51.

89 E.g., *Encuesta económica*, 41–42 and 113–14.

90 Vargas, *Intervención norteamericana*, 214–15.

91 USNA, RG 59, 817.00/3374, Bailie to Munro, 8 December 1923. On how Latin American labor movements frequently supported dollar diplomats' deflationary policies, see Drake, "Political Economy of Foreign Advisers," xxx.

6 · LANDLORDS, PEASANTS

1 E.g., Bulmer-Thomas, *Political Economy*, 25–47; Suter, *Prosperität und Krise*; Edelman, *Logic of the Latifundio*; Samper, "In Difficult Times"; and McCreery, "Wage Labor, Free Labor, and Vagrancy Laws."

2 E.g., Tony Smith, *America's Mission*, 37–83.

3 For how these views have been challenged by recent studies, see, e.g., Ayala and Bergad, "Rural Puerto Rico"; and LeGrand, "Living in Macondo," 337–42.

4 E.g., Thorp and Londoño, "Effect of the Great Depression."

5 For data on coffee production during the Zelaya era, see Charlip, *Cultivating Coffee*, 32.

6 See Bulmer-Thomas, *Political Economy*, 310 and 316–19.

7 Calculation based on Playter, *Nicaragua*, 43.

8 See table 2.2 in Bulmer-Thomas, *Political Economy*, 39.

9 USNA, RG 59, 817.1051/688, Guardia Newsletter, 21 August 1932, Lt. Weeks.

10 Merz, *Finanzhaushalt, Produktion und Handel*, 69, 74–76; Suter, *Prosperität und Krise*, 215–25; McCreery, *Rural Guatemala*, 307–11; Saavedra, *Bananas, Gold and Silver*, 46–47, 54.

11 For more on the Central American trade in Nicaraguan cereals and livestock, see Gobat, "Against the Bourgeois Spirit," 270–72.

12 Bulmer-Thomas, *Political Economy*, 80 (table 4.2).

13 USNA, RG 43, E996, box 1, folder General Records Executive, Capt. Durfee, July 1930.

14 Laird, "Technology versus Tradition," 80–105.

15 USNA, RG 43, E1004, box 6, folder Granada, Gladden to Johnson, 29 October 1930.

16 The most celebrated survey was Duque, *Informe del Jefe*.

17 E.g., *Encuesta económica*, 135.

18 On the ways that public improvements are critical to economic development, see Coatsworth, "Obstacles to Economic Development."

19 Figures based on B. R. Mitchell, *International Historical Statistics*, 529–32.

20 USNA, RG 59, 817.24/274, Lane to Secretary of State, 26 May 1934.

21 For the 1920s, public expenditures as percentage of total exports were twenty-four for Nicaragua, forty-eight for Costa Rica and Guatemala, fifty-four for El Salvador, and seventy for Honduras; B. R. Mitchell, *International Historical Statistics*.

22 Figures calculated from Cumberland, *Nicaragua*, 104; *Informe y cuadros de la Dirección General de Estadística: Año de 1928*, Guatemala City, 1928, 95; Suter, *Prosperität und Krise*, 284; Posas and del Cid, *Construcción del sector público*, 95; and Soley Güell, *Historia monetaria*, 287.

23 Between 1922 and 1929 Nicaragua's external public debt fell by 46%, while that of Guatemala, Costa Rica, Honduras, and El Salvador increased by 48%, 85%, 135%, and 187%, respectively. Calculation based on Young, *Central American Currency*, Appendix D; *Commerce Yearbook, 1924*, 576; and ECLA, *External Financing*, 27.

24 Suter, *Prosperität und Krise*, 145; Hall, *Café y desarrollo*, 114–15; Jones, *Guatemala, Past and Present*, 206.

25 Wünderich, *Sandino*, 40.

26 E.g., USNA, RG 43, E1004, box 6, folder Granada, Gladden to Johnson, 29 October 1930.

27 Suter, *Prosperität und Krise*, 59; Young, *Central American Currency*, 203; Soley Güell, *Historia económica y hacendaria*, 250.

28 Figures based on Playter, *Nicaragua*, 88; Cumberland, *Nicaragua*, 140; Suter, *Prosperität und Krise*, 187; and Government of Guatemala, *Informe y cuadros de la Dirección General de Estadística*, Guatemala City, 1928, 21.

29 Playter, *Nicaragua*, 30, 37.

30 Williams, *States and Social Evolution*, 105.

31 For more on the production process, see Charlip, *Cultivating Coffee*, 87–92.

32 Playter, *Nicaragua*, 26. For Matagalpa, see Gould, *To Die in This Way*, 50–57. For a contrasting argument that emphasizes the persistence of debt peonage in Granada's coffee sector, see Dore, "Debt Peonage in Granada."

33 Playter, *Nicaragua*, 26.

34 Per pound, labor then cost around six cents, which amounted to about two-

thirds of the total production cost. Computed from data presented in Charlip, *Cultivating Coffee*, 96–97 and 101.

35 Cumblerland, *Nicaragua*.

36 Analysis based on data taken from *Statesman's Yearbook* (various years).

37 Cumberland, *Nicaragua*, 133–34.

38 Dollar adjustment based on price index in B. R. Mitchell, *International Historical Statistics*, 690–92.

39 AMPG, 1916, leg. Demandas civiles, 113 fols.

40 See Suter, *Prosperität und Krise*, 178–80; and Acuña and Molina, *Historia económica y social*, 162.

41 For other Central American capital markets, see González Flores, *Crisis económica*, 33–37; Samper, "In Difficult Times," 173–74; Suter, *Prosperität und Krise*, 178; and McCreery, *Rural Guatemala*, 209–10.

42 Luis Cardenal, *Familia Cardenal*, 119.

43 In 1925, Lugo's thirty-four mortgage loans totaled $13,790. Twelve were for loans of less than $100 (for a subtotal of $1,150); sixteen for loans between $101 and $500 (subtotaling $4,840); two for loans between $501 and $1,000 (subtotaling $1,800); and four for loans over $1,000 (subtotaling $6,000).

44 As Julie Charlip's study of coffee growers in the neighboring department of Carazo shows, over the long run (1880–1930) the smallest producers were nearly five times more likely than the largest producers to default on their mortgage loans (respective percentages are 33% and 7%). See Charlip, *Cultivating Coffee*, 133.

45 RPPG, *Libro de propiedades*, vol. 60, fol. 252.

46 E.g., the Nicaraguan coffee census of 1909 in *Boletín de Estadística*, no. 14/15 (March 1911); and Munro, *Five Republics*, 78.

47 Ruhl, *Central Americans*, 118.

48 I analyzed the farm inscriptions made in the following years: 1881, 1893–94, 1903, 1907, 1912–13, 1915–17, 1919, 1928–29, 1932, 1934–37, and 1948. Totaling a bit over six hundred, these inscriptions are held in AMPG, *Libros*, 85, 169, 172, 186, 193, 218, 228, 256, 276, 289, and 314.

49 Granada's current property registry was established in 1904. Of the nearly 7,600 urban and rural properties registered between 1904 and 1932 (held in *Libros de propiedades*, vols. 1–85), I traced the history of 523 farms; this selection includes most of Granada's estates. In these years, more small farms were recorded in the property registry than in the hacienda surveys and agricultural censuses; for a contrasting case, see Edelman and Seligson, "Land Inequality."

50 This builds on the classification system developed in Baumeister, "Tres condicionantes." For how other Central Americanists have used similar

criteria, see Samper, "Significado social," 153; and Paige, *Coffee and Power*, 60. An important exception is Charlip, *Cultivating Coffee*, which defines medium coffee farms as ranging between 50 and 199 manzanas.

51 *Boletín de Estadística*, no. 14/15 (March 1911).

52 Rosa Aguirre, Gabriel Martínez, Manuel Vargas, Carlos Vega, Pedro Joaquín Arceyut, Leandro Abanza, and Dionisio Chamorro.

53 Salvador Cardenal, Agustín Chamorro, Joaquín Cuadra Zavala, Emilia and Adela Zavala, Mariano Zelaya, and the Gómez Rouhaud brothers.

54 Playter as cited in Charlip, *Cultivating Coffee*, 101.

55 Ibid.

56 Williams, *States and Social Evolution*, 173, 195; Suter, *Prosperität und Krise*, 142–50.

57 McCreery, *Rural Guatemala*, 218–28. For how service tenancy cushioned other Latin American coffee barons against the 1920–21 downturn, see Jiménez, "Traveling Far in Grandfather's Car."

58 RPPG, *Libro de propiedades*, vol. 43, fol. 308; vol. 45, fol. 220; vol. 41, fol. 32.

59 RPPG, *Libro de propiedades*, vol. 43, fol. 268.

60 ANN, Fondo Díaz, box 15, folder 5.1-C11, Román Reyes to Díaz, 30 January 1918.

61 Cuadra cultivated at least six hundred acres of coffee, with production costs then totaling about forty-five dollars per acre. Cost computed from data presented in Playter, *Nicaragua*, 26; and Charlip, *Cultivating Coffee*, 96–97 and 101.

62 AMPG, 1920–29, leg. Asuntos civiles, 114 fols. (26 February 1924).

63 AMPG, 1924, leg. Demandas civiles, 166 fols. (1 and 24 January, 29 February).

64 Cuadra Pasos, *Obras 1*, 468.

65 During the early 1920s, ranchers' profits fluctuated 5–9%; see Playter, *Nicaragua*, 46.

66 By the mid-1920s, Nicaragua exported nearly 90% of its coffee crop; see Bynum, *International Trade in Coffee*, 24–26.

67 The largest cattle rancher in Malacatoya loaned, free of charge, small plots of estate land to his workers on which they grew basic grains; see AMPG, 1917, leg. Demandas civiles, 161 fols., Urbina vs. Rodríguez. On the use of tenant farmers by Nicaragua's largest sugar estate (Ingenio San Antonio in Chinandega), see Gould, *To Lead as Equals*, 26–28.

68 Playter, *Nicaragua*, 44.

69 This figure is based on sales registered in Granada's property registry and thus does not include sales of nonregistered rural fincas. As such properties tended to circulate among popular sectors, the data underestimates peasant participation in Granada's land market.

70   See RPPG, *Libro de propiedades*, vol. 60, fols. 15, 97, 105, and 109; vol. 61, fols. 118, 182, 244, 248, and 255; vol. 64, fol. 254; vol. 65, fol. 164; and vol. 71, fol. 217.

71   RPPG, *Libro de propiedades*, vol. 55, fol. 255; vol. 56, fol. 261; vol. 60, fol. 177.

72   USNA, RG 80, file EF49/P9–3 (330125), Report of Chairman U.S. Electoral Mission, 1932.

73   The location of the remaining 8% remains unknown.

74   Medium-scale producers in Nicaragua's northern frontier region similarly expanded their economic power during the 1920s boom; see CIERA-MIDINRA, *Nicaragua*, 119–28 and 141.

75   "Crisis de hombres," *El Correo*, 11 May 1933.

76   Cumberland, *Nicaragua*, 12.

7 · CULTURAL ANTI-AMERICANISM

1   *El Diario Nicaragüense*, 22 March 1931.

2   E.g., Besse, *Restructuring Patriarchy*; Rock, *Authoritarian Argentina*; Deutsch, *Las Derechas*; and Rinke, "Voyeuristic Exoticism."

3   *La Noticia*, 17 January 1918.

4   On how the Jesuits helped found the Liga, see Cuadra Pasos, *Obras 1*, 479–82.

5   *Acción Social*, 21 June 1918, 1.

6   *El Mensajero del Corazón de Jesús y del Apostolado de la Oración* (hereafter *El Mensajero*), 3.26: 90 and 6.66: 305.

7   *La Noticia*, 13 April 1918.

8   E.g., "El liberalismo y la libertad moral," *El Católico*, 22 September 1920.

9   For Freemasons' cosmopolitan agenda, see the 1919–25 issues of *Astralia*.

10   See USNA, RG 59, 817.00/3276; and *El Diario Nicaragüense*, 15 January 1925.

11   Mena Guerrero, "Semblanzas granadinas," 38.

12   Committee on Cooperation in Latin America, *Christian Work*.

13   Ferris, "Protestantism," 212.

14   American Baptist Archives Center (hereafter ABAC), American Baptist Home Mission Society, 103rd Annual Report, 63.

15   See, e.g., Petty, "Three Weeks in Central America," 49.

16   Blackmore, "Nicaragua," 177.

17   My discussion of Caballeros' anti-Protestant discourse is based largely on articles appearing in *El Católico* and *El Mensajero*.

18   *El Católico*, 4 March 1920.

19   *El Mensajero* 3.35 (1922): 523.

20   Ibid., 6.70 (1925): 500.

21   For more on the views of Nicaraguan Protestants, see Parajón, *Veintecinco años*.

22   *El Católico*, 4 March 1920.

23   Ferris, "Protestantism," 120–21.

24   See the numerous reports published in *Missions* (journal of the American Baptist Home Mission Society) and *Ocean to Ocean* (journal of the Woman's American Baptist Home Mission Society).

25   ABAC, Woman's American Baptist Home Mission Society, group 13, box 7, folder 7–11, Ida Warnock to Katherine Westfall, 7 December 1931.

26   *El Católico*, 4 March 1920.

27   On how Baptists promoted the "Christian Americanization" of U.S. immigrants, see the 1920s issues of *Missions* and *Ocean to Ocean*. On how other institutions sought to Americanize immigrant women, see Sánchez, "Go After the Women"; McClymer, "Gender"; Barrett, "Americanization," 1012–13.

28   Sánchez, "Go After the Women," 254.

29   *El Mensajero* 6.70: 509–10.

30   "The Missionary Quiz," *Missions* 17.6 (June 1926).

31   AMPG, 1925, leg. Oficios y documentos, 155 fols., Bishop of Granada to Alcalde of Granada, 1 June 1925.

32   "Carta del Sr. Obispo a los protestantes," *El Diario Nicaragüense*, 9 June 1925.

33   AMPG, 1925, leg. Causas criminales, 207 fols., declaration made by Guillermo F. Aberle, 9 July 1925.

34   Ferris, "Protestantism," 171.

35   Ibid., 172.

36   Pike, *Hispanismo*, 182–84.

37   E.g., *El Mensajero* 3.35 (1922): 528.

38   For an evocative memoir, see Borgen, *Vida a la orilla*.

39   *El Diario Nicaragüense*, 14 January 1920.

40   See, e.g., Cott, "Modern Woman."

41   My analysis of Caballeros' view of the "modern woman" is based primarily on articles appearing in *El Diario Nicaragüense*, *El Mensajero*, *El Católico*, and *Acción Social*.

42   Vallejo, *Guia y reglas*, 15–19, 21.

43   Borgen, *Vida a la orilla*, 73–74.

44   For the case of Ocotal, see MCURA, Robert Denig Papers, box 2, Col. Robert Denig, "Diary of a Guardia Officer," 89.

45   E.g., "La mujer moderna," *La Patria*, September 1921, 117–18.

46   E.g., "Influencia de la mujer en la moralidad," *El Católico*, 15 January 1920.

47 E.g., *El Mensajero* 7.80 (1926): 476.

48 Mendoza, *Historia de Diriamba*, 300.

49 For the sexual violence perpetrated on Granadan coffee estates, see Dore, "Patriarchy from Above, Below," 227.

50 Contemporary novels, however, were a key means through which elite promiscuity was revealed. For one that focuses on Granadan elites, see Chamorro Zelaya, *Entre dos filos*.

51 Dore, "Patriarchy from Above, Below," 215.

52 Gould, *To Lead as Equals*, 232.

53 Interview with Dela Pérez Estrada, Granada, 6 June 2002.

54 Cuadra Chamorro, *Ama a tu prójimo*, i.

55 *La Prensa*, 23 April 1926.

56 Ibid., 1 May, 29 July 1926.

57 See *La Gaceta*, 20 November 1918; *La Noticia*, 16 May 1918; and Emiliano Chamorro, "Autobiografía," 74.

58 For how some Liberals had begun to advocate for female suffrage, see González, "From Feminism to Somocismo," 50–55.

59 *La Noticia*, 5 December 1917.

60 Obando Somarriba, *Doña Angélica Balladares de Argüello*, 44.

61 *El Diario Nicaragüense*, 11 July 1916.

62 E.g., Toledo de Aguerri, *Anhelos y esfuerzos*, 6.

63 "La mujer en el deporte," *El Gráfico*, 4.135 (3 March 1929). For how Nicaraguan feminists defended women's sports, see Sandoval, "Es peligroso el esfuerzo?"

64 "Plataforma política del Doctor Leonardo Argüello," *El Centroamericano*, 31 January, 1 February 1924.

65 E.g., "Feminismo," *El Católico*, 16 May 1920, 1; "La modestia cristiana en las mujeres sobre todo en sus vestidos y maneras," *El Mensajero* 7.80: 476; and "El principal 'deber' de las mujeres ante todo es el de ser heroinas," *El Diario Nicaragüense*, 14 June 1927.

66 Azarías H. Pallais cited in Argüello Lacayo, *Pobre de Jesús*, 362.

67 *El Católico*, 8 January 1920.

68 Interview with Graciela Bendaña, Managua, 9 March 2001.

69 *El Diario Nicaragüense*, 29 January 1920; *El Católico*, 14 January 1920.

70 This paragraph is based on interviews I conducted with Graciela Bendaña and Lola Coronel Urtecho (March 2001), both of whom played basketball in Granada in the 1920s; Dela Pérez Estrada (June 2002), who was an Hija de María in Granada during the 1920s and whose grandfather prohibited her from playing basketball; and Ana Gómez de Cuadra (June 2002), a Granadan tennis player of the same decade.

71 Interview with Ana Gómez de Cuadra, Granada, 10 March 2001.

72 *Mujer Nicaragüense*, 31 January 1933, 7.

73 Interviews with Graciela Bendaña, Managua, 9 March 2001, and Ana Gómez de Cuadra, Granada, 10 March 2001.

74 Cited in Whisnant, *Rascally Signs*, 397.

75 E.g., *El Católico*, 28 August 1920.

76 Cuadra Chamorro, *Liberalismo*, 83.

77 Ibid., 86.

78 E.g., *El Diario Nicaragüense*, 9 April 1930.

79 Ibid., 13 August 1924.

80 Cuadra Pasos, *Obras 2*, 68.

81 Ibid., 74–75. Within Choutales Indian communities persisted mainly in Boaco.

82 Josefa T. de Aguerri, "Una chontaleñada," 2, ANN, Fondo Adolfo Díaz, box 13, folder Corresp. Gral.

83 Cuadra Pasos, *Obras 2*, 338–39.

84 Ibid., *Obras 1*, 573.

85 Chamorro Zelaya, *Entre dos filos*.

86 J. P. de la Roche in *El Diario Nicaragüense*, 3 March 1928; Pedro Joaquín Cuadra Chamorro in *El Diario Nicaragüense*, 23 August 1932.

87 This concept is taken from Sommer, *Foundational Fictions*.

88 This term is taken from Baranowski, *Sanctity of Rural Life*.

89 For the idealization of the peasant in other Latin American nations, see Díaz Quiñones, "Enemigo íntimo"; and Shannon, *Jean Price-Mars*. For the idealization of the cowboy, see Delaney, "Making Sense of Modernity"; and Barr-Melej, "Cowboys and Constructions."

90 Chamorro Zelaya, *Entre dos filos*, 63.

91 This analysis draws much inspiration from Baranowski, *Sanctity of Rural Life*, 6–7.

92 Chamorro Zelaya, *Entre dos filos*, 36.

93 Cuadra Pasos, *Obras 1*, 131.

94 Chamorro Zelaya, *Entre dos filos*, 286.

95 *El Católico*, 19 August 1920.

96 "Igualdad," *El Católico*, 13 June 1920.

97 For the violence underpinning such relations in the coffee sector, see Dore, "Patriarchy from Above, Below."

98 ANN, Fondo de Gobernación, Sección: Jefatura Política, leg. 6.0 (Granada), box 69, folder 1937–1940, Jefe Político Enrique Chamorro to Ministro de Gobernación, 17 May 1937.

99 *El Diario Nicaragüense*, 23 August 1927.

100 Ruhl, *Central Americans*, 97–98.
101 E.g., Baranowski, *Sanctity of Rural Life*; Wiener, *English Culture*; Thornton, *Cultivating Gentlemen*; and Lears, *No Place of Grace*.
102 Moore, *Social Origins*, 490–91. My discussion of Moore is inspired by Jiménez, "At the Banquet of Civilization," 284–85.

8 · MILITARIZATION VIA DEMOCRATIZATION

1   USNA, RG 59, 817.00/4866, Stimson to Moncada, 11 May 1927.
2   *La Noticia*, 14 June 1927.
3   Julian Smith et al., *Review of the Guardia Nacional*, 52–53.
4   Renda, *Taking Haiti*; Calder, *Impact of Intervention*. On the U.S. military's more limited role in Cuba, see Louis Pérez, *Army Politics in Cuba*.
5   E.g., USNA, RG 59, 817.1051/481, memo by Thurston (Latin American Division), 12 January 1931.
6   Louis Pérez, "Intervention, Hegemony, and Dependency," 185. See also Rouquié, *Military and the State*, 117–28.
7   Two important exceptions are Kamman, *Search for Stability*; and Dodd, *Managing Democracy*.
8   USNA, RG 59, 817.00/7029½, Stimson's statement before the U.S. Naval Subcommittee, 3 February 1931.
9   Drake, "Good Men to Good Neighbors."
10 Ibid., 5.
11 E.g., Tony Smith, *America's Mission*; and Peceny, *Democracy at the Point of Bayonets*.
12 USNA, RG 80, General Correspondence—Secretary of the Navy, 1926–1940, file EF49/P9–3 (330125), box 2010, "Report of the Chairman U.S. Electoral Mission to Nicaragua, 1932," section 1, 30.
13 USNA, RG 43, E1004, box 6, folder Chontales, Stephenson to Intelligence Officer, 20 September 1930.
14 USNA, RG 80, General Correspondence—Secretary of the Navy, 1926–1940, file EF49/P9–3 (330125), box 2010, "Report of the Chairman U.S. Electoral Mission to Nicaragua, 1932," section 1, 31.
15 For more on these conflicts, see Dore, "Land Privatization"; Charlip, *Cultivating Coffee* (esp. chap. 3); Gould, *To Die in This Way*, 139–47; and Schroeder, "Horse Thieves to Rebels to Dogs."
16 USNA, RG 43, E981, box 23, folder V-1-c, Palacios to Moncada, 20 October 1928. For more on Palacios's leftist leanings, see Amador, *Siglo de lucha*, 52 and 59.

17 The following discussion of the U.S. electoral missions is based largely on documents held in USNA, RG 43, Records of the United States Electoral Mission in Nicaragua.

18 Between 1928 and 1932, Nicaragua had only thirteen departments, since Cabo Gracias a Dios and San Juan del Norte were not considered departments but were instead classified as "comarcas" (territories).

19 Dodds, "American Supervision," 488.

20 See Dodd, *Managing Democracy*, 64–75 and 127–39.

21 USNA, RG 59, 817.1051/474, enclosure no. 1, McCoy to Captain Johnson, 8 October 1930.

22 USNA, RG 59, 817.00/8160, enclosure no. 1, J. A. Willey to Allan Dawson, 18 October 1934.

23 USNA, RG 43, E 1004, box 7, folder Managua (Intell.), Final report, Chairman Departmental, 5 November 1930.

24 USNA, RG 43, E 1004, box 6, folder Chontales (Intell.), Stephenson to Intell. Officer, 20 September 1930.

25 USNA, RG 43, E 981, box 2, folder B-3-F, Smith to Dowell, 21 July 1928.

26 For landlords' efforts to control the placement of polling stations in rural Granada, see, e.g., AMPG, 1919, leg. Notas oficiales y particulares, 188 fols., jefe político de Granada to ministro de la gobernación, 8 November 1919.

27 For Granada, see USNA, RG 80, Gen. Corresp.—Sec. Navy, 1926–40, file EF49/P9–3 (290121), box 2011, Brixner and Stone to Senior Officer, 23 November 1928; RG 43, E 981, box 2, folder B-3-F, Smith to Dowell, 28 July 1928; RG 127, E 209, box 1, R-2 Report, 19 October 1928; and *El Diario Nicaragüense*, 11 October 1928.

28 USNA, RG43, E 981, box 12, folder I-5-F, Smith to McCoy, 29 September 1928.

29 McClellan, "Supervising Nicaraguan Elections," 37.

30 USNA, RG 43, E981, box 12, folder I-5-F [10f3], Smith to Crockett, 13 August 1928.

31 E.g., USNA, RG 43, E 1004, box 7, folder Managua (Intell.), Tate to Johnson, 4 November 1930, 11.

32 State Department's press release in USNA, RG 59, 817.00/7671a, 28 December 1932.

33 E.g., USNA, RG 80, General Correspondence—Secretary of the Navy, 1926–1940, file EF49/P9–3 (330125), box 2010, "Report of the Chairman U.S. Electoral Mission to Nicaragua, 1932," section 1, 30–31.

34 USNA, RG 43, E 996, box 1, folder General Records, Executive [2 of 3], "Political Situation in Nicaragua," 20 November 1930.

35 USNA, RG 43, E 1013, box 4, folder Periodical Intelligence Reports (Mission), "Confidential Intelligence Report: 1 to 31 October, 1932," 2.

36 USNA, RG 43, E 996, box 1, folder General Records, Executive [2 of 3], "Political Situation in Nicaragua," 20 November 1930.

37 See *Diario Moderno*, 29 October 1930.

38 Ochoa, "Rapid Expansion of Voter Participation."

39 For a contrasting view, see Vargas, *Elecciones en Nicaragua*.

40 E.g., Karl, "Dilemmas of Democratization," 1–2.

41 See USNA, RG 59, 817.00/6298, photo no. 173.

42 USNA, RG 43, E996, box 1, folder Gen. Records Executive [1 of 3], O'Donnell to Johnson, 10 November 1930.

43 E.g., USNA, RG 43, E1004, box 7, folder Leon, Departmental Chairman, "Observations of Lt. James Holloway" (August–September 1930).

44 USNA, RG 43, E 996, box 1, folder Gen. Records Executive [1 of 3], Duvall to Johnson, 12 November 1930.

45 Millett, *Guardians of the Dynasty*, 62, 116.

46 For more on the Guardia Nacional during the U.S. occupation, see ibid., 61–143.

47 For more on this war, see Macaulay, *Sandino Affair*.

48 Two recent studies that have explored this political struggle are Schroeder, "To Defend Our Nation's Honor"; and Grossman, " 'Hermanos en la Patria.' "

49 See MCURA, Robert Denig Papers, box 2, Col. Robert Denig, "Diary of a Guardia Officer," 35–37; and USNA, RG 59, 817.1051/552, Guardia News Letter 59, Capt. Arnett, Dept. Commander of Estelí, July 1931.

50 Julian Smith et al., *Review of the Guardia Nacional*, 220.

51 AMPG, 1928–38, Comunicaciones de los jefes políticos, de los Directores de policía a los alcaldes y presidentes de junta local, 205 fols., Erskine to Carazo, 1 July 1929.

52 USNA, RG 59, 817.00/7725, Talbott, 20 January 1933.

53 E.g., Buell, "Reconstruction in Nicaragua," 337.

54 E.g., Renda, *Taking Haiti*.

55 Julian Smith et al., *Review of the Guardia Nacional*, 52.

56 *La Prensa*, 29 June 1929.

57 *La Noticia*, 8 June 1927; Gould, *To Die in This Way*, 93–94.

58 See, e.g., the case of Bilway's indigenous community in Brooks, "Rebellion from Without," 152–54.

59 USNA, RG 59, 817.00/6588, Warnick to Hanna, 18 April 1930.

60 *El Diario Nicaragüense*, 2 October 1928.

61 See, e.g., Abelardo Cuadra, *Hombre del Caribe*, the memoirs of a Guardia lieutenant.

62 *La Prensa*, 13 January 1933.

63   This conclusion is partly based on interviews that I conducted in 1993–94 with nonelite Granadans who had experienced the U.S. occupation.

64   E.g., Rouquié, *Military and the State*, 128; and Grossman, " 'Hermanos en la Patria,' "245–61.

65   See, e.g., USNA, RG 59, 8160, Willey to Dawson, 18 October 1934; and Gould, *To Die in This Way*, 160.

66   USNA, RG 80, Gen. Correspondence—Sec. Navy, 1926–40, file EF49/P9-3 (330125), box 2010, "Report of the Chairman U.S. Electoral Mission to Nicaragua, 1932," section 1, 30–31.

67   Letter from Alejandro Cárdenas to Pedro Joaquín Cuadra Chamorro in *La Tribuna*, 10 November 1928.

68   E.g., Arellano, *Entre la tradición*; and Beverley and Zimmerman, *Literature and Politics*, 59–64.

69   Beverley and Zimmerman, *Literature and Politics*, 59.

70   *El Diario Nicaragüense*, 8 April 1930.

71   Ibid., 25 December 1929.

72   For more on this survey, see Arellano, *Entre la tradición*, 103–4.

73   USNA, RG 80, Gen. Corresp.—Sec. Navy, 1926–40, file EF49/P9-3 (330125), box 2010, "Report of the Chairman U.S. Electoral Mission to Nicaragua, 1932, section III (Personality Sketches—Prominent Citizens of the Republic of Nicaragua)."

74   Coronel Urtecho, Silva, and Gutiérrez, *50 años del Movimiento*, 71–74.

75   See, e.g., Cuadra Chamorro, "Dictaduras."

76   Cabrales's response to the 1932 survey as cited in Arellano, *Entre la tradición*, 107.

77   Coronel Urtecho's response to the 1932 survey in Coronel Urtecho, Silva, and Gutiérrez, *50 años del Movimiento*, 69.

78   Analysis based on Arellano, *Entre la tradición*, 74–75 and 186–92; Manolo Cuadra, *Gruñido de un bárbaro*, 198; Tirado, *Conversando*, 68, 112, 117; and Borgen, *Vida a la orilla*, 60–61.

79   On corporatism, see Charles A. Hale, "Political and Social Ideas," 293–99; Stepan, *State and Society*; and Williamson, *Corporatism in Perspective*.

80   Cuadra Pasos, *Obras 2*, 396.

81   Pike, *Hispanismo*, 265–66.

82   See Cabrales's response to the 1932 survey in Arellano, *Entre la tradición*, 107; and Cabrales, "Partido de productores."

83   E.g., "Entrevista con el Dr. Cuadra Pasos," *El Diario Nicaragüense*, 5 February 1932.

84   E.g., "Invitación a inscribirse en la Acción Católica," *El Diario Nicaragüense*,

1 October 1933; and "El comunismo: Su ambiente en Nicaragua," ibid., 24 February 1932.

85 "La conferencia de Coronel Urtecho," *El Diario Nicaragüense*, 4 December 1931.

86 "La acción social del conservatismo en el Congreso," *La Prensa*, 22 April 1932.

87 "Entrevista con el Dr. Cuadra Pasos," *El Diario Nicaragüense*, 5 February 1932. Managua's bishop, a Catholic corporatist, defended the demands of a labor group that many elites deemed a "Soviet movement"; see "Es peligroso el obrerismo organizado?," *El Diario Nicaragüense*, 10 September 1931.

88 See Cuadra Pasos, *Posibilidades de existencia del comunismo*.

89 E.g., "El Obrerismo Organizado propone al Presidente un plan para mejorar la condición de la clase trabajadora nicaragüense," *La Prensa*, 24 April 1932; and "El Partido Trabajador Nicaragüense presentó una exposición al Congreso," ibid., 8 June 1932.

90 See "Programa sustancial del Partido conservador," ibid., 18 August 1932.

91 See the speeches reproduced in *La Prensa*, 27 October 1931, and *La Renovación*, 29 October 1931; both papers were headed by Conservative corporatists.

92 Coronel Urtecho's testimony in Tirado, *Conversando*, 47, 116.

93 Interview with a member of a prominent Conservative family, Granada, Nicaragua, 22 March 1994.

94 "Los obreros y los no obreros," *La Prensa*, 13 January 1934.

95 Castillo, *Acotaciones*, 74–80.

96 E.g., Deutsch, *Las Derechas*. More generally on the diverse corporatist movements that emerged in Latin America during the 1920s, see Charles A. Hale, "Political and Social Ideas," 293–99.

97 MCURA, Robert Denig Papers, box 2, "Diary of a Guardia Officer," 9.

9 · REVOLUTIONARY NATIONALISM

1 For more on Sandino's personal history, see Wünderich, *Sandino*.

2 *El Mensajero* 6.66 (June 1925): 303.

3 On how elite Conservatives forged an alliance with Matagalpa's indigenous community, see Gould, *To Die in This Way*.

4 E.g., Selser, *Sandino*; Macaulay, *Sandino Affair*; and Torres Rivas, *Sandino*.

5 E.g., Wünderich, *Sandino*; Bendaña, *Mística de Sandino*; Hodges, *Sandino's Communism*; Vargas, *Floreció*; Dospital, *Siempre más allá*; and Navarro-Génie, *Augusto "César" Sandino*.

6 E.g., Schroeder, "To Defend Our Nation's Honor"; and Grossman, "'Hermanos en la Patria.'"

7 Paige, *Coffee and Power*, 181.

8 USNA, RG 127, entry 38, box 19, file N-4.45, Timeteo García to Pedro González, 9 March 1932.

9 Instituto de Estudio del Sandinismo, *Ahora sé*, 243.

10 *La Tribuna*, 19 August 1928. For more on Sandino's international fame, see Wünderich, *Sandino*, 120–29; and Vargas, *Floreció*, 250–58.

11 E.g., 15 January 1929 letter by Manolo Cuadra to his brother Luciano, reproduced in Manolo Cuadra, *Gruñido de un bárbaro*, 188.

12 E.g., Schroeder, "Horse Thieves to Rebels to Dogs."

13 USNA, RG 38, entry 192, box 1, file A-8, Portocarrero to T. T., 7 November 1931.

14 *La Prensa*, 27 October 1931; *La Renovación*, 29 October 1931.

15 Cited in Schroeder, "To Defend Our Nation's Honor," 523.

16 For their program, see *El Diario Nicaragüense*, 15 May 1928.

17 Sergio Ramírez, *Augusto C. Sandino*, 1:292.

18 Román, *Maldito país*, 36–37; Luis Cardenal, *Familia Cardenal*, 307–8.

19 Even Nicaraguans residing in El Salvador shared this perception; see ANN, Fondo Díaz, box 13, folder Correspondencia General, Alberto García (Santa Ana) to J. Francisco Martínez (Chinandega), 15 April 1928.

20 Tijerino, *Tratado Chamorro-Bryan*.

21 Dodd, *Managing Democracy*, 79.

22 E.g., *La Noticia*, 20 July 1927.

23 USNA, RG 127, entry 200, file J, Commander of Granada/Masaya to Jefe Director, 7 February and 28 May 1929.

24 Grossman, "'Hermanos en la Patria,'" 637.

25 Valle Castillo, "Prólogo," 31.

26 Pablo Antonio Cuadra, *Torres de Dios*, 219.

27 Manolo Cuadra, *Gruñido de un bárbaro*, 183–84.

28 *La Prensa*, 30 November 1930.

29 Macaulay, *Sandino Affair*, 150–56.

30 Grossman, "'Hermanos en la Patria,'" chap. 7; Schroeder, "To Defend Our Nation's Honor," chap. 6.

31 E.g., *La Noticia*, 19 November 1929.

32 Macaulay, *Sandino Affair*, 150–64.

33 E.g., Adolfo Ortega Díaz in *El Comercio*, 1 November 1929.

34 For more on this decision, see Kamman, *Search for Stability*, 193–207.

35 USNA, RG 59, 817.00 Bandit Activities, 1931/286, Beaulac to Sec. State, 24 November 1931.

36 USNA, RG 127, entry 38, box 19, file N-4.45, R. R. Hernández y Roblero to Capt. Aguilar, 12 November 1931.

37 USNA, RG 127, entry 43A, box 28, file GN-2, Intell. Reports, Weekly Summary, 7 March; November 1932.

38 USNA, RG 59, 817.00 Bandit Activities, 1931/333, Beaulac-Argüello conversation, 12 November 1931.

39 E.g., *El Diario Nicaragüense*, 25 November 1931.

40 For more on the origins of this event, see Gould and Lauria-Santiago, " 'They Call Us Thieves.' "

41 *La Noticia*, 23 February 1932.

42 *La Prensa*, 26 February 1932.

43 Quotes are from *El Diario Nicaragüense*, 15 February and 13 March 1932.

44 *El Diario Nicaragüense*, 24 February 1932.

45 "Programa sustancial del Partido Conservador," *La Prensa*, 18 August 1932.

46 *El Diario Nicaragüense*, 9 July 1931.

47 USNA, RG 38, entry 192, box 1, file A-8, Portocarrero to T. T., 7 November 1931; G. C. A. to Kessler, 11 February and 3 March 1932.

48 USNA, RG 38, entry 192, box 1, file A-8. Report Blank of Naval Attaché (Tegucigalpa, Honduras), 15 June 1932.

49 Interview with Dela Pérez Estrada, Granada, 6 June 2002.

50 USNA, RG 127, entry 200, file J, 22 June 1932.

51 *El Diario Nicaragüense*, 12 August 1932.

52 USNA, RG 59, 817.00/7580, Hanna to Secretary of State, 8 October 1932.

53 USNA, RG 127, entry 202, file 7.0. O'Neill, 14 October 1932; interview with Héctor Mena, Granada, 11 June 2002.

54 Conrad, *Sandino*, 416.

55 USNA, RG 59, 817.00/7654, Hanna to Secretary of State, 3 December 1932.

56 Editorial, *La Prensa*, 8 November 1932.

57 *La Prensa*, 11 November 1932.

58 U.S. fatalities totaled 136; the actual number of Nicaraguan guardsmen killed remains unknown. See Macaulay, *Sandino Affair*, 239.

59 Instituto de Estudio del Sandinismo, *Ahora sé*, 242–43.

60 For more on this mission, see Salvatierra, *Sandino*; and Calderón Ramírez, *Ultimos días de Sandino*; both are accounts by members of the peace mission.

61 *La Noticia*, 20 January 1933.

62 E.g., *El Diario Nicaragüense*, 3 February 1933.

63 *La Prensa*, 4 February 1933.

64 USNA, RG 59, 817.00/7785, Hanna to Secretary of State, 11 March 1933.

65 *El Diario Nicaragüense*, 1 March 1933.

66   Conrad, *Sandino*, 432–33, 440–42.

67   *La Nueva Prensa*, 16 February 1933.

68   For more on Sandino's strained relations with Nicaraguan communists, see Pérez Bermúdez and Guevara, *El movimiento obrero en Nicaragua*, 49–58.

69   Vargas, *Floreció*, 356–60.

70   Wünderich, *Sandino*, 298.

71   ANN, Sección Sacasa, box 29, "Reunión de los tipógrafos de Managua," 18 December 1932.

72   USNA, RG 59, 817.00/7776, Hanna to Secretary of State, 24 February 1933.

73   *La Prensa*, 18 August 1932.

74   *La Nueva Prensa*, 11 April 1933.

75   Ibid., 1 March 1933.

76   USNA, RG 59, 817.00/7807, Hanna to Secretary of State, 21 April 1933.

77   Conrad, *Sandino*, 468.

78   For the full text, see Sergio Ramírez, *Augusto C. Sandino*, 2:303–27.

79   E.g., *La Noticia*, 21 April 1933; and USNA, RG 59, 817.00/7807, Hanna to Secretary of State, 21 April 1933.

80   E.g., *La Nueva Prensa*, 18 April 1933.

81   Ibid., 14 February 1933.

82   *La Prensa*, 21 January 1928.

83   Villanueva, *Sandino en Yucatán*, 198–99.

84   U.S. Library of Congress, Motion Picture Division. Other movies of the era that similarly represent the Sandinistas include *Virgin Lips* (1928), *Cock-Eyed World* (1929), and *The Stoker* (1932).

85   *La Nueva Prensa*, 14 February 1933.

86   For early U.S. films about the wars of 1898, see Kaplan, *Anarchy of Empire*, 146–61.

87   Rosenberg, *Financial Missionaries*, 198–218.

88   Woll, *Latin Image*, 16–41.

89   Sandino in Hodges, *Intellectual Foundations*, 117.

90   *La Prensa*, 27 October 1931.

91   MCURA, Robert Denig Papers, box 2, "Diary of a Guardia Officer," 9.

92   MCURA, Thomas Watson Papers, box 3, file Oct. 17–30, 1932, George to Watson, 19 October 1932; interview with Dela Pérez Estrada, Granada, 6 June 2002.

93   Manolo Cuadra in Calatayud Bernabeu, *Manolo Cuadra*, 19.

94   E.g., *Vanguardia* 26.6 (1932); and *La Tribuna*, 8 December 1933.

95   Román, *Maldito país*, 80.

96   Sergio Ramírez, *Augusto C. Sandino*, 2:362–63.

97   On Sandino's cooperative, see Dospital, *Siempre más allá*, 168–77.

98 My views of utopian and reactionary strands of agrarianism have been influenced by Vlastos, "Agrarianism without Tradition."

99 Francisco Buitrago Díaz, *La Tribuna*, 22 September 1928.

100 Joaquín Pasos, *El Correo*, 2 August 1932.

101 E.g., Cuadra Pasos, *Obras 1*, 49–99.

102 For more on Sandino's mestizaje project, see Gould, *To Die in This Way*, 155–61. For a more general exploration of mestizaje's multiple meanings, see, e.g., Gudmundson and Scarano, "Conclusion."

103 *El Pez y la Serpiente* 22–23 (1978–79): 27.

104 Cardenal Ch., "Acerca de las 'Reflexiones.'"

105 USNA, RG 127, entry 38, box 19, folder 6, N-5.45, Nicaragua, Bandit Propaganda, 26 July 1927.

106 USNA, RG 38, entry 98, box 497, file C-10-d Reg 6473, "GN-2 Note No. 1," 7 August 1928, 7.

107 Cited in Grossman, "'Hermanos en la Patria,'" 276.

108 Sultan, "Army Engineer."

109 *El Diario Nicaragüense*, 8 May 1932.

110 E.g., Deutsch, *Las Derechas*, 170–71 and 280–81.

111 See, e.g., the appeal made by Pedro Joaquín Chamorro in *La Prensa*, 5 May 1933.

112 USNA, RG 59, 817.00/7823, Hanna to Secretary of State, 19 May 1933.

113 Francisco Estrada's letter of 30 May 1933 in Somoza García, *Verdadero Sandino*, 498.

114 See also USNA, RG 59, 817.00/7826, Hanna to Secretary of State, 25 May 1933.

115 *La Noticia*, 23 May 1933.

116 *El Comercio*, 25 April 1933.

117 While not a member of the Conservative Party, Ortega was nonetheless widely associated with conservatism since his father, Marco Antonio Ortega (director of the National Institute in Granada), was one of the party's leading ideologues.

118 ANN, Col. Sandino, box 1, folder 1, Dan. Ortega C. to Sandino, 19 May 1933.

119 All quotes are from the party's program as published in *La Nueva Prensa*, 26 May 1933.

120 E.g., *El Comercio*, 7 May 1933.

121 Conrad, *Sandino*, 472.

122 Wünderich, *Sandino*, 299–300.

123 *La Noticia*, 23 May 1933.

124 Salvatierra, *Sandino*, 267. More generally, see Hodges, *Sandino's Communism*, 56–67.

125 Cited in Somoza García, *Verdadero Sandino*, 488.

126 Conrad, *Sandino*, 474—75.

127 See, in particular, Staklo, "Harnessing Revolution"; and Dospital, *Siempre más allá*, 57—86.

128 These demands reflected the Comintern's recent shift from the "united front" strategy to the "class against class" line. Consequently, the Comintern opposed anti-imperialist movements led by "bourgeois" or "petit bourgeois" nationalists, and supported only those based on a Communist-led alliance of workers and peasants.

129 Letter from the Comintern's Caribbean Bureau of 14 February 1933 as cited in Staklo, "Harnessing Revolution," 140.

130 USNA, RG 165, Correspondence and Record Cards of the Military Intelligence Division Relating to General, Political, and Military Conditions in Central America, 1918—1941 (M1488), 2657-P-453 (6), Maj. Harris, 6 April 1934.

131 Prado, "Por que dejo de ser Sandinista."

132 For more on the Magnetic-Spiritual School of the Universal Commune, see Hodges, *Sandino's Communism*; and Navarro-Genie, *Sandino*.

133 For more on Sandino's cooperative, see Dospital, *Siempre más allá*, 168—77.

134 E.g., *La Prensa*, 7 June 1933.

135 Ibid., 9 June 1933.

136 Ibid., 18 February 1934.

137 See Ibarra Grijalva, *Last Night*; and Abelardo Cuadra, *Hombre del Caribe*; both accounts by Guardia officers.

138 Somoza's statement in USNA, RG 59, 817.00/8613, Ray to Secretary of State, 18 November 1936.

139 Conclusion based on the media's reaction to Sandino's death as well as interviews with various contemporaries.

140 Manolo Cuadra, *Gruñido de un bárbaro*, 228—30. Cuadra's book was published in 1942 under the title *Contra Sandino en la montaña*.

141 See, e.g., Calder, *Impact of Intervention*.

142 *La Reacción*, 5 April 1934.

EPILOGUE

1 See esp. Spalding, *Capitalists and Revolution*; and Paige, "Revolution and the Agrarian Bourgeoisie."

2 For more on the Marxist origins of the FSLN, see Zimmerman, *Sandinista*.

3 E.g., Vilas, *Sandinista Revolution*; and Gilbert, *Sandinistas*. For this view's persistent appeal, see Goodwin, *No Other Way Out*.

4   Compare, e.g., Vilas's *Sandinista Revolution* (1986) with his "Family Affairs" (1992).

5   For the boom's impact on rural society, see Gould, *To Lead as Equals.*

6   E.g., Everingham, *Revolution and the Multiclass Coalition.*

7   The most influential Sandinista work in scholarly circles was Wheelock, *Imperialismo y dictadura.*

8   One of the earliest and most significant studies was Torres Rivas, "Estado contra la sociedad."

9   Paige, *Coffee and Power*, 179.

10   USNA, RG 43, entry 1004, box 7, folder Leon, Dept. Chairman, Major del Valle to Johnson, 25 July 1930.

11   Tony Smith, *America's Mission.* See also Millett, *Guardians of the Dynasty*, 183–85.

12   See Gould, *To Lead as Equals*; and Amalia Chamorro, "Estado y hegemonía." An interesting parallel is the Trujillo regime, which ruled the Dominican Republic between 1930 and 1961. Like Somoza, Trujillo established a personalistic dictatorship based on a U.S.-created military. He also garnered widespread peasant support with populist policies. Still, it is important to stress that the rural populisms of Somoza and Trujillo were not identical. In particular, Somoza's populist project seems to have had a stronger antielite thrust, largely for three reasons. First, even though Nicaraguan landlords had been weakened by the U.S. occupation, they remained more powerful than their Dominican counterparts. To consolidate its control of the countryside, the Somoza regime had to carry out a more extensive attack on elite power. Second, because Nicaragua's commercial agriculture was more developed than that of the Dominican Republic, it had fewer areas with uncultivated land, and more rural people held definitive titles in the 1930s. As a result, the state's efforts to improve peasants' access to land were more likely to threaten elite interests in Nicaragua than in the Dominican Republic. Third, because U.S. agricultural investments in Nicaragua were far smaller than in the Dominican Republic, Somoza faced less U.S. opposition to his rural populist policies. My understanding of Trujillo's rural populism is based on Turits, *Foundations of Despotism.*

13   See Gould, *To Lead as Equals.*

14   Walter, *Regime of Anastasio Somoza*, 44–47.

15   Arellano, *Entre la tradición*, 145–53.

16   Coronel Urtecho, "Resistencia de la memoria," 106.

17   E.g., Argüello Lacayo, *Pobre de Jesús*, 176–80.

18   Luis Cardenal, *Familia Cardenal*, 316.

19 For more on Lane's opposition, see Clark, *United States and Somoza*, 1–30.

20 On Somoza's tense relations with the Guardia officer corps, see Abelardo Cuadra, *Hombre del Caribe*. A scion of Granada's Conservative oligarchy, Cuadra was a Guardia lieutenant who led a failed revolt of junior officers against Somoza in 1935.

21 Gould, *To Lead as Equals*.

22 Conclusion based on my analysis of credit data held in Granada's property registry. For a similar conclusion, see Laird, "Technology versus Tradition," 192–204. On how medium-scale producers maintained their economic strength throughout the Somoza dictatorship, see Zalkin, "Agrarian Class Structure."

23 Moore, *Social Origins*.

24 For the centrality of Moore's thesis to Central American scholarship, see Gudmundson, "Lord and Peasant." For more recent assessments, see Paige, *Coffee and Power*, 316–37; and Mahoney, *Legacies of Liberalism*, 268–74.

25 For a contrasting argument that stresses how Nicaraguan landlords perpetuated debt peonage well into the Somoza era, see Dore, "Debt Peonage in Granada," 557–58.

26 In Latin America, U.S. officials' faith in the middle sectors' democratic impulse most tragically underpinned the Alliance for Progress program of 1961–70. President John F. Kennedy and his advisors may have believed that this $20 billion program would engender peaceful, democratic revolution led by the middle classes; instead it produced an authoritarian nightmare as sixteen civilian governments were violently replaced by repressive military regimes that, initially at least, enjoyed strong middle-class support.

27 I explore this process in Gobat, "Soldiers into Capitalists."

28 On the rise of such a peasant movement, see Gould, *To Lead as Equals*.

29 For more on these U.S. efforts, see Pastor, *Condemned to Repetition*.

30 For more on the Sandinistas' "patriotic bourgeoisie," see Spalding, *Capitalists and Revolution*, 92–94.

31 See, in particular, Cardoso and Faletto, *Dependency and Development*.

32 USNA, RG 319, MID 000.245 Nica 4–20–43.

33 For their names, see Vilas, "Family Affairs."

34 See Gobat, "Oligarchs under Siege?"

35 E.g., Granda, "Contrareforma agraria en apogeo."

36 See Gobat, "Oligarchs under Siege?"

37 Ernesto Cardenal's grandparents were the wealthy Caballero Católico Salvador Cardenal and his wife, Isabel "la Católica," who had helped lead Granada's violent crusade against U.S. missionaries during the 1920s.

38 Conclusion based largely on conversations with various members of Gra-

nada's Conservative oligarchy, including José Joaquín Quadra Cardenal (brother of Pablo Antonio Cuadra and son of Carlos Cuadra Pasos), Alvaro Argüello Hurtado, Luciano Cuadra Vega, Jimmy Avilés, and Jorge Eduardo Arellano. The persistence of Conservatives' "antibourgeois spirit" is also evident in works like Tirado, *Conversando*; Chamorro Cardenal, *Diario político*; and Aguilar Cortés, *Memorias*.

39 Perhaps the best-known Conservative exaltation of Sandino's anti-U.S. struggle was Ernesto Cardenal's poem "Hora cero," which was written in 1956. For more on this poem, see Beverley and Zimmerman, *Literature and Politics*, 66–72. For more generally on Conservatives' anticommunist image of Sandino, see Hurtado González, *Sandino desconocido*.

40 Prominent Conservatives certainly cooperated with the Somozas, as evident in the infamous pacts made by Emiliano Chamorro and Fernando Agüero in 1950 and 1970, respectively. Still, many other elite Conservatives fiercely rejected the dictatorship, with some even leading unsuccessful uprisings against the Somozas. For more on Conservative opposition to the Somoza regime, see Instituto de Estudio del Sandinismo, "Maniobra, entreguismo y pactos"; and Alvarado Martínez, *¿Ha muerto el Partido Conservador?*

41 Observation based largely on my conversations with José Joaquín Quadra Cardenal, leader of the Juventud Conservadora. See also Ernesto Cardenal's memoir, *Los años de Granada*; and Beverley and Zimmerman, *Literature and Politics*, 59–72.

42 E.g., Coronel Urtecho, "Paneles de infierno."

43 For more on the peasantry's turn against the Sandinista revolution, see Horton, *Peasants in Arms*.

44 Johnson, *Blowback*, 8.

45 For more on the Sandinista challenge to U.S. power, see LeoGrande, *Backyard*; Zamora, *Conflicto*.

46 See, e.g., the calls made by Max Boot, a conservative editor of the *Wall Street Journal*, in "Case for American Empire," and Michael Ignatieff, a liberal professor of human rights practice at Harvard University, in "American Empire." For other U.S.-based pundits and officials advocating a contemporary U.S. empire, see Ferguson, *Colossus*, 4–6.

47 For the imperialistic thrust of U.S. foreign policy in the 1990s, see Bacevich, *American Empire*.

48 Ferguson, *Colossus*, 57. See also Boot, *Savage Wars*, 345.

49 See, e.g., Schmidt, *United States Occupation of Haiti*, 231–37; Calder, *Impact of Intervention*, 238–52; Louis Pérez, *Cuba under the Platt Amendment*, 333–40; Santiago-Valle, *"Subject People"*; and Briggs, *Reproducing Empire*.

50 E.g., Coatsworth, *Central America and the United States*; and LaFeber, *Inevitable Revolutions*.

51 According to one of its most prominent proponents, Niall Ferguson, a liberal empire is "one that not only underwrites the free international exchange of commodities, labor and capital but also creates and upholds the conditions without which markets cannot function—peace and order, the rule of law, noncorrupt administration, stable fiscal and monetary policies—as well as provides public goods, such as transport infrastructure, hospitals and schools, which would not otherwise exist" (Ferguson, *Colossus*, 2). This liberal agenda was essentially what the United States sought to implement in its Caribbean Basin protectorates; in some cases, such as post-1927 Nicaragua, it also tried to promote liberal democracy.

52 Quote is from the prepared text of President Bush's second inaugural address of 20 January 2005, www.npr.org.

53 Bolívar, "Letter."

Selected Bibliography

ARCHIVAL SOURCES

Nicaragua

Archivo de la Municipalidad y de la Prefectura de Granada (AMPG)
Archivo del Instituto de Historia de Nicaragua y de Centroamérica (AIHNCA)
    Fondo Díaz
    Colección José Angel Rodríguez
Archivo Nacional de Nicaragua (ANN)
    Colección Sandino
    Fondo Adolfo Díaz
    Fondo Juan Bautista Sacasa
    Fondo de Gobernación
    Fondo Presidencial
Biblioteca del Banco Central, Managua
    Correspondencia privada escrita y recibida por el General Emiliano Chamorro
        E. en los años 1904–1929 (CPEC)
Registro Público de la Propiedad, Granada (RPPG)
    Libro de Diario, vols. 9–29
    Libro de Personas, vols. 4–9
    Libro de Propiedades, vols. 1–363
    Protocolo Notarial del Dr. José Miguel Osorno, 1904–1907
    Protocolo Notarial del Dr. Ignacio Moreira, 1914–1917

United States

American Baptist Archives Center
    American Baptist Home Mission Society (ABAC, ABHMS)
Butler Library, Columbia University
    W. R. Grace and Company Papers
Marine Corps University Research Archives, U.S. Marine Corps, Gray Research
    Center, Personal Papers Collection (MCURA)
    Robert Denig Papers
    Joseph Henry Pendleton Papers
    Thomas Watson Papers
Rockefeller Archive Center

Rockefeller Foundation Archives
Tulane University
    Callander Fayssoux Collection of William Walker Papers, microfilm reels 1–4
U.S. National Archives (USNA)
    Record Group 43, Records of the American Electoral Commissions and Boards
        to Nicaragua, 1928–33
    Record Group 59, General Records of the Department of State
    Record Group 77, Records of the Office of Chief of Engineers
    Record Group 80, General Records of the Navy Department
    Record Group 84, Records of Foreign Service Posts of the Department of State
    Record Group 127, Records of the United States Marine Corps
Yale University Library
    Henry L. Stimson Papers, microfilm reel 144

NEWSPAPERS AND PERIODICALS

Acción Social. Granada, 1918
Amigo del Pueblo. Granada, 1922–23
Ariel. Masaya, 1933
Astralia. Managua, 1918–25
El Ateneo. León, 1881
Boletín de la Asamblea. Managua, 1911
Boletín de Estadística de la República de Nicaragua. Managua, 1910–12, 1919–20,
    1935
Boletín de Noticias. León, 1855
Boletín del Ejército democrático del Estado de Nicaragua. León, 1854
Boletín Oficial. Granada, 1855
Boletín Oficial. León, 1849, 1856
El Católico. Granada, 1920
El Centinela. Managua, 1910–11
El Centinela del Istmo en la América Central. Managua, 1864
Centro América. Granada, 1924–25
El Centroamericano. León, 1924
El Comercio. Managua, 1917, 1929
El Correo. Granada, 1917–18, 1933–34
Diario de Masaya. Masaya, 1917
Diario de Nicaragua. Managua, 1910–12
Diario Moderno. Managua, 1912
El Diario Nicaragüense. Granada, 1912–34
Los Domingos. Managua, 1920–24

El Eco de Occidente. Chinandega, 1875

El Eco Meridonial. Rivas, 1864

El Eco Nacional. León, 1924

El Escolar. León, 1875

From Ocean to Ocean: A Record of the Work of the Woman's American Baptist Home Mission Society. Chicago, 1916–36

La Gaceta de Nicaragua. Managua, 1867

La Gaceta Oficial. Managua, 1911–18

El Gráfico. Managua, 1925–30

La Juventud. León, 1868

La Información. San José (Costa Rica), 1912

El Mensajero del Corazón de Jesús y del Apostolado de la Oración. Granada, 1922–30

Missions. New York, 1916–33

La Mujer. Managua, 1931

Mujer Nicaragüense. Managua, 1929–33

La Nación. León, 1910

Nicaragua Informativa. Managua,1917–18

La Noticia. Managua, 1917–18, 1927–29, 1932–34

La Nueva Prensa. Managua, 1933–34

El 11 de Octubre. Managua, 1910–11

El País. León, 1887–88

La Patria. León, 1916–21

Paz y Bien. León, 1920–24

El Periódico. Granada, 1912

El Porvenir. Managua, 1912

La Prensa. Managua, 1926–34

La Reacción. Granada, 1934

La Revista Femenina Ilustrada. Managua, 1931

Revista Obrera. Managua, 1923–24

Las Revistas. Managua, 1913–16

La Tarde. Managua, 1910

La Tertulia. Masaya, 1875–79

La Tribuna. Managua, 1917

OTHER SOURCES

Acuña, Victor Hugo, and Iván Molina. *Historia económica y social de Costa Rica (1750–1950).* San José: Porvernir, 1991.

Aguado, Enoc. *Nuevos rumbos de la diplomacia yanqui.* León, Nicaragua: La Libertad, 1912.

Aguilar Cortés, Jerónimo. *Ramón Díaz*. Managua: Talleres Gráficos Pérez, 1930.

——. *Memorias: De los yanquis a Sandino*. San Salvador: Talleres Gráficos del I. T. Ricaldone, 1972.

Alvarado Martínez, Enrique. *¿Ha muerto el Partido Conservador de Nicaragua?* Managua: UCA, 1994.

Alvarez Lejarza, Macario. *Impresiones y recuerdos de la revolución de 1901 a 1910*. Granada, Nicaragua: Escuela Tipografía Salesiana, 1941.

Amador, Armando. *Un siglo de lucha de los trabajadores de Nicaragua (1880–1979)*. Managua: Imprenta UCA, 1992.

Arellano, Jorge Eduardo. *Una laica apostólica: Doña Elena Arellano (1836–1911)*. Managua: Alcaldía de Granada, 1991.

——. *El doctor David Arellano (1872–1928)*. Managua: privately printed, 1993.

——. *Entre la tradición y modernidad: El Movimiento nicaragüense de vanguardia*. San José, Costa Rica: Libro Libre, 1992.

——. *Historia básica de Nicaragua*. Vol. 2. Managua: CIRA, 1997.

Argüello, Leonardo. *Por el honor de un partido: Réplica a la Comisión mixta de reclamaciones de Nicaragua*. León: J. C. Gurdián, 1914.

Argüello Lacayo, José. *Un pobre de Jesús: El poeta de las palabras evangelizadas*. Managua: Hispamer, 2000.

Ayala, César, and Laird Bergad. "Rural Puerto Rico in the Early Twentieth Century Reconsidered: Land and Society, 1899–1915." *Latin American Research Review* 37.2 (2002): 65–97.

Bacevich, Andrew. *American Empire: The Realities and Consequences of U.S. Diplomacy*. Cambridge: Harvard University Press, 2002.

Baranowski, Shelley. *The Sanctity of Rural Life: Nobility, Protestantism and Nazism in Weimar Prussia*. New York: Oxford University Press, 1995.

Barcia, Pedro Luis, ed. *Escritos dispersos de Rubén Darío*. Vols. 1 and 2. La Plata: Universidad de La Plata, Argentina, 1968.

Barrett, James. "Americanization from the Bottom Up: Immigration and the Remaking of the Working Class in the United States, 1880–1930." *Journal of American History* 79 (1992): 996–1020.

Barrios de Chamorro, Violeta. *Dreams of the Heart: The Autobiography of President Violeta Barrios de Chamorro of Nicaragua*. New York: Simon and Schuster, 1996.

Barr-Melej, Patrick. "Cowboys and Constructions: Nationalist Representations of Pastoral Life in Post-Portalian Chile." *Journal of Latin American Studies* 30 (1998): 35–61.

Bauer, Arnold. *Goods, Power, History: Latin America's Material Culture*. Cambridge: Cambridge University Press, 2001.

Baumeister, Eduardo. "Tres condicionantes político-ideológicos en la formulación de las políticas agrarias en Nicaragua." *Boletín socio-económico* 7 (1988): 3–11.

Belausteguigoitia, Ramón de. *Con Sandino en Nicaragua*. Managua: Nueva Nicaragua, 1985 [1934].

Bendaña, Alejandro. *La mística de Sandino*. Managua: Centro de Estudios Internacionales, 1994.

Bermann, Karl. *Under the Big Stick: Nicaragua and the United States since 1848*. Boston: South End, 1986.

Berrios, Francisco. *Réplica al folleto conservador*. León, Nicaragua: La Patría, 1924.

Bertoni, Lilia Ana. *Patriotas, cosmopolitas y nacionalistas: La construcción de la nacionalidad argentina a fines del siglo XIX*. Buenos Aires: Fondo de Cultura Económica, 2001.

Besse, Susan. *Restructuring Patriarchy: The Modernization of Gender Inequality in Brazil, 1914–1940*. Chapel Hill: University of North Carolina Press, 1996.

Beverley, John, and Marc Zimmerman. *Literature and Politics in the Central American Revolutions*. Austin: University of Texas Press, 1990.

Binder, Caroll. "On the Nicaraguan Front." *New Republic*, 16 March 1927.

Blackmore, Eleanor. "Nicaragua." *From Ocean to Ocean* (1923–24), 177.

Bolaños, Pio. *Obras de don Pio Bolaños II*. Managua: Banco de América, 1977.

Bolaños Geyer, Alejandro. *El Testimonio de Joseph N. Scott*. Managua: Fondo de Promoción Cultural del Banco de América, 1975.

——. *William Walker: The Gray-Eyed Man of Destiny*. 5 vols. Lake Saint Louis, Mo: Privately Printed, 1988–91.

Bolívar, Simón. "Letter to Colonel Patrick Campbell." In *Latin America and the United States: A Documentary History*, ed. Robert Holden and Eric Zolov. New York: Oxford University Press, 2000.

Boot, Max. "The Case for American Empire: The Most Realistic Response to Terrorism Is for America to Embrace Its Imperial Role." *Weekly Standard*, 15 October 2001.

——. *The Savage Wars of Peace: Small Wars and the Rise of American Power*. New York: Basic, 2002.

Borge, Tomás. *The Patient Impatience*. Willimantic, Conn.: Curbstone, 1992.

Borgen, José Francisco. *La vida a la orilla de la historia (Memorias)*. Managua: Dilesa, 1979.

Bourdieu, Pierre. *Distinction: A Social Critique of the Judgment of Taste*. Cambridge: Harvard University Press, 1984.

Boyle, Frederick. *A Ride across a Continent: A Personal Narrative of Wanderings through Nicaragua and Costa Rica*. Vol. 1. London: Richard Bentley, 1868.

Briggs, Laura. *Reproducing Empire: Race, Sex, Science, and U.S. Imperialism in Puerto Rico*. Berkeley: University of California Press, 2002.

Brooks, David. "Rebellion from Without: Culture and Politics along Nicaragua's Atlantic Coast in the Time of the Sandino Revolt, 1926–1934." PhD diss., University of Connecticut, 1998.

Brown, Charles. *Agents of Manifest Destiny: The Lives and Times of the Filibusters.* Chapel Hill: University of North Carolina Press, 1980.

Buell, Raymond. "Reconstruction in Nicaragua." *Foreign Policy Association Information Service* 6.18 (November 1930): 315–43.

Buitrago Matus, Nicolás. *León: La Sombra de Pedrarias.* Vol. 2. Managua: Fundación Ortiz Gurdián, 1998.

Bulmer-Thomas, Victor. *The Political Economy of Central America since 1920.* Cambridge: Cambridge University Press, 1987.

——. *The Economic History of Latin America since Independence.* Cambridge: Cambridge University Press, 1994.

Burns, Bradford. *Patriarch and Folk: The Emergence of Nicaragua, 1798–1858.* Cambridge: Harvard University Press, 1991.

Butler, Smedley. *Old Gimlet Eye: The Adventures of Smedley D. Butler as Told to Lowell Thomas.* New York: Farrar and Rinehart, 1933.

Bynum, M. *International Trade in Coffee.* Washington, D.C.: Government Printing Office, 1926.

Cabán, Pedro. *Constructing a Colonial People: Puerto Rico and the United States, 1898–1932.* Boulder: Westview, 1999.

Cabrales, Luis Alberto. "Hacia un partido de productores." *La Nueva Prensa,* 30 March 1933.

Calatayud Bernabeu, José. *Manolo Cuadra.* Managua: Hospicio, 1968.

Calder, Bruce. *The Impact of Intervention: The Dominican Republic during the U.S. Occupation of 1916–1924.* Austin: University of Texas Press, 1984.

Calderón Ramírez, Salvador. *Ultimos días de Sandino.* Mexico City: Botas, 1934.

Canton, Alejandro. *El banco y el ferrocarril nacionales.* 1925.

Cardenal, Ernesto. *Los años de Granada.* Managua: Anamá, 2001.

Cardenal, Luis. *La familia Cardenal.* Managua: UCA, 1998.

Cardenal Ch., Rodolfo. "Acerca de las 'Reflexiones' de Coronel Urtecho." *Revista del Pensamiento Centroamericano* 15.1 (1976): 23–47.

Cardoso, Fernando Henrique, and Enzo Faletto. *Dependency and Development in Latin America.* Berkeley: University of California Press, 1979.

Carroll, Anna Ella. *The Star of the West: National Men and National Measures.* New York: Miller, Orton, 1857.

Casanova Fuertes, Rafael. "Hacia una nueva valorización de las luchas políticas del periódo de la Anarquía." In *Encuentros con la historia,* ed. Margarita Vannini. Managua: Instituto de Historia de Nicaragua, 1995.

Castillo, Alfonso. *Acotaciones.* Granada, Nicaragua: Canal, 1937.

Challener, Richard. *Admirals, Generals, and American Foreign Policy, 1898–1914.* Princeton: Princeton University Press, 1973.

Chamorro, Amalia. "Estado y hegemonía durante el somocismo." In *Economía y sociedad en la construcción del Estado en Nicaragua,* ed. Alberto Lanuza et al. San José, Costa Rica: ICAP, 1983.

Chamorro, Diego Manuel. *Discursos, 1907–1921.* Managua: Tipografía Nacional, 1923.

Chamorro, Emiliano. "Autobiografía." *Revista Conservadora* 1–18 (1960–62).

Chamorro Cardenal, Pedro Joaquín. *Diario político.* Managua: Nueva Nicaragua, 1990.

Chamorro Zelaya, Pedro Joaquín. *Entre dos filos: Novela nicaragüense.* Managua: Tipografía y Encuadernación Nacional, 1927.

Charlip, Julie. *Cultivating Coffee: The Farmers of Carazo, Nicaragua, 1880–1930.* Athens: Ohio University Press, 2003.

CIERA-MIDINRA. *Nicaragua: . . . Y por eso defendemos la frontera: Historia agraria de las Segovias occidentales.* Managua: MIDINRA, 1984.

Clark, Paul Coe. *The United States and Somoza, 1933–1956: A Revisionist Look.* Westport, Conn.: Praeger, 1992.

Coatsworth, John. "Obstacles to Economic Development in Nineteenth Century Mexico." *American Historical Review* 83.1 (1978): 80–100.

——. *Central America and the United States: The Clients and the Colossus.* New York: Twayne, 1994.

Collin, Richard. *Theodore Roosevelt's Caribbean: The Panama Canal, the Monroe Doctrine, and the Latin American Context.* Baton Rouge: Louisiana State University Press, 1990.

Committee on Cooperation in Latin America. *Christian Work in Latin America.* Vols. 1–3. New York: Missionary Education Movement, 1917.

Conant, Charles. "Our Mission in Nicaragua." *North American Review* 196 (1912): 63–71.

Conrad, Robert Edgar, ed. *Sandino: The Testimony of a Nicaraguan Patriot, 1921–1934.* Princeton: Princeton University Press, 1990.

Coronel Urtecho, José. "El americanismo en la casa de mi abuelo." *Revista Conservadora* 5.23 (1962): 25–31.

——. "Resistencia de la memoria." *Revista del Pensamiento Centroamericano* 150 (1976): 98–107.

——. "Paneles de infierno." In José Coronel Urtecho, *Pol-la d'ananta katanta paranta dedójmia t'élson.* Managua: Nueva Nicaragua, 1993.

Coronel Urtecho, José, Fernando Silva, and Ernesto Gutiérrez, eds. "50 años del Movimiento de Vanguardia de Nicaragua, 1928–29, 1978–79." *El pez y la serpiente* 22–23 (1978–79): 1–182.

Coronil, Fernando. Forward to Joseph, LeGrand, and Salvatore, *Close Encounters of Empire*, 1998.

Coronil, Fernando, and Julie Skurski. "Dismembering and Remembering the Nation: The Semantics of Political Violence in Venezuela." *Comparative Studies in Society and History* 33.2 (1991): 288–337.

Coto Conde, José Luis, ed. *Documentos históricos del 56*. San José, Costa Rica: Imprenta Nacional, 1985.

Cott, Nancy. "The Modern Woman of the 1920s, American Style." In *A History of Women in the West*. Vol. 5, *Toward a Cultural Identity in the Twentieth Century*, ed. Françoise Thébaud. Cambridge, Mass.: Harvard University Press.

Crahan, Margaret, and Peter Smith. "The State of Revolution." In *Americas*, ed. Alfred Stepan. New York: Oxford University Press, 1992.

Crispolti, P. F. M. *El mensaje de 24 de enero y el dictamen de 21 de febrero en el congreso de Nicaragua en 1882, relativos a la cuestión "Jesuitas" de 1881*. New York, 1882.

Crowell, Jackson. "The United States and a Central American Canal, 1869–1877." *Hispanic American Historical Review* 49 (1969): 27–52.

Cruz, Arturo J. *Nicaragua's Conservative Republic, 1858–93*. New York: Palgrave, 2002.

Cuadra, Abelardo. *Hombre del Caribe*. San José, Costa Rica: EDUCA, 1977.

Cuadra, Manolo. *El gruñido de un bárbaro: Visiones y confesiones*. Managua: Nueva Nicaragua, 1994.

Cuadra, Pablo Antonio. *Torres de Dios*. San José, Costa Rica: Libro Libre, 1986.

Cuadra Chamorro, Pedro Joaquín. *El liberalismo: Estudio histórico y filosófico*. Granada, Nicaragua: Centroamericano, 1920.

——. *Ama a tu prójimo, o Espejo del amor a Dios*. Granada, Nicaragua: Centroamericano, 1927.

——. "Las dictaduras y sus consecuencias." *El Diario Nicaragüense*, 1 September 1931.

Cuadra Pasos, Carlos. *Posibilidades de existencia del comunismo en Nicaragua*. Managua: Tipografía Nacional, 1937.

——. *Obras 1*. Managua: Banco de América, 1976.

——. *Obras 2*. Managua: Banco de América, 1977.

Cumberland, W. W. *Nicaragua: An Economic and Financial Survey*. Washington, D.C.: Government Printing Office, 1928.

Darío, Rubén. *El viaje a Nicaragua e intermezzo tropical*. Managua: Nueva Nicaragua, 1988.

Delaney, Jeane. "Making Sense of Modernity: Changing Attitudes toward the Immigrant and the Gaucho in Turn-of-the-Century Argentina." *Comparative Studies in Society and History* 39.3 (1996): 434–59.

Denny, Harold. *Dollars for Bullets: The Story of American Rule in Nicaragua*. New York: Dial, 1929.

Deutsch, Sandra McGee. *Las Derechas: The Extreme Right in Argentina, Brazil, and Chile, 1890–1939*. Stanford, Calif.: Stanford University Press, 1999.

Díaz Quiñones, Arcadio. "El enemigo íntimo: Cultura nacional y autoridad en Ramiro Guerra y Sánchez y Antonio S. Pedreira." *Op. Cit.* 7 (1992): 9–65.

Dodd, Thomas. *Managing Democracy in Central America: A Case Study, United States Election Supervision in Nicaragua, 1927–1933*. New Brunswick, N.J.: Transaction, 1992.

Dodds, Harold W. "American Supervision of the Nicaraguan Election." *Foreign Affairs* 7.4 (April 1929): 488–96.

Dore, Elizabeth. "Land Privatization and the Differentiation of the Peasantry: Nicaragua's Coffee Revolution, 1850–1920." *Journal of Historical Sociology* 8.3 (1995): 303–26.

——. "Patriarchy and Private Property in Nicaragua, 1860–1920." In *Patriarchy and Economic Development*, ed. Valentine Moghadam. Oxford: Clarendon, 1996.

——. "Debt Peonage in Granada, Nicaragua, 1870–1930: Labor in a Noncapitalist Transition." *Hispanic American Historical Review* 83 (2003): 521–59.

——. "Patriarchy from Above, Patriarchy from Below: Debt Peonage on Nicaraguan Coffee Estates, 1870–1930." In *The Global Coffee Economy in Africa, Asia, and Latin America, 1500–1989*, ed. William Clarence-Smith and Steven Topik. Cambridge: Cambridge University Press, 2003.

Dorfman, Ariel, and Armand Mattelart. *How to Read Donald Duck: Imperialist Ideology in the Disney Comic*. New York: International General, 1975.

Dospital, Michelle. *Siempre más allá . . . : El movimiento Sandinista en Nicaragua, 1927–1934*. Managua: Instituto de Historia de Nicaragua, 1996.

Doubleday, Charles. *Reminiscences of the "Filibuster" War in Nicaragua*. New York: G. P. Putnam's Sons, 1886.

Doyle, Michael. *Empires*. Ithaca: Cornell University Press, 1986.

Dozier, Craig. *Nicaragua's Mosquito Shore: The Years of British and American Presence*. Tuscaloosa: University of Alabama Press, 1985.

Drake, Paul. "From Good Men to Good Neighbors: 1912–1932." In *Exporting Democracy: The United States and Latin America*, ed. Abraham Lowenthal. Baltimore: Johns Hopkins University Press, 1991.

——. "Introduction: The Political Economy of Foreign Advisers and Lenders in Latin America." In *Money Doctors, Foreign Debts, and Economic Reforms in Latin America from the 1890s to the Present*, ed. Paul Drake. Wilmington, Del.: Scholarly Resources, 1994.

——. *The Money Doctor in the Andes: The Kemmerer Missions, 1923–1933*. Durham: Duke University Press, 1989.

Dunkerley, James. *Americana: The Americas in the World around 1850*. London: Verso, 2000.

Duque, Juan Pablo. *Informe del Jefe del Departamento Técnico sobre su viaje de estudio a algunos países cafeteros de la América Central*. Managua: Asociación Agrícola, 1938.

Economic Commission for Latin America (ECLA). *External Financing in Latin America*. New York: United Nations, 1965.

Edelman, Marc. *The Logic of the Latifundio: The Large Estates of Northwestern Costa Rica since the Late Nineteenth Century*. Stanford, Calif.: Stanford University Press, 1992.

Edelman, Marc, and Mitchell Seligson. "Land Inequality: A Comparison of Census Data and Property Records in Twentieth-Century Southern Costa Rica." *Hispanic American Historical Review* 74 (1994): 445–91.

Ediciones Ministerio de Educación. *Doctor y General Benjamín F. Zeledón*. Managua: Unión, 1980.

Encuesta económica propuesta a la consideración nacional por el Señor Presidente de la República don Bartolomé Martínez. Managua: Tipografía Nacional, 1924.

Everingham, Mark. *Revolution and the Multiclass Coalition in Nicaragua*. Pittsburgh: University of Pittsburgh Press, 1996.

"The Experience of Samuel Absalom, Filibuster." *Atlantic Monthly* (December 1859 and January 1860).

Fehrenbach, Heide, and Uta Poiger, eds. *Transactions, Transgressions, Transformations: American Culture in Western Europe and Japan*. New York: Berghan, 2000.

Fehrenbach, Heide, and Uta Poiger. "Introduction: Americanization Reconsidered." In *Transactions, Transgressions, Transformations: American Culture in Western Europe and Japan*, ed. Heide Fehrenbach and Uta Poiger. New York: Berghan, 2000.

Ferguson, Niall. *Colossus: The Price of America's Empire*. New York: Penguin, 2004.

Ferris, George. "Protestantism in Nicaragua: Its Historical Roots and Influences Affecting Its Growth." PhD diss., Temple University, 1981.

Findlay, Eileen. *Imposing Decency: The Politics of Sexuality and Race in Puerto Rico, 1870–1920*. Durham: Duke University Press, 1999.

Folkman, David. *The Nicaragua Route*. Salt Lake City: University of Utah Press, 1972.

Fumero Vargas, Patricia. "De la iniciativa individual a la cultura oficial: El caso del general José Dolores Estrada, Nicaragua, década de 1870." In *Nicaragua en busca de su identidad*, ed. Frances Kinloch Tijerino. Managua: Instituto de Historia de Nicaragua, 1995.

Gámez, José Dolores. "El canal anglo-japonés por Nicaragua." *La Patria* 21.8 (1916): 320–26.

——. "La Granada que yo conocí." In *Granada: Aldea señorial*, by Jorge Eduardo Arellano. Managua: CIRA, 1999.

"General Frederick Henningsen, Major-General in the Army of Nicaragua." In *The War in Nicaragua as Reported by Frank Leslie's Illustrated Newspaper, 1855–1857*, ed. Alejandro Bolaños Geyer. Managua: Banco de América, 1976.

Gilbert, Dennis. *Sandinistas: The Party and the Revolution*. Cambridge: Basil Blackwell, 1988.

Gobat, Michel. "Soldiers into Capitalists: The Rise of a Military Bourgeoisie in Pre-revolutionary Nicaragua (1956–67)." Unpublished ms. 1991.

——. "Oligarchs under Siege? The Impact of the Sandinista Agrarian Reform on Landed Elites in Revolutionary Nicaragua (Granada, 1979–1989)." Unpublished ms., 1995.

——. "Against the Bourgeois Spirit: The Nicaraguan Elite under U.S. Imperialism, 1910–1934." PhD diss., University of Chicago, 1998.

Goldstein, Warren. *Playing for Keeps: A History of Early Baseball*. Ithaca: Cornell University Press, 1989.

González, Victoria. "From Feminism to Somocismo: Women's Rights and Right-Wing Politics in Nicaragua, 1821–1979." PhD diss., Indiana University, 2002.

González Flores, Alfredo. *La crisis económica de Costa Rica*. San José: Trejos Hermanos, 1936.

Goodwin, Jeff. *No Other Way Out: States and Revolutionary Movements, 1945–1991*. Cambridge: Cambridge University Press, 2001.

Gould, Jeffrey. *To Lead as Equals: Rural Protest and Political Consciousness in Chinandega, Nicaragua, 1912–1979*. Chapel Hill: University of North Carolina Press, 1990.

——. "El café, el trabajo y la comunidad indígena de Matagalpa." In *Tierra, café y sociedad: Ensayos sobre la historia agraria centroamericana*, ed. Héctor Pérez Brignoli and Mario Samper. San José, Costa Rica: FLACSO, 1994.

——. *To Die in This Way: Nicaraguan Indians and the Myth of Mestizaje, 1880–1965*. Durham: Duke University Press, 1998.

Gould, Jeffrey, and Aldo Lauria-Santiago. " 'They Call Us Thieves and Steal Our Wage': Toward a Reinterpretation of the Salvadoran Rural Mobilization, 1929–1931." *Hispanic American Historical Review* 84.2 (2004): 191–237.

Granda, Darwin. "La contrareforma agraria en apogeo: Los nuevos terratenientes." *El Semanario*, 29 September 1994.

Greer, Virginia. "Charles Evans Hughes and Nicaragua, 1921–1925." PhD diss., University of New Mexico, 1954.

Grossman, Richard. " 'Hermanos en la Patria': Nationalism, Honor and Rebellion—Augusto Sandino and the Army in Defense of the National Sovereignty of Nicaragua, 1927–1934." PhD diss., University of Chicago, 1996.

Gudmundson, Lowell. "Lord and Peasant in the Making of Modern Central America." In *Agrarian Structure and Political Power: Landlord and Peasant in the Making of Latin America*, ed. Evelyne Huber and Frank Safford. Pittsburgh: University of Pittsburgh Press, 1995.

Gudmundson, Lowell, and Héctor Lindo-Fuentes. *Central America, 1821–1871: Liberalism before Liberal Reform*. Tuscaloosa: University of Alabama Press, 1995.

Gudmundson, Lowell, and Francisco Scarano. "Conclusion: Imagining the Future of the Subaltern Past—Fragments of Race, Class, and Gender in Central America and the Hispanic Caribbean, 1850–1950." In *Identity and Struggle at the Margins of the Nation-State: The Laboring Peoples of Central America and the Hispanic Caribbean*, ed. Aviva Chomsky and Aldo Lauria-Santiago. Durham: Duke University Press, 1998.

Gunn, Simon. *The Public Culture of the Victorian Middle Class: Ritual and Authority and the English Industrial City, 1840–1914*. Manchester: Manchester University Press, 2000.

Gutiérrez, Pedro Rafael, ed. *Partes de guerra del General Zeledón*. Managua: Lena, 1977.

Guzmán, Enrique. *Huellas de su pensamiento, política, literatura, historia, religión*. Granada, Nicaragua: Talleres Tipográficos el Centro Americano. 1943.

——. "Diario íntimo." *Revista Conservadora* 1–37 (1960–64).

Hale, Charles A. *Mexican Liberalism in the Age of Mora*. New Haven: Yale University Press, 1967.

——. "Political and Social Ideas." In *Latin America: Economy and Society, 1870–1930*, ed. Leslie Bethell. Cambridge: Cambridge University Press, 1989.

Hale, Charles R. *Resistance and Contradiction: Miskitu Indians and the Nicaraguan State, 1894–1987*. Stanford, Calif.: Stanford University Press, 1994.

Hale, William B. "With the Knox Mission to Central America." *World's Work*, June 1912.

Hall, Carolyn. *El café y el desarrollo histórico-geográfico de Costa Rica*. San José: Editorial Costa Rica, 1991.

Ham, Clifford. "The Revolution in Nicaragua." *American Review of Reviews* 46.5 (1912): 185–91.

Healy, David. *Drive to Hegemony: The United States in the Caribbean, 1898–1917*. Madison: University of Wisconsin Press, 1988.

Heater, Derek. *World Citizenship: Cosmopolitan Thinking and Its Opponents*. London: Continuum, 2002.

Heine, Wilhelm. *Wanderbilder aus Central-Amerika*. Leipzig: Hermann Costeno-ble, 1853.

Herrera, Miguel Angel. *Bongos, bogas, vapores y marinos: Historia de los "mari-neros" del río San Juan, 1849–1855*. Managua: Centro Nicaragüense de Es-critores, 1999.

Hertsgaard, Mark. *The Eagle's Shadow: Why America Fascinates and Infuriates the World*. New York: Farrar, Straus and Giroux, 2002.

Hill, Roscoe. *Fiscal Intervention in Nicaragua*. New York: Paul Maisel, 1933.

Hodges, Donald. *Intellectual Foundations of the Nicaraguan Revolution*. Austin: University of Texas Press, 1986.

——. *Sandino's Communism: Spiritual Politics for the Twenty-first Century*. Austin: University of Texas Press, 1992.

Hoganson, Kristin. "Cosmopolitan Domesticity: Importing the American Dream, 1865–1920." *American Historical Review* 107.1 (2002): 55–83.

Hollander, Paul, ed. *Understanding Anti-Americanism: Its Origins and Impact at Home and Abroad*. Chicago: Ivan Dee, 2004.

Horsman, Reginald. *Race and Manifest Destiny: The Origins of American Racial Anglo-Saxonism*. Cambridge: Harvard University Press, 1981.

Horton, Lynn. *Peasants in Arms: War and Peace in the Mountains of Nicaragua, 1979–1994*. Athens: Ohio University Press, 1998.

Houwald, Goetz von. *Los alemanes en Nicaragua*. Managua: BANIC, 1993.

Huete Abella, Rodolfo. *Los banqueros y la intervención en Nicaragua*. Managua: Tipografía Pérez, 1931.

Huezo, Francisco. "La caída de un presidente." *Revista Conservadora del Pensa-miento Centroamericano* 86 (1967).

Hurtado González, Armando. *Sandino desconocido*. San José, Costa Rica: Edi-ciones Populares Nicaragüenses, 1984.

Ibarra, Felipe Bartolomé. *Memorias y episodios del Coronel F. Bartolomé Ibarra*. Managua: Atlántida, 1944.

Ibarra Grijalva, Domingo. *The Last Night of General Augusto C. Sandino*. New York: Vantage, 1973.

Ibold, Frank. "Die Erfindung Lateinamerikas: Die Idee der *Latinité* in Frankreich des 19. Jahrhunderts und ihre Auswirkung auf die Eigenwahrnehmung des südlichen America." *Transatlantische Perzeptionen: Lateinamerika-USA-Europa in Geschichte und Gegenwart*, ed. Hans-Joachim König and Stefan Rinke. Stuttgart: Hans-Dieter Heinz, 1998.

Ignatieff, Michael. "The American Empire: The Burden." *New York Times Maga-zine*, 5 January 2003.

Instituto de Estudio del Sandinismo. *Pensamiento antimperialista en Nicaragua: Antología*. Managua: Nueva Nicaragua, 1982.

——. "Maniobra, entreguismo y pactos: Historia de la oposición burguesa en Nicaragua (1933–1979)." Unpublished ms., 1984.

——. *Ahora sé que Sandino manda*. Managua: Nueva Nicaragua, 1986.

Ivereigh, Austen, ed. *The Politics of Religion in an Age of Revival: Studies in Nineteenth-Century Europe and Latin America*. London: ILAS, 2000.

Jamison, James Carson. *With Walker in Nicaragua, or Reminiscences of an Officer of the American Phalanx*. Columbia, Mo.: E. W. Stephens, 1909.

Jiménez, Michael. "Traveling Far in Grandfather's Car: The Life Cycle of Central Colombian Coffee Estates—The Case of Viotá, Cundinamarca (1900–30)." *Hispanic American Historical Review* 69 (1989): 185–219.

——. "At the Banquet of Civilization: The Limits of Planter Hegemony in Early-Twentieth-Century Colombia." In *Coffee, Society, and Power in Latin America*, ed. William Roseberry et al. Baltimore: Johns Hopkins University Press, 1995.

Johnson, Chalmers. *Blowback: The Costs and Consequences of American Empire*. New York: Metropolitan, 2000.

Jones, Chester Lloyd. *Guatemala, Past and Present*. Minneapolis: University of Minnesota Press, 1940.

Joseph, Gilbert M. "Forging a Regional Pastime: Baseball and Class in Yucatán." In *Sport and Society in Latin America*, ed. Joseph Arbena. New York: Greenwood, 1988.

——. "Close Encounters: Toward a New Cultural History of U.S.–Latin American Relations." In Joseph, LeGrand, and Salvatore, *Close Encounters of Empire*, 1998.

Joseph, Gilbert, Catherine LeGrand, and Ricardo Salvatore, eds. *Close Encounters of Empire: Writing the Cultural History of U.S.–Latin American Relations*. Durham: Duke University Press, 1998.

Kamman, William. *A Search for Stability: United States Diplomacy towards Nicaragua*. Notre Dame, Ind.: University of Notre Dame Press, 1968.

Kaplan, Amy. *The Anarchy of Empire in the Making of U.S. Culture*. Cambridge, Mass.: Harvard University Press, 2002.

Karl, Terry Lynn. "Dilemmas of Democratization in Latin America." *Comparative Politics* 23.1 (1990): 1–22.

Katz, Friedrich. *The Secret War in Mexico: Europe, the United States and the Mexican Revolution*. Chicago: University of Chicago Press, 1981.

——. *The Life and Times of Pancho Villa*. Stanford, Calif.: Stanford University Press, 1998.

Keaseby, Lindley. *The Nicaragua Canal and the Monroe Doctrine*. New York: Putnam, 1896.

Kinloch Tijerino, Frances. "El canal interoceánico en el imaginario nacional: Nicaragua, siglo XIX." In *Nación y etnia ¿Identidad natural o creación cultural?*, ed. Frances Kinloch Tijerino. Managua: Instituto de Historia de Nicaragua, 1994.

——. *Nicaragua: Identidad y cultura política (1821–1858)*. Managua: Fondo Editorial, Banco Central de Nicaragua, 1999.

——. "La formación del Estado Nacional (1821–1909)." In *Enciclopedia de Nicaragua*. Barcelona: Oceano, 2002.

Krenn, Michael. *U.S. Policy toward Economic Nationalism in Latin America, 1917–1929*. Wilmington, Del.: Scholarly Resources, 1990.

Kuisel, Richard. *Seducing the French: The Dilemma of Americanization*. Berkeley: University of California Press, 1993.

Kutzinski, Vera. *Sugar's Secrets: Race and the Erotics of Cuban Nationalism*. Charlottesville: University Press of Virginia, 1993.

LaFeber, Walter. *Inevitable Revolutions: The United States in Central America*. New York: W. W. Norton, 1984.

——. *The Panama Canal: The Crisis in Historical Perspective*. New York: Oxford University Press, 1989.

Laird, Larry. "Technology versus Tradition: The Modernization of Nicaraguan Agriculture, 1900–1940." PhD diss., University of Kansas, 1974.

Lane, Wheaton. *Commodore Vanderbilt: An Epic of the Steam Age*. New York: Alfred Knopf, 1942.

Lears, T. Jackson. *No Place of Grace: Antimodernism and the Transformation of American Culture, 1880–1920*. Chicago: University of Chicago Press, 1981.

LeGrand, Catherine. "Living in Macondo: Economy and Culture in a United Fruit Company Banana Enclave in Colombia." In Joseph, LeGrand, and Salvatore, *Close Encounters of Empire*, 1998.

Lehoucq, Fabrice, and Iván Molina. *Stuffing the Ballot Box: Fraud, Electoral Reform, and Democratization in Costa Rica*. Cambridge: Cambridge University Press, 2002.

LeoGrande, William. *Our Own Backyard: The United States in Central America, 1977–1992*. Chapel Hill: University of North Carolina Press, 1998.

Lynch, John. "The Catholic Church." In *Latin America: Economy and Society, 1870–1930*, ed. Leslie Bethell. Cambridge: Cambridge University Press, 1989.

Macaulay, Neill. *The Sandino Affair*. Durham: Duke University Press, 1967.

Mack, Gerstle. *The Land Divided: A History of the Panama Canal and Other Isthmian Canal Projects*. New York: Alfred A. Knopf, 1944.

Madrigal Mendieta, Ligia. *La evolución de las ideas: El caso de los protestantes en Nicaragua (1856–1925)*. Managua: CIEETS/UNAN, 1999.

Mahan, A. T. *The Interest of America in Sea Power, Present and Future*. Boston: Little, Brown, 1898.

Mahoney, James. *The Legacies of Liberalism: Path Dependence and Political Regimes in Central America.* Baltimore: Johns Hopkins University Press, 2001.

Manning, William, ed. *Diplomatic Correspondence of the United States, Inter-American Affairs, 1831–1860.* Vols. 3 and 4. Washington, D.C.: Carnegie Endowment for International Peace, 1933–34.

Marr, Wilhelm. *Reise nach Central Amerika.* Vol. 2. Hamburg: Otto Meissner, 1863.

Matus, Ramón Ignacio. *Estudio crítico sobre dos órdenes de fusilación durante la guerra de 1912, atribuidas al general don Emiliano Chamorro.* Managua: Gutenberg, 1916.

May, Robert E. *The Southern Dream of a Caribbean Empire, 1854–1861.* Baton Rouge: Louisiana State University Press, 1973.

——. *Manifest Destiny's Underworld: Filibustering in Ante-bellum America.* Chapel Hill: University of North Carolina Press, 2002.

McClellan, Edwin. "Supervising Nicaraguan Elections, 1928." *United States Naval Institute Proceedings* 59.359 (1933): 33–38.

McClymer, John. "Gender and the 'American Way of Life': Women in the Americanization Movement." *Journal of American Ethnic History* 10.3 (1991): 3–22.

McCreery, David. *Rural Guatemala, 1760–1940.* Stanford, Calif.: Stanford University Press, 1994.

——. "Wage Labor, Free Labor, and Vagrancy Laws: The Transition to Capitalism in Guatemala, 1920–1945." In *Coffee, Society, and Power in Latin America,* ed. William Roseberry et al. Baltimore: Johns Hopkins University Press, 1995.

McCullough, David. *The Path between the Seas: The Creation of the Panama Canal, 1870–1914.* New York: Simon and Schuster, 1977.

McPherson, Alan. *Yankee No! Anti-Americanism in U.S.–Latin American Relations.* Cambridge, Mass.: Harvard University Press, 2003.

Mena Guerrero, Francisco. "Semblanzas granadinas." Unpublished ms. San Salvador 1992.

Mendieta, Salvador. *La enfermedad de Centro-América.* Vols. 1 and 2. Barcelona: Maucci, 1934.

Mendoza, Juan Manuel. *Historia de Diriamba.* Guatemala City: Electra, 1920.

Merz, Carlos. *Finanzhaushalt, Produktion und Handel der Republik Costa Rica.* San José: Universal, 1928.

Millett, Richard. *Guardians of the Dynasty: A History of the U.S.-Created Guardia Nacional de Nicaragua and the Somoza Family.* Maryknoll, N.Y.: Orbis, 1977.

Mitchell, B. R. *International Historical Statistics: The Americas, 1750–1988.* New York: M. Stockton, 1993.

Mitchell, Nancy. *The Danger of Dreams: German and American Imperialism in Latin America.* Chapel Hill: University of North Carolina Press, 1999.

Moncada, José María. *Social and Political Influence of the United States in Central America*. New York, 1911.

——. "Estados Unidos en Nicaragua." *Revista Conservadora del Pensamiento Centroamericano* 119 (1970).

Montalván, José. *Hace medio siglo*. León, Nicaragua: Centroamericano, 1963.

Montiel, Rafael. "La tierra del no vivir." *Ventana*, 3 October 1981.

Moore, Barrington. *Social Origins of Dictatorships and Democracy*. Boston: Beacon, 1966.

Moreno, Julio. *Yankee Don't Go Home! Mexican Nationalism, American Business Culture, and the Shaping of Modern Mexico, 1920–1950*. Chapel Hill: University of North Carolina Press, 2003.

Munro, Dana. *The Five Republics of Central America*. New York: Russell and Russell, 1918.

——. *Intervention and Dollar Diplomacy in the Caribbean, 1900–1921*. Princeton: Princeton University Press, 1964.

——. *The United States and the Caribbean Republics, 1921–1933*. Princeton: Princeton University Press, 1974.

Navarro-Génie, Marco Aurelio. *Augusto "César" Sandino: Messiah of Light and Truth*. Syracuse, N.Y.: Syracuse University Press, 2002.

Nearing, Scott, and Joseph Freeman. *Dollar Diplomacy: A Study in American Imperialism*. New York: B. W. Huebsch, 1925.

Needell, Jeffrey. *A Tropical Belle Epoque: Elite Culture and Society in Turn-of-the-Century Rio de Janeiro*. Cambridge: Cambridge University Press, 1987.

Ninkovich, Frank. *The United States and Imperialism*. Malden, Mass.: Blackwell, 2001.

——. "The United States and Imperialism." In *A Companion to American Foreign Relations*, ed. Robert Schulzinger. Malden, Mass.: Blackwell, 2003.

Nolan, Mary. *Visions of Modernity: American Business and the Modernization of Germany*. New York: Oxford University Press, 1994.

Obando Somarriba, Francisco. *Doña Angélica Balladares de Argüello, la primera dama del liberalismo*. Managua: Comercial, 1969.

O'Brien, Thomas. *The Revolutionary Mission: American Enterprise in Latin America, 1900–1945*. Cambridge: Cambridge University Press, 1996.

Ochoa, Enrique. "The Rapid Expansion of Voter Participation in Latin America: Presidential Elections, 1845–1986." In *Statistical Abstract of Latin America*, ed. James Wilkie and David Lorey. Vol. 35. Los Angeles: UCLA, 1987.

Orlove, Benjamin, and Arnold Bauer. "Giving Importance to Imports." In *The Allure of the Foreign: Imported Goods in Postcolonial Latin America*, ed. Benjamin Orlove. Ann Arbor: University of Michigan Press, 1997.

Ortega Arancibia, Francisco. *Cuarenta años de historia de Nicaragua (1838–1878)*. Managua: Fondo de Promoción Cultural, BANIC, 1993 [1912].

Outram, Dorinda. *The Body and the French Revolution: Sex, Class and Political Culture*. New Haven: Yale University Press, 1989.

Paige, Jeffrey. "Revolution and the Agrarian Bourgeoisie in Nicaragua." In *Revolution in the World System*, ed. Terry Boswell. New York: Greenwood, 1989.

——. *Coffee and Power: Revolution and the Rise of Democracy in Central America*. Cambridge, Mass.: Harvard University Press, 1997.

Palma Martínez, Ildefonso. *La guerra nacional: Sus antecedentes y subsecuentes tentativas de invasión*. Managua: Aldina, 1956.

Parajón, Arturo. *Veinticinco años de labor bautista en Nicaragua, 1917–1942*. Managua, 1942.

Pasos Arana, Manuel. "Granada y sus arroyos." *Revista de la Academia de Geografía e Historia de Nicaragua* 6.1–2 (1944): 69–124.

Pastor, Robert. *Condemned to Repetition: The United States and Nicaragua*. Princeton: Princeton University Press, 1987.

Peceny, Mark. *Democracy at the Point of Bayonets*. University Park: Pennsylvania State University Press, 1999.

Pérez, Jéronimo. *Obras históricas completas*. Managua: Fondo de Promoción Cultural, BANIC, 1993.

Pérez, Louis. *Army Politics in Cuba, 1898–1958*. Pittsburgh: University of Pittsburgh Press, 1976.

——. "Intervention, Hegemony, and Dependency: The United States in the Circum-Caribbean, 1898–1980." *Pacific Historical Review* 51.2 (1982): 165–94.

——. *Cuba under the Platt Amendment, 1902–1934*. Pittsburgh: University of Pittsburgh Press, 1986.

——. "Between Baseball and Bullfighting: The Quest for Nationality in Cuba, 1868–1898." *Journal of American History* 81.2 (1994): 493–518.

——. "1898 and Beyond: Historiographical Variations on War and Empire." *Pacific Historical Review* 65.2 (1996): 313–16.

——. *On Becoming Cuban: Identity, Nationalism, and Culture*. Chapel Hill: University of North Carolina Press, 1999.

Pérez-Baltodano, Andrés. *Entre el Estado Conquistador y el Estado Nación: Providencialismo, pensamiento político y estructuras de poder en el desarrollo histórico de Nicaragua*. Managua: IHNCA/UCA, 2003.

Pérez Bermúdez, Carlos, and Onofre Guevara. *El movimiento obrero en Nicaragua*. Managua: Amanecer, 1985.

Petty, Alonzo. "Three Weeks in Central America." *Missions* 15.9 (1924): 491–93.

Phelan, J. L. "Pan-Latinism, French Intervention in Mexico (1861–1867) and the

Genesis of the Idea of Latin America." In *Conciencia y autenticidad históricas*, ed. J. Ortega y Medina. Mexico City: UNAM, 1968.

Pike, Frederick. *Hispanismo, 1898–1936: Spanish Conservatives and Liberals and Their Relations with Spanish America*. Notre Dame, Ind.: University of Notre Dame, 1971.

Playter, Harold. *Nicaragua: A Commercial and Economic Survey*. Washington, D.C.: Government Printing Office, 1927.

Pletcher, David. *The Diplomacy of Trade and Investment: American Economic Expansion in the Hemisphere, 1865–1900*. Columbia: University of Missouri Press, 1998.

Posas, Mario, and Rafael del Cid. *La construcción del sector público y del Estado nacional de Honduras*. San José, Costa Rica: EDUCA, 1983.

Prado, Edgardo. "Por que dejo de ser Sandinista." *La Prensa*, 8 June 1933.

Quijano, Carlos. *Nicaragua: Ensayo sobre el imperialismo de los Estados Unidos (1909–1927)*. Managua: Vanguardia, 1987 [1928].

Ramírez, Pedro R. *Canal interoceánico: Algunos documentos relativos a esta cuestión*. Granada, Nicaragua: Centro-Americano, 1879.

Ramírez, Sergio, ed. *Augusto C. Sandino: El pensamiento vivo*. 2 vols. Managua: Nueva Nicaragua, 1984.

Ramírez Delgado, Rafael. *Narraciones históricas y cuatro novelas cortas*. Mexico City: Costa-Amic, 1963.

Rangel, Carlos. *The Latin Americans: Their Love-Hate Relationship with the United States*. New York: Harcourt Brace Jovanovich, 1977.

Ratterman, Elleanore. "With Walker in Nicaragua." *Tennessee Historical Magazine* 1 (1915): 315–30.

Reid, John. *Spanish American Images of the United States, 1790–1960*. Gainesville: University of Florida Press, 1977.

Renda, Mary. *Taking Haiti: Military Occupation and the Culture of U.S. Imperialism, 1915–1940*. Chapel Hill: University of North Carolina Press, 2001.

Reyes, María Auxiliadora, ed. *Granada: Historia y desarrollo urbano*. Granada, Nicaragua: Oficina de Preservación y Conservación del Centro Histórico de Granada, 1999.

Rice, Michael D. "Nicaragua and the U.S.: Policy Confrontations and Cultural Interactions, 1893–1933." PhD diss., University of Houston, 1995.

Rinke, Stefan. "Voyeuristic Exoticism: The Multiple Uses of the Image of U.S. Women in Chile." *North Americanization of Latin America? Culture, Gender, and Nation in the Americas*, eds. Hans-Joachim König and Stefan Rinke. Stuttgart: Hans-Dieter Heinz, 2004.

Robleto, Hernán. *Los estrangulados: El imperialismo yanqui en Nicaragua*. Madrid: Cenit, 1933.

Robleto, Hernán. *Nido de memorias: Poesía y tragedia en el Caribe*. Mexico City: Libro Mex, 1960.

Rock, David. *Authoritarian Argentina: The Nationalist Movement, Its History and Its Impact*. Berkeley: University of California Press, 1995.

Rodó, José Enrique. *Ariel*. Mexico City: Porrúa, 1991 [1900].

Román, José. *Maldito país*. Managua: El pez y la serpiente, 1979.

Roseberry, William. "Americanization in the Americas." In *Anthropologies and Histories: Essays in Culture, History, and Political Economy*. New Brunswick, N.J.: Rutgers University Press, 1989.

Rosenberg, Emily. *Spreading the American Dream: American Economic and Cultural Expansion, 1890–1945*. New York: Hill and Wang, 1982.

——. *Financial Missionaries to the World: The Politics and Culture of Dollar Diplomacy, 1900–1930*. Cambridge: Harvard University Press, 1999.

Rosenberg, Emily, and Norman Rosenberg. "From Colonialism to Professionalism: The Public-Private Dynamic in United States Foreign Financial Advising, 1898–1929." In *Money Doctors, Foreign Debts, and Economic Reforms in Latin America from the 1890s to the Present*, ed. Paul Drake. Wilmington, Del.: Scholarly Resources, 1994.

Rosengarten, Frederic. *William Walker y el ocaso del filibusterismo*. Tegucigalpa: Guaymuras, 1997.

Ross, Andrew, and Kristin Ross, eds. *Anti-Americanism*. New York: New York University Press, 2004.

Rouquié, Alain. *The Military and the State in Latin America*. Berkeley: University of California Press, 1987.

Ruhl, Arthur. *The Central Americans: Adventures and Impressions between Mexico and Panama*. New York: C. Scribner's Sons, 1928.

Saavedra, David. *Bananas, Gold and Silver*. Tegucigalpa: Talleres Tipografícos Nacionales, 1935.

Salisbury, Richard. *Anti-Imperialism and International Competition in Central America*. Wilmington, Del.: Scholarly Resources, 1989.

Salomon, Noel. "Cosmopolitanism and Internationalism in the History of Ideas in Latin America." *Cultures* 6.1 (1979). 83 108.

Salvatierra, Sofonías. *Sandino: O la tragedia de un pueblo*. Madrid: Europa, 1934.

Samper, Mario. "In Difficult Times: Colombian and Costa Rican Coffee Growers from Prosperity to Crisis, 1920–1936." In *Coffee, Society, and Power in Latin America*, ed. William Roseberry et al. New Brunswick, N.J.: Rutgers University Press, 1995.

——. "El significado social de la caficultura costarricense y salvadoreña: Análisis histórico comparado a partir de los censos cafetaleros." *Tierra, café y sociedad:*

Ensayos sobre la historia agraria centroamericana, eds. Héctor Pérez Brignoli and Mario Samper. San José, Costa Rica: FLACSO, 1994.

Sánchez, George. " 'Go After the Women': Americanization and the Mexican Immigrant Woman, 1915–1929." *Unequal Sisters: A Multicultural Reader in U.S. Women's History*, ed. Ellen Dubois and Vicki Ruiz. New York: Routledge, 1990.

Sandoval, Beatriz. "Es peligroso el esfuerzo en el atletismo femenino?" *Mujer Nicaragüense*, March 1930.

Santiago-Valle, Kelvin. *"Subject People" and Colonial Discourses: Economic Transformation and Social Disorder in Puerto Rico, 1898–1947*. Albany: SUNY Press, 1994.

Schmidt, Hans. *Maverick Marine: General Smedley D. Butler and the Contradictions of American Military History*. Lexington: University Press of Kentucky, 1987.

——. *The United States Occupation of Haiti, 1915–1934*. New Brunswick, N.J.: Rutgers University Press, 1995 [1971].

Schoenrich, Otto. "The Nicaraguan Mixed Claims Commission." *American Journal of International Law* 9.4 (1915): 858–69.

Schoonover, Thomas. *The United States in Central America, 1860–1911: Episodes of Social Imperialism and Imperial Rivalry in the World System*. Durham: Duke University Press, 1991.

——. *Germany in Central America: Competitive Imperialism, 1821–1929*. Tuscaloosa: University of Alabama Press, 1998.

Schoonover, Thomas, and Ebba Schoonover. "Statistics for an Understanding of Foreign Intrusions into Central America from the 1820s to 1930." *Anuario de Estudios Centroamericanos* 15.1 (1989): 93–118.

Schoultz, Lars. *Beneath the United States: A History of U.S. Policy toward Latin America*. Cambridge, Mass.: Harvard University Press, 1998.

Schroeder, Michael. " 'To Defend Our Nation's Honor': Toward a Social and Cultural History of the Sandino Rebellion in Nicaragua, 1927–1934." PhD diss., University of Michigan, 1993.

——. "Horse Thieves to Rebels to Dogs: Political Gang Violence and the State in the Western Segovias, Nicaragua, in the Time of Sandino." *Journal of Latin American Studies* 28.2 (1996): 383–434.

——. "The Sandino Rebellion Revisited: Civil War, Imperialism, Popular Nationalism, and State Formation Muddied Up Together in the Segovias of Nicaragua, 1926–1934." In Joseph, LeGrand, and Salvatore, *Close Encounters of Empire*, 1998.

Seager, Robert, and Doris Maguire, eds. *Letters and Papers of Alfred Thayer Mahan*. Vol. 3. Annapolis: Naval Institute Press, 1975.

Selser, Gregorio. *Sandino: General of the Free*. New York: Monthly Review Press, 1981.

Shannon, Magdaline. *Jean Price-Mars, the Haitian Elite and the American Occupation.* New York: St. Martin's, 1996.

Sheldon, Henry. *Notes on the Nicaraguan Canal.* Chicago: A. C. McClurg and Co., 1897.

Silva, Federico. *Jacinta.* Managua: Tipografía Pérez, 1927.

Slotkin, Richard. *Regeneration through Violence: The Mythology of the American Frontier, 1600–1860.* Middletown, Conn.: Wesleyan University Press, 1973.

——. *The Fatal Environment: The Myth of the Frontier in the Age of Industrialization.* Middletown, Conn.: Wesleyan University Press, 1986.

Smith, Joseph. *Illusions of Conflict: Anglo-American Diplomacy toward Latin America, 1865–1896.* Pittsburgh: University of Pittsburgh Press, 1979.

Smith, Julian, et al. *A Review of the Organization and Operations of the Guardia Nacional de Nicaragua.* Quantico, Va.: Marine Corps School, 1937.

Smith, Tony. *America's Mission: The United States and the Worldwide Struggle for Democracy in the Twentieth Century.* Princeton: Princeton University Press, 1994.

Soley Güell, Tomás. *Historia monetaria de Costa Rica.* San José: Imprenta Nacional, 1926.

——. *Historia económica y hacendaria de Costa Rica.* Vol. 2. San José: Universitaria, 1949.

Sommer, Doris. *Foundational Fictions: When History Was Romance.* Berkeley: University of California Press, 1991.

Somoza García, Anastasio. *El verdadero Sandino o el calvario de las Segovias.* Managua: San José, 1976 [1936].

Spalding, Rose. *Capitalists and Revolution in Nicaragua: Opposition and Accommodation, 1979–1993.* Chapel Hill: University of North Carolina Press, 1994.

Squier, E. G. *Nicaragua: Its People, Scenery, Monuments, and the Proposed Canal.* Vols. 1 and 2. New York: D. Appleton, 1852.

Staklo, Vadim. "Harnessing Revolution: The Communist International in Central America, 1929–1935." PhD diss., University of Pittsburgh, 2001.

Stepan, Alfred. *The State and Society: Peru in Comparative Perspective.* Princeton: Princeton University Press, 1978.

Stephanson, Anders. *Manifest Destiny: American Expansion and the Empire of Right.* New York: Hill and Wang, 1995.

Stimson, Henry. *American Policy in Nicaragua.* New York: Charles Scribner's Sons, 1927.

Stoler, Ann, and Frederick Cooper. "Between Metropole and Colony: Rethinking a Research Agenda." In *Tensions of Empire: Colonial Cultures in a Bourgeois World,* ed. Ann Stoler and Frederick Cooper. Berkeley: University of California Press, 1997.

Stout, Peter. *Nicaragua: Past, Present and Future.* Philadelphia: John E. Potter, 1859.

Stump, Joe. "El primer club de base-ball en Managua." *Nicaragua Informativa* 2.18 (1919): 9–10.

Sultan, Dan. "An Army Engineer Explores Nicaragua." *National Geographic Magazine* 61.5 (1932): 592–627.

Suter, Jan. *Prosperität und Krise in einer Kaffeerepublik: Modernisierung, sozialer Wandel und politischer Umbruch in El Salvador, 1910–1945*. Frankfurt on Main: Vervuert, 1996.

Téllez, Dora María. *¡Muera la gobierna! Colonización en Matagalpa y Jinotega (1820–1890)*. Managua: URACCAN, 1999.

Tenorio-Trillo, Mauricio. *Mexico at the World's Fairs: Crafting a Modern Nation*. Berkeley: University of California Press, 1996.

Teplitz, Benjamin. "The Political and Economic Foundations of Modernization in Nicaragua: The Administration of José Santos Zelaya, 1893–1909." PhD diss., Howard University, 1973.

Texas State Library. *The Papers of Mirabeau Buonaparte Lamar*. Vols. 4 and 6. Austin: Von Boeckmann-Jones, 1924.

Thompson, Arthur. "Renovating Nicaragua." *World's Work* 21 (March 1916): 490–503.

Thompson, Wallace. *Rainbow Countries of Central America*. New York: E. P. Dutton, 1926.

Thornton, Tamara Plakins. *Cultivating Gentlemen: The Meaning of Country Life among the Boston Elite, 1785–1860*. New Haven: Yale University Press, 1989.

Thorp, Rosemary. "Economy, 1914–1929." In *Latin America: Economy and Society, 1870–1930*, ed. Leslie Bethell. Cambridge: Cambridge University Press, 1989.

Thorp, Rosemary, and Carlos Londoño. "The Effect of the Great Depression on the Economies of Peru and Colombia." In *Latin America in the 1930s: The Role of the Periphery in World Crisis*, ed. Rosemary Thorp. London: MacMillan, 1984.

Tijerino, Toribio. *El tratado Chamorro-Bryan y sus proyecciones en la América Central*. Managua: La Prensa, 1935.

——. "Apuntes para la historia de la liberación económica de Nicaragua." *Revista Conservadora* 7.40 (1964): 55–81.

Tirado, Manlio. *Conversando con José Coronel Urtecho*. Managua: Nueva Nicaragua, 1983.

Toledo de Aguerri, Josefa, ed. *Enciclopedia nicaragüense*. Vol. 2. Managua: Nacional, 1932.

——. *Anhelos y esfuerzos*. Managua: Nacional, 1935.

Torres Rivas, Edelberto. "El Estado contra la sociedad: Las raíces de la revolución nicaragüense." *Estudios Sociales Centroamericanos* 9.27 (1980): 79–96.

Torres Rivas, Edelberto. *Sandino*. Mexico City: Katún, 1984.

Toruño, Juan Felipe. *La mariposa negra*. Ahuacahapán, El Salvador: Guttenberg, 1928.

Tulchin, Joseph. *The Aftermath of War: World War I and U.S. Policy toward Latin America*. New York: New York University Press, 1971.

Turits, Richard. *Foundations of Despotism: Peasants, the Trujillo Regime, and Modernity in Dominican History*. Stanford, Calif.: Stanford University Press, 2003.

U.S. Senate. "Instances of Use of United States Armed Forces Abroad, 1798–1945." *Situation in Cuba: Hearing before the Committee on Foreign Relations and the Committee on Armed Services*. Washington, D.C.: Government Printing Office, 1962.

Valle Castillo, Julio. "Zeledón." *Ventana*, 3 October 1981.

——. "Prólogo." In Luis Alberto Cabrales, *Opera parva*. Managua: Nueva Nicaragua, 1989.

Vallejo, Carlos, ed. *Guia y reglas del basket ball en América Latina*. Monterrey: Carlos F. Vallejo, 1948.

Vargas, Oscar René. *Elecciones en Nicaragua (Análisis socio-político)*. Managua: DILESA, 1989.

——. *La intervención norteamericana y sus consecuencias: Nicaragua, 1910–1925*. Managua: CIRA, 1989.

——. *Floreció al filo de la espada: El movimiento de Sandino, 1926–1939*. Managua: CEREN, 1995.

Venzon, Anne Cipriano, ed. *General Smedley Darlington Butler: The Letters of a Leatherneck, 1898–1931*. New York: Praeger, 1992.

Vijil, Francisco. *El Padre Vijil*. Granada, Nicaragua: Centro-Americano, 1930.

Vilas, Carlos. *The Sandinista Revolution: National Liberation and Social Transformation in Central America*. New York: Monthly Review Press, 1986.

——. "Family Affairs: Class, Lineage and Politics in Contemporary Nicaragua." *Journal of Latin American Studies* 24.2 (1992): 309–41.

Villanueva, Carlos. *Sandino en Yucatán, 1929–1930*. Mexico City: SEP, 1988.

Vlastos, Stephen. "Agrarianism without Tradition: The Radical Critique of Prewar Japanese Modernity." In *Mirror of Modernity: Invented Traditions of Modern Japan*, ed. Stephen Vlastos. Berkeley: University of California Press, 1998.

Wagnleitner, Reinhold. *Coca-Colonization and the Cold War: The Cultural Mission of the United States in Austria after the Second World War*. Chapel Hill: University of North Carolina Press, 1994.

Walker, William. *The War in Nicaragua*. Tucson: University of Arizona Press, 1985 [1860].

Walter, Knut. *The Regime of Anastasio Somoza, 1936–1956*. Chapel Hill: University of North Carolina Press, 1993.

Weinberg, Albert. *Manifest Destiny: A Study of Nationalist Expansionism in American History*. Baltimore: Johns Hopkins University Press, 1935.

Wells, William V. *Walker's Expedition to Nicaragua*. New York: Stringer and Towsend, 1856.

Wheelock, Jaime. *Imperialismo y dictadura*. Mexico City: Siglo XXI, 1976.

———. *Raíces indígenas de las luchas anticolonialistas*. Managua: Nueva Nicaragua, 1981.

Whelpley, Philip. "A Ranger's Life in Nicaragua: A Personal Narrative." In *The War in Nicaragua as Reported by "Harper's Weekly," 1857–1860*, ed. Alejandro Bolaños Geyer. Managua: Fondo de Promoción Cultural del Banco de América, 1976.

Whisnant, David. *Rascally Signs in Sacred Places: The Politics of Culture in Nicaragua*. Chapel Hill: University of North Carolina Press, 1995.

Wiener, Martin. *English Culture and the Decline of the Industrial Spirit, 1850–1980*. Cambridge: Cambridge University Press, 1981.

Wilkins, Mira. *The Emergence of Multinational Enterprise: American Business Abroad from the Colonial Era to 1914*. Cambridge, Mass.: Harvard University Press, 1970.

Williams, Robert. *States and Social Evolution: Coffee and the Rise of National Governments in Central America*. Chapel Hill: University of North Carolina Press, 1994.

Williamson, Peter. *Corporatism in Perspective: An Introductory Guide to Corporatist Theory*. London: Sage, 1989.

Wolfe, Justin. "Rising from the Ashes: Community, Ethnicity and Nation-State Formation in Nineteenth-Century Nicaragua." PhD diss., University of California, Los Angeles, 1999.

Wolfe, Patrick. "Imperialism and History: A Century of Theory, from Marx to Postcolonialism." *American Historical Review* 102.2 (1997): 388–420.

Woll, Allen. *The Latin Image in American Film*. Los Angeles: UCLA Latin American Center, 1980.

Wünderich, Volker. *Sandino: Una biografía política*. Managua: Nueva Nicaragua, 1995.

Young, John Parke. *Central American Currency and Finances*. Princeton: Princeton University Press, 1925.

Zalkin, Michael. "Agrarian Class Structure in Nicaragua in 1980: A New Interpretation and Some Implications." *Journal of Peasant Studies* 16.4 (1989): 575–605.

Zamora, Augusto R. *El conflicto Estados Unidos-Nicaragua, 1979–1990*. Managua: CIRA, 1996.

Zeitlin, Jonathan, and Gary Herrigel, eds. *Americanization and Its Limits: Reworking U.S. Technology and Management in Post-war Europe and Japan*. Oxford: Oxford University Press, 2000.

Zimmerman, Matilde. *Sandinista: Carlos Fonseca and the Nicaraguan Revolution*. Durham: Duke University Press, 2000.

Zúñiga, Edgar. *Historia eclesiástica de Nicaragua*. Managua: Hispamer, 1996.

Index

Italicized locators refer to illustrations.

205, 236, 246, 279. *See also* U.S. interventions: of 1927

Civil War (U.S.), 3, 23, 40, 48

Class (social): Caballeros Católicos' portrayal of their own, 194–95; differentiation of rural, 166–70, 174; discourse of struggles between, 85, 93, 95, 102, 110, 147, 225–26, 229–30; formation of elite, 62; of 1912 civil war leaders, 104–5, 117–18; Sandino Rebellion as struggle between, 235, 240–41, 265, 269; Sandino's vision of society without, 6, 263; sexual privileges of elite, 188. *See also* Artisans; "Bourgeoisie"; Caudillo(s); Conservatives; Elites; Labor; Landlords; Liberals; Nouveaux riches; Oligarchy; Peasants; Poor

Club Conservador de Artesanos, 80, 96

Club de Granada, 13, 63, 89–93, 104–5, 107

Clubes Sociales de Artesanos, 80

Cockfighting, 63, 64, 138

Coffee plantations, 12, 49, 57, 65, 89, 92, 117; awards won by, 59; cash crops produced by, 54, 166, 195; dollar diplomacy's effects on, 139, 149–52, 153, 154–55, 157–60, 166–73, 184; fictional depictions of, 133–34; labor on, 159–60, 168, 193–95, 273; Liberals' and Conservatives' ownership of, 14; missionaries on, 180; peasant ownership of, 56; quality of coffee produced on, 155, 168; Sandino raised on, 232, 239; World War I's effects on, 177

Coffee traders, 95. *See also* Immigration and immigrants

Cofradía del Taller San Lucas, 277

Cofradías, 105–6, 277

Colegio Centroamericano, 277

Colegio de Señoritas (Granada), 59, *60*

Colindres, Juan Gregorio, 249

Colombia, 236

Colonialism: by filibusters, 2–3, 34, 36,

37; by Spain, 13, 25, 34, 64, 90, 158, 166, 175, 194, 195, 197–99, 225, 255, 256. *See also* Imperialism (U.S.)

Colonization schemes, 21, 27–30, 33

Comintern. *See* Communist International (Comintern)

Comite Pro-Liberación de Nicaragua, 245, 249

Communism: in Cuba, 268, 274; elites' unity against, 26; in El Salvador, 232, 243, 263; in Mexico, 142; 1926–27 rebels described as advocates of, 145; Sandino and, 232–33, 236, 240, 246, 249, 262–66, 276–77. *See also* Liberation theology; Partido Trabajador Nicaragüense; "Social war"

Communist International (Comintern), 236, 249, 262–63

Compañía Mercantil de Ultramar, 134–35

Congress (U.S.), 47, 48, 66, 68, 130, 131

Congress on Christian Work in Latin America, 180

Conservatives: Americanization of, 5, 6, 8, 16, 65–66, 81, 82, 93, 101, 166, 174, 176, 184, 211, 221, 240, 256, 266, 269, 278; anti-Americanism of, 2, 5, 6, 8–9, 11, 16–17, 25, 82–86, 93–94, 115, 130, 174–201, 206, 221–33, 235, 238, 240, 245–59, 265–66, 272, 276–78; as Caballeros Católicos, 175, 177–84, 222–26, 238, 253, 255, 276–78, 322n.37; as caudillos, 207–8, 214, 220, 229, 240; as civil war leaders, 104–5, 111–20, 216; color associated with, 101; conflicts among, 76–80, 100–101, 104–5, 121, 125, 129, 135–37, 143, 144, 169; cosmopolitan ideals of, 12–13, 42, 77–78, 91, 176, 177, 184, 200, 259; calls of, for dictatorship, 260–61, 265; dollar diplomacy and, 11, 168–74, 224 embrace U.S. invaders after 1912 civil war, 120, 121; as entrepreneurs, 14, 57, 59, 91, 137–41, 148, 193, 195, 200; fascism

United States (*continued*)
sanctioned by, 26, 27; hegemony of, over Latin America, 69–71; interventions by, and democratization, 5, 13–14, 16, 17, 121–22, 146–47, 151, 231, 272–73; as model for other nations, 5–8, 21, 27–29, 31, 33, 41, 42, 44–45, 50, 65–67, 83–84, 111, 113, 117, 136, 147, 148, 238, 266, 280; national security of, and democracy, 207; Nicaraguans' request for invasion by, 21–22, 49, 103, 121, 136, 141, 143; occupations by, and democratization, 10, 70–71, 76, 99, 100, 268–69, 278, 279; opposition of, to Sandinista Revolution, 1, 278; reform movements in, 35, 126–27; results of imperialist policies of, 267, 278–80; September 11, 2001, attacks on, 279; Somoza dictatorships and, 269–70, 277; as threat to Nicaragua's sovereignty, 5, 8, 15, 16, 27, 45, 48, 67–68, 71, 75, 82–83, 280; transcontinental railroad in, 23, 47; treaty right of, to invade, 131

University of Granada, 224

U.S. expansionism: in Caribbean Basin, 9, 26, 67; in Central America, 27–28; in Mexico, 45, 71; myths supporting, 35; in Nicaragua, 1, 2–10, 21–41, 45, 69–71, 75–76, 144. *See also* Imperialism (U.S.); Manifest Destiny; Mexican-American War; War of 1898

U.S. interventions: by Accessory Transit Company, 23–25, 28; Conservatives on "bourgeoisie" as facilitating, 175; effects of, 1–2, 5–9, 13–14, 16, 17, 71, 146–47, 151, 205–28, 231, 272–73; by filibusters, 21–41; of 1910–12, 16, 71, 75–76, 88, 176, 269; of 1912, 75, 80, 100, 101, 103, 108–20, 143, 144–45, 176, 177, 267–80; of 1927, 126–27, 141–45, 147–49, 205, 216, 236, 253–54; number of, in Caribbean Basin, 3, 4; in ouster of

Zelaya, 5, 16, 68–71, 80; reformist impulses of some, 76; rise of nationalism in opposition to, 1, 8, 10, 82–88, 110, 131–32, 135–36, 175; variety of, 10–11. *See also* Dollar diplomacy; Imperialism (U.S.); Military; U.S. occupations

U.S. Navy, 40

U.S. occupations, 14, 270, 279–80; agroexport development impeded by, 3, 151–58; myths about, 269–70; of 1912–33, 1–3, 10, 12–14, 63–64, 100, 139, 148–51, 158, 163–64, 167–74, 192, 232, 233, 235, 242, 244, 246, 250–51, 267, 270–78; of 1855–57, 2–3

U.S. protectorate(s): in Caribbean, 3, 125, 126, 279–80; constabularies in, 205–6; Díaz's request for, 143; efforts to turn Nicaragua into, 29, 71, 75–99, 126–49, 177. *See also* Cuba; Dominican Republic; Haiti; Puerto Rico

Urban dwellers: anticosmopolitanism rebellion by, 50–52; canal proposal and, 46; growth of, 56, 94, 154, 175, 200; homosexuality among, 254–55; medium-scale agricultural producers as, 170; mobilization of, 85, 97–98; and 1927 U.S. invasion, 144–47; railroad nationalization and, 146; revolutionaries among, 105, 106; Sandino Rebellion and, 236–37, 242, 244, 249. *See also* Artisans; Granada (city); Landlords

Urbino, Coronado, 295n.82

Uriza, Sebastián, 171

Urtecho Cabistán, Juan Ignacio, 65, 66, 83

Urtecho family, 13, 65

Valle, José María (El Chelón), 33–34, 39

Vanderbilt, Cornelius, 10; transit company of, 23–25, 28, 30, 39–40

Vanguardistas, 221–28, 240

MICHEL GOBAT is an associate professor in

the Department of History at the University of Iowa.

Library of Congress Cataloging-in-Publication Data
Gobat, Michel.
Confronting the American dream : Nicaragua under U.S.
imperial rule / Michel Gobat.
p. cm.—(American encounters/global interactions)
Includes bibliograpical references and index.
ISBN 0-8223-3634-0 (cloth : alk. paper)
ISBN 0-8223-3647-2 (pbk. : alk. paper)
1. Nicaragua—History—1909–1937. 2. Nicaragua—History—
1838–1909. 3. United States—Relations—Nicaragua. 4. Nicaragua
—Relations—United States. 5. Intervention (International law)
I. Title. II. Series.
F1526.3.G595 2005
327.7285073—dc22 2005016089